gun control

Robert J. Kukla

edited by

Harlon B. Carter

Past President National Rifle Association

Stackpole Books

GUN CONTROL

Copyright © 1973 by
National Rifle Association of America

Published by
STACKPOLE BOOKS
Cameron and Kelker Streets
Harrisburg, Pa. 17105

Printed in the U.S.A.

Library of Congress Cataloging in Publication Data

Kukla, Robert J
    Gun control.

    1. Firearms—Laws and regulations—United
States. I. Title.
HV8059.K79   353.007'53   73-9505
ISBN 0-8117-1190-0

gun
control

To the memory of John and Antoinette Kukla, my parents, who instilled within me a keen appreciation for the twin bulwarks of progressive civilization, individual freedom combined with individual responsibility.

And to Barbara, my dear wife, who shares with me the optimistic conviction that the truth shall keep America free.

"Experience should teach us to be most on our guard to protect liberty when the Government's purposes are beneficent. Men born to freedom are naturally alert to repel invasion of their liberty by evil-minded rulers. The greatest dangers to liberty lurk in the insidious encroachment by men of zeal, well meaning but without understanding."

Justice Louis D. Brandeis
Olmstead v. United States
277 U.S. 438, 478 (1928)

Key to Major References

AA . . . Hearings before the Subcommittee to Investigate Juvenile Delinquency of the Committee on the Judiciary, U.S. Senate. Part 14: Interstate Traffic in Mail-Order Firearms. January 29 and 30; March 7, and May 1 and 2, 1963, Washington, D.C. U.S. Government Printing Office; 1963.

BB . . . Hearings before the Committee on Commerce, U.S. Senate. December 13 and 18, 1963; January 23, 24, and 30, and March 4, 1964. Serial No. 45. U.S. Government Printing Office; 1964.

CC . . . Hearings before the Subcommittee to Investigate Juvenile Delinquency of the Committee on the Judiciary, U.S. Senate. May 19, 20 and 21; June 2, 3, 8, 24, and 30; July 1, 20, 27, 1965. U. S. Government Printing Office; 1965.

DD . . . Hearings before the Committee on Ways and Means, House of Representatives. Part 1. July 12, 13, 14, 20, 21, 23, 26, 27, and 28, 1965. (Pages 1–355). U.S. Government Printing Office; 1965.

EE . . . Hearings before the Committee on Ways and Means, House of Representatives. Part 2. July 12, 13, 14, 20, 21, 23, 26, 27, and 28, 1965. (Pages 357–717). U.S. Government Printing Office; 1965.

FF . . . Hearings before Subcommittee No. 5 of the Committee on the Judiciary, House of Representatives. March 15, 16, 22, 23; April 5, 7, 10, 12, 19, 20, 26, and 27, 1967. Serial No. 3. U.S. Government Printing Office; 1967.

GG . . . Hearings before the Subcommittee to Investigate Juvenile Delinquency of the Committee on the Judiciary, U.S. Senate. July 10, 11, 12, 18, 19, 20, 25, 28, and 31; and August 1, 1967. U.S. Government Printing Office; 1967.

HH . . . Hearings before the Subcommittee to Investigate Juvenile Delinquency of the Committee on the Judiciary, U.S. Senate. June 26, 27, 28, and July 8, 9, and 10, 1968. U.S. Government Printing Office; 1968.

II . . . Hearings before the Subcommittee to Investigate Juvenile Delinquency of the Committee on the Judiciary, U.S. Senate. July 23, 24, and 29, 1969. U.S. Government Printing Office; 1970.

KK . . . Hearing before the Committee on Commerce, U.S. Senate. April 16, 1935. U.S. Government Printing Office; 1935.

MM . . . Hearing before a Subcommittee of the Committee on Interstate and Foreign Commerce, House of Representatives. June 22, 1937. U.S. Government Printing Office; 1937.

Acknowledgments

In the preparation of this manuscript the author has relied most heavily upon actual testimony in Congressional Hearings and upon the reports of various committees and commissions and press.

As might be expected, such original documentation, as raw material, contained many errors in spelling, punctuation, capitalization and the like. This manuscript has quite carefully preserved intact these multitudes of errors in an effort to be completely faithful to the available record. Doing so has exposed the author to frequent temptation to make corrections in the original documentation in the interest of what was obviously intended by the original speaker or his transcriber. This temptation has been consistently resisted; in some cases, a galling experience.

By adhering to the documented statements of those public figures who have taken positions for or against firearms legislation, the author has denied himself the interpretative advantages often taken by his opponents. He has instead given the reader what has been said and has quite squarely met those statements head on, leaving himself little in terms of flexibility for speculating upon what might have been meant. In doing so, he has denied himself the usual distortions, confounding to opponents, found in a polemic of this nature.

The author is grateful for the wise decision of Fred M. Hakenjos, President; C. R. Gutermuth, First Vice President; Merrill W. Wright, Second Vice President; Judge Bartlett Rummel, Past President; William Loeb, Executive Committee, all of the National Rifle Association, who served as an ad hoc committee to consider the need for such a book as this and the general suitability of this manuscript to supply that need.

The author especially wishes to thank his friends and colleagues Harlon Carter and Maryann Carter who have demonstrated, for many years, a vibrant spiritual affiliation and dedication to the principles expressed herein. They patiently edited and typed nearly a thousand pages of original drafting in order to bring forth this book in its present form.

There were indeed a thousand pages more which could have been written, and, we agree upon that, but in the interest of both readability and ready handling there had to be a stopping place.

Robert J. Kukla
Park Ridge, Illinois

Preface

It has become virtually a historic necessity that there be written a record of the efforts in America to abolish the private possession of firearms. Such a record cannot avoid, at the same time, suggesting the elimination, partially, if not completely, of that part of the United States military structure which so far has remained civilian and non-professional in character. The concept of a militia, of civilians individually possessing and bearing arms and familiar with their use, as opposed to large standing armies, has, since the birth of the Republic, been a substantial bulwark of American liberties.

There must also be suggested the inevitable and complete elimination of broad and democratic participation in the shooting sports in America, leaving them to those politically and economically privileged people approved by the government for such licensing or other exceptional procedures enabling them to possess firearms.

Similarly, the concept and acceptability of self-defense has been, and continues to be, diluted. Increasingly, women are told not to struggle when facing rape; that, if they do so, they may face greater injury or death. Prominent police chiefs, invading a realm of conduct to be judged by God and not men, advise citizens not to resist criminal attack or pillage, but to submit. As criminals, with increasing frequency, murder their victims or witnesses to their crimes, in order to prevent future identification, citizens are persuaded to avoid involvement. There are indeed cynical social forces at work to persuade them to "stay out of it"; not to be witnesses.

Mr. Robert J. Kukla of Park Ridge, Illinois, is an attorney well known throughout his State for his vigorous and clear-cut representations during the last 10 years before various legislative and administrative bodies in regard to gun control. Perhaps no one in America has spoken out in this controversy with more forceful logic and keen perception of the historical implications than Mr. Kukla.

Unfortunately, perhaps, for the stimulation of readership, an attempt to make a book of this kind attractive or titillating to the public mind comes dangerously close to subtracting from the serious burden it must carry. This burden is to report the various movements for, or which would have the eventual effect of, abolishing the private possession of firearms in America. Thus, it is that in pushing on through the chronological recitation of what actually happened and what was actually said by others, without added coloration or distortion, one is denied the brilliant wit of Mr. Kukla so many times flashed in legislative hearings and in televised debates with congressmen, state officials of Illinois and other public figures.

This book does not purport to furnish all the arguments for or against any given position. It is limited generally to the positions which were actually taken by key figures in the gun control controversy and to an honest recitation of the arguments presented and the actions taken by both sides.

As a recitation of what happened this book affords an insight into the motives of the principal characters in the gun control effort only as they themselves have stated their motives or as their motives can reasonably be made clear from what they have said or done.

Regrettably, it has not been possible within any reasonable book size, to set forth in a definitive manner, a full delineation of the proposition that generally those who have sought the most in gun control have also sought the most in steps to limit or to prohibit the shooting sports, or to denigrate the concept and conduct of natural and reasonable defense of self, family or home. Strangely, also, and overwhelmingly, while claiming to seek crime control, those who have sought the most in gun control have sought the least in the punishment of criminals. They have been adherents of a philosophy in command of the instruments of law and order and of punishment for crime in this country for nearly 40 years. During the last decade we have experienced the greatest rampancy of crime in our history. Also, at the same time we have annually had declining numbers of criminals in our prisons and capital punishment has been practically eliminated.

Lack of convincing evidence that crime control is really the goal of those who seek gun control, has led many reasonable and moderate men to conclude—though it does not necessarily follow—that the stoutest advocates of gun control in this country have, at the same time, been foremost in the aggravation of the conditions of crime which they say they deplore and which they pretend they seek to remedy.

As reasonable men become informed and concerned in regard to infringements of rights which they hold dear, and which they believe to be constitutionally guaranteed them, they become increasingly alerted to the whole panorama of their rights and possible infringements in other areas.

As a matter of fact, the whole package of our constitutional rights is under attack and most moderate thinking men agree that, when any part of that package is infringed, all of it is in jeopardy. Those who have sought to eliminate the right of the private citizen in America to keep and bear arms have pointed to England or to Japan as an example of domestic tranquility and they have often said that such tranquility is the consequence of the lack of privately owned arms.

What they do not point out is that in England the possession of arms for more than five centuries has been interwoven in hundreds of years of bitter religious conflict while, at the same time, as might be expected, the possession of arms has been reserved as a privilege of those who have been on the right side politically and on the well-fed side economically. The same could be said of Soviet Russia today.

As for the Japanese, these domestically tranquil people have never in thousands of years of their history permitted the immigration into their islands of racially different men. They are, perhaps, the most completely homogenous major race of people on earth. The introduction of new ideas into the mainstream of their social and economic structure has been accomplished in such a manner as to afford those ideas at least an external Nipponized character before full public exposure and presentation. Even the innovations in government brought by American occupa-

13

tion forces after the defeat of the Japanese, 1941–45, were fed into the Japanese system in a manner harmonious and acceptable to the Japanese spirit via the person and image of their Emperor Hirohito who successfully prevented, even in the fact of foreign occupation, a breakdown in the tranquil domestic society and economy of Japan. It is simply nonsense to point to other countries as either models or examples for America.

America faces a future fraught with still more turbulence and uncertainty, which on many future occasions will doubtlessly indicate to political figures, endowed with something less than the courage and stature of statemanship, that solutions lie in harsh and unhappy compromises of the rights and dignity of free men in favor of further domination by a highly centralized government with strongly developed national police dispositions.

The viability of our local and state structures, more immediately responsive to individual citizens close to home, are already under attack. They are in many cases being molded to a federal form planned and designed on the banks of the Potomac thousands of miles away.

Almost the entire television spectrum of expression has seemed to follow one political philosophy. Our citizens in ever increasing numbers do not read the news but, instead, see it and hear it molded and dramatized in their living rooms from a media which cannot afford to be without news, which is in competition with others to make news stimulating, titillating and even hysterical, no matter its real nature.

It is in the anguish of conflict, however, that people grow strong. Only in controversy and challenge do men become dedicated. Only in the study of history do men become wise in the social and political developments which affect their happiness and prosperity for the future. Herein lies our hope and to such involved perceptive students of life and politics this book is pointed.

Indeed, all Americans should study the history of the movement to eliminate the private ownership of firearms and the political careers, in every respect, of those engaged in it. If accomplished, such elimination will impose upon Americans many of the characteristics of oppression from which they thought they had been freed by the guarantees in America—and in America only—that the press shall be free; that the state shall not interfere with the nature of a man's worship; that law-abiding men may keep and bear arms; that a man's home shall be secure from unreasonable search and seizure; that a man may not be compelled to give evidence against himself and that a man shall be held to be innocent of any crime and free of any penalty until proved guilty of an offense in a court of competent jurisdiction.

14

This book has been more than a history of the movement for gun prohibition in this country during the last few years. It is a revelation that there exists here a political philosophy, distrustful of the people and willing to oppress them by measures which the arrogance of intellect has determined is good for them.

Gun prohibition is the inevitable harbinger of oppresson. It cannot be successful. It can only be pursued by "no-knock" laws under which jack-booted minions of government invade the homes of citizens; by "stop-and-frisk" laws under which the person of citizens can be searched on the streets at the whim and suspicion of authority; by confiscation of property having a legitimate use and which has not been used in crime, nor likely to be.

Just as mail-order controls, embargoes and discretionary statutory authority vested in bureaucrats, have been a convenient step to registration and licensing of guns, so is registration and licensing but a convenient step on the pathway to their confiscation and prohibition.

The liberties of the people can be nourished only where men are adequately punished for crime and where men, once free, are not coerced into a condition thought by government to be safe and good for them.

Harlon Carter

List of Illustrations

1

"Liberty cannot be preserved without a general knowledge among the people . . . Let us dare to read, think, speak and write."

JOHN ADAMS

A MOVEMENT EXISTS IN OUR COUNTRY WHICH, IF SUC-cessfully continued, will serve to eliminate virtually all privately-owned firearms in the hands of decent and law-abiding citizens. This abolition of arms would be accomplished by outright prohibition of possession in some cases. In other cases, possession of arms would be limited to an ever narrowing category of those who were willing and able: (1) to meet requirements of law and regulations imposed on law-abiding people but not upon criminal or violent people; (2) to become suspect in the eyes of the police and one's neighbors because one possessed a firearm and not because one had mis-used it or was even likely to do so.

Those requirements so far established—and proposed for wider imposition—are licensing of firearms owners, fingerprinting, photographing, identification and investigation in one's neighborhood, registration of privately held arms, police inspection and the decision and judgment of the police that the firearms owner is, or is not, dangerous to the peace and harmony of the community.

Police are human, but quite apart from the impossibility in a democratic society that they can pass judgment on the future actions of an individual whose conduct to the present has been blameless, there is the undeniable fact that criminal and violent men will not expose themselves to such identification, investigation or process. Neither criminals, nor the harborers of a criminal intent, will apply for gun owners licenses or register their guns and no one seriously expects them to do so.

Parenthetically, at this point, the Supreme Court has held that a man cannot be required to register a gun, if to do so is to incriminate himself. (Haynes vs U.S., 309 U.S. 85). In at least one city, Chicago, the law makers have dodged the question of constitutionality by simply excluding criminals and other gun-prohibited classes from the registration requirement. This is at least honest recognition that gun registration hits only honest men.

This movement to abolish private ownership of arms will end broad democratic participation in the shooting sports which has distinguished American participation in those sports from that of Europeans. In most of Europe, for generations, these sports have been reserved especially for the gentry—for the politically approved and economically privileged classes. For the most part, they remain so today.

This movement to prohibit the general and democratic possession of arms is neither of recent, nor American, origin. Every dictator, every absolute ruler, since the dawn of history has been sensitive to the consequences, or the possibilities, of arms in the hands of the people.

Charlemagne collected the swords, pikes and bows in the hands of his people when there was famine in the land of the Franks. He said his purpose was to protect the public graneries. The kings and nobles of France, England and Germany during the centuries of their autocratic rule forebade arms to the peasantry to insure against any popular uprising, and to insure the peasant had no means for poaching the king's deer or boar or hares—often a capital offense at that time.

In medieval Europe the people were almost completely disarmed. When pikes and long bows were being displaced by new developments in firearms these new weapons were too expensive for the people. Furthermore, the rulers feared them in the hands of men who were being stirred by a rennaissance of the arts and of the human spirit.

The people did, however, in a limited but decisive measure, obtain

18

arms in both Europe and America and the climactic actions of the Seventeenth and Eighteenth Centuries ended ages of faceless existence for the common man when the embattled farmers of George Washington successfully beat off the disciplined professional troops of George III—successful because they owned firearms and knew how to use them.

The development of the American concept of national defense grew out of the fear that vast professional armies were in peacetime a menace to a free people, and the confidence that in times of national danger courageous and ordinary citizens would rally to the cause of their country. It was not conceived, of course, that these would be citizens trained in war, but it was conceived that theirs would be the hardihood of youth inured to physical discomforts; born of strength developed and nourished on farms and woodlands and athletic fields, accompanied by a certain skill in their use of firearms.

We know today that this confidence can be buoyed by a degree of proficiency with firearms obtained in our schools, in ROTC programs—yes, in National Rifle Association programs.

Unfortunately there has been a change in attitude toward some of these concepts in the last decade. Lacking perspective in time, the causes have been difficult to identify precisely. Nor has it been possible yet to measure their impact or durability. Discussions concerning them are generally controversial. Conscientious men differ as to whether their origins and causes might lie with adherents to an alien philosophy—with those who deny, in the development and education of our youth, the virtues demanded and employed for their own.

In the last 40 years, millions of people have come to America whose only view of a gun has been from the muzzle. Many of these former subjects of distressing European tyranny have not yet found it possible to accept or understand the symbols of American free men.

Theirs has been an experience blurring the reality that a government which fears its citizens armed, is a government which cannot be trusted by its citizens when they are free to analyze it, to think of it, and speak of it.

The freedom of a people will not long remain after there has departed the spirit, the boldness, the enthusiasm and aggressiveness which made them free. Nor shall the spirit which made them free long survive the loss of the implements they have employed and the memories of their employment; these becoming, in fact, their respected symbols and traditions.

A cruel blow was struck in Dallas, by the assassination of President John F. Kennedy, November 22, 1963, when perhaps in hysteria and grief, powerful men in government spoke hastily and without facts, charging the crime against the traditionalist in American culture. Later, when those men found they had erred they lacked the political courage to say so. History then recorded that the villain was a rifle not a man. So it was that the monster—the object of hate—became an inanimate object of wood and steel, because men in high places did not have the courage to identify the man or his communist political background and likely reason for committing the murder.

Had the frustration, remorse and bitterness of the people been fixed upon the man and the political and social forces which moved him—who knows? Would Dallas have become a Serajevo bringing forth climactic political decisions our leaders did not have the courage to face? Would the spirit of the people have arisen to demand victorious wars when we are forced to fight? Would the political nature of Korea, or Southeast Asia or of Cuba been changed? And forcefully, if necessary?

The Chief Justice of the U.S. Supreme Court, appointed to head a commission of inquiry into the facts, only added to the rightful concern of the people—and their provocative speculation—when he announced some of the facts could not be known in our time.

Anyway, the weapon has become the deodand. Its forfeiture in all its forms to the government has been designed to satisfy the people that something has been done about crime.

After President Kennedy's assassination the curtain jerkily raised on the most strange and shrieking spectacle in all American history. Every instrument available to the news media was assembled and pointed in a single ideological direction. And never before in history had public attention, followed by concern and then hate, been so successfully moved from the murderer and his motivation, to the weapon which he employed.

It was as if we could no longer recall even the name of Cain, but identified and deplored the stone he used; no Brutus, but his knife; no Booth, but his derringer.

The murder weapon, a rifle, was found in Dallas. It was traced in six or seven hours to a man who only four years before had renounced his American citizenship and sworn allegiance to the Soviet Union; who in Russia had married the niece of an official in the MVD with whom she lived; who had only a short time before been engaged in activities in behalf of the communist government of Fidel Castro in Cuba.

These facts were soon to be conveniently forgotten by those who had prematurely and without foundation linked the crime to so-called right-wing elements instead of a known communist; a self-confessed Marxist. Sadly, stupidly and finally, all to be remembered was that

20

America's youngest President had been murdered with a foreign military war surplus rifle purchased from a mail-order company in this country.

The villain became the gun when it was discovered the murderer was not a "right-wing extremist" but, in fact, was a communist. The reaction against the gun has been seized upon and actively promoted by the news media, which ever since that time has incessantly railed against the gun and not against the alien philosophy of the assassin. The attack was against the means employed in the crime—without regard for its many legitimate uses—and not against the criminal.

There has arisen a clamor in the country for the enactment of legislation of a kind which, somehow, some people, perhaps by the weird reasoning of television, have come to think would forevermore prevent the recurrence of such a tragedy as that in Dallas. In support of that clamor the object of public wrath has been directed upon the mail-order sale of guns, the importation of foreign military surplus firearms and the National Rifle Association.

The forces of gun control—a euphemism for confiscation—have not been deterred by the historical evidence that prohibitions of such a nature as this are simply unworkable and unfair in a generally free society. They inevitably impose requirements in actual practice only on inoffensive, decent and law-abiding citizens and not upon criminals. Registration of firearms—an indispensable first step to their confiscation—discriminates against the decent people who comply. It can be ignored, generally with impunity, by those against whom it is purportedly directed. Thus, it is an ineffective device for revealing other law violations. Its enforcement would depend upon the cooperation of the classes who would defy it. Its defiance constitutes only another and lesser offense on the part of those who are already law violators, or who intend to be, and by such registration would reveal that fact. While making no contribution to law enforcement, it causes many people to think something effective is being done about crime when this is not true. Thus, while deceiving the people, it distracts their attention from the real problems of crime and diverts money and manpower which should be applied to their solutions.

It is amazing, indeed, how otherwise reasonable men have been lead to think that passing another law, and superimposing it upon others yet unenforced, will keep firearms out of the hands of criminals on our streets. The fact has been repeatedly demonstrated the past few years that we are not even keeping firearms out of the hands of convicted criminals in our penitentiaries—and all the might of England is not keeping them out of the hands of criminals on London's streets, nor out of the hands of the Irish Republican Army, even when death is a likely penalty for discovery.

After President Kennedy's assassination, Senator Thomas J. Dodd was suddenly propelled into the national limelight. The Senate Judiciary Subcommittee, of which he was chairman, had recently concluded hearings on a proposal which had as its purported purpose the control of mail-order sales of handguns to juveniles. Senator Dodd then quickly introduced a bill contemplating all firearms. In the glare of television lights he became the focus of American attention on the issues involving firearms generally.

The campaign had begun to eliminate the private ownership of firearms in America; to eliminate the shooting sports; to denigrate our historical posture and our traditions as they relate to arms; to eliminate hunting and to change or somehow disfigure the concept of citizen participation in military service as opposed to the concept of large professional armies so feared by our founding fathers.

The focus had now been successfully directed away from the assassin in Dallas. It has for years since remained upon the lawful firearms of law-respecting Americans in their homes, in the field and on the shooting ranges and not upon the distorted mind and actions of a puny little communist assassin and his likes.

This book contains the history of those years.

2

"I want to emphasize that we do not intend to tamper with the constitutionally guaranteed right of a free people to keep and bear arms"

SENATOR THOMAS J. DODD

THESE WERE THE SERENE AND PLEASANT DAYS IN THE gun control controversy. Senator Dodd was convincing in his role as the nation's foremost investigator in the problems of juvenile delinquency. As a good citizen embarked on a blameless mission to inquire into the problems of our youngsters and to recommend remedies for whatever he found of grievance and ill, Senator Dodd also appeared a paragon of all that was decent and good in our legislative processes.

Despite matters of personal conduct, which later were discovered to besmirch his career and to receive the censure of his colleagues in formal proceedings, Senator Dodd appeared then handsome, dignified, impeccable and unimpeachable.

The quotation above was among the first words spoken by him on

January 29, 1963, in the opening of hearings by the Senate Judiciary Subcommittee to Investigate Juvenile Delinquency on the general subject of the availability of mail-order firearms to juvenile Americans.

The work of the Subcommittee actually had begun nearly two years before and a great deal of preparation had gone into these public hearings, the purposes of which were to document the nature of the problem thought to exist and to present for examination, comment and perhaps constructive criticism, the general legislative framework by which the Subcommittee hoped to amend the existing Federal Firearms Act of 1938 in a manner substantially reducing the alleged abuses.

The evil, it was said, in existing gun control legislation began with an excessively permissive system of issuing Federal Firearms Dealer Licenses to virtually anyone who might apply for them. It was urged that this alleged fact permitted licenses for fly-by-night gun dealers plying their trade chiefly by mail order; trafficking in guns of poor design and shoddy manufacture; selling them indiscriminately to any mail-order purchaser who, through the anonymity of the transaction, could conceal either criminality or immature age. The prohibitions already imposed by the Federal Firearms Act of 1938 were ignored. The Subcommittee's attention was focused principally on handguns, as opposed to the rifle and shotgun, these last two being most frequently associated in the mind of the public as those suitable for sporting uses.

This point was clearly established by Senator Dodd at the beginning of the hearings by his disavowal of interest on the part of the Subcommittee in firearms used in sports. He said the Subcommittee's entire interest was in the availability of weapons to the undesirable elements in our society.

Senator Dodd acted promptly to dispel any apprehension that the subcommittee was entertaining measures which would prohibit firearms ownership by law-abiding private citizens.

Contrary to what many anti-gun proponents would have the public believe, the major domestic arms manufacturers and the various private not-for-profit sporting organizations had actually worked closely with Senator Dodd and his subcommittee for several years, and, far from acting as obstructionists, they provided much useful information and advice to his group. Dodd commended them for their attitude.

Also, to define the scope of the problem and to indicate that the serious abuses were limited to a minute few, Senator Dodd went on to say that such abuses were the clear exception among mail order firearms transactions, rather than the rule. Although this was true, he emphasized, it was equally true that a problem did exist.

In keeping with its mission to investigate juvenile delinquency, Sena-

24

tor Dodd's subcommittee initially concentrated its efforts on identifying the kinds of firearms most frequently encountered among youthful offenders. As might have been expected, these firearms were found quite overwhelmingly to be cheaper models, many of foreign manufacture. In a large number of examples they were so-called "starter pistols," designed to fire .22 caliber blank powder charges for use in athletic events. These starter pistols were often altered by youthful and ingenious owners in such a manner as to permit the discharge of live ammunition. As expected, the results were unpredictable and erratic.

During the five days of its hearings, Senator Dodd's subcommittee heard testimony from police officials who described in detail the manner in which youth gang warfare had evolved in recent years through the employment of progressively more convenient and lethal weaponry. Among the weapons displayed to the subcommittee were automobile snow chains; slung shots (not to be confused with sling shots) which consisted of a heavy weight, such as a one and one-half inch diameter brass ball or heavy fishing line lead sinker firmly attached to a flexible extension handle and wielded somewhat in the manner of a club; a garrison belt studded with nuts and bolts which cut, tear and bruise victims struck with it; an industrial conveyor belt into which were mounted thousands of razor-sharp tiny blades capable of rending and flaying flesh; and the usual array of more mundane street weapons; knives, razors, metal knuckles, bludgeons and other stabbing, cutting and striking weapons.

Testimony was convincing that lately there had been a sharp escalation in the nature and effectiveness of youth gang armament. The public was persuaded to believe that in a relatively short span youth gangs had graduated from bludgeons and wood instruments to cheaper mail-order handguns, identifying the zip-gun as sort of halfway station, in utilitarian terms, of juvenile street fighting.

Zip-guns, murderous little homemade instruments firing live ammution, could be made of various tubes from automobile radio aerials to gas pipes. Ingenious methods were employed to fasten them to a carved block of wood. Rubber bands used with an ordinary door latch might serve as a firing pin—altogether rather clear evidence that the subcommittee was going to be in trouble regarding any recommendation designed to disarm the nasty little hellions who were making the streets of some of our large cities a no-man's-land after night.

It was shortly clear that zip-guns, ranging from crude and unreliable specimens of the street to those manufactured in some of our prison work-shops with considerable skill and refinement, were going to serve for the most part as a reminder of the ease with which deadly weapons could be made by ordinary people from ordinary materials with very simple tools.

The complete lack of any proposals to deal with such deadly instruments in the hands of the murderously inclined must have been painful to the subcommittee. It seemed the discussions turned, and have continued to this day, to deal with the sort of thing in which law-abiding citizens have a legitimate interest. Both the subcommittee and the public put the zip-gun behind them.

The starter pistol sparked more interest. In spite of its legitimate use for decades as a starter for athletic events and theatrical productions, it appeared a real market was growing among those who, again, rather easily converted them at home into weapons for firing live ammunition. Evidence was presented, moreover, which suggested that certain domestic importers and retailers might actually have conspired with manufacturers to redesign starter pistols in such a way as to facilitate their illicit conversion; certainly not a difficult thing to do.

Testimony was presented that the practice of one Los Angeles mail-order company was to sell a starter pistol for $12.95 with the conventional solid blank barrel and to furnish separately a drilled and rifled pistol barrel. The mail-order purchaser could simply replace the barrel by unscrewing it and substituting in its place the useable barrel in a few minutes, without special tools.

Testimony was convincing that there had been a surprising failure to obtain any kind of enforcement of the Federal Firearms Act of 1938 or to obtain any effective enforcement of the stringent prohibition against handguns in both New York and South Carolina where the nation's most stringent prohibitions existed. Moreover, it was convincing that Federal Firearms Licensees, whose licenses were almost always issued without any investigation, were in some cases an irresponsible and unscrupulous bunch of people whose numbers had clearly increased since World War II. Some had criminal records for offenses in the field of pornography and for contributing to the delinquency of minors.

There was a problem. Neither the subcommittee, the news media, nor the public, seemed to want to come to grips with the fact that, for the most part, the problems described in the hearings represented violations of existing Federal law. The knowledgeable students of gun legislation were at first perplexed when it became clear this was a subject not to be explored in depth by the subcommittee. Strange helplessness and frustration came over the sportsmen's representatives. The clamor was for a new law, for new legislation, for extension of the Federal power in this field. It was all glossed over by kindly words from the chairman

26

with his warm reassurances that the law-abiding citizen's interest would be protected.

It was the testimony of James V. Bennett, Director of the U.S. Bureau of Prisons, which actually foretold the future. Here was a man who was destined to play a major role in all debates concerning gun control legislation for the next several years. He gave his warmest blessing to the approach taken by Senator Dodd and disarmingly observed that Dodd's bill was "a step in the right direction". He then proceeded with a number of suggestions "to strengthen its already meritorious provisions".

Franklin L. Orth, Executive Vice-President of the National Rifle Association, appearing before Senator Dodd's Committee.

From that moment on any speaker who used the phrase "a step in the right direction" was felt by firearms owners to be serving notice he was proposing only the first "step" down the pathway to confiscation and prohibition of privately owned firearms.

Among the important witnesses to testify was Franklin L. Orth, Executive Vice President of the National Rifle Association of America, an organization whose membership at that time was something over a half million. Orth's reply was mild. He recalled how often he and the National Rifle Association were vilified in the news media for allegedly taking harsh and extremist positions. The relationship which existed between the NRA and Senator Dodd's subcommittee can be readily seen from the following remarks by Orth to the committee:

> "It has been gratifying to note that the committee has definitely not developed any form of proposed legislation precipitantly. There have been a number of meetings in which the committee has sought the advice and opinions of sportsmen's groups who may be affected as well as dealers and manufacturers. National Rifle Association representatives have attended all meetings of this type. At each, everyone present have been both able and willing to speak frankly and vigorously, opposing any items advanced which seem objectionable. The committee is to be congratulated on its use of this approach which seems both logical and sensible. It is our opinion that the committee genuinely desires assistance in devising a practical plan of solving what is recognized by all to be the primary problem. The National Rifle Association wishes to place itself on record as being ready and eager to continue to offer to the committee the benefit of our vast experience in the field of firearms legislation." (AA–p. 3481)

Senator Dodd expressed his gratitude to the NRA with equal warmth and fervor. But this was early in 1963.

3

"DALLAS—President Kennedy was shot and killed Friday as he rode in a motorcade through downtown Dallas. The nation's Chief Executive was waving happily to thousands of cheering spectators along the street when he was cut down by a burst of at least three shots fired by a sniper armed with a high-powered rifle."

CHICAGO DAILY NEWS: NOV. 22, 1963

JOHN F. KENNEDY HAD NOT YET BEEN LAID TO REST when there burst forth across the country a most extraordinary and shameful display of political prejudice and bigotry. In blind rejection of the first reported facts concerning the character of the actual suspect apprehended in the assassination of President Kennedy, many persons and organizations frequently associated with leftist causes did not hesitate to attribute the crime to the influence of politically conservative Americans. Their behavior in attempting to impute collective guilt to those Americans whose political philosophy differed from their own was in itself a manifestation of the extremism that they so freely attributed to others.

A hint was captured of the vituperation that was to come in the

29

Chicago Sun–Times issue of November 23, 1963, which carried an Associated Press release entitled, "Kennedy Had Planned Blow At Right Wing" opening with these words:

> "He knew Dallas was a solid center of conservatism, and he meant to accuse his right-wing critics of talking 'just plain nonsense.' But that last Dallas speech was never delivered."
>
> * * *
>
> "Dallas, a white-collar town, has figured prominently as the conservative center of Texas. It is here that Adlai E. Stevenson, the U.S. chief delegate to the United Nations, was struck on the head with a sign by a placard-carrying picket protesting his speech here on the UN. It is here that former Maj. Gen. Edwin Walker lives. Walker, who espouses doctrines of the far right, has been very critical of the Kennedy administration. H. L. Hunt, a prominent and fabulously wealthy oilman who has long advocated a conservative approach to all matters, is another resident." (*Chicago Sun-Times*: Nov. 23, 1963)

Within an hour of the assassination, and apparently based solely upon wishful thinking, the Chief Justice of the United States Supreme Court, Earl Warren, reportedly issued a statement in which were included these injudicious opinions:

> "A great and good President has suffered martyrdom as a result of the hatred and bitterness that has been injected into the life of our nation by bigots, . . ." (*Chicago Sun-Times*: Nov. 23, 1963)

It is almost unbelievable that this man, having prejudged already the source or influence leading to the murder of a president, was selected by succeeding President Lyndon B. Johnson to head a commission which the public believed would be without prejudice.

The Chicago Branch of the National Association for the Advancement of Colored People, always quick to denounce prejudgments by others when directed at black people, unabashedly tendered the following explanation of the assassination:

> "The perpetrators of bigotry, of perverted patriotism and of contempt for law and decency bear the guilt for this blow to freedom. Americans of all races, creeds and nationalities must be alerted to the grave necessity to unite our efforts in bringing to a close an era of domestic subversion under the guise of patriotism and states' rights which has for too long a time been ignored by a majority of Americans." (*Chicago Sun-Times*: Nov. 23, 1963)

A spokesman for the Presbyterian Interracial Council did not hesitate to prejudge the motives for the assassination, nor to disregard the Biblical injunction of "judge not, lest ye be judged." It apparently was more emotionally satisfying simply to proclaim:

"The President's stand on civil rights apparently was responsible. There are some mighty sick people in our land who will take things in their own hands and do what is wrong for our country and all the people in it." (*Chicago Daily News*: Nov. 22, 1963)

Congressman Roman Pucinski summed up his view of the assassination as constituting more than an attack on the President by reportedly charging that it was an attack on America's system of self-government and adding that:

"It may awaken people to the danger of Birchites and fanatics in our country." (*Chicago Daily News*: Nov. 22, 1963)

The American Communist Party also was reported as having issued a statement to the widow of President Kennedy in which his killing was denounced as a political murder in these words:

"All true Americans, in tribute to your husband, will not only condemn this political murder but also will rededicate themselves with greater strength to the struggle for the democratic character of our country." (*Chicago Tribune*: Nov. 23, 1963)

Another Associated Press release datelined New York, Nov. 22, told how three "top leaders of the Communist party in America" sent their condolences by telegram to Mrs. Kennedy. Their message was said to have characterized the assassination as the "ultimate end of the rise of violence and terror in this land by racists and the forces of the ultra-right." (*Chicago Tribune*: Nov. 23, 1963)

In marked contrast to the uninhibited speculation over the nature, purpose and significance of the presidential assassination was the initial evidence adduced by authorities in Dallas as their basis for seizing Lee Harvey Oswald as a suspect in the killing. According to the reports the alleged assassin, Lee Harvey Oswald, was born in New Orleans on October 18, 1939. Seventeen years later, on October 24, 1956, he had enlisted in the U.S. Marine Corps at Dallas. While he still had a year of duty ahead of him, he requested release from active duty on grounds of hardship in order that he might support his mother. He was thereupon placed in the inactive reserve.

On October 13, 1959, Lee Harvey Oswald entered Soviet Russia and just two weeks later, November 1, 1959, he informed the U.S. Embassy in Moscow that he had renounced his American citizenship and had applied for Soviet citizenship. While living in Russia he married a Russian girl, the niece of an official in the MVD, with whom she had lived. His discharge from the inactive reserve was ordered on September 13, 1960, as an "undesirable discharge," which was upheld by the Board of Record Correction. It was also in 1960 that Oswald had reportedly described himself as being a student of "Das Kapital", the bible of Marxist Communism.

It should be noted that it was on the eve of the congressional elections in November, 1962, the press announced that President Kennedy had forced the Soviet Union to withdraw their missiles and bombers from Cuba. Just five months earlier Lee Harvey Oswald had been readmitted into the United States, and only two months before the assassination of President Kennedy he was serving as Chairman of a pro-Castro Fair Play for Cuba committee. It was during that period he and several Cubans were reported to have been arrested in Louisiana for distributing pro-Communist literature.

The United Press International release from Dallas told the story of Lee Harvey Oswald's arrest on the day after the assassination:

"Lee Harvey Oswald, 24, a pro-Castro Marxist who defected to Russia in 1959, was charged Friday with the assassination of President Kennedy, who was ambushed with a high-powered rifle." (*Chicago Sun-Times*: Nov. 23, 1963)

Interestingly enough, on the actual day of the assassination the *Chicago Sun-Times* reported this comment from Soviet Russia:

"Radio Moscow blamed the death on 'extreme right-wing elements'." (*Chicago Sun-Times*: Nov. 23, 1963)

In the months and years following his death, the memory of America's youngest and most popular president was repeatedly used in an attempt to engender public sympathy for the most highly restrictive firearms legislation ever proposed before the Congress of this country. Such distortions of the principles for which President John F. Kennedy stood will be readily grasped within the perspective provided by the following vignettes from his brief life.

Few, perhaps, were aware of John F. Kennedy's interest in, and appreciation of, fine firearms. Nor were many aware of his special relationship to the National Rifle Association of America, or of his enthusiasm for the training of young men in the basic skills of riflery, even in the so-called "age of intercontinental ballistic missiles."

At the time Senator John F. Kennedy was interviewed for an article which appeared in the April, 1960, issue of *Guns* magazine he was an owner and shooter of both high-powered rifles and shotguns. The following excerpt taken from that article incorporated his carefully considered opinion as to the relevance of the Second Amendment to Twentieth Century America:

"By calling attention to a well-regulated militia for the security of the Nation, and the right of each citizen to keep and bear arms, our Founding Fathers recognized the essentially civilian nature of our economy. Although it is extremely unlikely that the fears of governmental tyranny, which gave rise to the second amendment, will ever be a major danger to our Nation, the amendment still remains an important declaration of our basic military-civilian relationships, in which every citizen must be ready to participate in the defense of his country. For that reason I believe the second amendment will always be important." (BB–p. 95)

The favorable disposition of John F. Kennedy towards the National Rifle Association of America, its outstanding achievements in the field of competitive marksmanship and its notable contributions to the national defense effort, was clearly expressed in his letter of March 20, 1961, to Franklin L. Orth, Executive Vice President of the National Rifle Association of America:

"Dear Mr. Orth:
On the occasion of Patriots Day, I wish to offer my congratulations and best wishes to the National Rifle Association of America which over the past years has done credit to our country by the outstanding achievements of its members in the art of shooting.

Through competitive matches and sports in coordination with the National Board for the Promotion of Rifle Practice, the Association fills an important role in our national defense effort, and fosters in an active and meaningful fashion the spirit of the Minutemen.

I am pleased to accept Life Membership in the National Rifle Association and extend to your organization every good wish for continued success." (GG–p. 484)

In an appearance before the House Committee on Ways and Means, Congressman John P. Saylor narrated an experience he once had with President John F. Kennedy just prior to his having made an official trip to the Republic of Mexico:

"Knowing of the panic that some people have had in this matter since our late President's assassination, it was interesting for me to recall that several years ago John F. Kennedy, when President of the United States, made an official trip to Mexico, there to confer with the President of our neighboring country to the south and to talk about some of the problems that are common to our two countries, and at that time President Kennedy properly took with him a gift for the President of the Republic of Mexico, and I inquired as to what that gift was.

Members of the Ways and Means Committee, I would like to inform you that the gift was a Weatherby 303 high-powered rifle with an inscription placed on it, 'To the President of the Republic of Mexico' with his name 'With the hope that he may use it in the finest tradition of the great sport that he loves,' and then was followed a facsimile of the signature of John F. Kennedy, President of the United States.

I am sure that those of us who served in the House with John Kennedy and watched his political sunrise as he went to the other body, then became the President of all of the people of the United States, would realize that John Kennedy would not do anything or give a present to anyone that he thought would be dangerous, . . ." (DD–pp. 290–291)

As late as July 12, 1962, only four months before his decisive action forced Soviet Russia to withdraw her nuclear-armed missiles and bombers from their Cuban bases just ninety miles from the Florida coast, President Kennedy addressed the U.S. Marine Corps at the Marine Barracks in Washington, D.C., on the importance of individual riflemen to the security of the country:

"All of us, I am sure, 10 years ago, thought that the need for the man with the rifle would be passing away from the scene in the 1960's. And it is true that there are a good many Americans tonight who are stationed underground in a hardened silo whose duty is to watch some tables and some dials and a button. But the very size and magnitude of these new great weapons have placed a new emphasis upon what we call rather strangely conventional war, and they have made it even more mandatory than ever that we keep the man with the rifle . . ." (GG–p. 487)

34

It was against this backdrop that the next sequence was set in the drama of the gun control movement. A grief-stricken nation turned its attention to the first post-assassination Dodd bill.

The student will bear in mind Senator Dodd opened hearings of the Juvenile Delinquency Subcommittee of the Senate Judiciary Committee on January 29, 1963. These were the first formal hearings on the numerous "Dodd Bills" and their amendments which were to follow in the next several years. The Subcommittee had been studying the matter of mail-order sales of handguns to juveniles for two years prior to these first hearings.

Senator Dodd introduced his S.1975 on August 2, 1963, requiring only a simple notarized sworn statement for the mail-order purchase of handguns.

4

*"Fear of assassination often produces restraints
compatible with dictatorship, not democracy."*

JUSTICE WILLIAM O. DOUGLAS

PRESIDENT JOHN F. KENNEDY WAS ASSASSINATED ON
November 22, 1963. Five days later Senator Dodd introduced a series of amendments to his original S.1975 which produced
two major changes in its provisions. The most conspicuous modification
was to make his amended bill applicable to all firearms, including rifles
and shotguns. Only handguns had been the focus of interest for Senator
Dodd's subcommittee during its investigation of juvenile delinquency
seven months before.

The second significant change related to the notarized sworn affidavits which were to be provided by mail-order purchasers. Under Senator Dodd's new amendment there was the additional requirement that
the contents of such affidavits be certified by the chief law enforcement

officer of the purchaser's locality as being true to the best of his knowledge and belief.

Oddly enough, within less than two weeks, Senator Dodd changed his mind about requiring a certification of the affidavits by local police officials and on December 12, 1963, introduced another amendment. The procedure set forth in the latter amendment would have required mail order purchasers to include within their affidavits the name and address of the principal law enforcement officer of the locality into which the firearm was to be shipped. The amendment further provided that before being legally permitted to ship a firearm to a mail-order purchaser, the seller would first be required to mail to the police official named in the affidavit, by registered mail return-receipt requested, a duplicate copy of the purchaser's affidavit plus the description of the firearm to be shipped, and, further, to delay shipment until return of the receipt evidencing delivery and acceptance of the registered letter by the police.

It is important to note that the last amendment was filed by Senator Dodd only one day before commencement of the hearings on S.1975 by the Senate Committee on Commerce. The rapid succession of amendments and modifications of amendments to S.1975 proved extremely confusing to many persons interested in the proposed legislation, and was no doubt responsible for generating much inappropriate commentary and faulty criticism of S.1975 during the months which followed.

The first witness to testify on behalf of S.1975 was Senator Dodd. He cited instances wherein violent crimes and destructive acts had been committed by persons—many of whom were alleged to have had prior criminal records—whose firearms had been acquired through means of mail-orders. He then proceeded to explain his most recent amendments to S.1975, one of which had only been filed the previous day:

"The purpose of the amendment which I have introduced, and which I introduced after the tragedy of President Kennedy's death, is, first, to broaden the measure to include all firearms and not just handguns. I point out that the bill, as originally drawn, did include just handguns. But we have amended it to include all firearms; and, second, to put more teeth into the affidavit provision.

This legislation, as amended, contains the following provisions:

It prohibits the shipment in interstate commerce of guns to persons under 18 years of age.

It bars mail-order weapons to those who have been convicted of a felony.

It tightens up licensing requirements for manufacturers and sellers of guns in a manner designed to discourage fly-by-night mail-order houses and others who operate on the fringes of law.

It requires one seeking to buy a gun through the mails to State in an affidavit his name, address, age, whether he has a criminal record and whether the purchase would be contrary to local or State law.

It further requires that this affidavit shall include the true name and address of the principal law enforcement officer of the locality in which the affiant resides and that the affiant shall deliver the statement in duplicate to the seller, who must forward a copy of the statement to the law enforcement officer named in the affidavit by registered mail with a return receipt requested. Upon receiving that returned receipt, the dealer may then lawfully execute delivery of the firearm." (BB–pp. 11–12)

Senator Dodd admitted that S.1975 would not prevent all undesirable persons from obtaining firearms, and that it would not solve the "gun problem" in the United States, but he insisted the bill would, nevertheless, close off one avenue of access to lethal weapons for criminals which, in itself, was a solid step in the right direction. The impressive roster of support for S.1975, as amended, was then recited for the record by Senator Dodd:

"This legislation has the support, Mr. Chairman and members of the committee, of the administration. It has been approved by the Justice Department, by the Treasury, by the Commerce Department, by the State Department. And I am very happy to say to the committee that it has the support of the National Rifle Association, which is a very fine organization in this country. We have conferred many times with officials of the National Rifle Association. I don't know how many times altogether, because there have been many meetings, both in the course of our investigation and hearings on this bill, which took almost 2 years, and as recently as last night, and during this week. And we have their support.

I say, with their permission, that they approve of this bill. You know the National Rifle Association is made up of men who know most about guns in this country. And they are responsible people.

It also has the support of the arms industry. In my own State we have quite an arms industry. We have the Colt Co., we have Winchester, we have Remington, we have HI-Standard. It is quite a factor in the State of Connecticut. And I have talked with all of them, and I have talked to other manufacturers of firearms. We have their support for this measure. And perhaps most importantly, we have the support of law-enforcement officials all over this country." (BB–p. 15)

Following his formal statement to the Committee on Commerce, Senator Dodd answered questions put to him by various committee members and, in doing so, he just happened to comment on the general subject of gun registration. He stated to Senator Strom Thurmond:

"I suppose we could require total registration of all guns, maybe simply prohibit the sale or delivery through the mails. I think that is going too far, however. I don't want to go so far as that. I don't think we need it. I know there are some who urge that. But my own judgment is that this can be effective, this can help. It is better to try this way. Maybe we will have to come to a total prohibition of the interstate shipment of firearms. I don't think we do. I don't think the situation yet requires that we face up to that." (BB–p. 16)

Just a few minutes later Senator Cannon informed Senator Dodd that the Justice Department had made a proposal to ban all interstate shipments of firearms except as to dealers and manufacturers, and he asked Senator Dodd whether he supported that proposal. The response was:

"No, Senator. I think it goes too far. As I said to Senator Thurmond, I don't think we need to go that far now." (BB–p. 17)

Following the testimony of Senator Dodd, the committee heard from various other interested individuals, including representatives of major association of sportsmen, wildlife conservationists, several Members of Congress, government witnesses, and private citizens presenting either their own views or the views of local groups for whom they had been authorized to speak. With one exception, police officials representing their departments were conspicuously absent.

One of the most important government witnesses to be heard was John W. Coggins, Chief of the Technical Branch of the Office of Chief Counsel, Bureau of Internal Revenue, Department of the Treasury. It was in that capacity that Mr. Coggins presented the views of the Treasury Department on S.1975 and S.2345, both of which would have amended the Federal Firearms Act of 1938, enforced by the Alcohol and Tobacco Tax Division of the Internal Revenue Service as was also the National Firearms Act of 1934.

The Committee was informed as to how the authority of the Federal Government to control firearms stemmed from two Constitutional provisions, from the power of the Federal Government to regulate interstate and foreign commerce, and from the taxing power of the Federal

Government. A third basis for firearms controls, he observed, rested in the police power reserved to the several States. He then perceptively noted that:

> "The issues presented involve not only the question of constitutional authority, but the judgment as to how and by whom that authority is to be implemented or exercised." (BB–p. 65)

Mr. Coggins went on to say that the Federal Government's clear and exclusive authority to regulate interstate and foreign commerce was the basis for the enactment in 1938 of the Federal Firearms Act. This act, he explained, was designed to implement State firearms laws and to impose additional Federal control with respect to the commerce in firearms through the licensing of firearms dealers and manufacturers, among other things. He also briefly enumerated some of the prohibitions contained in the Federal Firearms Act of 1938:

> "Some of the prohibitions in the act are (1), to engage in business without a license; (2) to receive a firearm from an unlicensed dealer or manufacturer; (3) for a dealer or manufacturer to transport or ship a firearm to a person in a State which requires a license to purchase unless the required State license is exhibited; (4) for any person indicted for, or convicted of, a felony, or who is a fugitive from justice, to ship, to transport, or to receive a firearm in interstate or foreign commerce; and (5) to transport or to receive in interstate or foreign commerce a stolen firearm or one which has the serial number removed, obliterated, or altered." (BB–p. 66)

The second basis of the Federal Government's authority to regulate firearms, namely, the taxing power, was the principle underlying enactment by Congress in 1934 of the National Firearms Act which applied to all categories of small arms except those whose use was for predominantly sporting purposes or for personal defense. Mr. Coggins explained the scope of that Act's application in this manner:

> "The National Firearms Act is directed at the so-called gangster-type weapons, such as submachineguns and sawed-off shotguns, and includes firearms mufflers and firearms silencers, and weapons (other than pistols or revolvers) which are concealable on the person. This latter category includes flashlight guns, pen guns, palm guns, et cetera. and many other deceptive weapons which are made not to appear as weapons." (BB–p. 66)

It was then explained that the National Firearms Act of 1934 operated to control such gangster-type weapons through the imposition of a tax on those persons engaged in the business of importing, manufacturing, or dealing in such arms. In addition, a so-called transfer tax was assessed each and every time such a weapon was either sold or transferred from one owner to another. For example, the tax on the transfer of a submachinegun was $200.

It was for the purpose of enforcing payment of such transfer taxes that all weapons covered by the National Act were required to be individually registered by serial number and description. Extremely heavy penalties were provided for the possession of an unregistered machinegun, sawed-off shotgun, sawed-off rifle, and gadget-type guns, and the other paraphernalia covered by the law. Mr. Coggins explained:

"The possession of an unregistered national act firearm is a felony offense; and insofar as the firearms covered by this act are concerned, we believe that they are now effectively controlled under Federal law throughout the United States." (BB–p. 66)

John Coggins then touched upon an important point, one which should be carefully noted. He referred to one of the key provisions of the Federal Firearms Act of 1938, which flatly prohibited a firearms dealer or manufacturer from shipping any firearm to a resident of a State which required a license to purchase such a firearm unless the purchaser first exhibited his license. He then commented that:

"Since the enactment of the Federal Firearms Act in 1938, we understand that only seven States (Hawaii, Massachusetts, Michigan, Missouri, New Jersey, New York, and North Carolina) have seen fit to enact enabling legislation requiring a license to purchase concealable weapons, thereby affording the assistance granted by the provisions of section 2(c) of the act." (BB–p. 67)

The relevance of that statement became apparent during the subsequent questioning period when William T. Beeks, the professional staff member assigned to the hearings, asked John Coggins this penetrating question:

"We have the National Firearms Act now and the Federal Firearms Act, which are designed to implement State law. If the States passed adequate laws to implement the Federal Firearms Act, would Federal legislation be necessary?" (BB–p. 73)

Directing his reply to the narrow issue of controlling the interstate shipments of guns purchased by mail order, John Coggins commented:

"Although if each State passed laws tying in exactly with 2(c) of the act, which meant you had a permit to purchase, then it would not be possible to ship to an individual in that State, . . . unless the permit to purchase, issued by the State, was exhibited to the dealer." (BB–p. 73)

That particular fact was one which was frequently referred to by those persons who argued that the proper role and function of the Federal Government was simply to provide the means whereby individual States could, if they chose to do so, control the influx of firearms into their own jurisdictions. This argument had strong connotations of States' rights and was based squarely upon the Constitutional reservation of police powers to the individual States as opposed to the Federal Government. Furthermore, it was vigorously maintained that the crime problem varied from one State to another, and that firearms played a different and more important role in the less sparsely populated Western States than in the congested crime-ridden Eastern States. It was said repeatedly that it was the constitutional prerogative of each State, through its own general assembly, to make any law which its elected representatives deemed necessary for the full and proper exercise of its own police power. Many Members of Congress felt strongly that the issue of states' rights was of paramount importance, and the issue of gun control of very secondary importance. This fact was generally overlooked by most casual observers of the controversy.

John Coggins left no question in the minds of the members of the Committee on Commerce as to the complete endorsement by the Treasury Department of all the provisions contained in Senator Dodd's S.1975:

"The laws and ordinances of the States and local communities controlling the sale and possession of firearms are to an extent now being thwarted by the lack of Federal control over interstate mail-order-type shipments to individuals. The controls contained in S.1975 we feel are necessary and desirable and will clearly be an aid to States and localities that have made a serious effort to deal with firearms problems within their own jurisdictions. There would appear to be no reason for delay in dealing with this particular problem. In S.1975, the problem has been identified and practical and reasonable solutions to that problem have been carefully and thoughtfully developed over a period of years, taking into account the views of the firearms industry, organizations representing sportsmen, law enforcement representatives, and other interested groups. We feel that the fact that the National Rifle Association (certainly not a group inclined to support unreasonable firearms legislation) stated at the outset of this hearing that it would interpose no objections to the enactment of S.1975 (as it would be amended by Senator Dodd's proposals of December 12, 1963) is a clear indication that the enactment of this legislation would not unduly inconvenience or burden responsible citizens." (BB–p. 68)

It will be recalled that Senator Dodd's original S.1975 introduced August 2, 1963, only required a simple notarized sworn statement for the mail order purchase of pistols. Senator Dodd's amendment of November 27, 1963, added the requirement that the purchaser's affidavit also contain a certification by the chief police official of the locality into which the firearm was to be shipped. In turn, that certification requirement was changed by Senator Dodd's amendment of December 12, 1963, which simply substituted a provision requiring the forwarding of a duplicate copy of the affidavit to the local police official by registered mail with a return receipt requested. Inasmuch as the last amendment had been filed only one day before commencement of the hearings, John Coggins orally covered the Treasury Department's reaction to its effect:

"The Treasury Department has not submitted its views to the committee on the revision of this proposed subsection. Let me now state that the Department is of the view that the provisions of the proposed new subsection (1) of section 2 can be effectively administered and constitutes a generally more acceptable and reasonable alternative approach in achieving protection against abuses of mail-order shipments, as would have been the case under the scheme calling for authentication of the affidavit by the local police official." (BB–p. 69)

The official position of the National Rifle Association of America with respect to Senator Dodd's S.1975, as had been determined by its officers and Executive Committee, was presented to the Senate Committee on Commerce by Franklin Orth.

"The relative ease of accessibility of these handguns to certain undesirable elements of our society through advertisements in cheap pulp magazines and their subsequent delivery by mail or by common carrier was, and continues to be, a matter of much concern to the members of the National Rifle Association.
    Because of our concern with these problems and their possible effects on the interests of the many legitimate firearms users, the NRA worked closely with the staff of the subcommittee in conducting nu-

merous informal meetings to study the problems involved, assisted in the draft of S.1975 and spoke in favor of the original bill at the open hearings in May of this year.

S.1975, as originally introduced, represents the combined thinking and agreement of many segments of the shooting fraternity and is the product of more than 2 years of study and research. The terms of the bill were fairly and logically conceived and were the results of a sound approach to a solution to what has become a national problem." (BB–p. 49)

In order to eliminate any possible question as to whether or not the National Rifle Association of America supported the post-assassination amendment of November 27, 1963, by Senator Dodd, which had the effect of enlarging the scope of the original S.1975 so as to include rifles and shotguns as well as the originally covered pistols, Senator Philip A. Hart raised that issue with Franklin Orth:

"SENATOR HART. With respect to the first—the inclusion of rifles in the present Dodd bill as distinguished from the one introduced in August—have rifles been retained in the bill he introduced this morning?

MR. ORTH. Yes, sir.

SENATOR HART. And you have no objection to that?

MR. ORTH. We do not think that any sane American, who calls himself an American, can object to placing into this bill the instrument which killed the President of the United States." (BB–p. 55)

Franklin Orth also told the committee that the National Rifle Association had consistently favored increased and mandatory penalties where armed force had been used in the commission of a crime. He pointed out that violent crimes were acts of individuals and that such acts were not inherent in any instrument used, including firearms. He stressed that deterrent legislation must provide punishment for those criminal acts, and to be effective, those punishments must be firmly applied.

Interestingly enough, as time progressed, it developed that the concept of increased mandatory penalties for commission of crime was vigorously opposed by many of those same individuals who had most loudly demanded more restrictive gun controls, including confiscation of privately owned firearms. That is a fact worthy of careful consideration.

Because of the importance attached by many Members of Congress to the official position of the National Rifle Association of America,

Senator Hart once again pressed Franklin Orth on the question as to its support of Senator Dodd's S.1975:

"SENATOR HART. Lest a reader of this record or others present may have any doubt, does the association support the bill in the form introduced this morning by Senator Dodd?
MR. ORTH. In the form introduced this morning, the association supports the bill of Senator Dodd." (BB–p. 56)

During these hearings, the President of the National Rifle Association was the Honorable Bartlett Rummel, a Superior Court Judge from the State of Washington and a man who, by reason of having combined with his legal profession many years of studious interest in the specialized field of firearms legislation, was eminently well qualified to testify with respect to Senator Dodd's S.1975.

Judge Rummel recognized no inconsistency between his conservative and scholarly view of the Second Amendment to the United States Constitution and the specific methods for controlling the interstate shipments of mail order firearms as were provided in S.1975.

"We, as an organization, have supported the Dodd bill. As you know our people worked with Senator Dodd and his committee for many, many months, even prior to this very recent tragedy. We think that it is a good bill as it is now amended. As a matter of fact, it in itself is an amendment to the Federal Firearms Act and it does restrict in a reasonable way the mail-order business in guns. We have supported that, and we feel that is a proper thing." (BB–p. 123)

The National Wildlife Federation is the largest nonprofit organization in the United States dedicated to the conservation of wildlife through means of education. It is, as its name implies, a federation of affiliated independent local conservation organizations throughout each of the 50 States. Altogether, the individual members of those affiliates along with other supporters of the Federation numbered over 2,000,000 persons. Thomas L. Kimball, Executive Director of the National Wildlife Federation, was one of the witnesses who testified on December 18, 1963, before the Senate Committee on Commerce.

Compressing into remarkably few words the essence of what was encompassed by the American tradition of firearms ownership, Mr. Kimball also concisely described their role in the modern management of wildlife:

45

"Guns in the hands of responsible citizens have won our freedom and independence, rolled back our western frontiers, won two World Wars, provided millions of hours of pleasure and recreation for the sportsmen of our Nation, sustained an important industry vital to our Nation's economy and defense, and provided a continuing supply of meat and protein by cropping the Nation's wildlife surplus. Wildlife, a great renewable resource owned by the people must be managed to prosper and the removal of surplus animals by sport shooting protects the environment and is a vital and inseparable part of wise management." (BB–p. 80)

The position of the National Wildlife Federation with respect to Senator Dodd's S.1975 was one of support combined with an earnest request that the committee consider a slight modification of two of its less important provisions so as to guard against unintended problems and the possibility of abuses of its procedures.

The first of the two sections to which Mr. Kimball referred pertained to the provision that prohibited the firearms dealer from shipping the firearms to mail order purchasers until such time as the registered mail return receipt was returned to the dealer, signed by the purchaser's local police official:

"Only when receiving the return receipt may the seller lawfully execute delivery of the firearm. As I read the provision, the language provides police veto power over any and all gun purchases by mail order. There is no law requiring the intended recipient of registered mail to sign unless he desires to receive the message being conveyed. Without the return receipt, the gun dealer is powerless to conclude a sale. The provision requiring the seller to receive the returned receipt from the police should be eliminated and the penalties for executing a false affidavit should be increased." (BB–pp. 76–77)

The other provision over which Mr. Kimball showed concern related to the general language with which Senator Dodd's amendment of December 12th specified that the notice required to be sent by the firearms dealer to the principal law enforcement officer was to contain a description of the firearm to be shipped. Specifically, it was feared that in the event the Secretary of the Treasury were to define by regulations "description of the firearm" as including serial numbers, then this would undoubtedly lead to the establishment of firearms registration programs which were strongly opposed on principle by the National Wildlife Federation. Mr. Kimball's suggestion to the committee was direct and to the point:

46

"The Secretary should be prohibited from promulgating any regulations other than those specifically permitted by the Congress. More specifically there should not be a requirement for the serial number of a firearm as a condition of purchase. A requirement of both name of purchaser and serial number of weapons purchased would undoubtedly be used as a firearms registration device." (BB–p. 77)

Senator Cannon thanked Mr. Kimball for his statement and made a final inquiry of him to be certain that the position of the National Wildlife Federation was understood by members of the committee. He asked: "Do I understand, then, the thrust of your statement is that you see no objection to the provisions of the Dodd bill as it has now been amended?" Thomas Kimball's immediate answer was, "Yes."

Midway through the hearings by the Senate Committee on Commerce, Senator Dodd reconsidered the two minor provisions mentioned by Mr. Kimball and, although he knew that S.1975 had already been endorsed by both the National Rifle Association and the National Wildlife Federation, even with inclusion of those provisions, he voluntarily withdrew them from his bill. He accomplished the necessary changes by way of his letter dated January 22, 1964, addressed to Senator Warren G. Magnuson, Chairman of the Senate Committee on Commerce, stating that his subcommittee was not interested in recording the serial number of a mail-order weapon.

Senator Dodd further agreed to withdraw the provision prohibiting shipment of firearms by a dealer until the registered mail return receipt was returned to the dealer signed by the purchaser's local police official.

He withdrew these two provisions on the grounds, as he said, "the Federal Government has fulfilled its obligation if it enables local law enforcement to enforce its own laws," and, further, because in doing so he removed the objections expressed "by legitimate gun groups."

In another letter to Senator Magnuson dated January 29, 1964, the National Shooting Sports Foundation acknowledged Senator Dodd's changes in the two sections, expressed their full support and waived their scheduled oral testimony before the Senate Committee on Commerce in the interest of saving the committee's time.

Vaughn K. Goodwin, First Vice President of the National Muzzle Loading Rifle Association, presented their evaluation of Senator Dodd's S.1975 in terms of its potential effect on their activities and that of their individual members. The Subcommittee was informed the National Muzzle Loading Rifle Association believed that existing gun regulations were sufficient, but that there was a problem because existing laws were not being enforced. Accordingly, he indicated their full support for any efforts to enforce existing criminal laws, and predicted that crime waves and juvenile delinquency would continue until loopholes were closed and leniency discontinued.

A somewhat unique problem for muzzle-loading firearms enthusiasts was called to the committee's attention by Mr. Goodwin, namely, that there were less than a half-dozen people who manufacture muzzle-loading firearms. The consequence of that was that the majority of such guns were normally obtained by mail order. In spite of this prime consideration, which they anticipated would have a negative effect on their acquisition of muzzle-loading firearms, they were, nevertheless, prepared to give their support to Senator Dodd's S.1975.

Senator Cannon asked whether the National Muzzle Loading Rifle Association felt that the Dodd bill would deprive them of the right to be armed. Vaughn Goodwin replied in these words:

> "We feel, the way it is, that present legislation is sufficient to take care of this if it is properly enforced. If you have to go to some type, we back the NRA in this respect, that the Dodd bill as it presently stands would not be the best for our best interests, but we would at least back it in lieu of any other more serious. But we don't believe there should be any other legislation other than that." (BB–pp. 137–138)

The National Muzzle Loading Rifle Association and the Ohio Gun Collectors Association shared a similar problem in that they were both dependent on mail-order shipments to obtain unusual firearms not commercially available on the mass market. There was a significant difference between the two groups, however, in terms of the frequency of mail order transactions among gun collectors as opposed to shooters, and in the average financial value of those transactions.

Competitive muzzle-loading firearms shooters do not use antique guns for their activity, but instead purchase and use newly manufactured replicas of such arms providing more reliable accuracy and a greater margin of safety. The cost of such replicas is but a small fraction of the price for genuine original muzzle-loading firearms of a similar design and in a condition suitable of collecting purposes. Also, when once the required number of muzzle-loading firearms are acquired by the shooter, permitting his participation in the broad variety of competitive shoots conducted for such firearms, the occasions for adding to their number or disposing of those which are no longer desired, are inconsequential in comparison to the continual zig-zag movement of firearms among gun collectors.

It was, therefore, quite understandable that the Ohio Gun Col-

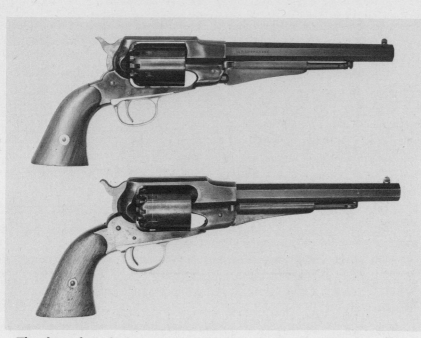

The above shows both original and replica examples of cap-and-ball pistols.

lectors Association would attempt to persuade the Senate Committee on Commerce that there existed a logical distinction between those firearms which were most obviously of an antique variety and those of a somewhat more modern character. The logic and reasonableness for such a distinction was presented by LaDow Johnston, President of the Ohio Gun Collectors Association:

"Those firearms falling within the scope of the term 'antique' weapons are highly prized by collectors and enthusiasts as specimens of a bygone era. They mark stages in the development of small arms through the process of experimentation, trial and error, and plain American inventiveness. Their sole value today lies in their historical associations and in their unique character. Clearly, Senator Dodd and this committee intend that legislation be directed towards those weapons favored by the criminal and not towards those firearms which have little or no utility and appeal for the lawless. Few people bent on committing crime will use matchlock, wheellock, snaphaunce, flintlock, per-

49

cussion lock, or similar weapons in preference of modern handgun or shoulder weapons. In connection with this observation, it should be noted that ammunition for many antique firearms is not available." (BB–pp. 170–171)

The solution to the gun collector problem was, in the view of LaDow Johnston, both simple and complex. Simple, because all that needed to be done was somehow to exclude antique firearms from the application of Senator Dodd's bill; complex, because it was virtually impossible to draw a definition that could satisfy the government and yet encompass the great variety of arms which were the legitimate subjects of gun collecting activities.

One of the witnesses to appear in support of Senator Dodd's S.1975 was George N. Craig, past National Commander of the American Legion and past Governor of the State of Indiana.

Governor Craig placed strong emphasis on the importance of maintaining marksmanship and safety training programs for the nation's youth. Governor Craig informed the committee that each year, through the joint efforts of the National Rifle Association and the American Legion, an average of 250,000 youths were taught the fundamentals of proper and safe use of firearms and taught to respect them for the lawful purposes for which they were intended. He then observed that that number of young men was approximately equal to six American Army Divisions, and also pointed out that military men throughout the nation's history have regarded the American soldier as being superbly efficient with small arms because of being familiar with them from an early age.

Among the several distinguished Members of Congress who addressed the Senate Committee on Commerce with respect to Senator Dodd's S.1975 were men who themselves had a lifelong interest in firearms and a personal understanding and appreciation of their legitimate role in American life. The message they brought reflected their deep and abiding concern for the preservation of the atmosphere of freedom which had been so uniquely enjoyed by law-abiding citizens since the Nation's birth. As Members of Congress to whom firearms had a special significance, they, nevertheless, left no question as to their willingness to support fully Senator Dodd's S.1975. Such a man was the Honorable Robert L.F. Sikes:

"Mr. Chairman and members of the committee, I am pleased to have this opportunity to express my feelings on the subject of additional gun laws now before this committee for consideration. During the years that I have had the privilege of holding elected office, the subject of the right of the law-abiding citizen to keep and bear arms, as guaranteed by our Constitution, has been, and continues to be, a subject of interest and deep concern to me. It is a matter of particular moment now, because of renewed agitation for tighter gun laws.

The tragic and senseless assassination of President Kennedy quite naturally resulted in a wave of hysteria against weapons and the ownership of weapons. However deplorable this inexcusable act was, it scarcely follows that a crime committed by one man should cause 35 million gun owners to be persecuted. I seriously question that the legislation now proposed would have prevented the purchase of a gun by Lee Oswald or would have resulted in tighter security measures than those which were in effect." (BB–pp. 91–92)

Congressman Sikes was not referring to Senator Dodd's S.1975 when he spoke of gun owners being persecuted, but, rather, his reference related to the vituperation against guns, and the people who owned and used them, which was rampant in the news media during this period. Firearms had become the vehicle by means of which many news writers, editorialists, and broadcast commentators vented their personal frustrations without restraint, rationality or conscience.

Congressman Sikes continued to point up the futility of attempting to legislate against human inconsistencies and portrayed firearms as being merely inanimate objects which, by themselves, possessed neither the capacity, nor the motive, to harm anyone. He reflected on the fact that the only people ever really affected by gun restrictions were the honest people, while those intent upon committing crime continued to procure deadly weapons by whatever means are necessary.

Congressman Sikes further made clear his intention to support any legislation which would make it more difficult for criminals or those inclined towards criminal activities, mental incompetents, drug addicts, habitual drunkards, and juveniles to obtain guns, and which would also severely penalize those persons perpetuating crimes while armed.

Paralleling to a large extent the views which had been expressed by Congressman Sikes were those of the Honorable John J. Flynt Jr. who deplored the efforts of those persons who sought to place the blame for the Dallas tragedy upon the ownership of a particular kind of gun, and who thereby made a whipping boy out of every gun owner, gun collector, sportsman, and gun dealer in the United States. The high esteem in which he held the right of private ownership of firearms was mirrored in these words:

"One of the prized possessions of Americans has been the right to own and possess firearms and to use these firearms in defense of country, in defense of home, in self-defense, provided that use is done in a legal and legitimate manner. The attitude towards firearms has become a historical tradition in the United States. I think it is safe to say that it represents a priceless freedom won by those preceding us as Americans, which few if any other nations enjoy. So strong was the conviction of early Americans about the right of law-abiding citizens to own, possess, and use firearms for lawful purposes, that there was included in an early amendment to the U.S. Constitution a provision that 'the right of the people to keep and bear arms shall not be infringed.' " (BB–p. 97)

Asserting that the right to keep and bear arms was exceedingly precious in the early days of the Republic, Congressman Flynt stoutly maintained that the right was still equally precious. In capsulizing the utility of firearms in modern America, he said:

"Guns have been and will continue to be constructive tools in America. Today they are used to build healthy minds and healthy bodies, to help develop self-discipline, initiative, and team spirit, to help prepare our young men to defend American ideals, both within and outside the armed services of our country. Hunting and shooting are wholesome forms of recreation which may be enjoyed for a lifetime. The development of firearms traces the historical progress of our Nation and the possession of them, individually and by law-abiding groups, offers a fascinating hope by too many Americans with real historic value." (BB–p. 97)

Congressman Flynt was responding to the increasing hostility against firearms marshaled by various persons who were seeking to exploit the nation's grief over the death of its young president. He soberly observed:

"Unfortunately, there has entered in the mainstream of American life a prejudice against firearms, a prejudice really against the simple ownership of guns." (BB–p. 97)

In spite of the impressive showing of support for Senator Dodd's bill by the country's largest organizations whose members would be most directly affected by its enactment, Dodd's principles did not enjoy either universal enthusiasm, or even grudging acceptance. Many entirely responsible, knowledgeable and sensitive individuals entertained grave reservations concering many aspects of Senator Dodd's S.1975 and its potential consequences. One such man was the Honorable Paul Fannin, Governor of Arizona.

The views of Governor Fannin were not exclusively his alone, but were shared by many Americans who lived in the States whose borders encompassed the great open plains, the vast arid desert regions, and the western mountain chains. Firearms, and access to them, had a different meaning in the lives of these people, and they were not at all disposed to reticence in this regard.

The written statement of Governor Fannin was presented to the Senate Committee on Commerce by Senator Carl Hayden, also of the State of Arizona. Highlights from that informative document follow:

"As Governor of Arizona it is my duty to uphold the constitution and laws of Arizona and to protect the rights and property of Arizona citizens. A study of S.1975 by Senator Thomas Dodd convinces me this bill would infringe the rights of our citizens under our constitution and convert to the whims of a Federal agency the time-honored principle that a man is innocent until proven guilty." (BB–p. 198)

Governor Fannin referred to the Constitution of the State of Arizona:

"I believe it is significant that a large majority of the States adopted strong constitutional provisions to guarantee the right of their citizens to keep and bear arms. And it cannot be argued that these provisions were a product of the frontier because Arizona's constitution was adopted in 1910, some 30 years after the last Indian war. It says: 'The right of the individual citizen to bear arms in defense of himself or the State shall not be impaired, but nothing in this section shall be construed as authorizing individuals or corporations to organize, maintain, or employ an armed body of men.' " (BB–p. 198)

One problem that was unique to the State of Arizona was its status as the custom gunsmithing center of the United States. Governor Fannin explained:

"This bill would also impose a restraint on trade that would virtually wipe out the lifework and businesses of a number of our citizens, some of whom are known nationwide for the quality of their work in building fine rifles, and accurizing rifles for this country's leading competitive shooters, including some of the top marksmen of the Air Force and the Army."

* * *

"All of these depend upon mail-order business for their existence, but theirs is not a traffic in cheap arms with criminals. Some of the rifles they turn out cost hundreds of dollars, and their barrels draw premium prices throughout the country." (BB–p. 198)

The concern expressed in Governor Fannin's concluding appeal to the members of the Senate Committee on Commerce was echoed time and time again by many others in the years that followed. It was ridiculed and scoffed at by those who would have hidden the truth from the public, but it has proved to be far more prophetic than even the Governor might have dreamed:

"I appeal to you, gentlemen, not to be carried away by the hysteria of our President's assassination. The antigun people of our country have seized upon this as an opening wedge to disarm the citizens of this country so they will quickly forget the skill of marksmanship. But I must remind you that our country must depend on its citizenry in time of grave peril, and there never is time to train expert marksmen." (BB–p. 198)

It should be understood that from the moment of President Kennedy's assassination there was an extraordinary volume of news coverage pertaining to Senator Dodd's bill and to related congressional hearings. Also, virtually every prominent personality interviewed by the press or on radio or television had some kind of personal theory concerning the gun control laws needed. Few, if any, such persons were acquainted with the nature and provisions of Senator Dodd's bill other than that such a bill was pending in Congress.

Even those sportsmen whose knowledge of Senator Dodd's bill had been, for the most part, gleaned from various articles appearing in the sports magazines became quickly confused because of conflicting interpretations of what provisions it did, or did not, contain. This was, of course, aggravated because of Senator Dodd's relatively rapid-fire amendments to his bill. It is also important to understand that although the primary legislation before the Senate Committee on Commerce was S.1975, the committee's attention was by no means directed only to that measure, and, therefore, the field of discussion, debate and deliberation was wide.

The hearings by the Senate Committee on Commerce provided the source for many news stories which purported to report the content of testimony given by the more prominent witnesses. However, the hearings were separated by lengthy intervals and it would be unreasonable to expect that news reporters, usually knowing little of the background of Senator Dodd's bill or the role played in its development by the National Rifle Association and the firearms industry, could accurately portray the real issues, even if one charitably granted that they were inclined to do so.

Contributing to this vexacious situation was the fact that several witnesses appearing before the committee submitted proposals which did less to advance the cause of enacting Senator Dodd's bill than to alarm people who were already confused but who had accepted the leadership of the National Rifle Association in its support of S.1975.

Bear in mind Senator Dodd had broadened S.1975 to cover rifles and shotguns and had strengthened the affidavit provisions immediately following the assassination of President Kennedy. Many members of the large sports and conservation organizations were, therefore, disturbed. Nevertheless, the leadership of these organizations had steadfastly continued their support of S.1975. It can be imagined the shocking effect produced by the following remarks of Mr. James V. Bennett, representing the Department of Justice:

"The bill S.1975, introduced by our mutually good friend, Senator Dodd, is a step in the right direction. I would recommend it. I would recommend, however, that, if anything, this committee undertake to strengthen its already meritorious provisions. It was, as you know, written before November 22, 1963, and was intended largely to discourage mail-order sales to juveniles only." (BB–p. 101)

From that moment forward, Bennett's choice of the words, "a step in the right direction", would send chills of apprehension down the spines of lawful firearms owners across the country. Those words were from a prominent man in government, representing the Attorney General, who had earlier recommended registration—historically, in other countries, a first step, and a necessary prerequisite, to confiscation of privately owned firearms.

Bennett proceeded to recommend a total ban on the interstate shipment of firearms consigned to private citizens. So, even while supporters of Senator Dodd's S.1975 were concerning themselves over the niceties of the language contained in its various provisions, so as not to produce needless problems or hardships unintentionally, Bennett suggested that the entire system of purchasing firearms by mail-order be totally abolished. Yet, he was not finished. He was still to suggest gun registration despite the gun-owning American's justified fears of it. Not a man to proceed by half measures, Bennett proposed the centralization in federal record-keeping of all firearms sales records in the Treasury

55

Department. Bear in mind dealer's records of gun sales had been a requirement since the Federal Firearms Act of 1938 had become effective.

Senator Dodd was to wonder in the days following what had stirred so many people to write their congressmen protesting gun registration when there was nothing whatever within S.1975 requiring the registration of firearms. The enthusiasm of some of its backers exceeded the force of its content and they spoke recklessly. Within minutes after proposing the establishment of a procedure to systematically collect and centralize all gun dealer's sales records, Bennett did not hesitate to make this confusing disavowal:

> "We are not suggesting a gun registration bill, not suggesting a bill that would in any way infringe the right to keep and bear arms."
> (BB–p. 104)

By some perversion of logic, Bennett first proposed amending Senator Dodd's S.1975 so as to establish national record-keeping for which national gun registration would clearly be indispensable; then calmly went on and assured the committee that it really wasn't gun registration, but that whatever it was it would not infringe on "the right to keep and bear arms." A few minutes later he proceeded to deny that the right to keep and bear arms was a basic freedom:

> "The wording of the constitutional amendment, as I recall, says that a 'well-regulated militia, being necessary to the security of a free people, the right to keep and bear arms shall not be infringed.'
> It is not one of the basic freedoms. It is hooked up with decisions that have said time and time again, with the notion that applies to the militia, well-regulated militia." (BB–p. 105)

Bennett played a major role during the years which followed in the national controversy over gun control. His name continued to be linked ever more firmly with the anti-gun movement in the United States.

The shooting sports world did not have long to wait until his proposal to abolish completely the sale of guns by mail order was incorporated in a bill and submitted to Congress. It appeared in the House of Representatives as H.R. 9757 and was known as the Lindsay bill, after John V. Lindsay, who at that time was a Congressman from the State of New York.

Congressman Lindsay testified before the Senate Committee on Commerce on January 30, 1964, the final day of the regularly scheduled hearings. Before explaining the details of his bill, the Lindsay bill, he volunteered that it had actually been drafted by his friend James V. Bennett and "his people in the Bureau of Prisons and the Department of Justice." He also paid the following compliment to Senator Dodd:

> "I certainly want to compliment Senator Dodd on his advancement of his proposal and I should like to compliment him and his office and assistants on the wonderful job they have done in persuading the Rifle Association to, as I understand it, back the provisions of his bill. I am very optimistic, therefore, that we may see a result." (BB–p. 232)

Several other comments made by Congressman Lindsay during his testimony are worth noting for future reference. One was his reaction to the volume of mail which he received following the publication in the *Saturday Evening Post* of an article written by him entitled "Too Many People Have Guns":

> "And my mail is pouring in at a very great rate. And I am amazed at the rapid assumptions that people make, that just because some kind of regulation is proposed, they think that they are going to be deprived of a very basic and historical, traditional right in this country to own a firearm. No legislation that I know of, State or Federal, is proposed to impinge upon that right." (BB–p. 233)

He was evidently not prepared to proceed quite as far as did James V. Bennett when it came to playing down the importance and significance of the Constitution's Second Amendment, and instead uttered this assurance to the committee:

> "Certainly in framing gun-control laws we must think carefully about the constitutional aspects of the question. Surely there is no reason why we should prevent responsible adults or even minors from possessing licensed firearms—for self-protection, hunting, target shooting or gun collections. But it should also be apparent that the unrestricted traffic in death weapons must be stopped." (BB–p. 234)

One of the most interesting witnesses to grace the Senate Committee on Commerce hearings was a Deputy Commissioner of the New York City Police Department, Leonard E. Reismann. Although Reisman did not directly address his testimony to Senator Dodd's bill, he did provide some fascinating insights into the thinking of the New York City Police Department which administered the State's so-called Sullivan Law in that city. A self-proclaimed afficionado of sporting firearms,

Reisman seldom neglected to mention that fact in such a way as to suggest that he sympathized with legitimate firearms owners in the pursuit of their interests:

"Mr. Chairman, members of the committee, before proceeding to my prepared text, may I point out that I am not insensitive to the interests of the sportsmen and the gun enthusiasts. I, too, am one. I, too, competed at Camp Perry, before the war, and shot an impossible at a thousand yards. I am a member, probably not in good standing any longer, of various gun clubs. So my remarks are the result of the consideration that should be and has been given to the interests of the sportsmen, the hunter, and the lobbyist." (BB–p. 210)

The major thrust of the highly restrictive New York State's Sullivan Law was described by Mr. Reisman in this manner:

"In the State of New York, no one (the short list of exemptions is of no relevance in this discussion) may legally possess a pistol, revolver, or other firearm of a size which may be concealed upon the person unless he has first obtained a license.
The procedure whereby a person applies for and receives a license is very detailed and involves an intensive investigation both of the applicant and of his need to possess the firearm." (BB–p. 210)

Note his use of the words, "his need to possess the firearm". The key to that phrase and to the Sullivan Law is the word "need", a clue to the subjective criteria which is at the root of much of the justifiable criticism of the thoroughly despised Sullivan Law. A flash of insight into the philosophy that guided the New York City police in their administration of the Sullivan Law was provided by Mr. Reisman's candid statement:

"We do not consider that the issuance of a license is an inalienable right in the city of New York." (BB–p. 215)

At the time of these hearings the New York State Sullivan Law was unquestionably the most severely restrictive pistol licensing and permit law in the country, and the myriad injustices suffered by entirely law-abiding citizens were legend. The very name "Sullivan Law" was anathema to the country's organized firearms owners.

Detailing plans to extend the provisions of the Sullivan Law Reisman provided harassed New York firearms owners with additional food for thought with which to occupy their idle moments for the next several years:

"To implement this, we are also asking for the licensing of dealers in rifles and shotguns, the registration of all rifles and shotguns now possessed by individuals, the obtaining of a certificate of eligibility which recites that the individual has not been convicted of a felony or serious misdemeanor and has not been institutionalized for mental illness before a rifle or shotgun may be purchased.

Finally, we propose to limit the sale of ammunition to those persons who possess a certificate of registration or of eligibility for the weapon for which the ammunition is designed. These proposals may seem hard but they are logical, fair and of no inconvenience to the sportsman or gun enthusiast." (BB–p. 212)

New York residents were not the only people to take note of Reisman's bold candor. From one end of the country to the other American gun owners were quietly observing the gradual constriction of proposals for new laws—and each constituted a "step in the right direction."

For all practical purposes the official hearings before the Senate Committee on Commerce came to a close on January 30, 1964, but one month later they were reconvened for a brief 45 minutes at the specific request of Senator Dodd who, during the interim, had become disturbed over mounting public opposition to S.1975. Senator Dodd explained to the committee members why he requested being heard once again:

"I have asked to appear here again because I feel that the bill which I and members of the Juvenile Delinquency Subcommittee introduced has been the target of an irresponsible lobbying campaign.

On December 10, 1963, 18 days after the assassination of President Kennedy, Chairman Magnuson of this committee announced the first public hearings on S.1975, a bill which I had introduced some 4 months prior to the assassination. When the bill was introduced, it was with the approval of the major Federal, State, and private groups concerned with firearms legislation. The amendments I sponsored after President Kennedy's death with a mail-order gun likewise have the approval of the important leaders in Government, industry, and sports groups. And, as of today, it is a matter of record that these same groups publicly support the amended S.1975 as it is currently being considered by your committee.

However, despite all these years of research by Government, business, industry, and groups of sportsmen; despite their cooperative effort in drawing the bill; despite the several public hearings on the bill in each phase of its development, I have become aware of a concerted attempt to kill the bill, attempts to see that the bill, S.1975, never becomes law. There is no doubt in my mind at all that this is the intention of the opposition.

One of the principal devices used by the opposition is the attribution of certain concepts to S.1975, which are in no way a part of the bill.

Even the press can become confused by witnesses who are supposed to be for the bill, who then object to a host of ideas which have no relation, whatever, to the bill before this committee. Thus, de facto support of S.1975 has frequently been interpreted through the press to the public as opposition.

Let me give you an example. There is a news story covering the Commerce Committee hearings from the Washington Post. It is headlined, 'Police Powers in Gun Control Bill Rapped.'

The same story is in the Washington Star. It is headlined:

'Control of Firearms Sales Backed by Two Groups.' " (BB–pp. 273–274)

Senator Dodd's point about the kind of news emphasis given to the testimony concerning his bill was too obvious to miss, even in the opening lines of the two articles. Although he was unaware of it at the time, this pattern of "news reporting" would continue and eventually result in a spirited crusade against both private ownership of firearms and against the National Rifle Association of America.

The opening lines from the *Washington Post* article of December 18, 1963, were as follows:

"The National Wildlife Federation proposed amendments yesterday to key sections of legislation before Congress restricting the sale of mail-order guns. The federation, backed by the National Rifle Association, urged removal of a requirement in the bill that the serial number of a gun be given to police in the jurisdiction to which it is to be shipped. It also objected to a provision that the mail-order house hold up shipping the guns until a registered letter is received that police have been notified of the sale." (BB–p. 274)

The opening lines from the *Washington Evening Star* article of December 18, 1963, were as follows:

"A bill to establish controls on firearm sales today won support from two organizations." (BB–p. 275)

It is obviously easy to accentuate either the positive or the negative aspects of a news story. This is frequently done by the choice of words in the caption establishing the tone of the article in the mind of the reader. It is also done by emphasizing information carefully selected either to heighten or diminish the apparent importance of any particular facet of the subject. Recent apologists for this kind of journalism have euphemistically characterized it as "interpretative journalism."

Senator Dodd continued his lamentation to the committee:

"Mr. Chairman, these two reporters are writing about the same hearing and the same witnesses. I am not charging the reporters here with anything except to support what I said a minute ago, that the campaign against the bill has been such that it is almost impossible to make clear what the truth of the matter is and what the efforts of the opposition are." (BB–p. 275)

To dissuade the committee members from any inclination to reject his bill because of any misunderstandings they might have harbored concerning it, Senator Dodd valiantly answered each of the allegations which he believed had been unfairly leveled at S.1975.

Accompanying Senator Dodd to this special session of the committee was Franklin Orth, Executive Vice President of the National Rifle Association. Senator Dodd commented about Mr. Orth's presence:

"I have been particularly concerned because I think there has been a studied effort to have it appear that the National Rifle Association is opposed. As a matter of fact, I have even received mail from members of that organization who apparently got this impression some way or another. That just is not so. And I worked rather closely with the NRA when I originally drew up this bill. We were in consultation all of the time with the NRA, because I felt and I feel now this is a very responsible organization in this country. Mr. Franklin Orth is here, and I asked if he could be here today in case you wanted him to tell you what the attitude of his organization is about this matter." (BB–p. 280)

At that point Senator Cannon acknowledged Franklin Orth and inquired of him as to whether there was anything he desired to add to what had been said by Senator Dodd. Franklin Orth replied:

"Senator, the position of the organization, its elected officers and officials, has not changed in respect to the Dodd bill.

Now obviously in an organization the size of NRA, with 625,000 individual members and some 400,000 members in our affiliated clubs, which represents over a million sportsmen in the United States, there are some individuals among that group who may not agree with the officers and officials. But that does not mean the NRA is not solidly behind what Senator Dodd is trying to do, namely, to stop the criminal, the mentally incompetent, the drug addict, and the habitual drunkard from obtaining arms through the mail, along with the juvenile, who is unsupervised.

That is our stand, and we stay with Senator Dodd all of the way in that effort, because we feel that sportsmen in the United States who want to use guns should be able to use them for all reasons, for sporting in the field, shooting in competition, and for personal defense in their home or place of business. These things have not been infringed in the Dodd bill. And we believe therefore that the Dodd bill should be supported." (BB–p. 281)

Orth might well have added it was small wonder ordinary citizens were confused, considering the kind of news reporting by those striving to support the bill—a thing which drove even Senator Dodd to complain.

5

"Every avenue of solution will be studied. But the solution must not be one conceived in hysteria, born of ignorance, intended to foster complacency and destined to futility. The solution must be total, not partial. It must be dictated by the voices of reason not emotion."

SENATOR WARREN G. MAGNUSON

FROM A SIMPLE MECHANISM INTENDED TO LIMIT THE mail-order acquisition by juveniles of foreign-made starter pistols, flare guns, and inexpensive foreign-made .22-caliber pistols, the scope of Senator Dodd's S.1975 had been enlarged by his frequent amendments to encompass all mail-order guns including the highest priced and finest quality domestic, foreign and custom-built target and hunting firearms.

From a cooperative effort to obtain workable legislation on the part of sincere people in government, industry, conservation, and the shooting sports organizations, there gradually developed an erosion of confidence which eventually broke down many fine relationships of long standing. The result was bitter recriminations and undisguised hostility.

63

The stupid and fallacious misinterpretations by mass media played a major role in contributing to that deterioration. Senator Dodd complained bitterly of their errors as they tried to support him. Imagine, if you can, the frustrations of sportsmen as the press attempted to crucify them while affording them meager, if any, opportunity for response.

Three months after the special session of the Senate Committee on Commerce, and at a time when the official position of the National Rifle Association of America with respect to Senator Dodd's S.1975 had remained entirely consistent with what it had been throughout the hearings, CBS-Television produced a special telecast entitled "Murder and the Right to Bear Arms". The moderator opened the program with these words:

"The world's greatest arsenal of privately held small arms, consisting of 150 to 200 million guns, is owned by citizens of the United States. For the next hour we will examine the controversy which swirls about the acquisition and use of these weapons. Gun owners opposing restrictive legislation claim that the Second Amendment to the Constitution gives them the right to keep and bear arms for sport, national defense, and personal protection." (CBS-TV June 10, 1964)

A few minutes later in the program the moderator inserted this little paragraph for the benefit of its audience:

"Hunters and shooters are against any proposed gun legislation that might restrict their freedom to keep and bear arms. Many of these sportsmen are members of the National Rifle Association, a non-profit organization with headquarters in Washington. The NRA is the recognized watchdog on the alert to defeat bills they do not approve." (CBS-TV June 10, 1964)

In the apparent interest of still further emphasizing their message to the millions of persons viewing the program, there was included a discussion of the so-called Second Amendment issue which began in this manner:

"The opposition to legislation restricting the sale of guns takes many forms, including an objection on constitutional grounds. The National Rifle Association, other sporting groups, and hunters and shooters, cite the Second Amendment to the Constitution as basic authority for their positions." (CBS-TV June 10, 1964)

64

It is not difficult to imagine the kind of impression that these statements must have had on those persons hearing for the first time about the National Rifle Association. Furthermore, the disproportionate amount of time allotted to contrivance of a debate of sorts over the question of what the Second Amendment provided, was completely misleading. Not only did the program create the erroneous impression that the National Rifle Association was opposed to Senator Dodd's bill, but that it was opposed to it on the basis of some nebulous theory of constitutional application.

The emotion laden film then took its viewers to the funeral of a Los Angeles police officer who had been killed by a felon who had recently been conditionally-released from a Federal penitentiary, as if a gun law would have prevented the murder.

The police official who spoke a few words in eulogy for his slain comrade then commented about the dangers faced by policemen from criminals:

> "He can, with a five-cent stamp and a few dollars, get weapons of warfare that are prohibited even for law enforcement use." (CBS-TV June 10, 1964)

The warden of the penitentiary from which the convict had been released was interviewed and had this to say about the felon:

> "Smith has lived a life of violence and, of course, he relies on weapons, and the first thing he would think of, when he gets out, is to get a weapon so he could enforce his will, and Smith could have purchased a gun within 30 minutes after we released him, if he had not been released in custody." (CBS-TV June 10, 1964)

Can you visualize CBS-Television calmly interviewing a zoo keeper who had recently released a ravenous tiger that promptly devoured the first person it encountered? Suppose the zoo keeper replied:

> "Tigers are vicious flesh eaters. This one had been vicious all of his life, and the first thing he would think of when he gets out of his cage is to tear some person to shreds."

The first rational question that would come to mind is, why are admittedly vicious animals continually released on a decent society? Without dwelling on this point, it suffices that one consider the analogy because it constitutes the basis of the belief by many persons that crimes of violence committed with any kind of a weapon should be punished with severe mandatory penalties so as to assure that such animals do not return among human beings and wreak their violence a second time. Statistics show approximately three-fourths of our crime is committed by those guilty of serious crime before!

Continuing heavily on emotionalism the film went on to the pitiful report of a husband whose wife, twice committed and twice released from an institution, purchased a revolver and after killing their four children took her own life. She had not used a gun purchased by mail order, but the incident, nevertheless, added undeniable emotional content to the program.

The one hour show was also liberally laced with numerous references to submachineguns and machine guns, with mortars, flame throwers and aerial bombs included in a segment purporting to describe activities of the so-called "Minutemen" organizations.

In another portion of the show that caused serious competitive pistol shooters to seethe with indignation, CBS-Television described the pistol shooting sport allegedly participated in by "200,000" quick-draw artists. As though an adult attired in authentic western regalia and firing wax bullets at a man-shaped target were not sufficiently dramatic, CBS-Television chose to focus on a scene where a small girl with revolver in hand was being given these instructions by her mentor:

"Try to hit the man about in the chest. Are you ready? Now, when I say, draw. Draw! (the child draws and fires) A good shot! A beautiful shot!" (CBS-TV June 10, 1964)

In another segment of the program, a half-dozen interviews which were conducted with various inmates from Cell House "B" in a State penitentiary produced this horror story from a convict who had rented his pistol specifically for use in the crime for which he was then imprisoned.

CONVICT: "Well, I rented this gun. I rented this gun from a fellow. I paid $150 just for this particular job. The more money you make on a job, the more you pay for this pistol. In other words, if you rob a bank or something for ten or twenty-thousand dollars, it might cost you a good $1,000, $500 for a gun. In other words, the more money you make, the more the gun costs you."
REPORTER: "What kind of guns do they have for rent?"
CONVICT: "You can rent any kind of gun, a machine gun, a sawed-off shotgun, any make of pistol, a .45, a .38. Any kind of gun you want." (CBS-TV June 10, 1964)

66

That bit of intelligence, while irrelevant to Senator Dodd's bill on mail order sale of firearms, probably enlivened the show and may have kept some people from switching channels.

It would be inconceivable that such a program would not include at least one interview with the omnipresent James V. Bennett, suggesting techniques for gun control. He was interviewed, and the reporter asked him flatly: "Mr. Bennett, what kind of legislation would you propose?" Back came this reply, candid and directly to the point:

"Well, the ultimate in firearms legislation would be a Federal statute which imposed an excise tax on those who own, purchase or possess firearms. This law would require the identification of each and every gun. It would make it possible to feed this information into a data processing machine and, within an hour or so, the police could trace any gun that they found had been used in the commission of a crime." (CBS-TV June 10, 1964)

There he did it. He admitted an intent he had previously denied—and all with the help of CBS-Television. During the course of a nationally telecast program, clearly associated in the minds of nearly every sportsman in the country with the pending Dodd bill, S.1975, Bennett recommended gun registration and added federal taxes on every American gun owner.

In the one hour presentation, "Murder and the Right to Bear Arms", originally released June 10, 1964, CBS-Television managed in one degree or another to leave the impression that the National Rifle Association and other equally responsible sporting and conservation organizations unreasonably opposed all firearms legislation. Completely false.

Finally, of the numerous excellent reasons why certain kinds of gun control laws were opposed by knowledgeable American firearms owners, CBS-Television selected only the one concerning the Second Amendment to the Constitution which had about as much relevance to the issue presented in S.1975 as did the criminal who had rented his crime gun from the underworld.

The role of both the printed and broadcast media clouding the gun control issue will become increasingly and painfully obvious as this subject is further explored. It may indeed have been the news media which, more than any other factor, prevented some reasonable action by the Congress in this period after the assassination of President Kennedy.

6

"Those who cannot remember the past are condemned to repeat it."

GEORGE SANTAYANA

SENATOR DODD'S S.1975 QUIETLY PASSED AWAY WITH the 88th Congress toward the end of 1964. With the convening of the new Congress in January, 1965, an identical bill was introduced by Senator Dodd and was assigned a new number, S.14. The emergence of Senator Dodd's S.14 was immediately reported in the nation's press with the same confusion of content and purpose long misleading to the public and long an irritant to the sportsmen who, fearing to become the victim, studied such bills in some detail.

The *Chicago Tribune*, January 6, 1965, reported that S.14 was actually the same bill as S.1975, which had not been brought to a vote in the last Congress, and quoted Senator Dodd to the effect that he had been defeated by an unreasonable and "well organized hard-core minority". This minority may have been hard to identify, however, because Dodd went on to say that the legislation had the prior approval of the Treasury Department, which was the enforcement agency, the National Rifle Association, firearms manufacturers and importers.

The readers of the *Chicago Daily News* of January 18, 1965, were exposed, however, to an entirely different impression: "(Senator Dodd) blamed a 'hard core minority' for killing this bill (S.1975) in committee last year. The core of that hard core—the National Rifle Association—this year has seen fit to support Dodd's bill—a change of tactics in the hope of warding off tougher laws".

Six months later the *Chicago Daily News* was still attributing the death of old S.1975 to the opposition of the National Rifle Association and the National Shooting Sports Foundation, which by this time had come to be identified by journalistic license and convenience as the "gun lobby". This distortion of the history of S.1975 and S.14 was continued and embellished by the *Chicago Daily News*.

Thus, it was that in some segments of the press the National Rifle Association was an irresistible target. It made no difference to certain reporters what the facts were as to legislation NRA supported or did not support. The press had eagerly joined the vendetta marking every paragraph with lurid phrases, "machine gun like efficiency", "gun lobby" and associating it with "weapons manufacturers" and "merchants of death".

In this manner the press aroused the membership of the National Rifle Association as the organization itself could hardly have done. Many staunch members had not been happy with NRA support of Dodd's first bills anyway. Then, notwithstanding this support, when they found the organization pilloried in the press for opposing them, sportsmen's cries of anguish were heard all over the country and the press did not understand them and, for the most part, did not seem want to understand them.

S.14 never had a serious chance for Congressional approval. Within three months it was replaced by another Dodd Bill, S.1592, at the request of President Lyndon B. Johnson. S.1592 would have prohibited entirely the interstate mail-order sale of all firearms to private citizens. As was the case with Dodd's two earlier bills, S.1592 was designed to amend the Federal Firearms Act of 1938 and, in certain provisions, similarly to amend the older National Firearms Act of 1934.

The National Rifle Association was once again the spokesman for the position it regarded as being in the best interest of law-abiding

69

Americans. This was not a new role for NRA, nor was it a new role even back in 1961 when Senator Dodd's subcommittee first began working with the National Rifle Association on the development of proposals which eventually emerged in the first Dodd Bill, S.1975. Actually, this role had begun in the early 1930s in deliberations on those measures which were finally enacted into law as the National Firearms Act of 1934 and the Federal Firearms Act of 1938.

Literally, every proposal and every argument presented in the 1960s has been scrutinized 30 years before.

Someone has suggested that the principal reason behind the enactment of the National Firearms Act of 1934 was the attempted assassination of Franklin D. Roosevelt on February 15, 1933, in Miami, Florida. This is interesting speculation but there is nothing in the record to support it; granting, of course, that each congressman and senator might have had his own reasons for the position he took at that time.

The 1930s reflected the era of prohibition-spawned gangsters. It was the period of such bank robbers and "cop killers" as Pretty Boy Floyd, John Dillinger, Baby-face Nelson and others. The hysteria of the times zeroed in on the Thompson submachine gun. The press in following its usual wont, called it the "Chicago chopper" and its emphasis and description was designed to terrorize the public and perhaps the police as well.

There was then, as there frequently is now, an imperative that problems be identified to the public with something of excitement and drama; naming simple and tangible things as the cause. Simplistically, an instrument might be offered as its cause.

What better, in the era of crime made possible by the prohibition of liquor, than the submachinegun? It had been the subject of a long period of press reporting which had endowed it with magical qualities of lethality; a fear-producing character which, as an inanimate object, it could never legitimately possess. The press made the submachinegun in prohibition days not only the cause of crime, but the symbol of it. Politicians oratorically, loudly and solemnly, denounced it. No ordinary citizen could defend it. No sportsman wanted to do so.

At that time the serious national controversy over the right of a law-abiding citizen to keep and bear arms in this country had just begun. The record of the controversy at that time reveals no one standing forthrightly on the proposition that, once having conceded any inanimate object as evil, independent of the character and purpose of the man who uses it, it would be almost impossible later to point the virtuous finger of scorn and condemnation convincingly and effectively at politicians who, in seeking to duck the real and unpleasant confrontation with criminal men, sought to imbue other inanimate objects of the same family of things with evil of and by themselves. With no one to defend such a weapon it was easy for those seeking simplistic answers to identify its abolition with the control of crime.

No one at the time even identified the temptation to yield something of individual freedom in order to obtain something of collective security, because in the history of weapons control from ancient times to the present there has been no evidence of a causal relationship between the availability of a weapon and the incidence of crime. When man in some particular place or age has been deprived of one means of effective assault or murder he has always, with seeming facility, found another.

In its approach to firearms control, the National Firearms Act of 1934 was patterned after the previously enacted Harrison Narcotics Act, which had been based upon the tax power of the Federal government. This Act applied only to machine guns, submachine guns, sawed-off rifles, sawed off shotguns, gadget guns disguised to resemble some innocent device, gun silencers and the like. A special tax was attached to each and every transaction involving the transfer of weapons within the purview of the Act. For example, in the case of the submachine gun, a $200 tax was imposed on each occasion of the transfer of one by sale, gift or trade. In order to force compliance with the revenue provisions there was the additional requirement that every weapon within its purview be registered by specific terms and serial number with the Alcohol, Tobacco and Tax Division of the Internal Revenue Service.

The reason the National Firearms Act had been established under the taxing powers of the Federal Government was because the narcotics legislation, which had been set up along similar lines, had already been successfully court-tested as to its constitutionality in the lawful exercise of Federal taxing power. It must be remembered that such a circuitous route was necessary in the opinion of the then U.S. Attorney General, Homer S. Cummings, because of a two-fold problem. There was no constitutional grant of police powers to the Federal Government. There was the glaring presence of the Second Amendment to the Constitution, combined with the embarrassing appropriateness of machine guns and submachine guns to any conceivable militia.

The original proposal out of which the National Firearms Act was derived included pistols and revolvers. The Congress, however, refused to add the privately owned firearms of law-abiding citizens to this morass of bureaucratic red tape and pistols and revolvers were excluded from its provisions.

71

The reaction of the American public to the threat to restrict the private ownership of handguns doubtlessly had much to do with bringing the issue before the Congress in this light. Senator Royal S. Copeland of New York, a sponsor of the bill, said there had been a storm of

Reproduction of famous 1934 cartoon by Orr, which originally appeared in *Chicago Tribune* in opposition to the Copeland bill.

protest "as a result of the introduction of our original bill" on the ground that it was too drastic because it interfered with the possession of firearms by law abiding citizens. Responsible segments of the press at that time identified the Copeland Bill as one which would promote burglary and robbery.

Statistics at that time were, perhaps, abused about as much as they were to be abused 30 years later in support of Senator Dodd's bills. In 1934 Attorney General Homer Cummings in hearings before the House Ways and Means Committee stated that there were more than a half-million armed men in the underworld. This dramatic statement had its effect in shocking and astonishing his listeners. It was subsequently revealed, however, that the Attorney General—as has also happened lately—contrived these statistics to suit his own purpose. He had added up each crime reported by 1,264 of the country's largest cities during the previous year. He had assumed that each of those crimes had been committed by different criminals armed at the time of the crime. Then, because the population of those largest cities had constituted less than half the population of the United States at that time, he simply doubled his figures.

Irresponsible and farfetched! Yes. But, not more so than the fabulously contrived canard so often repeated by Congressmen and Attorneys Generals alike during the last 10 years that some 20,000 Americans are shot to death annually and that, since the year 1900, casualties from civilian gun fire have exceeded the total military casualties of all our wars from the Revolution to the present. Contrived statistics and unfounded suppositions have been used for nearly 40 years in efforts to stampede the Congress and the public into the acceptance of confiscatory gun laws.

And, when the machine gun law had been in effect for 30 years no one on either side of the gun control controversy seriously argued that it had done anything to control crime in this country. Some of the old cliches, however, seemed to have been born during this legislative battle over gun control in the 1930s. Attorney General Cummings gave birth to one which is still heard today, "Show me the man who doesn't want his gun registered and I will show you a man who shouldn't have a gun"—as though good citizens could not object to registration on the grounds it had little or nothing to do with crime control and was a prerequisite to future efforts to confiscate guns—such confiscation now (by 1972) being embodied in measures before the Congress.

Hearings on proposals out of which came the Federal Firearms Act of 1938 commenced in 1935. Senator Copeland sponsored S.3, a bill to regulate commerce in firearms. A committee was formed consisting of General Milton A. Reckord, Executive Vice President of the National Rifle Association, a representative of the senate committee and a representative of the Department of Justice. These three gentlemen drafted S.3.

Hearings were conducted on a cordial note and both General Reckord and Mr. Karl T. Frederick, President of the National Rifle Association, were congratulated by Senator Copeland during the hearings for their help and cooperation. As far back as 1935 the officers of the NRA were compelled, as in later decades, to defend themselves against completely unfounded allegations that they somehow represented or were associated with American firearms manufacturers. Testimony of the two responsible officials of the NRA made it abundantly clear that the NRA never had been subsidized or supported by the firearms manufacturers or any commercial interests.

There was then, as there is today, reference to advertising in the NRA magazine *The American Rifleman*. It was pointed out, however, that the firearms manufacturers . . . "like many other people, buy advertising space in our magazine. They buy it on the same terms as other people do".

Interestingly, S.3 contained a provision that the possession of a firearm or ammunition was presumptive evidence that such was transported in violation of the Act. Mr. Frederick in persuasive debate pointed out, over the objection of some of the senators, that the provision was unconstitutional. As a matter of fact, however, some senators thought "its the best thing in the Act".

The criticism of a gun bill by a NRA spokesman was hardly believed to possess merit. Nevertheless, the Congress passed the bill with that specification in it. However, the NRA position was vindicated by the U.S. Supreme Court a few years later when that subsection was declared unconstitutional in the case of Tot vs United States, 319 U.S. 463.

It had been shown, as there would be shown time after time in the future, that the men of the National Rifle Association would support good firearms legislation and would honestly and intelligently criticize that which was not good. It has too often been true that too few have been willing to listen and to believe. Mr. Frederick's testimony contained another statement equally true and clearly prophetic. The following statements should be recorded for the benefit of future generations and not hidden away in the dusty archives of Congress.

"We have had a great number of suggestions or bills with respect to the control of firearms. I think without exception they have been offered ostensibly for the purpose of diminishing or controlling crime and the criminal use of firearms. Beyond the motto or the flag at the masthead, most of them have immediately departed from that in practice, and instead of actually being aimed at the criminal use of firearms and at crooks in the use of firearms, they have, in fact, been aimed at the law-abiding citizen. He is the one that is the easiest to reach. The problem of firearms regulation is a difficult one."

* * *

"I think that the legitimate use of firearms has been rather overlooked in the discussion of the situation, and in the practical approach of most of the bills which have come to my notice—and I think I have seen most of them—the real effect of the bills would have been to make criminals of a whole lot of honest people, and to have acomplished little or nothing with respect to the suppression of crime or the stopping of the criminal use of firearms." (KK–p. 9)

Important and prophetic testimony was also presented on S.3 by Mr. Charles V. Imlay, of the National Conference of Commissioners on Uniform Laws. Mr. Imlay highly commended the cooperation of Mr. Frederick and General Reckord and particularly referred to the co-operative attitude of these gentlemen as reflecting a broad legal knowledge and experience with legislation and the techniques of firearms use.

Mr. Imlay criticized the fact that with regard to the National Firearms Act of 1934, the assessment of the so-called transfer tax on the various weapons it controlled was merely a contrivance to cloak a federal gun registration law with some semblance of constitutionality. As a matter of fact, it had been revealed during the 1934 hearings that this was the case. Thirty-two years later Mr. Imlay was proved correct. On January 29, 1968, in Haynes vs United States, the U.S. Supreme Court invalidated perhaps the most important part of the National Firearms Act of 1934 on the grounds that it violated the constitutional guarantee of the Fifth Amendment against the self-incrimination to which a criminal would be subjected by forcing him to register his submachine gun or any other firearm covered under the Act.

The most significant provision of Senator Copeland's S.3, and one which was generally ignored in subsequent years despite its intention to assist individual States to control firearms within their own borders, was section 2(c), which read:

"It shall be unlawful for any licensed manufacturer or dealer to transport or ship any firearm or ammunition in interstate or foreign commerce to any person other than a licensed manufacturer or dealer in any State the laws of which require that a license be obtained for the purchase of such firearm, unless such license is exhibited to such manufacturer or dealer by the prospective purchaser." (KK–p. 2)

This important section required that any firearms dealer who received a mail-order for a gun from an out of state purchaser must make certain that the purchaser had a license to possess such a gun, if a firearms license were required by the law of the purchaser's State. In common practice, purchasers who lived in such States would merely enclose a copy of their current firearms license along with their purchase order. This meant that any states whose legislatures decided that it wanted to control the out of state mail order purchases of guns by its residents could do so simply by enacting a licensing law covering such purchases.

The heart and soul of that provision was recognition that, as Charles Imlay expressed it, ". . . firearms regulation is primarily and traditionally a matter of State regulation." The function of the Federal Government, therefore, was confined simply to providing the individual states with the means through which their internal laws could be enforced, without evasion by the mail-order purchase of guns which could not be bought within their borders without a license.

It was frequently argued in the 1960s that the legislation needed was interstate control by the Federal government enabling the individual states to enforce their own laws. Such legislation had been on the books for 30 years.

Furthermore, not only does this kind of legislation protect the states which desire licensing of individual possessors of firearms; at the same time it protects the residents of all the other states who have not desired restrictive licenses.

At that time, as is true today, there were those who sought far more stringent controls than that contained in the legislation being considered. In this regard Assistant Attorney General Joseph B. Keenan wasted few words. Concerning S.3, he stated the matter of possession and transportation of firearms "should have more drastic treatment" than the bill contained, and then he went on to state that the objective of his department was to obtain general licensing of those who possessed any concealable weapon.

Colonel Calvin C. Goddard, Director of the Scientific Crime-

Detection Laboratory of Northwestern University at Chicago, implied that the representatives of the shooting-sports would not protest the most stringent legislation if it would in any measure reduce crime. He added, and it is still true, that there have never been any figures to show that stringent gun legislation reduces crime. Strong words indeed from the father of modern scientific crime detection in the United States.

Colonel Goddard was a most unusual man—a Doctor of Medicine and an ordnance expert. He had traveled extensively in thirteen Western European countries and had spent considerable time studying scientific crime detection laboratories and medical legal institutions in Europe. His opinions, however, in conflict with dilettantes or theoreticians, were the opinions of a man intimately acquainted with the violent misuse of guns and the problems presented.

> "The law which Mr. Keenan advocates requires the licensing and the registration of pistols and revolvers. As sportsmen, I think we may assume that that is merely a beginning, that the next step would be the licensing of rifles and shotguns. Such steps have already been taken, and there is now a bill pending which requires the licensing of shotguns and pistols, rifles, revolvers by the police department.
>
> One of the most active proponents of the bill, a judge in the city of Chicago, at a luncheon held last year, which I attended stated without blushing that the intent of those who had drawn the bill was to bring in the arms by the legislation and then confiscate them, and that very few arms would get back to the hands of their present owners." (KK–p. 41)

One set of figures arose in the 1930s which have not received the attention that might merit at the present time. A presentation was made as to the number of hoodlums killed by the police and then another showing the number of hoodlums killed by individual citizens defending their lives and property. In Chicago in the early 1930s the figures ran about 55% for the police and 45% for the citizens, which raises questions yet unanswered. Do our present homicide statistics reflect the percent of homicides later revealed by the courts to have been justified? How is any set of statistics of this nature to be held to reflect upon the law-abiding nature of the citizenry unless the subsequent disposition of the courts is known?

The 1930s were afflicted as were the 60s with silly propositions. One obviously naive and impractical proposition by a Mr. Hector Pocoroba was that the bullet in every cartridge manufactured be numbered and that these numbered bullets be sold only to a buyer who gave his name and a set of fingerprints. In recent years metallic cartridges and shotgun shells are being manufactured in the United States in excess of 4 billion annually. If the Congress should take seriously some of the proposals made, most of the budget and the energies of the United States could be devoted to the job.

Another proposal made at that time, and which recurs from time to time today, is the naming of dates for the surrender of millions of pistols and revolvers voluntarily, making it a crime thereafter to possess one without a license. Upon reflection, the concensus of many sane men then was, as it is today, that the deacons and elders and all other good people would probably surrender their guns, leaving criminals and crooks armed.

Among those who also supported Senator Copeland's S.3 were Colt's Patented Firearms Company, Smith and Wesson; and Harrington and Richardson. Mr. Harold Wesson, President of Smith and Wesson, fairly well summed up their position with the statement that to restrict sale of arms to sales through recognized jobbers and dealers, would result in a pretty good record of sales—a good thing.

The American Legion at that time was carrying on a firearms education program involving nearly 400,000 boys annually between 15 and 18 years of age. It could hardly have been dreamed then that these young men would be in their early twenties when only a few years later American troops stormed the beaches of Western Europe to break the back of Nazi Germany.

7

"... the objects of this Association are to promote
social welfare and public safety, law and order, and
the national defense; to educate and train citizens
of good repute in the safe and efficient handling of
small arms, and in the technique of design, production
and group instruction; to increase the knowledge of
small arms and promote efficiency in the use of such
arms on the part of members of law enforcement
agencies, of the armed forces, and of citizens who
would be subject to service in the event of war; and
generally to encourage the lawful ownership and use
of small arms by citizens of good repute."

BYLAWS OF THE NATIONAL RIFLE ASSOCIATION
OF AMERICA (AS AMENDED APRIL 7, 1971)

FREQUENT REFERENCES HAVE BEEN MADE TO THE
National Rifle Association and its efforts in the area of
legislation relating to the possession and the use of firearms. Legislative
matters, however, were not among the original reasons for the founding
of the NRA. Nevertheless, the Association was early compelled to enter
the legislative fray in order to influence, where possible, the legislative
effort in such a way as to avoid restraints on good citizens which, in any
event, would have no effect on criminals. Clearly, the NRA effort to preserve the right to keep and bear arms was one to preserve a spirit and
capability important to the national welfare, to the shooting sports (and
it is questionable the two are separable) and to a man's right to defend
that which is lawfully his.

National Rifle Association Headquarters Building, Washington, D.C.

The National Rifle Association was founded in 1871. It was incorporated as a non-profit organization in New York. Its members were initially a small group of National Guard officers brought together at the invitation of Colonel William C. Church, editor of a newspaper called, for short, *The Army-Navy Journal*.

Colonel Church was wounded in the Civil War and returned to civilian life in June, 1863, to accept the post of Editor of the *Army-Navy Journal*. During his part of the war he had received an unfavorable impression of the combat performance of volunteer militia units in the United States Army, and he immediately began a series of articles and editorials exposing the inadequacies of American marksmanship compared to that he had witnessed while a correspondent in Europe. He recited specific feats of marksmanship regularly performed by British volunteers, none of which, he said could be remotely approached by the New York National Guard which was renown for its spit-and-polish precision marching.

In Great Britain a volunteer rifle association has been formed in 1859 to promote marksmanship among the British. That organization was associated with and encouraged by the British War Office which provided 1,000 Long Enfield Rifles on loan. The British club called itself the NRA of Great Britain and its now famous 1,000 yd. rifle range, the Wimbledon, was officially and personally opened by Queen Victoria.

Col. Church wrote an editorial in August 12, 1871, *Army-Navy Journal*, "An association should be organized in this city to promote and encourage rifle shooting on a scientific basis. The National Guard is today too slow in getting about this reform. Private enterprise nust take up the matter and push it into life. We would suggest that a meeting of those favorable to such a project be called, and should be only too happy to hear from representatives of the different commands of the First and Second Divisions relative to this subject. The subject has already been presented to several enterprising officers and ex-officers of the National Guard, and they have been found enthusiastic in the matter. It only requires hearty cooperation and an actual start to make the organization successful. Let us have our rifle practice association, also a Wimbledon on American principles."

The rifle practice association called for was organized and named the National Rifle Association of America. During the century of its existence its goals have come to include the education, training, and promotion of efficiency in the U.S. with small arms on the part of members of the armed forces, law enforcement agencies and of citizens who would be subject to service in the event of war. It has encouraged the lawful ownership and proper use of small arms by American citizens of good repute. Literally hundreds of congressmen, senators and also presidents of the United States have been among its members. One President of the United States has also been President of the National Rifle Association, General Ulysses S. Grant, 1883–1884. President Theodore Roosevelt was a Life Member and he added great strength to the objectives of the National Rifle Association, when through his efforts Congress, in February 1903, established the National Board for the Promotion of Rifle Practice. When the Secretary of War Elihu Root appointed the first members of the NBPRP on April 21, 1903, the first meeting of that board brought forth the following recommendation, "That every facility should be offered citizens outside of the Army, Navy, Marine Corps, and organized militia to become proficient in rifle shooting, and that this purpose can best be accomplished by means of rifle clubs. The board therefore respectfully recommends the encouragement by the War Department of the organization of rifle clubs composed of those who would be eligible for service in time of war, but without special obligation for war service on account of such membership, under such regulations as may be prescribed by the Secretary of War."

The first National Matches were held in September 1903. Congress authorized the sale of rifles to rifle clubs under regulation of the NBPRB in 1905. President Roosevelt included the following statement in his message to the Congress in 1908:

"There should be legislation to provide a complete plan for organizing the great body of volunteers behind the Regular Army and National Guard when war has come. Congressional assistance should be given those who are endeavoring to promote rifle practice so that our men, in the Services and out of them, may know how to use the rifle. While teams representing the United States won the Rifle and Revolver Championships of the World against all comers in England this year, it is unfortunately true that the great body of our citizens shoot less and less as time goes on. To meet this we should encourage rifle practice among schoolboys, and indeed among all classes, as well as in the military services, by every means in our power. Thus, and not otherwise, may we be able to assist in preserving the peace of the world. Fit to hold our own against the strong nations of the earth, our voice for peace will carry to the ends of the earth. Unprepared, and therefore unfit, we must sit dumb and helpless to defend ourselves, protect others, or preserve peace. The first step—in the direction of preparation to avert war if possible, and to be fit for war if it should come—is to teach our men to shoot."

The National Defense Act carried additional recommendations for the furtherance of the civilian marksmanship program including considerable details for supply in 1916. General Pershing called for more recruits who knew how to shoot and pointed out the need for competence with the rifle in battle in 1917. The NRA Marksmanship Training Program was identified and maintained as a program for peace time preparedness and Franklin D. Roosevelt, Assistant Secretary of the Navy, was appointed Chairman of the NBPRP in 1918. The National Defense Act was again amended and the civilian marksmanship program was further expanded in 1924 to the condition in which it remained until the late 1960s.

Thus, the NRA, in line with American traditions, responded as Col. Church called for in 1871. Private enterprise engaged in the effort and pushed "it into life" under civilian leadership with the enterprise of volunteer citizens and without profit motivation. The Congress and the Armed Forces gave support for the purpose of preserving the goals of our founding fathers—goals indispensable to the preservation of the freedoms we take for granted but which would be restricted or even crushed were America to be compelled, as in most European countries, to depend upon massed professional standing armies in pursuit of long term national goals. Those liberties which are not likely to survive, and which never have survived, under the national influence of great professional armies, are freedom of the press, freedom of assembly, freedom from unreasonable search and seizure, and freedom to keep and bear arms.

8

*"... the Civilian Marksmanship Program...
contributes significantly to the development of rifle
marksmanship proficiency and confidence in the
ability to use a rifle effectively in combat. ..."*

ARTHUR D. LITTLE, INC., 1966

FROM THE EARLIEST DAYS OF OUR REPUBLIC THE DE-
fense structure of America has been based upon a small
professional military force with which to meet peacetime requirements,
backed up and reinforced in time of emergency by citizen soldiers who,
while they were civilians, were inspirited and trained for that purpose.

Provision was made during the 1930s to protect the government in
shipment of firearms in the Civilian Marksmanship Program of the
Army.

As finally adopted in the Federal Firearms Act of 1938, the provision read as follows:

"Provided, That nothing contained in this section shall be construed to prevent the shipment of firearms and ammunition to institutions, organizations, or persons to whom such firearms and ammunition may be lawfully delivered by the Secretary of War, nor to prevent the transportation of such firearms and ammunition so delivered by their lawful possessors while they are engaged in military training or in competitions."

At the time of this provision's original consideration by the Congress in 1937, the United States was enjoying its twentieth year of peace following the great war to end all wars, World War I. In spite of that fact, the provision to protect the Civilian Marksmanship Program was neither dismissed as irrelevant, nor considered to be a bellicose manifestation of militarism.

Such language became highly controversial thirty years later during the considerations of Senator Dodd's bills. He purposely omitted it when to do so was to do great, and perhaps irreparable, damage to the Civilian Marksmanship Program.

Title 10, U.S.C. 4308, provides for the instruction of able-bodied citizens of the United States in marksmanship with rifled arms. To carry out this provision, ranges are to be built, arms to be sold to the members of the National Rifle Association at cost, national rifle and pistol matches are to be held, trophies and medals are to be awarded and all other necessary steps taken to establish, to maintain and to encourage participation in a program for civilian marksmanship.

Our Founding Fathers had long been students of European history. They had seen how it was that inevitably the large professional armies of Europe—the standing armies—had been a burden on the people. To avoid this oppression—the burden of taxes, continual war, or the threat of war, and the relating autocratic political forms—every step possible was taken in the establishment of our government to rely instead upon citizen armies in time of need.

If civilians, arising in time of national need, are to serve effectively as an alternative to the economic and political evils of large professional standing armies, then they must become aware of their responsibility and respond to it. Awareness is the product of education, of the study of history; the study of the course taken by countries before us, their options, their decisions and the consequences. The logical result of awareness is loyalty of the people; their affinity for certain ideals and national goals. Having established an intelligent appraisal among the people of the course of nations and having brought them together in pursuit of national ideals and goals it only remains for a realistically motivated government to establish and maintain leadership in the realization of the means by which the people and their representative, the civilian soldier, can be effective.

Whether fortunate or unfortunate may not be ours to say, but there is nothing in the history of mankind to indicate that a civilization can survive leisure, easy living and the inevitable satiation and boredom which follows. As a result, a vital and surviving people must have work, inspiration, struggle and finally, accomplishment, in their daily lives. From this there follows also physical ability and spiritual willingness to participate in those activities which built good health and sustain, where necessary, a military character.

Forty years after the great Civil War, President Theodore Roosevelt, and his Secretary of War Elihu Root, foresaw the need for establishing again a national program for promotion of civilian marksmanship. It was not true then, and it is not true now, that the whole burden of victory—the burden of national survival—rests with riflemen. It is more likely to be instead that an adequate program of rifle training inculcates desirable attitudes and establishes a training platform offering many convenient and necessary departures.

The foremost qualification of a man skilled in arms is self-discipline. He may be puny of stature, his eyes may not be sharp and clear, he may in fact suffer a number of physical disabilities, but if he has self-discipline and the other qualities indispensably related, he will be able to handle small arms satisfactorily and experience has shown, in many cases, expertly.

With self-discipline come accomplishment and personal pride. And accomplishment and personal pride come in no other way. These are the indispensable qualities of the citizen soldier. But, this is not all. The man who has self-discipline and pride in accomplishment, who is qualified in his discipline, who attends to the many details of arms and is determined to overcome the difficulties in qualifying with them—this man has many skills which are readily transferable and which readily form the foundation for other skills.

While we have described the qualification of a man skilled in arms, we have at the same time described substantially the basic ingredient in a man skilled in flying an airplane, in performing tedious surgery and in resting a steady finger on the nuclear push-button.

Many thinkers have expressed themselves, during the last decade of somewhat delicately balanced nuclear terror, to the effect that a nuclear war is not an economically or politically practical war. The interlinking economies of the earth, the dependence of the prosperity of one country on the trade and the prosperity of other countries, do not indicate the practicability nor the desirability of nuclear obliteration of any one of them.

However that may be, it is undeniably true that more security to the people exists when the minds behind the button, and literally the finger upon it, are guided and controlled by self-discipline—a quiet and steady intent, a calm confidence. The wisdom of Theodore Roosevelt and Elihu Root has borne fruit nourishing our national successes. It has been recognized and expressed in strongest terms of encouragement and appreciation by many national leaders including General John J. Pershing, General, later President, Dwight D. Eisenhower, President John F. Kennedy and many others. It has been known for a long, long time that no sport, and no military related activity, affords more in terms of training in self-discipline, steadiness of mind and body and individual confidence, than marksmanship with rifles and handguns.

It is, indeed, a sad chapter in the description of our national character and the pursuit of our national political and military goals with civilian soldiers instead of massed professional standing armies as in Europe, that after the sad assassination of President John F. Kennedy in November 1963, many leading American political figures, by the frustration introduced into their own personal and political lives and by the hysteria-inducing attitudes of much of the news media, have been stampeded into unrealistic responses regarding gun ownership—unrealistic and historically unconscionable.

On June 13, 1967, the following letter, reproduced in its entirety, was transmitted to the Honorable Robert S. McNamara, Secretary of Defense, over the signature of Senator Edward M. Kennedy:

"Dear Mr. Secretary:
The Washington Post performed a distinct public service this morning by drawing attention to the Defense Department's involvement with and support of the National Rifle Association. This is a matter which has long concerned me and which I have discussed at length with officials of your Department. It is also a subject which the members of the Senate Juvenile Delinquency Subcommittee expect to look into next month when the Department and N.R.A. witnesses testify on the proposed State Firearms Control Assistance Act of 1967 and other weapons control proposals.

I have serious doubts about the justification for continuing the entire Civilian Marksmanship Program in this nuclear age, and especially about the privileged position given the N.R.A. under that program despite certain developments in the N.R.A's finances, purposes, and activities. These questions will certainly be reviewed at our hearings. But there is one facet of this problem which should be resolved immediately and to which I wish to draw your attention at this time, namely, the appropriateness of holding the National Rifle Matches this year in light of the pressure of the Vietnam conflict on the personnel and budget of the Defense Department, and in light of alternative possible uses for its facilities and equipment.

I understand that the National Matches, held annually at Camp Perry, Ohio, in conjunction with the N.R.A., cost the Defense Department $2,717,300 in 1965. This was broken down as $197,150 for the office of the Director of Civilian Marksmanship, $1,816,250 for the Second Army, $36,000 for the Army Materiel Command, $272,800 for other Army sources, $234,900 for the Navy, and $160,200 for the Air Force. These expenditures were applied to the rental of Camp Perry; the provision of support personnel; supplies and equipment to house and feed the competitors and service personnel; travel expenses and subsistence for civilian competitors, service personnel, and officers and staff of competing teams and the N.R.A.; and ammunition and other firearms supplies. I would assume that this estimate is conservative since it does not include depreciation of non-expendable equipment used for the matches. The most recent figures I have seen indicate that about 3,000 members of the armed forces are assigned for support duty alone at the matches, but again the total would be significantly higher if military participants were included, perhaps as high as 5,000.

Camp Perry itself is a facility of great size and flexibility, capable of providing room and board for about 10,000 people for the matches. It is reserved during the months of August and September exclusively for the matches, and no other activities are programmed for that period.

It seems to me that it is impossible to justify the use of 5000 military men and $3 million dollars and a large military facility for the purpose of a weapons competition during the present Vietnam conflict. In the month of August you have asked that 29,000 American men be drafted, and it seems patently unfair to ask these young men to interrupt their lives when 5000 men in uniform are assigned to what must be considered non-essential, if not unproductive, duties. Moreover, the President has asked that the expenditures for all non-essential activities and programs be curtailed to alleviate the budgetary strain of the Vietnam conflict. Certainly the rifle matches are such an activity, and there is precedent in the suspension of the matches during World War I, the Depression, World War II, and part of the Korean War.

On the other hand, the nation does have a pressing need for the space and facilities at Camp Perry during the summer months. A great deal has been accomplished to provide training and employment programs for our urban youth, particularly through the Youth Opportunities Campaign under the leadership of the Vice-President. But these programs offer little in the way of recreation or self-improvement to those under the age of 16, who form a substantial part of the urban youth population and who have been deeply involved in some of the urban disturbances over the recent years.

I know that Congressman Vanik of Cleveland has ascertained that there are over 12,000 children in this group in the Hough area of Cleveland alone. He has suggested that the local government, citizen groups, and others in Cleveland are prepared to provide financial and staff support for a program of recreation and training outside the city if a site can be obtained. I am sure there are other cities in the Midwest which could prepare similar programs.

It would appear to me that such programs would certainly constitute a much more sensible use of Camp Perry this summer than the holding of weapons competitions requiring great expenditures of military funds and manpower. I would, therefore, most urgently suggest and request that the matches be cancelled this year and that the camp be turned over to nearby cities for youth programs. I am confident that the N.R.A., with its traditional concern for our military efforts and its new concern for problems of urban tension, would gladly support such a change in plans, and might perhaps be able to assist in providing youth counselors and other aid from its membership.

I want to emphasize that I would certainly support the rescheduling or relocation of any activities carried on in connection with the national matches which are an integral part of conventional battle training for members of the armed forces on active duty. I understand, however, that any such purely military part of the program would require only a small fraction of the expense, manpower, and facilities used for the national matches, and could be held at a time other than the summer or at another training facility.

Of course fast action is necessary if the cities are to be able to prepare their programs, and I look forward to hearing from you promptly."

Senator Edward Kennedy's letter created a stir as its contents were "interpreted" for the readers of newspapers across the country. Typical "facts" liberally circulated by the news media included this excerpt from a San Francisco newspaper:

"The annual rifle matches at Camp Perry, Ohio, are an additional expenditure. About 7000 riflemen compete in the matches each year, about 3000 of whom are members of the NRA and the rest servicemen. Participants receive travel expense to and from Camp Perry and free lodging, meals, ammunition and trophies while they are there." (*San Francisco Chronicle*: June 15, 1967)

On the day that Senator Edward Kennedy's letter was forwarded to Secretary of Defense Robert McNamara, Congressman Richard D. McCarthy offered an amendment in the House of Representatives which would have had the effect of destroying the Nation's Civilian Marksmanship Program. His opening words were:

"Mr. Chairman, this amendment is very simple. It would strike $428,-000 for the National Board for the Promotion of Rifle Practice. This money is used for ammunition and the loan of rifles to National Rifle Association clubs. The present law requires that groups which want this Federal aid must join the National Rifle Association." (*Congressional Record*: June 13, 1967)

Among the remarks Congressman Richard McCarthy had to make about the National Rifle Association were the following:

"I suggest to you that because of the lack of effective firearms laws, we have permitted the arming of very militant far left and far right antagonistic groups, groups like the Black Panthers and the Minutemen. This situation represents a force for instability, especially in the coming hot summer.
    Mr. Chairman, I think this whole practice is at best questionable, and I certainly think that the record shows that the NRA is not a proper or responsible conduit for Federal guns and ammunition, and that we could save the taxpayers $428,000 by adopting this amendment." (*Congressional Record*: June 13, 1967)

Joining in with Congressman McCarthy was Congressman Jonathan B. Bingham and Congressman James H. Scheuer. Scheuer said with regard to the relationship between the NRA and the NBPRP:

"It is a relationship between a private group and our defense agencies that is bad in principal and worse in practice. It should be brought to a prompt halt by the passage of this amendment." (*Congressional Record*: June 13, 1967)

Rising in opposition to the amendment was Congressman Robert Sikes, one of the Members of Congress familiar with all of the facts concerning the NRA, whose incisive remarks penetrated to the very heart of the issue:

"The National Rifle Association, by helping to carry out the duties and responsibilities which are assigned by law to the National Board for the

Promotion of Rifle Practice, is actually subsidizing the U.S. Treasury. What is done represents a service to the Government which is not paid for from Government funds."

* * *

"Nothing is taken from the active forces by making arms and ammunition available for this purpose. The rifles and the ammunition which are used generally are obsolescent or overage, but in the hands of the National Board for the Promotion of Rifle Practice they serve a very useful purpose."

* * *

"I would like to point out that this program has been going on since 1903 when Elihu Root, as Secretary of War, sponsored the program. During that time the program has worked well. The people have found it useful. No one has tried before in my 27 years here to kill the program. Now, when we are at war it is an inopportune time to do so." (*Congressional Record*: June 13, 1967)

Joining in opposition to Congressman McCarthy's amendment were several other Members of Congress, including Congressman John J. Flynt Jr. who, knowing the full facts behind the lengthy history of both the NRA and the NBPRP, observed that:

"The author of the amendment undoubtedly has not reviewed the 64-year history of this board and the functions which it has performed. If he had done so, I am confident he would have come to the unmistakable conclusion that it has been a good program, and has justified its existence and continuance over the years." (*Congressional Record*: June 13, 1967)

More newspaper articles and editorials flooded the country in vigorous attacks not only upon the NBPRP and the NRA, but also upon the National Matches. The same pattern ran through news article after news article, much as though to suggest that their "facts" emanated from a single fountainhead. With few exceptions such articles also made one or more references to Senator Edward Kennedy. Consider the "facts" in the following excerpt from a Pennsylvania newspaper:

"The NRA is upset because there is some talk of ending its federal subsidies. This puts it in the position of supporting federal aid, but opposing federal regulations such as proposed gun legislation. Specifically, Sen. Edward M. Kennedy of Massachusetts has urged Secretary of Defense Robert S. McNamara to cancel the NRA's national rifle matches slated for Camp Perry, Ohio.

91

Sen. Kennedy said it would make much more sense to use Camp Perry as a recreation center for the slum children of Toledo and Cleveland. These month-long matches will cost the Defense Department $3 million. The government not only makes available the military base and many allied services, but also pays for the contestants' travel expenses, lodging and meals. In addition to this, throughout the year, NRA rifle team members are entitled to free ammunition, the loan of military weapons, and the right to buy others at cost." (*Delaware County Daily Times*: July 14, 1967)

Such news articles distorted the facts and engendered resentment towards the National Rifle Association. The purpose served by the rash of news releases containing such misinformation, accepted uncritically by the media and disseminated as though Gospel, seemed to be quite obvious. Closely coordinated with the attacks on the National Matches were articles blaming the National Rifle Association for the failure of Congress to enact Senator Dodd's various bills. Consider the following excerpt taken from a thirty-column-inch article purportedly having been written by Senator Edward Kennedy during this controversy over the continuation of the National Matches:

"And why hasn't something been done about this carnage? Because the anti-gun bill lobby, led by the National Rifle Association, has opposed responsible federal gun control legislation at every step. Much of this opposition has been hysterical, with slogans like 'Register Communists, Not Firearms,' and talk of firearms control legislation as part of a subversive plot." (*San Francisco Examiner*: July 30, 1967)

The extent to which the press misrepresented the gun control issue may be gauged by the reader after reviewing the following opening paragraph taken from a Delaware newspaper, again timed during the controversy over the National Matches at Camp Perry. The article obviously included within its scope all of the Dodd bills, including the original S.1975 which enjoyed the support not only of the NRA, but of every major shooting, conservation and industry group in the country:

"Every year since the assassination of President Kennedy, Congress has thought and thought about control of firearms. And each time, pressure from the National Rifle Association, other sportsmen's groups and the firearms industry have kept legislation in abeyance, despite the need for some real degree of public control over deadly weapons." (*The Morning News Opinion*: July 15, 1967)

The kind of highly emotional undercurrent running through many of the attacks upon the NRA and the National Matches by the mass media can be quickly gleaned from the following patently vicious remark which appeared in an Eastern publication:

"Well, you don't learn combat by shooting at paper targets and cardboard pop-up silhouettes. What you need are moving targets, live ones that shoot back. If the NRA will simply arrange its competitions in that format—for members only, of course—that should satisfy its severest critics." (*Evening Star*: July 6, 1967)

On June 27, 1967, Secretary of Defense Robert S. McNamara replied to Senator Edward Kennedy's letter of June 13, 1967. His letter follows in its entirety:

"I have considered with care the points you raise in your letter of June 13.

In my view, the central responsibility in this whole matter lies with Congress. What is fundamentally at issue here is the responsible use of firearms.

I frankly am shocked that Congress has been so remiss in enacting the necessary controls to assure that the sales and use of weapons are effectively kept out of the hands of those who use them to threaten the right of free dissent.

There have been a number of gun control proposals before Congress during the past three years, but wholly without final effect.

The matter dragged on through the 89th Congress, and never emerged from committee in either the House or the Senate.

The current Administration proposals, incorporated in H.R. 5384, and in Amendment 90 to S.1, are sound, but languish on without decisive action.

Even in the case of the National Matches, and the N.R.A.'s involvement in them, Congress has circumscribed the issues by statute, in 10 U.S.C., paragraphs 4312 and 4313. If Congress is dissatisfied with these statutes, then it clearly has the responsibility to change them.

But in any event, while Congress deliberates we now face the prospect of another summer which may well witness more bloodletting in our streets with weapons—from whatever source—that have found their way into the hands of bigots and extremists.

The absence of sensible gun control legislation is not only unreasonable; it is an open and permanent invitation to violence and disorder.

I would hope that you would continue to use your influence in Congress to bring an end to this serious legislative deficiency."

Secretary of Defense Robert McNamara's letter to Senator Kennedy drew a sharp reaction in some quarters and, in the interest of perspective on the period, are worth repeating in part. The following interesting view was advanced by a Connecticut newspaper:

"If there has been any doubt during the past several years that Defense Secretary McNamara's ideas are dangerous to the nation, this should settle it."

* * *

"While American soldiers fight with rifles in Asian jungles, he offered no defense or support for the National Rifle Assn., mainstay of civilian rifleman training in this nation, or for its time-honored national matches.

The Secretary of Defense has loaned the prestige of his office to a political move to disarm the citizens of this nation. Traditionally, disarming of citizens becomes a political necessity when they must be rendered unable to oppose a government which is to be imposed upon them.

Secretary McNamara's record is composed of underestimates of our military needs, erroneous forecasts and costly blunders. The monetary savings which he offers as justification are smeared with the blood of American servicemen.

His letter to Sen. Kennedy goes even beyond that. He now has taken part in a political attack upon the Constitution of this nation. Congress and the President must control McNamara, or get rid of him." (*Connecticut Sunday Herald*: July 16, 1967)

One Kentucky newspaper nominated Defense Secretary McNamara as America's No. 1 "bleeding heart" and expressed disgust over his remark that "I am frankly shocked that Congress has been so remiss in enacting the necessary controls to assure that the sales and use of weapons are effectively kept out of the hands of those who use them to threaten the right of free dissent." The editorial characterized the implications of that statement as follows:

"In other words, McNamara isn't worried about the guns owned and used by those who wish to demonstrate, to protest, to dissent. He is worried about the weapons owned and used by those who are the targets of these demonstrations, those who would defend themselves against the 'dissenters.'

As long as the 'law of the land' is 'loot, shoot, and burn, baby, burn,' we just think we'll keep our guns despite McNamara's tears and fears. There just might come a time when we will want to shoot back at his 'free dissent' rabble which McNamara—with 'bleeding heart'— defends." (*Mt. Sterling Advocate*: July 5, 1967)

Senator Edward Kennedy responded to Secretary of Defense Mc-Namara's letter very quickly, by another letter on June 30, 1967, in which he continued to press for cancellation of the National Matches, and to raise further questions about the Civilian Marksmanship Program. That letter follows, again in its entirety:

"I was very pleased to receive your response to my letter of June 13. It is encouraging to have your enthusiastic support for S.1—The State Firearms Control Assistance Act of 1967. I hope that when we hold hearings on this bill in the coming weeks, you will find it possible to attend and to express your support for this legislation in person.

I am also glad to have your acknowledgement of the need for a Congressional review of the Defense Department's Civilian Marksmanship Program. In the light of the vastly changed circumstances since this program was initiated, I believe that the 90th Congress should undertake a thorough reconsideration of the statutory provisions in this area.

Since it appears that you have not yet made a final decision as to whether the Camp Perry shooting matches should be suspended as they have been in prior times of warfare and budgetary restraint, and whether the leased premises at the Camp should be made available for summer recreation and training programs for urban youth from Midwest cities, I would like to point out three developments since my last letter which may bear on your decision.

First, on June 20th your Department announced the cancellation of Exercise Kitty Hawk, a large military combat training maneuver planned for August and involving military units which might well be called upon to utilize such training in the near future. The reason given by the Department spokesman for the cancellation was the need for curtailing the Department budget because of the rising cost of the War in Vietnam. I should think that it necessarily follows that the National Matches, involving nearly $3 million and consuming the time and energies of three thousand uniformed personnel for support purposes alone, but producing only the most marginal and tenuous contribution to military preparedness, should also be cancelled this year.

Second, on June 21st your Department agreed to make available to the City of New York military facilities in that area for summer youth programs. This is certainly an exciting and promising break-through and should surely be extended as expeditiously as possible into a nation-wide effort this summer to provide the urban youth of America with an opportunity for self-expression and self-improvement away from the city streets. In particular, the children of Cleveland and other Midwestern cities should surely be given an opportunity to use Camp Perry during the periods it is leased to the Federal Government but is not being fully utilized for purely military purposes.

Third, also on June 21st, the New York City Police arrested 16 members of a terrorist group, known as the Revolutionary Action Movement (RAM), who had allegedly been plotting to assassinate national civil rights leaders. The group was charged with forming the Jamaica Rifle and Pistol Club as a cover and front for illegal possession of weapons. This Club apparently was affiliated with and received a certificate of endorsement from the National Rifle Association, and thus under present regulations was entitled to participate in the Civilian Marksmanship programs of the Department of Defense. As a result the Club was issued .22 caliber rifles and M-1 rifles, free of charge, by the Department of the Army, and was given access to National Guard Armories for the purpose of weapon practice. Its members were also given the opportunity, exclusively reserved to N.R.A. members, to purchase surplus military weapons at cost from the Department of the Army, and at least one of the arrested persons had availed himself of this opportunity. About a third of the weapons which were seized by the police when the arrests were made had originated in the Department of Defense Civilian Markmanship Program.

While I am aware that the Director of Civilian Marksmanship and the N.R.A. have cooperated fully with Federal and local investigatory agencies during the past several months in an effort to assure both the safety of the alleged targets of the group and the arrest of the alleged conspirators, the fact is that for over a year this group had the approval and endorsement of the National Rifle Association and thus the right to participate fully in your Department's equipment, facilities, sales, and competitive programs. I am also fully aware that the vast majority of the N.R.A. and D.C.M.—affiliated firearms groups are made up of highly reputable sportsmen, competitors, and hobbyists, and that the officials of the N.R.A. and of the Office of the Director of Civilian Marksmanship are dedicated and sincere individuals who do their assigned duties in the utmost good faith.

Neverthless, the New York incident is not the first instance of the use of the N.R.A.—D.C.M. program by extremist groups. In the past similar circumstances have developed involving the Minutemen and the Ku Klux Klan. The New York disclosure merely emphasizes the need for much more careful screening of participating groups so long as the program continues, and for an immediate re-screening of existing groups to get the very few questionable ones out of the program. It would seem that it would be impossible to complete such a re-screening before August, and, on the other hand, that if the officials of the N.R.A. and the D.C.M. were relieved of the necessity for preparing for the National Matches, they would be able to address themselves fully and deliberately to the re-screening task.

Once more let me express my sincere appreciation for your support for effective controls on the unfettered flow of firearms in the United States and my hope that you will seriously consider the suggestion that Congressman Vanik and I have made that Camp Perry be made available to city youths this summer."

Although the obvious target of the unremitting assaults upon the National Matches at Camp Perry was the National Rifle Association, it is nonetheless necessary to pause for a moment and respond to the allegations concerning the Jamaica Rifle and Pistol Club. Stephen Ailes, Secretary of the Army, had testified before Senator Dodd's subcommittee in 1965 and, in doing so, commented on the method of screening clubs that applied for NRA and DCM affiliation. By coincidence he cited the specific procedure followed in New York where the all-Black club in question was organized:

"Before accepting a club's application, the NRA institutes a check through the State adjutant general and the rifle and pistol association of the State in which the club is located to determine that the club's officials are American citizens without criminal backgrounds and not members of subversive organizations.

The actual investigation varies somewhat from State to State, depending upon facilities available and local regulations. In New York, for example, the names furnished are checked through the State Criminal Investigation and Identification Division. Prior to final approval of NRA affiliation, the club must also obtain endorsements from two community leaders." (CC–p. 59)

That was the overall procedure employed in New York for such club applicants. The testimony of Franklin Orth as to additional details concerning the club to which Senator Edward Kennedy referred will complete the facts:

"The application of the Jamaica Gun Club—we might as well run through the history of it, because I think your questioning is aimed in this direction—reached the NRA on September 8, 1965. We received biographical questionnaires and the required endorsement certificates September 28, 1965. Signing that certificate was an accountant, Walter Winfree, listed as president of a firm named Promon, Inc., and another man listed as a New York patrol officer.

The police check reported to us by the adjutant general's office indicated two minor police reports which we followed up. One was a gambling charge; the other resulted from participation in a civil rights demonstration. The latter was a matter of public record and the individual, as an assistant principal within the New York Department of Education, had not been adversely affected by it.

On January 4, 1966, the report from the State Rifle and Pistol Association indicated that there was no reason for denying the club's affiliation, and this procedure was completed.

Sometimes it appears that the critics of NRA, including someone from New York City, demanded a higher standard of NRA than they maintain themselves. While we take it as a compliment, it seems to me that it is hardly fair to them or to us." (GG–pp. 531–532)

Some of the additional information brought out by Franklin Orth as to the composition of the Jamaica Gun Club membership also proved to be highly revealing to Senator Dodd's subcommittee:

"Four of them are employees of the city of New York. In addition, two others were admitted from West Africa as exchange students of the U.S. Government. Thus, it would appear that nearly half of the alleged conspirators had some official status, recognition, or approval. One is described as a U.S. management analyst, one is assistant principal in the New York schools, one is a teacher in the New York school system, one is a custodial engineer of New York schools, one is a New York Department of Welfare clerk, and so on.

I think it may be properly asked, Why expect the NRA to screen out these people from their official credentials when the State Department and the city of New York fail to do so? They have better machinery than we have, and we try our utmost to keep these extremists out. We have repeatedly said we want none of these people in our organization, have publicly so declared, have placed it in a full two pages in our magazine in August of 1964. I do not know what more we can do." (GG–p. 532)

These facts, like so many others, were never presented to the public by the news media. It appeared to many persons that all too often the object of certain news articles was not so much to inform, as it was to discredit and undermine the National Rifle Association by whatever method proved most effective at the moment.

Paralleling the attempts to obtain the cancellation of the National Matches at Camp Perry, and the efforts to sabotage the Civilian Marksmanship Program, there were sharp criticisms directed simultaneously at the Nation's R.O.T.C. and military cadet programs. Although, in the majority of cases, such cadet corps were not affiliated with the National Rifle Association, they were eligible for the benefits of the Civilian Marksmanship Program and, therefore, were targets of the anti-gun forces. Consider these words of remonstration from the *Washington Post*:

> "The educational benefit of military drill is zero. The military value of training high school students is negligible. Consequently, the military cadet corps in the Washington schools is an expensive waste of time that should be ended at once." (*Washington Post*: Aug. 29, 1967)

In yet another *Washington Post* story, a spokesman for Senator Robert F. Kennedy was quoted as follows:

> "A spokesman for Sen. Robert F. Kennedy (D-N.Y.) said that the Senator was especially concerned about the 10 to 15 hours that cadets must spend on school rifle ranges practicing with .22 caliber rifles and ammunition supplied by the Army.
> 'Like the NRA-sponsored and Government-subsidized rifle matches at Camp Perry,' the spokesman said, 'it would appear that this type of program is not only unnecessary but detrimental in a society which is already troubled by too many guns and too much violence.' " (*Washington Post*: Aug. 28, 1967)

Unbelievable as it might seem, the diatribe went on and on, and readers were told of the shock of one member of the Board of Education to learn that real ammunition was used in cadet training practice with .22 caliber rifles:

> "Albert A. Rosenfield, another member of the Board of Education, said that he was 'shocked and amazed' to learn that cadets fire live ammunition. It was reported yesterday in The Washington Post that cadets fire between three and five million rounds a year." (*Washington Post*: Aug. 28, 1967)

Eventually, the one-sided onslaught produced its desired result and the U.S. Army announced the cancellation of the 1968 National Matches. The official grounds were the ones that had been repeatedly suggested by Senator Edward Kennedy, reasons of economy. That announcement was joyously proclaimed by the *Boston Herald Traveler* in an editorial entitled, "A Victory for Reason". The editorial quoted Senator Edward Kennedy as describing the announced cancellation as "a victory for reason and good government." After carefully pointing out that "some observers feel the Defense Department cancellation is a slap at the NRA", the editorial ended with these truculent words:

"We draw two hopes from these developments. First, that the matches will be cancelled permanently. Second, that the NRA, in this mood of reasonableness, will withdraw its powerful opposition to the Administration's firearms control bill." (*Boston Herald Traveler*: Nov. 3, 1967)

The reaction of Senator Thomas Dodd to the cancellation of the National Matches was reported by a Kentucky newspaper as follows:

"Sen. Thomas J. Dodd, D-Conn., another advocate of gun control legislation, also praised cancellation of the matches. He said the matches have 'repeatedly been used by the gun industry to advertise its wares, and by the opponents of effective firearms laws to proselytize shooters with propaganda in the form of literature and posters to oppose firearms legislation.' " (*The Courier Journal*: Nov. 2, 1967)

The entire matter was seen in a different light by people who had knowledge of the facts concerning the background of the National Matches, and a Phoenix newspaper editorial did not hesitate to express its disgust with the cancellation:

"When the Army foolishly cancelled the National Rifle Matches for 1968, it offered as a reason that the matches 'do not make a substantial contribution to the current defense effort.' That isn't true and the Pentagon knows it.

Only last year, the Arthur D. Little Co., a renowned research firm, completed a study—requested by the Army—on the national matches and the nation's civilian marksmanship program. The study held that the matches served a useful purpose and that the civilian marksmanship program was of definite value to the Army.

Quite obviously, the Army cancelled the matches at the behest of Sen. Robert Kennedy and others who have convinced themselves that crimes involving the use of firearms can be reduced by disarming the honest people and dismantling rifle ranges." (*Phoenix Gazette*: Nov. 3, 1967)

A Pennsylvania newspaper editorial also expressed its opinion that the only real factor involved in the cancellation of the National Matches was bitter animosity by those whose gun control legislation was opposed by the National Rifle Association. After citing the background of the Arthur D. Little, Inc. study, the editorial concluded:

"It is unfortunate that Dodd through his unremitting pressure on this issue has forced cancellation of a training program which encourages small arms skills at a time when guerrilla warfare rages in Vietnam and threatens in several other hot spots.

No, Dodd, this might be a personal political victory. It is a loss for the nation. To claim 'economy' on a program involving so relatively little is to flout the intelligence of the public." (*Altoona, Pa., Mirror*: Nov. 4, 1967)

The testimony of Stephen Ailes, Secretary of the Army, before Senator Dodd's subcommittee in 1967 will serve to provide the background necessary to understand and appreciate the developments which occurred at that time regarding the Civilian Marksmanship Program. The Secretary of the Army presented his personal opinion as to the value of that program to the members of Senator Dodd's subcommittee:

"I think past studies have shown that, in Korea, something less than 50 percent of the riflemen in combat fired at anything. Men who have some talent as marksmen are more liable to shoot at something than men who do not. The range of the weapon is extended in the hands of the marksman. We have a great interest in this. We still depend on the rifleman and his being able to shoot his rifle well. The fact that the recruit has been shooting squirrels as a boy enables him to be a better marksman when he comes into the Army, and that is to our advantage." (CC–p. 63)

Secretary Ailes admitted, however, that neither the Army nor any of its agencies had ever conducted a comprehensive study attempting to measure the effectiveness and value of the Civilian Marksmanship Program. He then announced that the Army planned to have exactly such an evaluation undertaken by a private research firm:

"For a long time, many military and civilian leaders have considered that the instruction in marksmanship and the experience with firearms provided to citizens of the United States under the civilian marksmanship training program have been beneficial to the national security, by creating a reservoir of personnel trained in a basic military skill, on which the Armed Forces may draw in time of need, and I might add by providing us with a fair number of new recruits who have had some previous experience with the rifle.

However, this benefit has never really been measurable, and a solid body of facts on which to base a judgment has never been gathered together. I have recently approved undertaking a study designed to cover from an independent point of view, four areas related to the basic question of the extent to which the program enhances national security.

First, the study will give us a basis for determining the benefits which actually accrue to the military from the activities of the National Board for the Promotion of Rifle Practice.

Second, the study will review the organizational structure which carried out these activities.

Third, it will evaluate the program controls.

Fourth, it will subject the program to a cost analysis. The firm of Arthur D. Little has been chosen to carry out this study, and the contract negotiations were completed on May 13. We expect to have a draft of the study in 6 months." (CC–p. 61)

The study to which Secretary of the Army Stephen Ailes referred was completed and published in 1966, one year before the introduction of Senator Dodd's S.1. The information which it contained, as well as its evaluations, were available to all interested persons, including the proponents of Senator Dodd's newest bill. Franklin Orth called attention to that study as well as to some of its conclusions:

"At this point, Mr. Chairman, since this subcommittee has heard some wholly gratuitous statements questioning the value to the United States of the pittance spent by the Federal Government to preserve rifle marksmanship among civilians who would be called upon to fight in time of war, I should like to quote certain conclusions from a study made by Arthur D. Little, Inc., a private industrial and management research firm engaged by the Department of the Army in May 1965. This firm was requested to make recommendations as to the necessity for the civilian marksmanship program and its possible implementation." (FF–pp. 624–625)

Franklin Orth then read into the record brief excerpts taken from the Arthur D. Little study. He had to be brief because of his limited time allotment. We are not so burdened, however, and can consequently do justice to that report's findings and recommendations. As its basic premise concerning the future need of riflemen, even in the nuclear age, the report observed:

"In spite of recent technological developments in the modes of waging war, the Army's Light Weapons Infantrymen (LWI) and the Marines are almost certain to be employed in any 'shooting wars' in which our nation becomes embroiled. Since the basic individual weapon of such combat arms is the rifle, it is important that the men in such units become thoroughly proficient in its use." (A. D. Little Rept. to Dept. of the Army, 1966, p. 14)

102

The Arthur D. Little report then proceeded to state its overall conclusions as to the effectiveness of the Civilian Marksmanship Program. It was this portion that Franklin Orth read for the benefit of Senator Dodd's subcommittee:

"The results of our study indicate that the Civilian Marksmanship Program sponsored and supported by the Army, directed by the National Board for the Promotion of Rifle Practice (NBPRP), and administered by the Director of Civilian Marksmanship (DCM) contributes significantly to the development of rifle marksmanship proficiency and confidence in the ability to use a rifle effectively in combat on the part of those who participate in the program or benefit indirectly from it." (Op. cit. p. 15)

A perfect example of indirect benefits derived from the Civilian Marksmanship Program was that which took place during World War II when several thousand men who themselves had been directly trained through such programs then became instructors and, in turn, trained millions of inductees both prior to, and subsequent to, induction. Such highly trained men formed the nucleus through which many times their number were trained.

In making their evaluation as to the differences between those men having had marksmanship training prior to entering the military service, as compared to those which had not, the Arthur D. Little report found that men who had previously been members of gun clubs:

"Are more apt to enlist
Are more apt to prefer a combat outfit
Are more apt to choose outfits where they are more likely to use their rifle (Infantry and Airborne)
Liked firearms and shooting more
Had more shooting experience
Received more marksmanship instruction
Are more confident of their ability to use their rifle effectively in combat
Are more likely to want to become a marksmanship instructor
Competed in more and higher level shooting matches
The differences noted above are even greater and more apparent when trainees who belonged to gun clubs affiliated with the DCM are compared with trainees who were not members of gun clubs." (Op. cit. p. 16)

An interesting discovery was also made by Arthur D. Little, Inc. to the effect that members of organized gun clubs actually furnished rifle instruction to approximately three times the number of Army trainees who were not members of such clubs than who were members of gun clubs. It was, therefore, clearly apparent that the training value of such clubs far exceeded the number of persons who were actually former members.

In an attempt to place some degree of value on pre-induction rifle training, the Arthur D. Little, Inc. research team conducted individual structured interviews with 34 distinguished combat commanders. Their findings were that:

> "A serviceman who demonstrates minimal proficiency with his rifle tends to have a correspondingly low degree of confidence in his ability to use his rifle. Further, there was almost universal agreement that the *degree* of a serviceman's confidence in his own marksmanship skill is significantly and highly correlated with the *degree* to which he actually uses his rifle in combat." (Op. cit. pps. 22 and 23)

As a pattern gradually began to emerge from their research into the factors involved in pre-induction marksmanship exposure, the following determination was made:

> "Thus, a chain of relationships was established which indicates that, in general, the more marksmanship instruction, practice, competition and shooting experience individuals get before entering service, and the greater the density of such prior experience in the population of young men entering service, the more effective rifle units will be in combat and the fewer casualties they will suffer. Since the DCM program stimulates and supports broader prior service experience in shooting and provides and supports marksmanship instruction, it appears to have significant value." (Op. cit. pps. 23 and 24)

So impressed with the findings of its research team was Arthur D. Little, Inc. that it not only placed a stamp of approval on the Civilian Marksmanship Program, but went so far as to recommend that it be enlarged and expanded:

> "We believe that those aspects of the DCM program which relate to the stimulation of broader interest and participation in rifle shooting among the youth of our country (primarily club activities) should be emphasized more and pursued even more effectively to reach a greater percentage of those young men likely to enter military service." (Op. cit. p. 24)

104

Another finding of the Arthur D. Little study related to a matter which at first glance might have seemed somewhat distant from any military significance, namely, international shooting competitions:

"The NBPRP and DCM programs contribute substantially to the emergence and development of competitors for international competition. Key elements in this contribution are the club and competition programs which stimulate interest and facilitate participation in shooting on the part of young men. This is essential in generating a broad base of participants from which a number of international caliber shooters can emerge." (Op. cit. p. 25)

Further developing that point, the report then went on to relate international shooting matches to the military posture of the country:

"It is significant to note that development of successful shooting teams is either a major goal of or important to a number of nations who wish to project an image of growing strength, competence and power. This is probably because shooting is essentially a military art and thus success in international shooting competitions connotes a national defense capability rather directly. In the 1964 Olympic Games, only four sports had more nations represented in competition than shooting." (Op. cit. p. 26)

Before proceeding further with the Arthur D. Little report, we should take a brief excursion to the other side of the world for an examination of a remarkably similar pattern in the development of the civilian marksmanship training program of Soviet Russia, including that country's emphasis on the importance of international shooting matches. The material that follows has been taken from the translated Russian book entitled *The Development of Marksmanship in Russia* by A. A. Yur'yev, published in 1957 by the State Publishing House for Physical Culture and Sport in Moscow. It is a very fine book on the techniques of marksmanship training. The opening paragraph of its preface reads as follows:

"In the Soviet Union marksmanship is one of the most popular and most mass-scale types of sport. The mass nature and accessibility of this type of sport were a necessary condition for the revealing and the competitive growth of a considerable group of capable competitive marksmen who, by unceasingly working to improve themselves, have achieved a high level of competitive mastery."

The history of Russian marksmanship covered by the book went back as far as the 5th Olympic Games which were held in 1912. One of the embarrassed Russian participants in those shooting matches contributed this painful recollection:

". . . In 1912, along with the best Russian marksmen I left for the Stockholm Olympiad, where contests were held in all types of sport. Even now it is unpleasant for me to remember that Olympiad. No one was interested in us except the American riflemen, who manifested a not too flattering attention for our guns. . . . They were enraptured by our Russian-produced rifles, but were astonished at the poor aiming devices and front sights on those rifles. Many Americans exchanged their Winchesters for our rifles. . . . Without waiting for them to give out the prizes, most of the Russian sportsmen, myself included, literally ran home in complete disgrace." (Op. cit.)

Twenty years and one World War after the United States adopted its Civilian Marksmanship Program, the Russian counterpart was created:

"In 1924 the All Union Central Executive Committee issued a decree concerning the organization of a marksmanship section at the Higher Council of Physical Culture (VSFK), which constituted a major step in the development of marksmanship in our country. The organization of a marksmanship section at the VSFK created a firm basis for the solution of very important tasks: the selection of the organizational forms of the development of marksmanship in our country; the supplying of rifle clubs with guns and ammunition; the construction of firing ranges; the training of instructor cadres and the publication of methodological literature." (Op. cit.)

This seems quite similar to the National Board for the Promotion of Rifle Practice (NBPRP) and its administrative agency, the Director of Civilian Marksmanship (DCM) in the U.S. Finally, as might have been expected, the Russian equivalent of the NRA was formed in 1927. The book explained it in this way:

"In the same year (1927) the Society of Cooperation with Aviation and Chemistry (Osoaviakhim) was created. In 1928 that society was given the responsibility of directing competitive marksmanship work in civilian organizations. Osoaviakhim played an exceptionally large role in developing marksmanship. Osoaviakhim rifle clubs organized everywhere throughout the country have contributed to a considerable extent to the popularization of marksmanship among the workers and helped them to master the art of accurate shooting." (Op. cit.)

The continuing support by the Russian government combined with obligatory training furthered the development of riflery in the Soviet Union:

"In 1931 the all-union physical-culture complex 'Ready for Labor and the Defense of the USSR' was adopted. In addition to the fulfillment of the standards for various types of sport, standards for shooting were included among the obligatory ones. The passing of 'Ready for Labor and the Defense of the USSR' standards for shooting increased sharply the mass development of that type of sport." (Op. cit.)

The progress of the Russian riflemen was particularly rapid during the 1930s. During those years in America, the U.S. Attorney General, Homer Cummings, was exerting his best efforts to restrict possession of arms and shooting. The Russian text continued:

"The call of the Central Committee, All Union Lenin Communist Youth Society and the Central Council of Osoaviakhim, to master the art of accurate shooting, was taken up ardently by the youth of our country. The movement among the workers for the fulfillment of the standards for the rank of 'Voroshilov Riflemen' took on very broad scale. In two years more than 500,000 'Voroshilov Riflemen' were trained, and three years later, that is, in 1935 the number of 'Voroshilov Riflemen' who were members of the Osoaviakhim society alone was more than 2 million." (Op. cit.)

The period 1929 to 1934 saw widespread construction of firing ranges and their equipping with necessary operating gear by Soviet trade unions. Virtually all national enterprises were represented by teams of trade-union youth, and shooting matches were held between factories, plants and kolkhozes.

Continuing with a remarkable parallel between the Russian and American experiences with their respective civilian marksmanship programs, Yur'yev told of the coming of World War II and the role played in it by the Russian marksman:

"The Great Patriotic War confirmed the exceptional importance of the development of marksmanship in our country during the prewar period. Competitive-marksman training carried out under peacetime conditions helped Soviet patriots to use weapons skillfully against the enemies of their Motherland. With the complete support of the party and Communist Youth League organizations, a sniper movement began to develop and expand on all fronts from the very first days of the Great Patriotic War. The initiators of that patriotic movement of deadly snipers were, for the most part, soldiers and commanders—recent members of rifle clubs of various volunteer sport societies—who exchanged their frontline experience by grouping around themselves young, beginning snipers. Hundreds of thousands of sportsmen, including riflemen, were awarded decorations and medals of the Soviet Union for successful combat operations at the front and in the enemy's rear area." (Op. cit.)

In the postwar years, Russian marksmanship training continued and began to take on an international significance along with other sports:

"A tremendous role in the further development of sport in our country was the decree of the Central Committee of the VKP dated 27 December 1948, in which it was indicated that the principal task in the field of physical-cultural work lies in the development of a mass-scale physical-culture movement, the raising of the level of sport mastery, and the winning by sportsmen of worldwide preeminence on that basis." (Op. cit.)

The pervasiveness of the marksmanship philosophy of Soviet Russia was also seen in the post-war German Federal Government where the following quotation appeared in a bulletin issued by that Russian dominated government through its Press and Information Office on August 2, 1960:

"TOO MANY YOUNG PEOPLE STILL CANNOT SHOOT
The Soviet zone authorities have long furthered the premilitary training of young people in Central Germany. Now the regime has increased its demands for stressing premilitary training at institutes of higher learning.
    A new directive has been issued by Herr Richard Staimer, chairman of the Soviet zone's organization for premilitary training, the 'Society for Sport and Technology'. According to this directive, the society is to intensify secondary school instruction in the sports that are called the military sports, chiefly target-practice and signalling. At the universities, the 'military pentathlon' is to be included in the programmes of all student sports meetings.
    The Communist trade unions in the Soviet zone were called upon by Herr Staimer to emphasise target-practice in their youth work, since, as he put it, 'there are still too many young people who cannot shoot'. He added that the society's chief form of sport continued to be shooting."

On May 20, 1966, the *New York Times* announced the Soviet Union had ordered an intensification of "paramilitary training for civilians to meet present day needs". The Soviet Government and the central committee of the Communist Party in 1966 issued a decree to their military training society for civilians, instructing that society to take immediate steps toward "strengthening the military defense capabilities of the nation, increasing the vigilence of all the Soviet People and training them in constant readiness to defend their homeland". The very first item on the list of steps to be taken by this Soviet society with millions of members was to order preparation of youngsters for military service by training them in rifle shooting. This was the first qualification on the list of qualifications for Soviet youth. At this time, when the U.S. program enrolled about a half million youngsters, the Soviet Union enrolled 17 million in their counterpart organization.

Not long before, the East German Shooting Association had recorded that the aims of its association was "to demonstrate the superiority of the socialist physical culture against that of capitalism also in the sport of shooting. The performance of the selected teams must . . . beat all capalist countries . . ." (*Official Bulletin of the International Shooting Union*, April 1958)

Similar responses have come from Red China. A young Chinese world champion marksman carried a written pledge in his pocket at tournaments, "Overcome all difficulties, be ready to make any sacrifices . . . World records must be broken to bring greater honor to the mother country." (*International Shooting Sport*, Weisbaden, West Germany, April 1966)

Thus, incredibly, substantial American politicians have been persistent in their efforts to eliminate from the American scene those marksmanship activities so vigorously encouraged and maintained by our only prospective enemies on earth as a contribution to their own defense capability to meet present day needs.

Returning to the Arthur D. Little report there were found to be two significant nonmilitary benefits provided by DCM affiliated gun clubs. The first of those related to the civilian police departments in the country:

"The organized shooting groups of U.S. law enforcement agencies which are affiliated with the DCM believe that the DCM program is quite valuable to them in supporting marksmanship training and practice and in stimulating participation in shooting competitions." (A. D. Little Rept. to Dept. of the Army, 1966, p. 29)

A few words of background at this point will help to explain the operation of the Police Firearms Training Program sponsored by the National Rifle Association of America. That superlative program was initiated over a decade ago, and in the course of its relatively short life has already certified over 250,000 law enforcement officers who have completed the NRA police firearms instruction course. The program is available to every police department in the United States without charge and without any special qualifications.

Just as was true in the case of the Civilian Marksmanship Program, the key to its entire operation was in its training of instructors who, in turn, taught other men in their departments. In brief, it was designed to be a course for instructors.

The course was taught by NRA Staff Personnel whose salaries, travel and living expenses were all paid for by the National Rifle Association without cost of any kind to the various participating police departments. That public service program included the following subjects: Teaching Techniques in Knowledge of Guns and Ammunition; Fundamentals of Instruction; Developing Training Aids; Fundamentals of Marksmanship; Double Action Shooting; Combat Shooting; Firearms Safety; The Police Shotgun; Shotgun Ammunition; Fundamentals of Shotgun Shooting; and The Police Use of the Shotgun. Actual range firing for weapons familiarization was done with both police service revolvers and with shotguns. The NRA also provided an excellent training manual entitled "NRA Police Firearms Instructor Manual", as well as professional filmstrips covering special aspects of the handling of police firearms.

The following evaluation of the overall NRA program was summed up in *Law and Order* magazine, October 1968, widely read by professional law enforcement officers:

> "The NRA program is totally professional. The knowledge and techniques gleaned from many years of experience in the training field form the foundation on which NRA police firearms training is based. The competence of the Training Activities Section Staff comes from the contribution of exceptional teaching ability, personal skill with police weapons, actual police experience and a deep interest in getting firearms training to every possible police officer."

Police personnel also developed and maintained their proficiency in the use of the service revolver through the stimulation of match competition, which permitted a comparison of relative skill, through the NRA National Police Course which included both bullseye shooting and practical combat shooting. It is important also to note another fact concerning the NRA program:

"This is not a 'public relations' program of the NRA. There is no sales pitch in the course." (*Law and Order* Oct. 1968, p. 83)

The A. D. Little, Inc. reported another major collateral benefit associated with DCM clubs:

"Many DCM-affiliated gun clubs throughout the country provide NRA designated 'Hunter Safety Programs' to neophyte hunters in an organized effort to reduce shooting accidents among hunters." (A. D. Little Rept. to the Secy. of the Army, 1966, p. 50)

The program to which the report referred was the Hunter Safety Training Program which had been started by the National Rifle Association in 1948 and which presently exists on a state-wide basis in 41 States and 6 Canadian Provinces. Since its inception it has trained approximately 4,700,000 persons, primarily youngsters, in the safe, proper, and responsible use of firearms while hunting afield. The success of that program has been measured in the constantly decreasing number of hunting accidents in proportion to the increasing number of hunters with each passing year. The NRA Hunter Safety Training Program was administered through private gun clubs, through organizations such as the Boy Scouts of America, the Boys Clubs of America, the American Legion, the Veterans of Foreign Wars, the Izaak Walton League, and many others.

One of the most spectacularly successful of the NRA affiliated Hunter Safety Training Programs was the one which has been adopted in the State of Utah during 1956. A concise description of the experience in that State over a ten year period was presented to the House subcommittee by Congressman Laurence J. Burton:

"The Utah Department of Fish and Game started a hunter safety program in 1956. That year, with 165,000 hunters in the field, we had 128 gun accidents, 79 percent of which were caused by juveniles. Almost every year since 1956 we have had an increase over the previous year in numbers of hunters afield, a decrease from the previous year in gun accidents, and a decrease in the part of those accidents that was caused by juveniles. In 1966, 10 years later, with 231,000 hunters afield, there were 19 gun accidents, 16 percent of which were caused by juveniles. Attached to this statement is a compilation of these statistics for the period 1956 through 1966. The hunter safety courses were conducted with the aid of junior rifle clubs and were broadcast over an educational television station. The National Rifle Association was a cooperator in this endeavor and a most welcome one." (FF–p. 766)

Individual NRA members have given unselfishly of their time, effort, money, range facilities, and more, to provide assistance to youngsters who were fortunate enough to have been given the opportunity to learn at an early age not only the mechanical functioning of firearms and marksmanship techniques, but also the importance of a responsible attitude which goes along with the ownership of a firearm. Those youngsters are not the ones who ended up either inflicting accidental injuries upon others, or upon themselves. They grew up to understand that a firearm is to be used only under proper conditions. Having had those conditions provided them by conscientious adults, they did not resort to the more destructive and frequently deadly uses of guns typical of those children whose parents "can't stand guns" and are too selfish to take the time, or too lazy to make the effort, to insure that their children are properly instructed by competent people.

In the process of its study, the Arthur D. Little firm also directed its attention to an inquiry into the nature of typical DCM gun clubs and in a period of widespread fears over various kinds of political extremist groups made the following reassuring observation:

"Our impression of the club officers we interviewed is that they are typically enthusiastic devotees of the sport of shooting. We found no instances, of direct orientation towards any political programs or extremist activities and, in almost all instances, club officers readily responded that it was club policy to reject applicants known to have extremist views. These general impressions were reinforced in our series of systematic interviews with police and other civic officials. We found no instances where the civic officials linked clubs or club members to criminal or politically extreme elements." (pp. 34–35–ADL Rept.)

Quite apart from political extremists, the Arthur D. Little study also explored the question of whether Government arms or ammunition had ever been converted to criminal purposes by persons having access to such items, and this is what they reported:

"At the outset it should be emphasized that, based on (1) our personal interviews with the officers of 100 DCM-affiliated clubs and with police and civic officials in the vicinities of these clubs, (2) our interviews and correspondence with FBI, Treasury, and State Police officials, and (3) our contact with several members of the Congress (a few of whom are critical of the DCM program), we were unable to uncover a single incident where a DCM-affiliated club or its members have been convicted of using firearms, ammunition, and/or government property improperly or where DCM arms have been used in crimes of violence. We believe that our investigations were sufficiently thorough to uncover information regarding such incidents if they had occurred, especially in view of the publicity that currently would be attached to an unfavorable incident involving firearms or a shooting club. Therefore, we conclude that NRA/DCM control procedures have at least been adequate in the past." (p. 41–ADL Rept.)

It should also be noted that all rifles and pistols issued by the DCM on a loan basis to qualifying clubs were secured by having club officers bonded and held financially accountable for any losses of such arms as might occur. The ammunition allotment for a DCM club was an annual total of 150 cartridges per member, but only provided that members fired the prescribed qualification course of shooting. For senior rifle clubs, the ammunition alloted was .30 caliber rifle cartridges. For adult pistol clubs, the ammunition was .45 caliber pistol cartridges. Junior rifle clubs, on the other hand, firing only .22 caliber rimfire ammunition, were issued 300 rounds of ammunition per youngster, per year.

The reader should understand that for any adult rifle or pistol shooter, 150 cartridges of any kind of ammunition constituted about the equivalent of one day's practice quota. The greatest value to such shooters of Government ammunition lay in the fact that the empty cartridge cases could then be reloaded many times before being discarded. In addition, the .30 caliber rifle ammunition was usually too old for use by the Armed Forces, or consisted of the unpopular armor piercing variety, which produced much grumbling among those receiving it. In either case, if such ammunition had not been issued through the DCM Civilian Marksmanship Program, it would have been destroyed by being dumped into the ocean. The primary purpose of stimulating adult rifle and pistol clubs was to establish the human and physical resources through which the junior shooters could be trained and, when old enough, given the opportunity to familiarize themselves with the military rifles and pistols issued to the senior clubs for that purpose. The differences between such adult and junior clubs was noted in the Arthur D. Little report in this manner:

"In contrast with senior clubs, most junior clubs or junior divisions of senior clubs rely to a major extent on the use of DCM arms and ammunition in conducting their instructional and competitive programs. We estimate that about 57% of all junior members would be unable to participate in club shooting programs without DCM support. It is also in the junior programs that the Army appears to be getting its most direct value from the DCM program in terms of pre-service training. As an extreme example of what can be accomplished through a well organized junior program, we contacted a Boy Scout Council Camp in Kentucky which each year has about 1000 Scouts who fire the DCM Qualification Course utilizing only ten .22 Caliber rifles and an average issue of 100,000 rounds of ammunition per year from the DCM. The success of junior shooting programs, however, depends largely on the availability of dedicated adult leaders and instructors." (p. 39–ADL Rept.)

In addition to the recommendation that the youth-oriented DCM programs be further emphasized, it was also suggested that ammunition allotments might be increased provided that such additional issues be employed in the furtherance of hunter safety programs, or other worthwhile community shooting activities.

Each year the Nation's finest competitive marksmen participated in the National Championship shooting matches held at an old Ohio National Guard camp on the shore of Lake Erie. Those were the famous Camp Perry National Matches to which Senator Edward Kennedy had so strongly objected. The responsibility for conducting the National Matches was vested in the Secretary of the Army by Act of Congress, but the actual planning and coordination for those events fell to the President of the National Board for the Promotion of Rifle Practice, with the National Rifle Association assisting him in an advisory capacity.

Actually, the National Matches really consisted of two sets of national competition, the National Trophy Rifle and Pistol Matches, for which awards were issued by the NBPRP, and the NRA National Rifle and Pistol Championship Matches, for which awards were issued by the National Rifle Association. Most people, including many competitors, generally blurred this distinction when referring to these competitions. In any event, each match consisted of a prescribed course of fire in terms of the kind of firearm that had to be used, specific caliber designations, number of shots fired, distance to the targets, and amount of time permitted to do the shooting. At the conclusion of these matches there would emerge new national champions in each category of marksmanship, and in each category of competitor, with recognition going to separate classes of military, civilian, police, reservists, women and juniors. These matches were, by far, the most important rifle and pistol competitions in the country and they attracted well over 8,000 competitors, most of whom were military shooters, during the month of August when they were fired at Camp Perry.

As an integral part of the National Trophy Matches, there also was included the Small Arms Firing School, the function of which was often misunderstood by many persons not thoroughly familiar with their purpose. Quite obviously, persons in attendance at national shooting championships did not attend a marksmanship school to learn how to shoot or to improve their own proficiency, but rather to acquire the specialized training which developed their capabilities as instructors who could then properly teach others how to shoot. This, of course, was the basic principle upon which the NRA Police Firearms Training Program had also been established. It has worked well. The Small Arms Firing School was conducted by the Army and was open to all individuals, military and civilian, whether or not they were actually competing in the matches. Attendance at the school, however, was mandatory for any competitor who received any kind of Government travel allowance.

One should understand that of the approximately 8,000 participants at the National Matches, the majority were members of the Armed Forces and were attending the matches as a part of their assigned military duties with food and lodging provided to them as well as transportation to and from their home bases. Of the remaining competitors, a substantial number were members of official police teams. Some of these teams received small allowances from their departments but most of them paid their own way entirely out of their own pockets, as did nearly all civilian competitors.

In order to encourage each state to designate and send rifle and pistol teams to compete in the National Trophy Matches, a small travel and food allowance was authorized for the members of such teams. The maximum number of civilians eligible for such allowance was 700 out of the 8,000 competitors, and the amounts to which they were entitled were 5¢ per mile for travel and $1.50 per day for meals, or about one-third of their actual expenses. This information is mentioned at this time because that pittance played a role out of all proportion to its relevance or significance. The overwhelming majority of civilian participants at the matches paid for their own travel, lodgings, meals, and match entry fees.

In all of the NRA-sponsored National Championship Matches, each competitor was required to furnish his own ammunition, and was permitted to use either freshly manufactured commercial target-grade ammunition, or he could use his own homemade reloaded ammunition, according to his choice. Incidentally, a pistol competitor normally would fire a total of 90 rounds each of .22 caliber, .38 caliber, and .45 caliber ammunition over a three day match period.

It was a different matter, however, in the case of the National Trophy Rifle and Pistol Matches sponsored by the National Board for the Promotion of Rifle Practice, where competitors were required to fire Government issued ammunition. The rule was as follows:

> "In the National Trophy Matches service ammunition will be issued by range personnel at the firing line. Competitors are required to fire this ammunition and none other. A competitor will be disqualified if any other ammunition of the same caliber as issued is found about the person while in position at the firing line." (Rules & Regulations for the National Matches, June 30, 1967, p. 15)

The purpose of that rule was not to subsidize the shooters with a few rounds of ammunition, but to insure that the matches, fired with military weapons, measured the true performance capabilities of men firing standard military ammunition, rather than commercial target loads, or handloaded cartridges. The net result was the expenditure of a quantity of both .30 caliber rifle and .45 caliber pistol military ammunition during that phase of the championships.

The subject of the National Matches was included in the evaluation of the Civilian Marksmanship Program by the Arthur D. Little firm because of the extent to which the military services were involved in these matches. Their findings were as set out below:

> "The National Matches at Camp Perry are regarded as the 'World Series' of shooting in America. The advantages to the military departments accruing from participation in the National Matches include the following: (1) The process of preparing and qualifying for the National Matches stimulates a continuing source of knowledgeable and qualified marksmen and potential instructors in marksmanship at all levels; (2) Such competitions are directly related to the development of an essential combat skill; (3) Successful performance in National Matches presents a public image of military services capable in the use of their individual weapons; (4) Individual and team achievements are a source of pride to the individual, to the unit, and to the military services; (5) The Matches serve as an effective arena for testing shooting techniques and training methods; and (6) Successful shooters in the National Matches add luster to their reputation which makes them more believeable and effective as marksmanship instructors." (p. 28– ADL Rept.)

In costing out the program of civilian marksmanship, it was found

Overhead view of facilities at Camp Perry, Ohio. Rifle ranges in background.

that, depending upon which of two methods of accounting was used, the cost to the government of each DCM-affiliated club member in 1965 ran from $1.14 to $8.70. The total number of individuals participating during the year examined was 417,000, most of whom were juniors. The report went on to make this additional observation:

"Even these figures tend to overstate the per person cost since our questionnaire data from Army trainees suggest that many thousands of people in addition to actual DCM members receive training benefits from DCM-club personnel and programs." (p. 32–ADL Rept.)

The final conclusion of the Arthur D. Little research study commented upon the relationship which had existed since 1903 between the National Rifle Association and the National Board for the Promotion of Rifle Practice:

117

"The aims and proposes of the NRA are quite similar to those of the NBPRP. The network of NRA clubs is the primary vehicle through which the DCM applies its programs and benefits in stimulating shooters and shooting activities. NRA club officers and members provide range facilities, instruction and manpower on a volunteer basis to carry out the club programs of the DCM. The NRA magazine, 'The American Rifleman', is an excellent organ for informing, stimulating, and communicating with individuals interested in various aspects of shooting. Therefore, it is not only appropriate but essential that the NRA and the NBPRP achieve effective liaison and work closely together. We endorse the arrangement through which the NRA provides three members to the NBPRP." (pp. 46–47–ADL Rept.)

The report of the highly respected Arthur D. Little, Inc. research firm had been released in January 1966 after it had been approved by the Department of the Army and ordered implemented. It was only too clear, however, that Senator Dodd's newest bill, S.1, introduced nearly a year later, still had not made any attempt to restore the important protective clause contained in the original Federal Firearms Act of 1938 quoted near the end of the preceding chapter. Imagine the puzzlement of Franklin Orth as he addressed himself to that issue before Senator Dodd's subcommittee and inquired of them:

"In my opinion, the present system is working well, and any change in it does not seem to be justified. So why leave it out of the present bill?" (GG–p. 550)

The question of Franklin Orth was a futile one, because, at the time he had asked it, the die had been cast.

The domestic assailants of the Civilian Marksmanship Program, however, were not alone in their opposition. The Communist Party, also opposed the program as seen in the testimony of Franklin Orth to the Dodd subcommittee:

"Gentlemen, this is a great patriotic service and has nothing to do with a subsidy whatsoever. Those who call it subsidy are either ill informed or for some reason are determined to end the program which has done so much good for our servicemen in the past. I have recently asked some prominent Americans this question: 'Who is NRA's enemy? Who is intent on destroying it and who would be best served by doing so? Certainly, not the American people.' It is established that the Communist Party did attack the NRA in its official organ, The Worker, on June 18, 1967, in a double spread 'open letter' to President Johnson, signed by National Chairman Henry Winston and General Secretary Gus Hall of the Communist Party, U.S.A." (GG–p. 487)

Franklin Orth continued with his defense of the Civilian Marksmanship Program by calling the attention of the subcommittee to these facts:

"NRA provided similar service in each of our wars since 1903 with the aid of the Government. Today we are engaged in a war to maintain the freedom of the peoples in Southeast Asia. Many young men are today in Vietnam who have been trained with the service rifle at NRA clubs under the National Board for the Promotion of Rifle Practice program, largely at NRA expense, with the exception of some loaned rifles and some 150 rounds per trainee of corrosive ammunition, surplus and unuseable in military stocks. It costs NRA clubs five to 10 times as much in dollars as the amount furnished by the Government, and a hundred times as much in time and effort. NRA clubs train members and nonmembers alike in the use of the service arm on their ranges, with their instructors and with their range personnel, to insure safety, to pull and score targets, and to perform a score of other similar duties." (GG–p. 487)

Bear in mind this controversy was occurring at precisely the same time the Soviet Union was argumenting its own civilian marksmanship program, and the NRA was being attacked by the Communist Party.

A number of conscientious people for social, political or personal reasons, deny the value of the A. D. Little conclusions. Many among them accept the truth of the report but deny its application; they deny its relevancy in a world of nuclear sufficiency, if not over-abundance. Many of them may not have considered the nature of the several wars fought between the world's two greatest conflicting ideologies since Hiroshima and Nagasaki. In them the powers have scrupulously avoided the presentation of an issue or a target permitting an acceptable nuclear solution.

The United States has been so narrowly fixed on the concept of the nuclear solution and "more bang for a buck" that so far no acceptable military or political means have been found for coping with the issues presented by the North Koreans, the Red Chinese, the North Vietnamese, the Castro Government in Cuba, Juan Bosch in Santo Domingo, the Soviet menace to Israel and the Suez, or for that matter even the defense of the Panama Canal. The world's most sophisticated weapons systems simply seem unable to come to grips with little wars or a little man armed with a rifle. The unimaginable fire-power of the superpowers is frustrated. No suitable targets are provided.

9

"... it is highly important that infantry soldiers should be excellent shots ... I, therefore, strongly renew my previous recommendations that all troops be given a complete course in rifle practice prescribed in our firing manual before leaving the U.S."

GEN. JOHN J. PERSHING
WORLD WAR I

"In early 1940, ... the United States Army mirrored the attitudes of the American people, as is the case today and as it was a century ago. The mass of officers and men lacked any sense of urgency. Athletics, recreation, and entertainment took precedence in most units over serious training ... The Springfield rifle was outmoded; ... small-arms ammunition for range firing had to be rationed ... the American people, in their abhorrence of war, denied themselves a reasonable military posture."

GEN. DWIGHT D. EISENHOWER
WORLD WAR II

decades between the National Rifle Association of America and the Department of Defense through the National Board for the Promotion of Rifle Practice, had never before been so evident as during the turbulent period which followed the news on September 1, 1939, that Germany had invaded Poland. The NRA helped America prepare for war with every means at its disposal. The record it achieved was truly a great one and a source of continuing pride by all of its members.

Between 55 and 60 percent of all civilian members on the rolls of the National Rifle Association in 1941 served in the Armed Forces during the war. The civilian members of the NRA who were commissioned in the Army, Navy, Marine Corps, Coast Guard and Air Force for the purpose of conducting small arms training programs, directly supervised the small arms training of 1,667,000 officers and men, or over 10 percent of those in the Armed Forces.

NRA civilian rifle clubs in 1,278 communities conducted a total of 2,862 Pre-Induction Small Arms Training Schools approved by the War Department. Small arms training in this manner was given to 158,956 men without expense to the Government, and, in addition, 150 rifle ranges owned by NRA civilian clubs were loaned or leased to Armed Forces units in areas where no National Guard or Regular Service ranges were available for small arms training.

During the first two years of the war, no small arms training films were available in the Armed Forces, and during that period the Army Services Forces, Air Force, Navy and Coast Guard utilized hundreds of 16mm training film prints made from master prints prepared by the National Rifle Association prior to the war and furnished without cost to the Government. Similar master prints were furnished without charge to the Canadian and Australian Forces.

At the beginning of the war, neither the Air Force nor Navy had available working drawings for the purpose of rifle range construction, and the National Rifle Association supplied such drawings without charge to several contractors engaged on range construction projects for these two branches of the Armed Forces.

In the majority of States the National Guard units were sent to training camps without any advance planning for their replacement with Home Guard Units. After study and analysis of the British Home Guard organization and the World War I Home Guards in the United States, the National Rifle Association prepared a plan for Home Guard organizations utilizing established civilian rifle clubs as a nucleus, and distributed it to all Governors. That plan served as the basis for the Home Guard organizations established in many of the states during the war.

Utilizing the experience of members familiar with plant protection techniques, the National Rifle Association prepared and distributed a manual on Plant Protection which was widely recommended and used by the Provost Marshal General's office. In addition, more than one hundred war defense plants utilized the services of NRA civilian members as instructors in small arms practice for plant guard forces.

Through its broad contacts with other civilian sportsmen, the National Rifle Association recruited both dogs and dog trainers for Coast Guard Beach Patrols.

When the United States Army requested sportsmen to sell various small arms to the Government for the arming of Bridge Guards and similar such units, the National Rifle Association, with the aid and assistance of its local affiliated clubs, established, without cost to the Government, 200 inspection stations throughout the country where arms could be properly inspected and screened to insure the acquisition of suitable weapons.

When the scarcity of suitable rifles and ammunition made it necessary to arm internal security units with shotguns, the National Rifle Association prepared and distributed the only manual available during the entire war on the training and tactical use of the shotgun for internal security missions.

Eventually, when the shortage of brass cartridge cases made it difficult for police, plant guards and home guardsmen to obtain adequate quantities of ammunition for training purposes, the National Rifle Association recruited 250 experienced and already equipped handloaders of ammunition to reload fired cartridge cases. During the period of greatest emergency in this field these "over-age" civilians furnished approximately 2,000,000 rounds of reloaded cartridges to internal security units. Also, over 1,000 NRA competitive pistol shooters, over-age for military service, served as small arms instructors and officers of Auxiliary Police units. In addition, hundreds of other members, already equipped with high grade binoculars and telescopes as part of their hunting and target shooting equipment, served as aircraft spotters.

Over 500 experienced gunsmiths and ammunition handloaders were also recruited for positions as foremen and inspectors in war-built arms and ammunition defense plants where their special "know-how" was of great value in training and supervising "green" crews.

Throughout the war special requests from Government and private plants were filled by the National Rifle Association from its "over-age" membership for individual specialists in the purchasing and processing of such items as wood for gun stocks, leather for holsters, optical glass, specialized gear for the Arctic and for the tropics, etc., and the National Rifle Association also served continuously in a liaison capacity by placing government departments and contractors in touch with small manufacturers who had specialized equipment and know-how to do typically small-shop jobs, frequently very far removed from the field of small arms but requiring kindred skills.

Following the British evacuation in early 1940 of 338,226 men from Dunkirk with their attendant loss of 7,000 tons of ammunition, 90,000 rifles, 8,000 Bren guns, and 400,000 antitank rifles, Britain was in imminent danger of invasion. Its vaunted Home Guard was virtually defenseless and literally forced to supplement its few sporting guns with clubs and spears! These words of Winston Churchill described its predicament:

"All over the country, in every town and village, bands of determined men came together with shotguns, sporting rifles, clubs and spears." (HH–p. 486)

It was in response to the plight of the disarmed British civilians that concerned NRA members unselfishly donated personal rifles, shotguns, pistols and binoculars to the American Committee for Defense of British Homes after a full page plea was printed in the November 1940 issue of the NRA magazine, *The American Rifleman*. Over 7,000 small arms collected in this manner were shipped to the Civilian Committee for Protection of Homes in Birmingham, England. Recognition of the superb and unselfish contribution to the war effort of the United States, which had been made by the National Rifle Association of America and its many thousands of members, came from many sources none of which were more proudly received than the following letter from the White House, dated November 14, 1945, and signed by President Harry S Truman. Addressed to the National Rifle Association, the letter read:

"The tradition of citizen soldiery is firmly, and properly imbedded in our national ideals. Initiative, discipline, and skill in the use of small arms are essential for the development of the finished citizen soldier.

The National Rifle Association, in the periods between our last four wars, has done much to encourage the improvement of small arms and small arms marksmanship in the Regular services, as well as in the National Guard, Reserve units, and the civilian population.

123

SEND
A GUN
TO DEFEND
A BRITISH HOME

British civilians, faced with threat of invasion,
desperately need arms for the defense of their homes.

THE AMERICAN COMMITTEE FOR DEFENSE
OF BRITISH HOMES

has organized to collect gifts of

PISTOLS—RIFLES—REVOLVERS
SHOTGUNS—BINOCULARS

from American civilians who wish to answer the call and aid in defense
of British homes.

These arms are being shipped, with the consent of the British Government, to
CIVILIAN COMMITTEE FOR PROTECTION OF HOMES
BIRMINGHAM, ENGLAND
The members of which are Wickham Steed, Edward Hulton, and Lord Davies

YOU CAN AID

by sending any arms or binoculars you can spare to

AMERICAN COMMITTEE FOR
DEFENSE OF BRITISH HOMES
C. Suydam Cutting, *Chairman*
ROOM 100
10 WARREN STREET, NEW YORK, N. Y.

World War II "Guns for Britain" Advertisement.

During the war just ended, the contributions of the association in the matter of small-arms training aids, the nationwide preinduction training program, the recruiting of experienced small-arms instructors for all branches of the armed services, and technical advice and assistance to Government civilian agencies aiding in the prosecution of the war—all contributed freely and without expense to the Government—have materially aided our war effort.

I hope that the splendid program which the National Rifle Association has followed during the past three-quarters of a century will be continued. It is a program which is good for a free America." (CC–p. 205)

The National Rifle Association of America also was honored by General George C. Marshall, Chief of Staff, United States Army. In his letter of October 30, 1945, General Marshall expressed his feelings in this manner:

"I wish to express to you and to the members of the National Rifle Association of America my appreciation for the service rendered the Army by the Association during World War II.

Through the conduct of pre-induction small arms training schools, the preparation of manuals and charts required for instruction in rifle marksmanship, by making available to the Army training films on rifle and pistol marksmanship and allied activities, the Association greatly facilitated small arms training throughout the Army. The record of the National Rifle Association during the war has been one in which its members should take great pride. The nation is fortunate in having such an organization upon which it can rely for the continued development of proficiency in the use of small arms by the citizens of this country.

I take this opportunity to extend to you my best wishes for the future." (GG–p. 485)

It should, therefore, be evident why there existed such intense and uncompromising loyalty to the National Rifle Association, and why NRA members were outraged when efforts were made to besmirch the reputation and character of that patriotic organization and to tear apart the programs upon which it had been founded.

Remarks such as the following one, made by Senator Dodd, were destructive of any possible confidence in Senator Dodd's comprehension of the relationship between that program and the national defense:

"I have never been able to convince myself about the value of gun experience with respect to national defense. There is something to it. But I do not think it is that much." (CC–p. 669)

The U.S. Attorney General, Nicholas Katzenbach, obviously detected the emotionalism, which was mirrored in the tremendous opposition to S.1592, when he was prompted to make this observation to Senator Dodd's subcommittee:

"These opponents feel their views most deeply, as is evident from the bitterness and volume of their opposition." (CC–p. 39)

The question remains whether or not he ever understood the reason. It appears doubtful he did. Franklin L. Orth, Executive Vice President of the National Rifle Association understood.

Backed by a distinguished career in World War II as a combat officer in Merrill's Marauders and later in government as Deputy Assistant Secretary of the Army, Orth understood clearly the importance of the Civilian Marksmanship Program and the omission of the special language which protected it in the Federal Firearms Act of 1938. He tried to explain to Senator Dodd's subcommittee:

"Mr. Chairman, the effect of this omission of existing law from the terms of S.1592 could spell the end of that extremely valuable contribution to our National Defense Establishment, the program for civilian marksmanship, the responsibility of the National Board for the Promotion of Rifle Practice, under the Secretary of the Army." (CC–p. 204)

Appearing as one of the witnesses speaking to this entire issue was the Honorable Stephen Ailes, Secretary of the Army, who told the subcommittee that enactment of S.1592 would require that the practice of distributing firearms on a loaned basis to qualifying clubs would have to be modified, but that, in his opinion, the modification probably could be accomplished and the program effectively continued. His general statement superbly described how the Civilian Marksmanship Program operated at that time, and the Army's general experience with it:

"Since 1903, the Congress has directed the Secretary of the Army to provide a civilian marksmanship training program under the direction of the National Board for the Promotion of Rifle Practice.

The Board consists of 25 members appointed by the Secretary of the Army and includes representatives of the three military services, the Coast Guard, the Armed Forces Reserve components, the Selective

Service System, the National Rifle Association of America (NRA), and the country at large.

The activities of the Board are authorized and directed in sections 4307 to 4313 of title 10, United States Code, and are supported every year by a separate appropriation in the Defense Appropriation Act.

The President's budget for the coming fiscal year requests $459,-000 for this purpose.

The principal functions of the Board are (1) to promote small arms practice among citizens who are not members of the Armed Forces, (2) hold small arms competitions, and (3) issue, loan, or sell small arms, ammunition, and targets necessary for this program.

The Board's programs are administered for the Board by the Office of the Director of Civilian Marksmanship in my office.

The Board's promotion of rifle and pistol practice is accomplished primarily through supporting civilian rifle and pistol clubs enrolled with the Director of Civilian Marksmanship.

On January 1 of this year, there were 5,697 clubs enrolled with the Director of Civilian Marksmanship. The total enrollment in these clubs was 413,371 persons.

The clubs are of three main types—senior clubs, composed of members 17 years of age and over; junior clubs, composed of members between 12 and 18 years of age, supervised by an adult; and clubs affiliated with colleges or with schools maintaining National Defense Cadet Corps programs.

To be eligible for enrollment with the Director of Civilian Marksmanship, the senior clubs must have 10 or more civilian members, and junior clubs must have a certified adult instructor.

All clubs must have access to adequate range facilities and must agree to conduct marksmanship training for 9 months of the year.

The clubs must be operated without regard to race or creed, and they must be affiliated with the National Rifle Association. Before accepting a club's application, the NRA institutes a check through the State adjutant general and the rifle and pistol association of the State in which the club is located to determine that the club's officials are American citizens without criminal backgrounds and not members of subversive organizations.

The actual investigation varies somewhat from State to State, depending upon facilities available and local regulations. In New York, for example, the names furnished are checked through the State Criminal Investigation and Identification Division. Prior to final approval of NRA affiliation, the club must also obtain endorsements from two community leaders.

The Board supports these clubs by distributing ammunition and issuing caliber .30 rifles, caliber .22 rifles, and caliber .45 automatic pistols on a loan basis. These are issued to clubs on a ratio of approximately 1 weapon for every 11 members. The clubs are responsible for the safety and care of the weapons. Ammunition is issued once a year on the basis of the number of members in the club who have fired approved marksmanship qualification courses during the previous year.

Currently, there are about 18,000 caliber .22 rifles, 12,500 caliber .30 rifles, and 4,300 caliber .45 pistols on loan to the clubs.

The Director of Civilian Marksmanship is accountable for all these weapons and maintains an accurate list of them by serial number.

The Board conducts the National Rifle and Pistol Matches at Camp Perry, Ohio, each year. As an integral part of the matches, Small Arms Firing Schools are conducted by the U.S. Army Infantry School under the general supervision of the National Board. These schools provide the latest information and techniques concerning marksmanship instruction.

The law which directs these activities of the Board also provides for the sale, at cost, of weapons and ammunition necessary for target practice. Such weapons and ammunition as may be sold have, of course, been determined to be no longer needed by the Government. The principal types of weapons sold under this program have been caliber .30 1903-A3 'Springfield' rifles, caliber .30 M1 carbines, and caliber .45 pistols.

Under the Army's policy, no more than one weapon of each type may be sold to any one purchaser. Under the law, sales may be made only to members of the National Rifle Association.

To be a member of the National Rifle Association, an individual must pledge that he is a citizen of the United States, not a member of an organization which seeks the violent overthrow of the U.S. Government or any State or local government, and not a person convicted of a crime of violence.

In addition to providing his NRA membership, the purchaser must also comply with all applicable State laws concerning purchase and ownership of weapons and must submit the forms and certificates required by such laws at the time of purchase.

In general, we believe that the civilian marksmanship program is being carried out properly, responsibly, and in accordance with the purposes intended by the Congress. We know of nothing to indicate that guns lent or sold under this program have been used for any improper purpose." (CC–pp. 58–60)

That was *not* the kind of information typically presented to the American public by the press.

Consider, if you will, what manner of reader reaction had been produced by the following lurid excerpt taken from an article which appeared in the October 8, 1964, issue of the *Reporter* magazine.

"And the Minutemen, an anti-Communist guerilla organization that claims to have 25,000 members, urges its followers to join NRA-affiliated clubs in order to obtain the ammunition, targets, and surplus or rented weapons—including machineguns, flamethrowers, and aerial bombs—that the Defense Department issues to the NRA each year in order to improve civilian marksmanship." (CC–p. 557)

Imagine that: "machineguns, flamethrowers, and aerial bombs". Is it supposed that that report was the result of poor research, interpretative journalism, or vicious falsehood?

Another witness who touched on the Civilian Markmanship Program in passing was Frank Foote. Mr. Foote appeared before the House Committee on Ways and Means representing the Nebraska Game, Forestation and Parks Commission. After a brief explanation of how the program was constituted, Frank Foote informed the committee that much of the ammunition issued under the program was so old that if it were not issued for this particular purpose it would have to be destroyed:

"This has cost the U.S. Government the cost of loaning us the weapons and in issuing ammunition which was near the end of its effective age and would, I assume, have no longer found a use. A lot of our issue comes from 1952 and 1954 near the end of its storage shelf life." (EE–p. 389)

It should be noted that, although the Secretary of the Army testified that the distribution program would have to be modified under S.1592 because of omission of the protective clause of the old Federal Firearms Act of 1938, he, nevertheless, had said that it would still be possible to administer the program. This would have involved going through a complex and unwieldy State-by-State maneuver involving the various State National Guard Units. Despite the best intentions of the Secretary of the Army, there existed in the minds of knowledgeable persons grave doubts as to whether his optimism was justified.

The omission of that protective clause from S.1592 was by design, and not inadvertence. It should be noted that anti-gun pressures had already built up to the point where as of April 15, 1965, a month prior to the commencement of the hearings on S.1592, all sales of military surplus weapons to civilians had been administratively terminated.

10

"You do not examine legislation in the light of the benefits it will convey if properly administered, but in the light of the wrongs it would do and the harms it would cause if improperly administered."

LYNDON B. JOHNSON

THE GUN CONTROL CONTROVERSY OF 1965 WHICH CENtered around Senator Dodd's new bill, S.1592, was heralded early in January of that year by a spate of news articles released across the country carrying a story similar to that reported by the *Chicago Tribune* on January 6, 1965, in a piece captioned "Dodd Cites Illegal Sales To Chicagoans." The two paragraphs in that news story which shocked and appalled readers were:

"Dodd said that President Kennedy was killed with a mail order gun, and that the subcommittee's investigation disclosed that over a recent three year period two Los Angeles firms sent 4,069 firearms to consignees in Chicago."

* * *

" 'Subcommittee investigators with the help of the Chicago police found that 25 per cent of these consignees had criminal records,' Dodd said."

The allegations made with respect to those 4,069 Chicagoans, continued to reverberate across the country not only for the duration of the hearings on S.1592, but for sometime thereafter when the topic of mail-order firearms was debated. Moreover, Senator Dodd did not hesitate to project those figures to a nationwide basis and suggest that they typified the experience throughout the country. For example, on one occasion he addressed one of the witnesses appearing before his subcommittee and asserted:

"In one city after another, anywhere from 25 to as high as 30 percent of those who buy mail-order guns have prior criminal records." (CC–p. 279)

Reference to the Chicagoans with "criminal records" was even incorporated in the opening remarks of the Honorable Nicholas Katzenbach, Attorney General of the United States, where he distilled the story into this succinct comment:

"It has also been disclosed that over a 3-year period in Chicago, 4,000 persons bought weapons from only two mail-order dealers and that of these, fully one-forth had criminal records." (CC–p. 36)

The impressive nature of those statistics, their wide-spread dissemination, and the importance attached to them by so many of those persons who labored so vigorously to eliminate the mail order sale of firearms, requires a more critical examination of them. Do you recall the half-million "armed criminals" of Attorney General Homer Cummings of the 1930's, with which he attempted to shock and astonish both the Congress and the public?

On July 13, 1964, the Chicago Police Department issued a news release on the subject of this particular investigation conducted for Senator Dodd's subcommittee. The release reported that, of 4,069 persons who bought guns through mail-order advertisements from three California firms during 1963, a total of 948 of them were found to have had a police record of some kind with the Chicago Police Department. Their breakdown was as follows: 406 for traffic violations; 426 for disorderly conduct; 111 for various kinds of assaults; 83 for carrying concealed weapons; 42 for burglary; 58 for robbery; and 13 arrests for murder.

Assuming that one can trust the accuracy of the news release from the Chicago Police Department, there then arises several inescapable conclusions from the facts reported. It would appear that either Senator Dodd consciously equated traffic violations with the kind of criminality that should bar offenders from possessing a gun, or that he consciously included traffic violations so as to contrive a large and impressive percentage of "criminal records". The reader is free to decide which theory is more plausible.

It also should not escape our attention that arrest records are not the same as criminal records because criminal records refer to persons who have been finally convicted in a court of law of a specific offense. If, therefore, the persons referred to were actually convicted criminals, rather than mere suspects, then of necessity they would have fallen within the provisions of the Federal Firearms Act of 1938 which, as will be recalled, provided:

> "It shall be unlawful for any person who has been convicted of a crime punishable by imprisonment for a term exceeding one year or is a fugitive from justice to receive any firearm or ammunition which has been shipped or transported in interstate or foreign commerce, . . ." (GG–p. 71)

Now, if the persons alleged to have had "criminal records' were actually convicted criminals, then it seems reasonable that by using the proof that they had received firearms illegally in interstate commerce they each should have been prosecuted and convicted of violating the Federal Firearms Act of 1938, which carried a maximum penalty of a $2,000 fine and/or imprisonment in the penitentiary not exceeding five years.

On the other hand, if these persons only had arrest records which had never resulted in conviction, then it would appear that these persons were characterized by Senator Dodd as having "criminal records" for the sole purpose of deceiving the American public and arousing sympathy for the enactment of S.1592. As a former agent of the Federal Bureau of Investigation, Senator Dodd was well aware of the distinction between an arrest record and a criminal record.

Could it have been that the tacit implication was that an arrest record was to be regarded in qualifying for gun ownership as the equivalent of a criminal record in violation of the fundamental precept of American jurisprudence which holds that a man is presumed innocent

132

until proved guilty in a court of law by a jury of his peers? That would, indeed, be an interesting proposition, and one that was pregnant with ramifications for "due process."

The first of the Congressional hearings on Senator Dodd's S.1592 were scheduled to commence on May 19, 1965, before Senator Dodd's own Senate Judiciary Subcommitte to Investigate Juvenile Delinquency. They occupied eleven days interspersed through July 27, 1965, with only slight overlapping, the House Committee on Ways and Means began its hearings on July 12, 1965, and spread its eleven day total on through July 28, 1965.

At the outset it will be helpful to present an abbreviated enumeration of the general provisions which were contained in Senator Dodd's S.1592. The bill was designed generally to do the following:

(1) Prohibit interstate mail order sales of firearms to private citizens by limiting such firearms shipments only to those occurring between licensed dealers, manufacturers and importers.

(2) Prohibit sales of pistols by Federal licensees to persons under 21 years of age, and prohibit sales of rifles and shotguns to persons under 18 years of age.

(3) Prohibit a Federal licensee from selling a handgun to any person who was not a resident or businessman of the State in which the licensee's place of business was located.

(4) Curb the importation into the United States of surplus military weapons and other firearms not regarded as being suitable for sporting purposes.

(5) Bring so-called destructive devices such as bazookas, grenades, antitank guns, bombs, missiles, and rockets under Federal controls.

(6) Increase the annual Federal license fees for firearms and ammunition dealers from the $1 fee to $100.

It evidently was felt by certain legislative experts that in order to goad an unenthusiastic Congress into enacting S.1592 it first would be necessary to arouse the quiescent public and manufacture the appearance of a wide-spread demand for the proffered legislation sufficient in degree to overcome the strong opposition that such an obnoxious measure predictably would produce.

In addition to the continual repetition of scare-statistics based upon the distorted allegation that 25 percent of some 4,069 Chicago purchasers of mail-order firearms had been found to have had "criminal records", a sampling which incidently was based on purchasers virtually all of whom lived in the city's Negro ghettos, there was also interjected

133

into the subject of firearms controls the diversionary issue of destructive devices. This was a bugbear which also strongly appealed to the fears of middle class Americans who were cast in the role of pawns in that incredible legislative chess game.

In spite of the fact there was no substantial controversy over the proposed controls for destructive devices, and that minor questions as to their definition were capable of immediate correction, this essentially simple legislation was not separated from the firearms issue for prompt enactment. This fact appears to have been primarily because of the greater value of various explosives and crew-served ordnance in facilitating the sensationalization and dramatization of Senator Dodd's S.1592. Destructive devices had an obvious usefulness in gaining the attention, sympathy and support of many persons who might have otherwise remained largely indifferent to the pending legislation.

Historically, deliberations pertaining to the control of firearms have proceeded upon the premise there existed a legislatively recognizable distinction between concealable handguns and the longer, bulkier rifles and shotguns. It will be recalled that Senator Dodd's first bill—the originally introduced S.1975—was limited solely to the establishment of an affidavit system as a prerequisite to the purchase of mail-order pistols, and that it was only in the throes of hysteria immediately following the assassination of President Kennedy that Senator Dodd added the so-called "long guns" to his bill. How, then, during a period of relative calm, could the Administration hope to justify the inclusion of long guns in a bill so drastic that it would totally ban their interstate shipment to private citizens other than licensed dealers?

At the very least it was realized by the Administration that opponents of Senator Dodd's S.1592 would try to persuade Congress that long guns should be excluded from its harsh restrictions on the grounds that they were significantly less often associated with crimes of violence than were handguns. The record is almost ludicrous in the manner in which it reveals the efforts exerted by Senator Dodd in his attempt to overcome that contention and to implicate the use of long guns in a sufficiently high percentage of serious crime as to justify their retention in his bill. The official statistic fastened upon and repeated ad nauseam was that 30 per cent of all murders committed by firearms were committed with rifles and shotguns. In spite of the fact that one Administration witness after the other could not even come close to substantiating that percentage within their own communities, Senator Dodd, nevertheless, did not waver for a moment in stoutly maintaining its accuracy.

In order to entice the Congress to assume controls which had been traditionally reserved to the individual States because of the absence of

134

any constitutional grant of police power, it became necessary to establish that the Federal Government merely intended to provide the assistance necessary to permit the States to enforce their own internal laws. The assertion was made that the States were powerless to act by themselves to control the shipment of mail-order guns into their jurisdictions, and that their only salvation lay in the total prohibition of the interstate shipment of mail-order firearms by means of Senator Dodd's S.1592, which had been so thoughtfully advanced by a kindly and benevolent government. The general public could hardly be expected to be familiar with the provisions of the Federal Firearms Act of 1938, which carefully gave to the States precisely the power sought in S.1592, providing, of course, that the legislatures of the respective States chose to exercise their power.

In effect, the Administration decided to remove that right of decision from the States, whether they wanted it removed or not. The glaring fact was that the legislatures of fourteen States specifically adopted resolutions vigorously opposing S.1592 on grounds that they did not want it and did not feel any need for such legislation. This is not at all difficult to understand when it is known that the total number of murders committed annually in the four cities of Chicago, Los Angeles, New York, and Washington, exceeds the total number of murders committed annually in thirty States, even though the population of those States is substantially higher than the population of those cities.

Through means of numerous press releases concerning the subcommittee's alleged "Findings of Fact" which were regularly carried and editorially elaborated upon by the 93 percent of the country's newspaper circulation that reportedly supported Senator Dodd's S.1592, the general public gradually became saturated with the anti-gun litany. In an attempt to capitalize upon the resulting conceptual conditioning, popularly referred to as brainwashing, anti-gun proponents continually cited various public opinion polls which they then interpreted as indicative of a vast burgeoning of public sentiment for that specific piece of legislation. It was almost humorous to observe the manner in which efforts were made to substitute the national opinion polls—taken on samples of approximately 1,600 people—for the collective voice of all America.

Anxious to establish a more impressive number of annual deaths which could be attributed to firearms than was already provided by the nation's murder rate, it was decided to include in the total deaths cited, all suicides and accidents which had been inflicted through means of firearms. The annual suicides by gun more than doubled the criminal homicides committed by shootings, and that was further enlarged by the accidents. It was common practice, however, when referring to those figures to simply lump them altogether and present them as the number of persons "killed with firearms" each year, thus conveying the impression to the casual reader that all such unfortunate persons were the victims of deliberate murders. One cannot help wondering whether or not the idea occurred to anyone to employ the panic technique originated by Homer Cummings back in 1934 in an effort to stampede the Congress into including handguns in the National Firearms Act of 1934. Of course, in this more sophisticated era, how many persons could really be expected to believe that the nation harbored over 3,500,000 armed criminals?

Before proceeding any further, the reader should once again refer to the key provision of the Federal Firearms Act of 1938 with respect to so-called "license" States which provided:

"It shall be unlawful for any licensed manufacturer or dealer to transport or ship any firearm in interstate or foreign commerce to any person other than a licensed manufacturer or dealer in any State the laws of which require that a license be obtained for the purchase of such firearm, unless such license is exhibited to such manufacturer or dealer by the prospective purchaser." (GG–p. 71)

That particular section had been explained back in the 1963 hearings held before Senator Dodd's subcommittee by John Coggins of the Alcohol and Tobacco Tax Division of the Internal Revenue Service:

"So there are only seven States, although this act has been on the books for 25 years, there are only seven States which have requirements tying in with this permit to purchase firearms. Those States are—I have it here. The States which tie in with the provisions of section 2(c) of the Federal Firearms Act are Hawaii, Massachusetts, Michigan, Missouri, New Jersey, New York, and North Carolina. So only in those States would it be a violation for the out-of-State dealer to ship into the State, unless the purchaser within the State exhibited their license." (AA–p. 3410)

It is therefore clearly evident that it would constitute a violation of the Federal Firearms Act of 1938 for a dealer to ship a gun into one of those States to which Mr. Coggins referred unless the purchaser had exhibited a license for such firearm. It will now prove most enlightening to examine the efficiency with which that thirty year old law had been enforced by those who had been charged with that responsibility.

136

The reader will observe that two of the States mentioned by Mr. Coggins as having a license law that interlocked with the Federal Firearms Act of 1938 were New Jersey and New York. Consider that fact in light of this remarkable statement by Arthur J. Sills, Attorney General for the State of New Jersey:

"In 1964 a survey was conducted by the State police to determine if purchase permits had been obtained by residents in New Jersey who had received mail-order guns from Seaport Traders, Inc., and Weapons, Inc., both California-based corporations.

It was discovered that of the 126 guns sold and shipped by mail by Seaport Traders, Inc., of Los Angeles, Calif., permits were issued for the legal purchase of 63, no permits were issued for 56. Of the 28 handguns sold and shipped by Weapons, Inc., permits were issued for 22, no permits were issued for 5. Of the 154 guns sold and mailed by these two outfits, 61 were sold and mailed without permits being issued. It was also ascertained that 26 persons with criminal records were among those who had purchased the 61 weapons from these 2 mail-order houses." (CC–p. 405)

Before rushing into all manner of commentary, let the reader first examine similar testimony on the part of Leonard Reisman, Deputy Commissioner of the New York City Police Department:

"As you know, in New York we have a law which requires that common carriers have the packages which contain concealable firearms so marked and it is required that these common carriers notify the police department before delivery is made.

From 1950, until the present, the ballistics bureau which is sent to check these, has checked 2,676 of which some 1,200 were proper shipments, they were shipments to licensed individuals, and they have disapproved 1,439, which means 1,439 pistols and revolvers were shipped in, if you will, mail order or common carrier, to persons who would not have been authorized to receive them, and accordingly those guns were never delivered." (CC–p. 610)

Just one more fact is all that will be necessary for the completion of this particular point, and that has to do with the kind of records that firearms dealers were required to keep under the Federal Firearms Act of 1938. The general public was never informed of the fact that firearms dealers, wherever they happened to be based, were required by Federal law to be licensed. If they were not, then that fact of itself constituted a violation of the Federal law. As licensed dealers, they

137

were further required to maintain detailed records of all transactions regarding firearms sales according to a certain prescribed format. Also, those records were required to be preserved for a number of years and available for authorized investigatory inspections.

Remember the penalties which were provided for a violation of any of the provisions of the Federal Firearms Act of 1938:

> "Any person violating any of the provisions of this chapter or any rules and regulations promulgated hereunder, or who makes any statement in applying for the license or exemption provided for in this chapter, knowing such statement to be false, shall, upon conviction thereof, be fined not more than $2,000, or imprisoned for not more than five years, or both." (GG–p. 72)

It seems to be clear that the various investigations produced more than sufficient evidence to have permitted the successful prosecution and conviction of both firearms dealers and criminals who apparently violated the Federal Firearms Act of 1938. Why were such persons not prosecuted?

The fact that the subcommittee's investigators were able to establish as many violations of the law as had been alleged should dispel the notion that the task was burdensome. Were not such continual investigations the very essence of what formerly was regarded as good routine police work? After all, the major mail-order firearms dealers conducted their business by openly and conspicuously advertising their wares for sale, hence it would not have been very difficult to determine which of them were the suppliers of those inexpensive pistols which were said to appeal most to the criminally-inclined individual. Then, what prevented a periodic inspection to ascertain whether the dealers were in proper compliance with all applicable laws? Clearly, it was no secret as to which states required a license for the purchase of a firearm. The purchase orders of persons residing in such states could have been spot-checked to verify that they had submitted documentary evidence of having possessed a valid license? Why was this not done?

If the Alcohol and Tobacco Tax investigators had regularly secured the successful prosecution of those mail order firearms dealers who allegedly shipped guns into license states without having received evidence that the purchaser had a license, then would that fact alone not have put such undesirable firearms dealers promptly and permanently out of business by withdrawal of their licenses? Why was this not done under Federal Firearms Act of 1938?

If the Federal Government could cooperate with the police de-

138

partments of such municipalities as Chicago by providing them, as it did, with information as to which of their residents had purchased mail-order handguns could they not have secured the prosecution of all persons with "criminal records" who had violated the Federal law by illegally having received firearms in interstate commerce? Why was this not done?

What was the Administration's attitude with respect to this matter? To what did they attribute the lack of enforcement? In what manner did they present the problem to the Congress? An enlightening insight into these questions was provided by none other than the Honorable Sheldon S. Cohen, U.S. Commissioner of Internal Revenue, on the occasion of his appearance in support of Senator Dodd's S.1592 before the House Committee on Ways and Means. In attempting to justify the need for still more laws, he stated:

"The pivotal problem with regard to this traffic as it exists today is that neither the State nor city into which the firearm is shipped has any practical way of exercising any effective control over the importer, manufacturer, or dealer who sells the firearm and ships in it from another State." (DD–p. 31)

That statement is in direct conflict with the provisions of the Federal Firearms Act of 1938. Perhaps an insight into the nature of the national problem of enforcement which existed can be gleaned from the following very illuminating exchange which occurred between Congressman Thomas B. Curtis and Sheldon Cohen:

MR. CURTIS. "How many employees in the Internal Revenue Service devote full time to the enforcement of this act?

MR. COHEN. As I mentioned the other day, we don't use these people full time. We use our alcohol and tobacco tax agents in a variety of tasks in the alcohol, tobacco, and gun field.

MR. CURTIS. My memory is a little better than yours. You testified to that. In fact, you said that they were mingled. Then I said, 'How many are on this particular assignment full time?' because I said there must be some, and you said that you didn't have the figure but you would get them.

MR. COHEN. I do have the man-year figure. We have 52.

MR. CURTIS. Fifty-two who are on full time.

MR. COHEN. No, sir, that is a compilation of time. That includes some people part time.

139

MR. CURTIS. Do you have anybody in the Internal Revenue Service whose job it is, and sole job it is, to operate and direct enforcement of interstate traffic in firearms and ammunition?

MR. COHEN. Five people in the national office who direct the operation of these fifty-two people around the country.

MR. CURTIS. Well, those five are full time on this job?

MR. COHEN. Yes, sir.

MR. CURTIS. What are their names?

MR. COHEN. I can get them.

MR. CURTIS. I can get some information. Let's have their names.

MR. COHEN. Mr. Neal and Mr. Darr are two of them. I will have to get the rest of them for you.

MR. CURTIS. Can any of the gentlemen with you tell me what their titles are and what their instructions actually are?

MR. COHEN. May I supply that for the record, sir? It may be easier.

MR. CURTIS. Yes, but I still want to get it, because frankly, I want to talk to them.

MR. COHEN. You will have it, sir.

MR. CURTIS. What I would really like would be an organizational chart.

MR. COHEN. We can give you an organizational chart.

MR. CURTIS. Are they in an office together?

MR. COHEN. They are in an office adjacent to one another.

MR. CURTIS. I meant on your chart structure.

MR. COHEN. Yes, sir; yes, sir, this would be one unit of the alcohol and tobacco tax unit.

MR. CURTIS. And each has one assistant and clerk; is that the way it is?

MR. COHEN. I am not sure exactly how it is.

MR. CURTIS. Let me express wonderment. Here you come in and ask the Ways and Means Committee to change laws and you have ready figures justifying your need for additional personnel. But you don't have the evidence at your fingertips or anyone with you to help you answer the very basic question of how you are presently structured.

You have demonstrated the reason for my worry about how much you people have been trying to dig in depth to find out what is wrong with the law. If you haven't tried to find out what is wrong with your own organization by even knowing how you are set up, how in the name of heaven can you recommend legislation because you are going to have to enforce whatever we put on the books, and a lot of your proposals are really redundant. You are going to have the same kind of difficulties in enforcing your new proposals that you are experiencing in enforcing the present law. So the wonderment I am expressing, to emphasize, is that you are unable to tell this committee at this time how you are structured in your own organization to carry out the law that we presently have.

MR. COHEN. No, sir; I didn't say that.

MR. CURTIS. I have said it." (DD–pp. 161–163)

In another, less hectic, portion of the hearings before that same committee, Sheldon Cohen did manage to answer the question which had been put to him by Congressman John W. Byrnes with regard to the powers of his division to punish firearms dealers for infractions of the Federal Firearms Act of 1938:

"MR. BYRNES. What if a person does not maintain proper records? You can take away his license?

MR. COHEN. We can take away his license. He might be subject to other penalties. There would be a prosecution, of course, if there were a willful criminal sanction for failure to maintain his proper records and withdrawal of his license." (DD–p. 54)

Now, to provide the reader with some manner of gauge as to the lack of vigor with which the two national firearms control acts were enforced during the year prior to these congressional hearings, it is only necessary to review Sheldon Cohen's answer to the following questions raised by Congressman James F. Battin:

"MR. BATTIN. Do you know or does anybody sitting at the table there with you know how many prosecutions have been initiated—

MR. COHEN. Something like 340 or so the year before last.

MR. BATTIN. And this dealt with what type of violations?

MR. COHEN. Under the national act last year there were 274 prosecutions recommended. Under the Federal act there were 48 recommended. Joint, that is, under both acts, there were 16, or a total of 338.

MR. BATTIN. This dealt with improper recordkeeping?

MR. COHEN. This is a combination of all of those, all types of violations. I don't have a breakdown as to the specific instances of the 338, but there were 338 violations of one sort or another varying from recordkeeping all the way to the unlawful possession of machineguns, sawed-off shotguns, or that sort of thing." (DD–pp. 125–126)

Considering the number of violations previously alleged, the miniscule number of prosecutions is nothing short of astounding. The question posed is obvious. If these violations were so readily discoverable, then why were the offenders not prosecuted and promptly punished? In addition to the firearms dealers being subject to the penalties of the Federal Firearms Act of 1938 so also were the persons with "criminal records" who flouted it, assuming of course that something more serious than a traffic citation or parking ticket lurked in their backgrounds. Why, then, were these criminals not prosecuted when they were discovered?

It seems all too apparent that the abuses of the Federal laws which were reported during the course of the various hearings on Senator Dodd's S.1592 were not the routine product of a normally vigorous and inquisitive Alcohol and Tobacco Tax Division of the Internal Revenue Service in the customary discharge of their responsibilities as the enforcement arm of the Treasury Department, but seem instead to have been the spectacular discoveries made during the course of special intensive investigations for the sole purpose of producing evidence to support the alleged need of another new law.

One of the several controversial aspects of Senator Dodd's S.1592 arose as a result of the belief of many that, if enacted into law, it could lead to the establishment of a national gun registration system through the exercise of the exceptionally broad rule-making authority vested in the Secretary of the Treasury. Whether it would, or would not, have done so is not, for the moment, important. What was important were the opinions concerning that aspect of S.1592 which troubled the nation's sportsmen so deeply and caused them to fear its enactment. The U.S. Attorney General, Nicholas Katzenbach, addressed himself to that apprehension and made the following positive statement of assurance with regard to that point:

"This legislation will not force sportsmen to register their guns, and it will not prevent them from carrying their guns." (DD–p. 72)

Over on the Senate side of the Capitol building, Senator Dodd was being less dogmatic and less reassuring in his statement concerning that fear:

"You know one of the arguments made by opponents of this bill is that it will lead to ultimate legal registration. Maybe it should." (CC–p. 125)

Sportsmen did not have too much longer to wait, however, before

142

another witness on behalf of the government, Arthur Sills, Attorney General of the State of New Jersey, confirmed their suspicions:

> "The N.R.A. says, in fact, they have no addicts, alcoholics, or criminals among their 600,000 members. If this is true, then they have absolutely no fear of legislation which will have them register their guns or legislation like S.1592 which will make registration feasible and effective." (CC–p. 405)

To what conclusion would the reader be drawn upon comparing the three preceding statements? Were those statements necessarily inconsistent with each other, or were they each literally accurate?

Early in the course of the hearings before Senator Dodd's subcommittee, Nicholas Katzenbach flatly asserted the importance of including rifles and shotguns within S.1592 on the grounds that statistics demonstrated that such long guns were involved in at least 30 percent of all murders committed with guns.

One would quite naturally be led to believe that the police records of the major cities in the United States would tend to corroborate the statement of the U.S. Attorney General that 30 percent of all murders by guns involved rifles and shotguns. Not so.

Notwithstanding careful and leading questions of his own witnesses Dodd failed repeatedly to obtain support for the 30 percent figure. Less than half that would have been closer to the fact.

Still later, and still vainly trying somehow to support the "official" statistic that long guns accounted for "fully 30 percent of all murders committed by firearms", Carl Perian, the subcommittee Staff Director, pursued the same line of questioning with J. Preston Strom, the Director of the South Carolina State Law Enforcement Division. The dialogue went as follows:

> "MR. PERIAN. We have found that, nationally, rifles and shotguns account for about 30 percent of the murders or homicides by firearms. From your experience or from any information you have available, would this 30-percent figure hold true in South Carolina?
> MR. STROM. It would not in our State. The small arms would by far outweigh the shotgun or the rifle." (CC–p. 666)

It should also be noted that as of the time that testimony was elicited, the State of South Carolina for years had totally prohibited both the manufacture and sale of handguns. Consequently, one would have expected that if the use of long guns were to meet the continually alleged 30 percent ratio, then it should have been in South Carolina.

The techniques employed to establish whatever facts are deemed necessary to support a predetermined objective are interesting indeed!

One item which was continually exploited by the anti-gun claque in numerous newspaper and magazine articles, and during radio and television commentaries, was the so-called fountain-pen gun. The sensationalism associated with that ridiculous device was a consequence both of its bizarre nature and the misleading advertisements through which it was offered to the public. A typical ad would feature an illustration of the device which resembled a pen, and the accompanying text would read something as follows:

"New Amazing 'BALL POINT PEN GUN'. . . . $4.95 postpaid Novel and different. Looks like a ball point pen . . . writes like a ballpoint pen, BUT cleverly built into the other end is a .22 caliber pistol. Only $4.95 ppd." (AA–p. 3196)

The repetitive references to that device and its descriptive ad copy which were cited as a compelling reason for the prompt enactment of Senator Dodd's S.1592 were naturally taken seriously by many good people who believed that they were being told the truth. Who could possibly have blamed the uninformed public for reacting with shock and horror at the casual mail-order availability of what they were encouraged to believe was a lethal weapon selling for less than $5.00? How were they to know the truth? Hardly through the news media.

The advertisement was obviously a natural for exploitation merely by quoting it verbatim and allowing gullible readers and listeners to draw their own predictable inferences. Credibility of such inferential conclusions also was enhanced by the prestigious source of some of the references. One allusion to that particular kind of ad was even incorporated in the written statement filed with Senator Dodd's subcommittee in 1965 by Congressman John Lindsay who later became Mayor of New York City. It is, therefore, especially appropriate that the item's non-lethal function be fully exposed.

The following quotation was taken from a statement made by Sergeant Patrick W. Murphy of the Los Angeles Police Department during the course of a general panel discussion relating to various problems concerning firearms back in 1961. The full text of that panel discussion was published in the appendix to the hearings of Senator Dodd's subcommittee all the way back in 1963:

"Regular ball-point pen. It is advertized as being a .22 to be carried on the person. These ads are run each month in these pulp magazines. I

144

have copies of them here, and I will distribute them. However, our crime lab- we did obtain one from the dealer, and our crime lab tried to fire a .22 through it. It would not work with a .22. However, the ad says that it shoots a regular .22. It actually shoots a blank cartridge." (AA–p. 3508)

While on this temporary excursion into the realm of anti-gun fantasy and crafty stratagems, there is yet another kind of item the innocent nature of which also was continually exploited in the news media along with the ball-point pen gun. This was the item of cheap handguns and how cheap they were. Originally, this inclusion in the official record of the first Dodd subcommittee proceeding was of no great importance, because, as you will recall, there was virtually unanimous support for Senator Dodd's S.1975. The cheap handguns were casually dismissed at that time by those who knew better, thinking references of the kind Dodd made were mere errors attributable to an excessive enthusiasm for documenting the alleged availability of unbelievably inexpensive "deadly weapons". Such statements having repeatedly worked their mischief on the public mind must now be exposed.

Legitimate firearms owners had long thought someone had been deliberately misrepresenting certain facts to the press when stories began to circulate about the incredibly low prices for which certain well known and costly handguns were allegedly being sold by mail-order. Perhaps, now, the mystery can be explained more accurately.

One of the witnesses who had appeared before Senator Dodd's subcommittee in 1963, prior to assassination of President Kennedy, was Sergeant K. T. Carpenter of the Los Angeles Police Department. He had brought with him certain exhibits which, subsequently, were incorporated into the final printed record of those hearings. He presented one set of exhibits with these accompanying words of explanation:

"Here is a group advertisement, advertising various guns from various dealers with a Reporter magazine article on how any youngster can buy a gun; it is just that simple." (AA–p. 3198)

There was featured in one of the ads, which was published in the official record of Senator Dodd's subcommittee, an illustration of a snub-nosed .38 caliber revolver. The advertisement was captioned "Colt Cobra .38" and the prominently displayed price was shown to be $3.95 post paid. Can you visualize the ecstatic excitement that advertisement produced among the ranks of the anti-gun claque? Why, it was even more sensational than the ball point pen gun, and, also, less expensive.

There was just one small detail which no one ever bothered to tell the general uninformed public who simply were allowed, as usual, to draw their own erroneous conclusions. The very fine print within the body of the advertisement recited these additional illuminating facts, which every experienced gun owner understood without the necessity of reading the copy:

> "Authentic Replicas Reproduced in Actual Size, Design and Balance. Solid Cast Aluminum. Finished in Gunmetal Black. He-man trophies for Den, Rumpus Room, Cabin, Etc." (AA–p. 3202)

Why was such an advertisement permitted to be included in the subcommittee record? What relevance did it have to the issues under consideration by the Congress? Was its inclusion innocent, or calculated? Interesting. One thing is certain, however, neither Senator Dodd nor any member of the Administration came forward to denounce such misleading materials and to explain their true nature in order to avoid deceiving the public.

Bear in mind there were two distinct sets of hearings on Senator Dodd's bill during 1965, one held before Senator Dodd's own subcommittee, the propriety of which will not even be discussed, and the other held before the House Committee on Ways and Means. A rather sharp insight into the difference in attitudes prevailing within those two committees can be perceived from the following incidents, one which concerned a cartoon drawn by the talented but anti-gun cartoonist of the *Washington Post*, Herblock, and the other which concerned a public opinion poll on the subject of gun control.

Sheldon Cohen, Commissioner in the Internal Revenue Service, appeared before both committees, but first testified before Senator Dodd's subcommittee. While doing so, he tendered what he evidently regarded to be a worthwhile contribution to the subcommittee's deliberations. His proffered exhibit was accepted by Senator Dodd who ordered it marked "Exhibit No. 11" and placed in the files of the subcommittee. Mr. Cohen explained the nature of his document:

> "I have here the Herblock cartoon which appeared in the Washington Post on December 29, 1964, entitled 'You Don't Even Need to Limit Yourself to a Few People,' which so aptly illustrates the subject which I am discussing, and I would like the members of the subcommittee to see it, and with your permission, Mr. Chairman, I would like to have it inserted in the hearing record." (CC–pp. 69–70)

"You don't even need to limit yourself to a few people"

Herblock cartoon of Dec. 29, 1964, which was made a part of the official record by Senator Dodd.

Thus reassured and encouraged by the subcommittee's receptivity to emotional and irrelevant materials, Sheldon Cohen bolstered his contention that there existed a wide-spread public enthusiasm for Senator Dodd's S.1592 by referring to a recent public opinion poll on gun control:

"I think there was a Gallop poll, sir, some while back that indicated the general population at large, 70 or 75 percent of the people supported it." (CC–p. 75)

Mr. Cohen was not allowed to get away with such irrelevancies, however, when he testified before the House Committee on Ways and Means where he was told the following by Congressman Thomas B. Curtis:

"I might say this committee is not interested in the Gallop poll and cartoons by Herblock or anyone else. We are concerned with trying to get the information as to what the law is and how it has been interpreted, where it seems inadequate, and that way we can direct our attention to it." (DD–p. 61)

Another Administration spokesman who appeared before that same committee, but who apparently hadn't received the message, was James V. Bennett who tried in vain to impress the committee members with the wisdom of the majority of the country's newspaper editors who favored S.1592, and with the results of the Gallup Poll. He was rebuked by Congressman James F. Battin:

"If we were to follow through with your suggestion as to the number of editorial writers that favor this bill or some control, why have a Congress? Why not then just submit their opinion to the President and have him endorse whatever they believe and make that the law of the land?" (DD–p. 253)

Some of those persons in the forefront of the anti-gun movement evidently decided that if they were ever to succeed in steering Senator Dodd's S.1592 through the Congress, it would be necessary to stifle, and possibly even destroy, their most credible, respected, and influential opponent. They cast the National Rifle Association in the role of a villain and began their insidious work.

James V. Bennett included in his testimony before Dodd's subcommittee various aspersions as to the legitimacy of objections to S.1592 which had been presented by opposing witnesses. He began with this historical reference to the old Copeland hearings on S.3 which had become the Federal Firearms Act of 1938:

> "As I have listened here to the testimony, I marvel at your patience and long-suffering tolerance toward witnesses who have come before you in opposition of this bill. They give the same old timeworn and tired arguments that have been raised against bills of this type since the hearings Senator Copeland of New York held on the original Federal Firearms Act some 30 years ago." (CC–p. 496)

It seems quite likely that anyone who had not been familiar with the substance of those Copeland hearings would have gained the impression the National Rifle Association had testified in opposition to enactment of the Federal Firearms Act of 1938, instead of having assisted with its drafting and supporting it. Such an interpretation of Bennett's remark might very well have been accepted by representatives of the news media as fact.

Continuing with his testimony, Bennett apprised the members of the subcommittee of the details of a case with which he was familiar and which concerned an actual killer whose fascination with guns had been reflected in his ten-year criminal career from the time he was only 18 years old. Describing the contents of the killer's arsenal, which had been seized by authorities during a raid, James Bennett included this amazing statement:

> "The arsenal included 4 bulletproof vests, several thousand rounds of ammunition, an automatic carbine rifle, a dozen semiautomatic and submachineguns, 17 revolvers and hand grenades, and two 10-foot-long antitank guns. Nussbaum purchased nearly all of these weapons from what were alleged to be legitimate sources. Clearly the Federal Firearms Act didn't work. No questions were asked. None are really required by the law." (CC–p. 497)

An extraordinary disregard for existing law and the facts. Here's an arsenal which included an automatic carbine and submachineguns, and Bennett asserted that no questions were required by the law. Were some uninformed person to accept his statement on its face they would probably conclude that there was no such law as the National Firearms Act of 1934 with its strict registration provisions and transfer taxes, and that one could simply purchase a machine gun as easily as a sporting rifle. Such a law did exist and one can safely assume all of the members of Senator Dodd's subcommittee knew it. It seems obvious, however, that the majority of news reporters covering the hearings did not know it. They presumably attended the hearings to learn the facts from honest and knowledgeable experts. Accurate communication is at best difficult. Who is to be blamed here if an occasional press misunderstanding resulted from the spoken or written word? Who is to be blamed if a regular pattern of misunderstandings resulted over a long period of time?

The consequences of an incorrect interpretation of faulty information can be illustrated by these lines from a responsible and competent journalist, Ralph McGill, taken from an article in the *Chicago Daily News* captioned "Some Reasons to Seek Control of Gun Sales":

"Guns may be bought in shops or by mail. If one wants a machinegun, it may be had. A bazooka and rockets to fire in it? Why, certainly. Just fill out the blank and mail it in."

After having carefully expounded the details of the Nussbaum arsenal and the killer's penchant for firearms, especially for machineguns, James Bennett then blandly made the following assertion:

"Nussbaum is opposed to firearms controls. As he told me, personally, he doesn't believe that they will work.
    He shares the arguments of the National Rifle Association." (CC–p. 497)

Continuing, Mr. Bennett then added:

"He was, as a matter of fact, once a member of the National Rifle Association. One reason may be that he was a member of the National Rifle Association and several other gun clubs." (CC–p. 497)

Persons old enough to remember the McCarthy hearings on the alleged infiltration into high positions of government by Communists will also recall the outrage expressed by many liberals concerning what they characterized as a reprehensible technique of attempting to establish "guilt by association". They were correct. It is a reprehensible technique. It is also an effective technique for those enjoying a special influence with, or privileged access to, the mass media, or those who are a component part of it.

It will be recalled from the testimony of Colonel Calvin Goddard before Senator Copeland's committee in the 1930s, there has been a firm conviction in the minds of both knowledgeable and responsible citizens that the inevitable result of progressively restrictive firearms legislation would be the ultimate loss of firearms to private citizens through some mechanism of governmental confiscation or through pressures, persuasions and complicated procedures. That was true in the 1930s. It is equally true today, but far more clearly evident. The prospect was referred to in an NRA Legislative Bulletin concerning certain aspects of Senator Dodd's S.1592 which had been mailed to NRA members on April 9, 1965. The U.S. Attorney General, Nicholas Katzenbach, responded to that apprehension by labeling it "preposterous" during his testimony before Senator Dodd's subcommittee:

> "One last comment on the specific NRA objections, as expressed in the letter sent to its membership. The letter described this measure as one which conceivably could lead to the elimination of 'the private ownership of all guns.'
> I am compelled to say that there is only one word which can serve in reply to such a fear, and that is preposterous." (CC–p. 40)

In the discussion of some of the objections to Senator Dodd's S.1592, expressed at the hearings by spokesmen for the National Rifle Association, the U.S. Attorney General made this supposition before the House Committee on Ways and Means:

> "Both of these objections suggest that the NRA's principal concern may be less for the hundreds of thousands of legitimate shooters than for the very small number of commercial gun dealers who have flourished as the result of public neglect." (DD–p. 72)

One of the witnesses to appear before Senator Dodd's subcommittee ostensibly to discuss the merits of S.1592, but who instead used the opportunity in an apparent attempt to discredit the National Rifle Association, was Leonard S. Blondes, an Assemblyman from the State of Maryland. Mr. Blondes, it should be noted, was introduced to the subcommittee by Senator Joseph D. Tydings, also of Maryland, of whom more will be learned later. The main thrust of the testimony presented by Leonard Blondes was exactly as follows and should be read with care:

> "In my freshman year, I introduced house bill No. 233, not realizing the force and effect of an organization which, I think we have heard about during the last many months and years, the National Rifle Association. The bill proposed a 72-hour waiting period which, of course, required a check into the person himself; whether or not he was a

felon, dope addict, or derelict. This also required a compulsory training program and restrictions as to juveniles and to mail orders.

Shortly after the introduction of the bill I was deluged with letters, telegrams, and telephone calls in opposition thereto. However, several of the letters suggested that my thoughts were good and that the National Rifle Association would like to be helpful in correcting a few of the problems existing in the bill. This was the first time I began feeling the effect of the NRA.

I appreciated the offer. I proceeded to make an appointment with the gentlemen on 16th Street and spent several hours with them preparing a new bill, later to be known as house bill 1072. It was recommended that for the final touches I discuss the matter with General Reckord of the State of Maryland. It was a real honor to discuss the bill with the gentleman, and I felt that I really had a partner in my firearms legislation. However, I felt then after lengthy discussion with the general that the NRA was basically a cosponsor of the bill. It was interesting, however, that by the same day house bill 1072 was dropped in the hopper, that is March 21, 1963, the NRA 'informative' letter was mailed, knifing each and every proposal of house bill 1072. It was mailed to all the members of the house of delegates and to the committee members of the judiciary committee and the chairman giving each and every provision of house bill 1072 and, of course, they knew every item of the bill because we had worked them out item by item so they were one step ahead of me at that point, and any point where I thought we were working together. By taking certain words and phrases out of context, it was suggested that I was trying to disarm the Nation and deprive our youth of their right to firearms instruction." (CC–p. 425)

The bill, Mr. Blondes added, finally died a glorious death under the pressures of the unregistered, unrecognized, nonlobbying entity known as the NRA. Senator Dodd preoceeded to extend his appreciation for this "very important and expert" testimony:

"Thank you for your testimony. It is a very important piece of testimony because you are obviously an expert since you have been through this." (CC–p. 428)

The damaging nature of the statement made by Leonard Blondes in open public hearings before Senator Dodd's subcommittee is too apparent to require comment. The reader should now bear in mind that the materials which follow were not published until many months later when they were incorporated into the record of those proceedings, long after the damage had been done; long after it could be remedied. Speculate, if you will, on the number of persons whose opinion of the National Rifle Association was adversely influenced by the testimony of Leonard Blondes. Reflect upon the number of anti-NRA news articles which may have been kindled and fueled by that "very important piece of testimony."

Two weeks following the Blondes testimony, Franklin Orth, Executive Vice President of the National Rifle Association, sent a letter of refutation complete with attached exhibits to Senator Dodd. The contents of that letter appear below with only certain details omitted for brevity:

"Dear Senator Dodd:

I have considered, for some time, how best to react to the testimony given before your Subcommittee on Juvenile Delinquency on Tuesday, June 8, 1965, by Maryland Assemblyman Leonard S. Blondes. I have decided to put the facts in a letter to you and to rely on your fairness and sense of justice to 'set the record straight'.

It was apparent, I think, that the presence of Mr. Blondes before the committee was not so much to testify in favor of the provisions of S.1592 as to discredit the National Rifle Association of America and to represent us as a 'lobbying' organization that would resort to almost any means, fair or foul, to prevent any firearms legislation from being enacted, no matter how worthwhile or constructive it might be. Delegate Blondes said many things in his testimony that were slanted to bring discredit upon the association and its members, but two comments in particular were so damaging in their implication and so completely false, that I cannot permit them to go unchallenged.

I am enclosing, as exhibit A, an excerpt from Mr. Blondes' testimony containing the statements to which I refer. I would direct your attention first to the statement in the opening paragraph in which Mr. Blondes says, with respect to Maryland House bill 233, that the bill, '* * * proposed a 72-hour waiting period, which, of course, required a check into the person himself; whether or not he was a felon, dope addict, or derelict. This also required a compulsory training program and restrictions as to juveniles and to mail orders.' I am sending you, as exhibit B, a copy of Maryland House bill 233 and would point out to you that this bill does not propose a 72-hour waiting period; it does not require a check of the person himself; it does not mention a compulsory training period or any other training period. What this bill would have done would have been to bring to a complete halt every NRA or other junior marksmanship program in the State of Maryland.

I send you, as exhibit C, a copy of our Legislative Bulletin reporting this bill to our members in the State of Maryland. I think you will find it a fair and objective digest of the bill's provisions.

As a result of the public reaction to this bill, Delegate Blondes did, indeed, make an appointment with us and visited here for several hours on February 27, 1963. He discussed his legislative proposal with Mr. Jack Basil and Mr. Dan Mountin of this staff. Following this visit, and in a further effort to be helpful, we wrote Delegate Blondes at some length and I enclose a copy, marked 'Exhibit D,' of our letter to him dated March 7, 1963. This represents the last contact we had with Delegate Blondes. We have not spoken nor corresponded with him since that time."

* * *

"I am sending you, marked 'Exhibit E,' a copy of Maryland House bill 1072, also a photocopy of the introduction notice provided us by the Commerce Clearinghouse. You will note that this bill was not introduced on March 21, 1963, as Mr. Blondes testified, but on March 13. We had absolutely no knowledge of the provisions of the bill until a draft copy was sent to us from Annapolis, reaching us on March 20. Our legislative bulletin was dated March 21, 1963. This bulletin was mailed to NRA members in the State of Maryland and only to NRA members. We do not and we have never mailed NRA legislative bulletins to members of State legislatures or committee members. I send you, marked 'Exhibit F,' a copy of our legislative bulletin with reference to Maryland House bill 1072. I believe you will find that it does not take words or phrases out of context and that it is, in fact, an objective and correct digest of the bill's provisions. Mr. Blondes' implication that we had advance knowledge of the provisions of the bill, that we had worked them out with him, and that we then worked to defeat the bill behind his back, is absolutely false.

You may wish to check with General Reckord. He tells me that, to the best of his recollection, he has never met Delegate Blondes nor spoken with him. General Reckord has served the State of Maryland for many years. His reputation for fearless honesty is well known. That he would resort to the sort of double dealing implied by Delegate Blondes would stagger the credulity of anyone who knew the general." (CC–pp. 431–432)

The following excerpt was taken from a letter addressed to Senator Joseph Tydings by Milton A. Reckord, Lieutenant General, the Adjutant General of the State of Maryland:

"Dear Joe:
My attention has been invited to the fact that Mr. Leonard S. Blondes, a member of the Maryland Legislature representing Montgomery County, testified on June 8 at the hearings on the proposed amendments to the Federal Firearms Act.

I am writing you, as a member of the committee before which the hearings are being held, to advise you that certain statements made by Mr. Blondes are not true; and I request that you take the necessary action to correct the record. Specifically, I refer to Mr. Blondes' statement regarding a conference had with me. Mr. Blondes has never had any conference whatever with me on any firearms legislation, and I wish to categorically deny his statement: 'After lengthy discussions with the gentleman I felt that I really had a partner in my firearms legislation.'

In reading Mr. Blondes' statement before the committee, it appears to me that he made an attempt to discredit the National Rifle Association, as well as myself, rather than to give testimony for or against the bill now under consideration." (CC–p. 442)

The third and final excerpt was taken from a letter dated August 19, 1965, which had been addressed to Senator Thomas J. Dodd, and signed "Leonard S. Blondes."

"Dear Senator Dodd:
The past several days I have had the opportunity to review the comments made by Franklin L. Orth in a memorandum to you dated June 22, 1965. I feel that this is a perfect example of the 'rifling' ways and means of the NRA. There is no question that I made an error in my presentation as to the contents of house bill 233. But, did it really make any difference?" (CC–p. 443)

Blondes flippant disregard for the facts was felt by many law abiding gun owners to be typical of their opponents.

At this point the reader may also find interesting an exchange which took place on the first day of the hearings on S.1592 between U.S. Attorney General Nicholas Katzenbach and Senator Dodd. These were the first words uttered by the U.S. Attorney General to the members of Senator Dodd's subcommittee:

"Thank you, Mr. Chairman. I picked up the May 15 issue of the Shotgun News as I was coming down here and I thought the committee might be interested in this full page ad that makes a series of misstatements about this bill. I thought members of the committee might be particularly interested in the following quotation indicative of the accuracy of the ad: 'Write every member of the hearing committee: Chairman Senator Thomas Dodd and Senators Philip Hard, Birch Bayh, Quentin Burdick, Joseph Tidings, Roman H. Hruska, Herman Fong,' and if you have any mail for Herman Fong, you will know the source of it. They do have Jacob Javits correct. It might be well, Senator Fong, for you to let your mail room know that mail for

Herman Fong is intended for you and too, I thought the committee might be interested in seeing this ad. It is typical of the propaganda and the misstatements that are being made about this bill and this happens to be from the American Sportsmen's Foundation, Inc., of Hanover, N.J." (CC–pp. 33–34)

Senator Dodd approved the inclusion of the ad as part of the official hearings record, as he had done with the "valuable and informative" cartoon by Herblock on another occasion. Incidently, for those not familiar with the spelling errors to which the Attorney General referred, they were: Senator "Hard" instead of Senator Hart; Senator "Tidings" instead of Senator Tydings; and Senator "Herman" Fong instead of Senator Hiram Fong. Now, this was the immediate response of Senator Dodd:

"The point is, Mr. Attorney General, this is characteristic of the outrageous misrepresentations that are spread across the country about this bill." (CC–p. 35)

It clearly appeared that Senator Dodd was anything but insensitive to misrepresentations, depending of course on the nature of the misrepresentations and, perhaps more importantly whose ox was gored.

The hundreds of thousands of letters and telegrams which rained down upon the Congress protesting S.1592 were the heartfelt expressions of concern by their senders over the actual, probable or conjectural effect which Senator Dodd's bill would have on some important, as well as unimportant, aspects of personal, commercial or national interests relating to the legitimate use of firearms. In many instances, some were misinformed, some uninformed and some were seeking to become informed.

In the vast majority of cases, however, they were quite well informed about the provisions of the bill, drew their own conclusions as to its effect on their particular area of greatest interest, and, in the very best of American traditions they informed their representatives in Congress of their opinions—many in no uncertain terms. Was that a fair and proper exercise of their right to petition Congress? Some people didn't think so. After all, did not the editorial writers of the country know what was best for the American public? How dare the common citizen raise such a clamor of protest! As if by medieval imprecation— off with their heads!

Let there be no doubt as to the extent of informed and legitimate opposition to Senator Dodd's bill. The legislatures of the following 14

States adopted resolutions opposing enactment of S.1592: Alabama; Arizona; Arkansas; Louisiana; Michigan; Nebraska; New Hampshire; New Mexico; Ohio; Oklahoma; Texas; Vermont; Washington; and, Wisconsin. The volume of personal mail to the Members of Congress may be gauged from this comment by Senator Jacob K. Javits, a member of Senator Dodd's subcommittee:

"Finally, like other Senators—and perhaps more so, because I have 18 million constituents—I have received an enormous amount of mail, really enormous, almost unbelievable, Mr. Chairman, expressing opposition to this bill. Some of it is from very well-intentioned people who use their firearms for sports and other recreation." (CC–p. 25)

Another member of Senator Dodd's subcommittee, Senator Roman L. Hruska, confirmed Senator Javit's experience:

"My mail, like that of most Members of Congress, has been extremely heavy. In fact, I have received many more letters on this question than any other so far this year. It has been evenly divided between residents of my own State and others from across the country. The mail has been virtually unanimous in its opposition to S.1592. By actual count only 3 letters supporting the bill have been received so far out of more than 3,000." (CC–p. 25)

In marked contrast to its previous support of the original Dodd bills, S.1975 and S.14, the National Rifle Association felt obliged to withhold its support from so much of S.1592 that the net effect required it be actively opposed. Franklin Orth, the NRA Executive Vice President, capsuled its general position before presenting detailed specifics:

"We agree with the President that the sale of firearms in interstate commerce, as ordered through the mail, is a proper subject for legislation by the Federal Government. However, we view such highly restrictive legislation as herein proposed in S.1592 as being unsound and premature.

The National Rifle Association has been seeking ways and means to assist law-enforcement organizations in accomplishing legitimate objectives and at the same time insure that the citizen and sportsman not be disarmed. We have worked with this committee for more than 4 years in order to obtain a bill which would be meaningful and helpful, aimed at preventing criminals and juveniles from obtaining firearms by order through the mails. Last year I thought we had agreed on such a bill, S.1975, which was developed by this committee and by sportsmen and members of the firearms industry." (CC–p. 196)

Recall that not everyone who had testified before the old S.1975 hearings had been satisfied, particularly James V. Bennett and John V. Lindsay, both of whom had wanted Senator Dodd to go further than the provisions of S.1975. Congressman Lindsay even then had touted his own "Lindsay bill" to ban interstate sales of mail-order firearms, and he had stated to the subcommittee that he would have preferred to have it enacted rather than Senator Dodd's S.1975. Indeed, not everyone had agreed on S.1975. Does that have any significance? What influences and considerations could have arisen to explain the radical difference between the old S.1975 and S.1592? Interesting.

Franklin Orth continued with his general position statement:

"As shown by our support of the enactment, years ago, of the National and Federal Firearms Acts, the National Rifle Association has studied this matter of firearms control legislation for many decades. We will support legislation which can effectively reduce the criminal use of firearms, but the NRA stands squarely on the premise that the ownership of firearms must not be denied American citizens of good repute so long as they use them for lawful purposes." (CC–p. 198)

The complexities of the controversy which raged over S.1592 eluded those who lacked the background to understand or appreciate the issues actually involved. In the uncritical minds of many the whole matter was simply reduced to the question of whether or not criminals and juveniles should be able to buy guns by mail. Nothing else seemed to concern them. Simplistic.

11

"For it is a truth, which the experience of all ages has attested, that the people are commonly most in danger when the means of injuring their rights are in the possession of those of whom they entertain the least suspicion."

ALEXANDER HAMILTON

ANOTHER FACET OF THE CONTROVERSY OVER S.1592 involved a subject concerning which, at first glance, it appeared difficult, if not impossible, to find fault; namely, the imposition of stringent controls over all so-called destructive devices through means of the provisions of the National Firearms Act of 1934. (The reader is again cautioned that there were actually two Dodd bills pending in each of the two Houses of Congress, each with its own separate identifying number, for a total of four separate bill numbers. For reasons of clarity, and to avoid unnecessary confusion, the only bill number which will be used to refer to the entire "package" of Dodd bills will continue to be S.1592.)

Despite a lack of evidence presented to establish that such items

159

constituted a law enforcement problem, the so-called destructive devices were of such a nature as to repel most people. Not one person or organization protested the imposition of the most rigorous control over destructive devices. The Congress was urged to deal promptly and effectively with all such contraptions, yet the issue of controls over destructive devices became the subject of controversy. Why? We shall see.

Under Senator Dodd's proposal to control destructive devices, the scope of the National Firearms Act of 1934, which covered such gangster-weapons as machineguns, sawed-off shotguns, and gadget guns would have been enlarged to include such items as bombs, grenades, rockets, missiles, mortars, antitank guns, bazookas, etc. As might be expected, it was the "etc." that caused the furor. All items, which were classified as destructive devices, would have become subject to the terms of the National Firearms Act of 1934 and persons engaging in business as importers, manufacturers, and dealers in such weapons would have been required to register and pay a special occupational tax. In addition, the same kind of taxes applicable to the transferring of machineguns would have become applicable to the transfer of destructive devices. Naturally, it also would have been unlawful for any person to possess a destructive device unless it were registered with the Secretary of the Treasury. What could possibly be objectionable with so simple a proposal? What, indeed?

In addition to two separate incidents which had occurred many years previously which involved youths firing 20mm antitank guns and touching off a fire in a California forest in one case, and damaging a utility shed located on a New Jersey rifle range in the other, the only other documented report of an illegal use of a destructive device took place in New York City towards the latter part of 1964. Some benighted individuals were said to have tried to launch a bazooka rocket into the United Nations headquarters building from across the East River. The rocket fell harmlessly into the river, possibly because it had been fired from a cut-down bazooka, recovered from the launching site, or possibly because the rocket had been propelled by an ineptly concocted homemade propellant mixture. In any event, it was clear that destructive devices had to go.

In order that there be no misunderstanding, the reader should understand that, at no time, were live rockets, bazooka missiles, mortar shells, or artillery projectiles available anywhere on the commercial market for sale. Such shells and missiles as were sold had been completely deactivated, if ever they had been loaded in the first place. They were sold, as were the destructive devices themselves, as ornaments for court house lawns, VFW halls, museums, and the like. The single exception was the 20mm antitank guns, for which shells were available at a cost of approximately $1 each. A 20mm projectile measures just over three-fourths of an inch in diameter.

Senator Dodd acknowledged to his subcommittee that "live" shells for the large devices were not commercially sold, but he expressed concern that they might be re-activated by experts.

These facts are not presented herein as criticism of the effort to remove essentially crew-served war weapons from ordinary commercial channels. They are set forth for the purpose of clarifying their exact nature. Their mere presence as exhibits adorning the subcommittee's hearing room produced confusion in the minds of many persons, who promptly and unquestioningly associated them with the National Rifle Association, the Civilian Marksmanship Program, and other activities equally far removed from their use, a fact which may explain some of the erroneous and misleading news stories flooding the country concerning such items. As has been previously mentioned, the awesome appearance of such instruments of warfare created a macabre atmosphere during the hearings and provided the mass media with an ample source of photo-illustrations with which to impart morbidity to anti-gun and anti-NRA newspaper and magazine articles.

In the absence of credible evidence of the serious misuse of destructive devices, the next logical rationale for their elimination was their alleged potential for such misuse. By whom? By members of various kinds of groups referred to in the collective as "extremists", regarded by some as constituting a Twentieth Century equivalent of Quantrill's raiders. Concern over such extremists was voiced to Senator Dodd's subcommittee by Thomas C. Lynch, Attorney General of the State of California:

"Our troubles with machineguns and 'destructive devices' in California involve mainly members of private armies in our State. In California, we have self-styled saviors of our Nation. They operate under such names as Minutemen and the Christian Defense League. These groups train and arm themselves—in Nazi terms—for 'Der Tag.' They don't quite specify 'Der Tag.' The Minutemen say that it will occur when they decide that Communists are in control. The Christian Defense League is not that clear. Since the latter group is known to be linked with the Ku Klux Klan, perhaps their day of reckoning is much more racially oriented." (CC–p. 105)

As a result of Dodd committee testimony such as that quoted above, with nebulous indications as to crimes committed, many news articles casually began to equate legitimate sportsmen and NRA members with extremists in such a manner that one virtually became indistinguishable from the other in the minds of many uninformed people.

Senator Robert F. Kennedy, younger brother of the late President John F. Kennedy, delivered a brief presentation to Senator Dodd's subcommittee in which he directed a portion of his remarks to the necessity of controlling extremist groups:

> "The national interest will be served by the speedly enactment of S.1592. I support every one of its provisions.
>
> Durings its deliberations, I would urge the subcommittee to consider also ways by which the private arsenals of secret groups—such as the Ku Klux Klan, the Black Muslims, and the so-called Minutemen—could be curtailed and eliminated. At a minimum, all weapons in the possession of these organizations or members of these organizations should be registered. Further, all large-caliber heavy weapons should be removed from private hands. Private citizens have no need of anti-tank guns, mortars, or machineguns." (CC–p. 88)

Senator Kennedy's recommendation that, "At a minimum, all weapons in the possession of these organizations or members of these organizations should be registered" no doubt sounded highly appealing to many people and contributed to their desire to have the Congress enact S.1592 with "every one of its provisions". Such exhortations, coming as they did from a former U.S. Attorney General, were curious, to say the very least, in view of the fact that such power had been vested in the U.S. Attorney General ever since 1940. It was the very essence of the Voorhis Act of 1940.

In brief, the Voorhis Act of 1940 required the registration with the U.S. Attorney General of every organization, whose purpose was to control, seize or overthrow the Government or any of its subdivisions by force or threat of force. All firearms or other weapons owned by such organizations were included in the registration process. A few excerpts from that Act will clearly establish these facts for the reader:

> "(B) (1) The following organizations shall be required to register with the Attorney General:
>
> * * *
>
> Every organization, the purpose or aim of which, or one of the purposes or aims of which, is the establishment, control, conduct, seizure, or overthrow of a government or subdivision thereof by the use of force, violence, military measures, or threats of any one or more of the foregoing.
>
> * * *

162

(3) Every registration statement required to be filed by any organization shall contain the following information and documents:

* * *

(k) A description of all firearms or other weapons owned by the organization, or by any chapter, branch, or affiliate of the organization, identified by the manufacturer's number thereon;" (U.S.C. Title 18, Chapter 115, Section 2386)

The above-quoted provisions of law had been on the statute books since 1940 and, yet, the Congress, and the press, and the public, were told by a former U.S. Attorney General that the country needed another law under which to register the weapons of extremist groups. Many people never quite seem to grasp the simple axiom that any law the enforcement of which depends upon the cooperation of the criminal is doomed to failure.

Although it makes for grand rhetoric to demand boldly the eradication of an indefensible evil, the practitioners of such political strategy must exercise great caution lest the evil be too quickly vanquished, thus depriving them of the continuous opportunity to exploit ostentatiously its ugly presence—to fascinate, to frighten and to enthral the intended audience for what otherwise might prove a sideshow too prosaic to gain the desired attention. The destructive device matter was carefully nurtured, cultivated and presented as something from which only Senator Dodd's bill could rescue the Nation.

The following is an excerpt from testimony presented to Senator Dodd's subcommittee and is of a most interesting and enlightening nature:

"Mr. Chairman and members of the committee, my name is Robert N. Margrave. I am the Director, Office of Munitions Control, Department of State.

By section 414 of the Mutual Security Act of 1954, as amended (22 U.S.C. 1934), the President is authorized to control the export and import of arms, ammunition, and implements of war. This control is to be exercised 'in the furtherance of world peace and the security and foreign policy of the United States.' The President is further 'authorized to designate those articles which shall be considered as arms, ammunition, and implements of war.' The President has delegated this authority, by Executive Order 10973, to the Secretary of State. Within the Department of State, the Office of Munitions Control has the functional responsibility for controlling the exportation and importation of munitions and this Office administers the control under the international traffic in arms regulations which went into effect on March 1, 1960.

Groupings of so-called "destructive devices", shown in the Senate's hearing room, which the President already had authority to control without the additional legislation then sought.

Inclusion of this authority in the Mutual Security Act underscored the specific terms of the provision, and was consonant with the stated purpose of that act; namely, 'to promote the security and foreign policy of the United States.'

The preceding legislative authority, section 12 of the Neutrality Act of 1939, empowered the Secretary of State to issue import licenses. Section 414 of the Mutual Security Act permits the denial of imports when such action is necessary in the interest of national security or foreign policy." (CC–p. 126)

The implications of Robert Margrave's testimony were astonishing and shocking, at least to a few people. Senator Roman Hruska, a member of the subcommittee before which the testimony had been presented, reacted strongly to this testimony, as evidenced by his written statement filed for the official record. The applicable portion stated as follows:

"On May 20 Mr. Robert Margrave of the State Department testified before the subcommittee. I was shocked and appalled by his testimony. Mr. Margrave indicated that section 414 of the Mutual Security Act of 1954 gives the President more than ample authority to control the importation or exportation of firearms, ammunition, and implements of war. There is authority to ban even the importation of bows and arrows, dartguns, and blunderbusses, if need be. The language of section 414 says in part:

'The President is authorized to control, in furtherance of world peace and the security and foreign policy of the United States, the export and import of arms, ammunition, and implements of war* * *.'

This is broad language—much broader than the comparable language in S.1592, which alludes only to the public interest. No further legislation is necessary in this area. All that is required is judicious enforcement of that law. The destructive devices we have sitting back of this room were probably imported under a license approved by Mr. Margrave himself—assuming that he has any records of the transaction. He or one of his predecessors in all probability approved the shipment that contained the rifle which was used by Lee Harvey Oswald."

* * *

"Other language of section 414 requires registration of manufacturers and importers of firearms and ammunition and to set fees therefor. Strict penalties are set forth with up to a 2-year term and a $25,000 fine authorized.

If foreign imports are a problem, why aren't these provisions being enforced at the present time? * * * * * Mr. Chairman, I would like to find out the answers to these questions and more. Mr. Margrave should be recalled. One point is very clear: There is ample legislative authority to curb, indeed stop entirely, the flow of not only surplus military weapons, but all firearms into this country by enforcing present law." (CC–p. 26)

Setting aside for the moment any further discussion of the relevancy of Senator Dodd's bill to the control of crew-served implements of war, attention may now be directed to some of the collateral problems for legitimate sportsmen which its language precipitated. A review of the definition of "destructive device" as was contained in the bill will be helpful:

"The term 'destructive device' means any explosive or incendiary (a) bomb or (b) grenade or (c) rocket or (d) missile or (e) similar device, or launching device therefor (except a device which is not designed or redesigned or used or intended for use as a weapon or part thereof); and the term shall also include any type of weapon by whatsoever name known (other than a shotgun having a barrel or barrels of 18 or more inches in length), which will, or which is designed to, or which may be readily converted to, expel a projectile, or projectiles by the action of an explosive, the barrel or barrels of which have a bore of one-half inch or more in diameter: *Provided*, That, the Secretary or his delegate may exclude from this definition any device which he finds is not likely to be used as a weapon." (DD–p. 7)

It is not necessary to struggle with the entire definition, as the problem arose over the simple words "the barrel or barrels of which have a bore of one-half inch or more in diameter". Therein lay the problem. Why did the definition specify a bore of one-half inch or more in diameter? At first glance one might conclude that the criteria of a one-half inch bore diameter was selected so as to include within its scope the smallest bore diametered destructive device, the nasty 20mm antitank gun, which fired a huge cartridge tipped with a 2-ounce steel armor-piercing projectile that measured slightly more than three-fourths of an inch in diameter. Now why does the reader suppose the definition did not simply specify that the minimum bore diameter was to be three-fourths of an inch? If it had done so, then there would have been no problem and no controversy over that little detail.

Little detail? Hardly. By reason of the one-half inch bore definition, stubbornly insisted upon by many proponents of the bill, automatically there was included within its application literally hundreds of thousands of antique firearms and many thousands of high-powered big game hunting rifles. Was that result a product of error or of design, of inadvertence or of calculation? But, did it really make any difference?

One of the persons to whom it did make a difference, a very substantial difference, was Dr. Harmon Leonard, President of the American Society of Arms Collectors, a group which he described as representative of some 800,000 arms collectors in the United States. Dr. Leonard's plea to the subcommittee included the following explanation:

"The primary interest of the arms collector in the American Society lies in antique and historical arms. These include 16th century match locks, Revolutionary War flint locks, Civil War musket, and the arms that settled and established law in our western lands. In the 20 years I have been collecting arms, I do not know nor have I heard of one of these collector arms being used in a crime. Nor would the remote possible incidence in which one might have been involved be any more incriminating than any handy object which might be used. Therefore, we earnestly and sincerely request your initial exclusion to the entire act antique, historical, and collector arms." (CC–pp. 269–270)

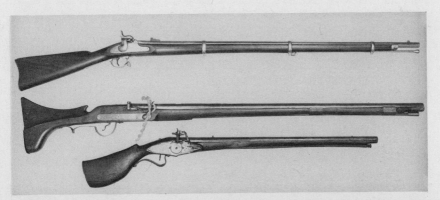

Examples of miscellaneous antique firearms having a muzzle diameter of one-half inch or larger, such as (top-bottom) Civil War musket, matchlock and wheel lock.

The National Rifle Association of America, whose membership included thousands of gun collectors and hunters, in addition to competitive rifle, pistol and shotgun shooters, also spoke out against the poor choice of language used in Senator Dodd's bill. Franklin Orth expressed the problem in the following manner to the subcommittee:

"We take exception to the definition of a 'destructive device' that includes any weapon having a bore of one-half inch or more in diameter. Our objections are based on the simple fact that many legitimate sporting arms and collectors' items are included in this definition. Most muzzle-loading rifles and pistols, whether a part of a collection or used in so many Civil War enactments, are of a caliber greater than .50. Many famous and expensive big-game rifles are more than .50 caliber. The fact that the Secretary of the Treasury may exclude from this definition any device which he considers not to be a firearm is of small consequence in the long run when you consider that each type of firearm would have to receive a separate ruling by the Secretary, or his delegate (in all likelihood, the Alcohol and Tobacco Tax Division), as is presently the case in the 'any other weapon' category in the National Firearms Act. The time and redtape involved in receiving such a ruling, together with the expense of engaging in hearings before the Treasury Department is, in many cases, a discouraging factor that is detrimental to the legitimate use of certain types of sporting weapons by the ordinary citizen. To state that the Secretary of the Treasury can take steps to remove certain inequities contained in the bill, if he deems such steps to be necessary, is easy to say; getting him to take such steps or, in some cases, to correct certain errors made by Treasury Department clerks, is quite another thing." (CC–p. 199)

In a sincere effort to effect a reconciliation between the general proscriptions of Senator Dodd's S.1592 and the effect which they would have had on millions of obsolete and antique firearms which were legitimately part of antique firearm collections, Orth offered the suggestion that the following language might accomplish that purpose without in any way affecting the intent of the bill:

"Provided, that nothing contained in this section shall be construed to include those firearms that are designed for use with loose powder and ball, or which are incapable of being fired with self-contained primed cartridges, or to firearms held as a curiosity or decoration that would require cartridges of an obsolete pattern no longer manufactured and readily available through commercial channels. These exemptions shall apply only to those firearms of all types manufactured prior to 1898." (CC–p .199)

Most people who have never extensively engaged in the collection of genuine early American or European antique and obsolete firearms generally fail to understand the basis for the grave concern which was expressed by serious gun collectors whose personal collections often are valued in many thousands of dollars. Two incidents taken from the actual experience of such collectors should prove instructive.

One of the country's foremost gun dealers to testify before the House Committee on Ways and Means was Leon C. Jackson, a man of impeccable credentials and a highly regarded specialist in early American firearms. During the course of his formal presentation, Jackson touched upon several well known incidents wherein the capricious nature of the regulations, issued by the Treasury Department and enforced by the Alcohol and Tobacco Tax Division, had produced consternation and a loss of confidence in the Department among gun collectors. He then cited a personal experience:

> "In another case in Pennsylvania, photographs of firearms, all antiques, were submitted to the Department for a decision as to whether or not they must be registered. Two pictures of the same gun—a flintlock blunderbus approximately 200 years old—were submitted taken from opposite sides of the weapon. The Department ruling was that it must be registered on one side but was not subject to registration on the other." (DD–pp. 352–353)

Flared-muzzle blunderbuss.

Ludicrous? Laughable? Yes, but not to the man whose property was involved when the penalty for a violation of the law included heavy fines and a prison sentence. That occurance was only one of a number with which all serious gun collectors were well acquainted and which did not contribute to their confidence in the Treasury Department's knowledge or skill.

One might ordinarily be inclined to think that an occasional clumsy bungling of a particular matter, in the long run, would be more than offset by the paternalistic benevolence which some people still foolishly associate with a powerful central government. Any illusions along that line were irrevocably shattered back in 1956 by an outrageous occurrence which was neatly documented in an excellent statement filed for the records of Senator Dodd's subcommittee by George R. Whittington.

Although primarily in the investment business, George Whittington was also an attorney admitted to practice before the U.S. Supreme Court, a past president of the National Rifle Association, a civilian member of the National Board for the Promotion of Rifle Practice, and an outstanding competitive marksman holding several national records. He also was a discriminating collector of fine firearms.

The incident which he described took place following the seizure of three obsolete pistols from the premises of a California gun dealer by agents for the Alcohol and Tobacco Tax Division of the Internal Revenue Service. The seizure was made pursuant to the provisions of the National Firearms Act of 1934 which, as the reader will recall, included a special category of gangster-type weapons referred to as gadget guns. Gadget guns, for the most part, were deceptive weapons, disguised so as to resemble something other than a normally shaped pistol or revolver, as for example, a fountain pen gun, a cane gun, a cigarette lighter gun, etc. The firearms which were seized in this instance were so-called palm pistols.

Palm pistols were manufactured in an exceedingly small quantity near the turn of the century and were unique in design and function, as well as extremely impractical. Shaped somewhat like a round snuff box, they featured a stubby little barrel which, in use, projected out from between the fingers of the user's hand. The pistol had a rotating circular magazine and fired a special type of cartridge which hadn't been manufactured for seventy years. It was operated by being held in the palm of the hand and having the curved lever which projected from its rear circumference squeezed by the hand. Never very popular as a practical pistol, production of it was soon discontinued. Such surviving specimens, as still exist, are highly prized by gun collectors as relics of earlier

Chicago and Minneapolis palm pistols.

years when newly perfected self-contained metallic rim-fire cartridges produced a plethora of oddly designed pistols, most of which were destined to become nothing more than curios from a bygone age.

The mere fact that so innocuous a collectors' item would be the object of a seizure under the National Firearms Act, in itself, was cause for dismay among gun collectors, but it was only the prelude.

The owner of the pistols filed suit for their recovery, denying that such pistols were the proper subjects of registration and the transfer tax imposed by the National Firearms Act of 1934. Eventually, the case was decided in his favor by the U.S. District Court for the Southern

District of California, Central Division. The following excerpts were taken from the findings of fact by the District Court:

> "That the evidence adduced by the respondent established that said weapons were and are pistols and/or revolvers and that said weapons did not have to be registered under the National Firearms Act or under any other regulation or law of the United States; that said weapons were an exception to taxation under the National Firearms Act and that the amendments to the Code of Federal Regulations effective November 1, 1955, do not alter the status of said weapons for they are pistols and/or revolvers under said amendments.

> V.

> That the United States of America, libelant, has failed to prove that said weapons, either at time of seizure or at any time of the trial, were other than pistols and/or revolvers, and further did not prove that said weapons, or any of them, are a 'gadget device,' a gun altered or converted to resemble pistols, or was a small portable gun erroneously referred to as pistols." (CC– p. 835)

Continuing, the U.S. District Court rendered the following conclusion of law, which, in turn, was followed by a decree ordering that the palm pistols must be immediately returned to their owner from whom they had been taken:

> "That the Minneapolis palm protector pistol and the Chicago palm protector pistol are pistols and/or revolvers as defined in the Code of Federal Regulations, title 26, section 179.35 and section 179.37 as well as is so commonly known and considered in the weapon trade and industry; that the said weapons, and each of them, are not required to be registered, nor are they taxable under the provisions of the National Firearms Act; that said weapons are not 'gadget devices,' but that on the contrary are recognized established pistols and/or revolvers." (CC–p. 836)

The U.S. District Court also took note of the fact that one of the pistols had been broken while in the hands of the Government.

The U.S. District Court's decision was handed down on March 27, 1956, and the results of its findings were published as an item of great interest to gun collectors in the May 1956 issue of *The American Rifleman* magazine published by the National Rifle Association of America. Four weeks later the National Rifle Association received the following letter dated June 4, 1956, from the Director of the Alcohol and Tobacco Tax Division. It stated that, in the opinion of the Alcohol and Tobacco Tax Division, the court decision was strictly limited to the jurisdiction of the Southern Judicial District of California and that it was their intention to continue to regard the palm pistol as a device subject to the National Firearms Act elsewhere in the United States. Unbelievable? Here is the text of that letter:

"Gentlemen:
On page 52 of the May 1956 issue of the American Rifleman, you announce that, as the result of a decision rendered on March 27, 1956, by the U.S. District Court for the Southern Judicial District of California, a device identified as the 'Chicago palm pistol' is not subject to registration and taxation under the National Firearms Act.

The court decision to which you refer affects the classification status of the device mentioned only within the jurisdiction of said court, specifically the Southern Judicial District of California. Revenue Ruling 55–44 published on January 24, 1955, in Internal Revenue Bulletin No. 4 (Rev. Rul. 55–44 C.B. 1955–1,129.), takes precedence elsewhere.

To avoid any misunderstanding which may result from your published article, it is suggested that you consider the propriety of clarifying this important point as a public service. Your cooperation in this matter will be appreciated." (CC–p. 837)

George Whittington summarized the reactions of the many thousands of arms collectors by asking this question:

"It readily becomes apparent if this Division of the Treasury Department assumes this kind of an attitude towards a judgment of a Federal district court, then how can a mere individual hope to uphold his rights except at great loss in time and money?" (CC–p. 837)

The plight of the gun collector will be considered further at a later point, but before leaving the general area of destructive devices the following acknowledgement made by Sheldon Cohen of the official position taken by the National Rifle Association with regard to heavy crew-served military weapons should be noted:

"I would also like to note that the National Rifle Association has recognized the need for action in this area and that in their April 3, 1965, statement at the annual meeting, the National Rifle Association declared: 'That it would support properly drawn legislation to outlaw dangerous devices such as bazookas, bombs, antitank guns, and other military-type weapons that have found their way into trade channels across America.' " (CC–p. 69)

173

It should now be quite apparent why the qualifying words "properly drawn legislation" were so important to the National Rifle Association. It is one thing to outlaw bazookas and mortars. It is quite another thing to outlaw along with them antique and obsolete collector guns and big game sporting rifles. After all, what organization other than the National Rifle Association should better understand the distinction between the two?

A brief resume of some of the more modern and completely legitimate sporting rifles, which would have come within the definition of destructive devices, spans that class commonly referred to by non-shooters as "elephant guns." Many such rifles have a bore diameter of one-half inch or slightly larger, and they are usually chambered to fire one of the following big game cartridges: .50-70 Winchester; .500 Jeffrey Magnum Nitro Express; .505 Gibbs Rimless Nitro Express; .577 Nitro Express; and the .600 Nitro Express. Rifles designed to fire such potent cartridges are most frequently custom built in Europe to the specifications of their purchaser. They not infrequently cost as much as a new American-made automobile and sometimes much more.

It was not only the gun collecting organizations which feared the extensive use of catch-all phraseology in S.1592. Except for those persons who appeared in unequivocal support of the Administration, there was virtually a continuous procession of witnesses who protested one or more of the broad, discretionary powers which were to be granted to the Secretary of the Treasury. Their fear was that such extensive powers

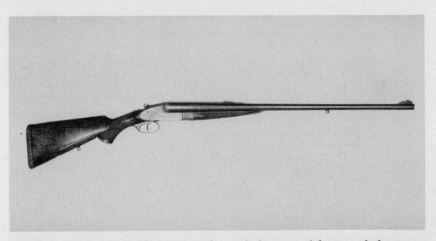

So-called "elephant" double gun popular with hunters of large and dangerous game.

might be used to surround sales and transfers of firearms with arbitrary and burdensome regulations and restrictions, including gun registration.

These apprehensions were not in the least relieved by such statements as that which had been made by the Attorney General of New Jersey, who asserted that Senator Dodd's bill would make gun registration both feasible and effective. Furthermore, the very strong overtones of hostility and animosity, which were directed towards the National Rifle Association by some of the witnesses in support of S.1592, did little to promote either trust or respect.

Typical of the many witnesses who called for specifics in one or more of those areas of Senator Dodd's bill which used such words as "subject to discretion of the Secretary", was Thomas L. Kimball, the Executive Director of the National Wildlife Federation:

"Mr. Chairman, I have read this S.1592 many times. I would like to state for the record that there are seven different places in this bill which gives the Secretary of the Treasury the authority to further regulate, and that we feel that in matters of this import, that the committee itself should spell out these regulations which govern the sale, possession, and use of firearms for lawful purposes, and not leave this, so much of it, to the administrator or the executive discretion of one man who changes with the administration each time." (CC–p. 258)

Senator Gordon Allott informed the subcommittee that much of the mail which he had received from his constituents reflected anxiety over the wide latitude afforded the Secretary of the Treasury, and, in particular, he referred disparagingly to one provision of S.1592 which permitted the Secretary to refuse to issue a Federal Dealer License to anyone whom he believed was not likely to maintain operations in compliance with the act "by reason of his business experience, financial standing, or trade connection." Senator Allott characterized such absolute discretion by this colorful analogy:

"Such discretion reminds me of the words of Lewis Carroll, the eminent author of 'Alice's Adventures in Wonderland': "I'll be judge, I'll be jury,' said cunning old Fury, 'I'll try the whole cause, and condemn you to death.' " (CC–p. 250)

The president of the country's largest import-export company for surplus military small arms also advised the subcommittee of the dangers inherent in the broad delegation of discretionary authority. Samuel

175

Cummings, whose International Armament Corp. warehoused from 100,000 to 500,000 firearms at any given moment, described one experience which the commercial trade had undergone during past years as the basis for his opinion:

"For instance, it took 25 years of continual effort to change a small detail of the original national firearms law pertaining to barrel length, so that a certain category of sporting rifle could be legally included. The barrel length was set originally at 18 inches, strictly because of the lack of knowledge of standard commercial barrel lengths when a certain category was 16 inches. For 25 years efforts were made, supported by the National Rifle Association and the various firearms dealers to change that. They finally succeeded. But it takes 25 years to change a barrel length requirement, we shudder to think what would happen under the present bill with the tremendous discretionary powers and the large areas of confusion in the present bill which are not really spelled out as to what the Treasury Department would do. Such words as—'The Secretary may issue, subject to discretion of the Secretary,' and so forth and so on. I frankly am afraid of such words in a national law." (CC–p. 708)

James V. Bennett, in contrast to those witnesses fearing broad discretion, sharply denounced their apprehensions as utterly groundless and he boldly issued this challenge to prove his point:

"Let them cite any case where the Secretary of the Treasury has abused the powers given him under the present Federal or National Firearms Act to issue regulations." (CC–p. 499)

Bennett never lacked audacity!

12

*"If a gun bill will pass because of the politics of the
situation, you must see to it that its burdens are imposed
upon a man because of a criminal background and not
because he is an ordinary citizen and perhaps poor."*

GEN. JAMES H. DOOLITTLE

AMONG THE MANY ISSUES INVOLVED IN THE CONTRO-
versy over S.1592, which quickly became utterly and
hopelessly blurred in the mass media, and in the minds of the general
public as well, was the one that concerned imported war surplus military
small arms. That result can be attributed to several causes, not the least
of which was the frequent reference to the fact that President Kennedy
had been killed by a surplus foreign military rifle. The role of the
assassin, his period of residence in Soviet Russia, and his self identification as a Marxist was conspicuously de-emphasized by the news media.
Consequently, the scapegoat turned out to be war surplus rifles, in
general, and Italian Carcanos, in particular. It was as though the latter
type of rifle had been specially selected by Lee Harvey Oswald because
of some unique properties it possessed, which, in some mysterious manner, contributed either to its lethal capabilities or to its suitability for
criminal use.

177

The words "military war surplus" meant different things to different people. Rarely, if ever, was there any attempt to distinguish between war surplus destructive devices and war surplus military rifles. The recognition by some people that there was, in fact, a very substantial and legitimate basis for distinction between the two classifications led to strenuous protests from some quarters over the proposal to ban entirely the importation of small arms through Senator Dodd's bill. The general language of the bill which pertained to military surplus weapons read as follows:

"No person shall import or bring any firearms into the United States or any possession thereof, except that the Secretary may authorize a firearm to be imported or brought in if the person importing or bringing in the firearm establishes to the satisfaction of the Secretary that the firearm—

* * *

(3) is of a type and quality generally recognized as particularly suitable for lawful sporting purposes and is not a surplus military weapon and that the importation or bringing in of the firearm would not be contrary to the public interest; . . ." (CC–p. 11)

It should be noted parenthetically that other exceptions to the importation of firearms were provided for antiques, unserviceable firearms (not readily restorable to firing condition) brought in as curios or museum pieces, firearms having scientific or research value, firearms to be used in connection with competition or training purposes, and those firearms previously taken out of the United States. The discussion here, however, is limited solely to war surplus foreign military rifles and, to a much lesser extent, handguns of a similar origin.

There appears to have been three distinct motives for the movement to ban the importation of foreign military surplus small arms; (1) residual emotionalism over the assassination of President Kennedy; (2) professed concern over the general availability of so-called inexpensive firearms, and (3) a protectionist attitude towards the interests of domestic arms manufacturers.

The emotional overtones of the issue, for the most part, were confined to the outpouring of newspaper and magazine articles which, in the course of propagandizing for the enactment of S.1592, never passed up an opportunity to remind their readers that President Kennedy had been shot with a foreign-made imported 6.5mm Manlicher-Carcano carbine fitted with a telescopic sight and costing only $19.95. Not infrequently, this fact was coupled with a recollection of how John F. Kennedy, as the junior Senator from the State of Massachusetts, in 1958, had introduced legislation calling for an embargo of the importation of war surplus small arms. The obvious implication being that Senator Kennedy's effort in this regard sprang from his recognition and concern over the potential danger posed by the presence of such guns in the United States, and that had he only been successful he might not have been shot five years later in Dallas. The first implication was incorrect and the second was illogical.

It was in the early 1950s that significant quantities of foreign-made military rifles began entering United States markets as a result of their technical obsolescence as bolt-action rifles, and as a result of the international standardization of the new North Atlantic Treaty Organization cartridge. Those bolt-action rifles and carbines included the well known and desirable U.S. Springfield, the British Enfield, and a variety of excellent Mauser-action models. Calibers ranged from 6.5mm to 8mm with many variations of the popular .30 caliber, as well. In addition to European rifles, there also were a number of Japanese arms, although far fewer in number.

As the volume of imports increased year by year, stimulated by their low cost and the discovery made by American shooters that they could easily be modified into eminently satisfactory hunting rifles, a serious impact on the domestic arms industry was reported. In the face of sharply decreased sales and profits, a group of manufacturers petitioned the Department of Defense and the Department of State as early as May 1957 and again in January 1958 for an administrative decision to terminate imports of military rifles. Both Departments, however, declined the request.

Typical war surplus military rifle before and after sporterization to hunting or target rifle.

Undaunted, the American manufacturers took their case to Congress, where hearings were held on March 25, 1958, before the House Foreign Affairs Committee. The firearms industry's problems were presented to that committee by Mr. E. C. Hadley, President of the Sporting Arms & Ammunition Manufacturers' Institute:

"There are four sources of the industry's problem. First, the importation of American-made rifles declared surplus by our allies abroad; second, the importation of surplus used and new foreign made military surplus rifles; third, the importation of foreign made commercial arms; fourth, the sale of surplus military firearms by the U.S. Government within the United States." (CC–p. 717)

On the other side of the issue, the Government's reason for refusing to cut-off such imports was reflected in the following statement made to that same House Foreign Affairs Committee on the same day by Mr. R. L. O'Connor, Administrator of the Bureau of Security and Consul Affairs of the Department of State:

"I am frank to say that when there are questions of surplus arms cropping up abroad, which another area is bidding for it, may very often be the better part of valor and indeed the best part of our foreign relations to have them imported into this country rather than float around." (CC–p. 715)

It would appear as though the presence of large quantities of small arms on the open world market was a source of concern to the U.S. Government, which evidently feared that they might become channeled into illegal international trade and jeopardize world peace and security. The alternative was to permit their importation into this country for absorption by hundreds of thousands of hunters, collectors and shooters.

It was just one month later, April 28, 1958, that Senator John F. Kennedy introduced bill S.3714 to amend the Mutual Security Act of 1954 so as to exclude from importation or reimportation into the United States either firearms or ammunition which had been originally manufactured for military purposes. Senator Kennedy explained the purpose and intended effect of his bill to the Senate:

"The effect of the proposed amendment to the law would be to exclude from importation only arms or ammunition originally manufactured for military purposes. Ammunition and guns imported into the United States have helped spoil the domestic market and the market for imported guns which were originally manufactured for game purposes. So I think the bill is in the interest of a great many jobbers, and at least 125,000 retailers located in all 48 States, and of particular importance to 5 arms manufacturers in Massachusetts, including Savage Arms, Harrington & Richardson, Nobel Manufacturing Co., Smith & Wesson, and Iver-Johnson Arms & Cycle Works." (*Congressional Record*: April 28, 1958, p. 6696)

Senator Kennedy's bill was identical to one which had been filed previously in the House by Congressman Albert P. Moreno. After being reported favorably by the House Foreign Affairs Committee, however, the Moreno amendment was defeated by a House vote. Subsequently, the amendment was modified so as to make it applicable only to those firearms which had been originally manufactured in the United States and shipped abroad under a lend-lease program or as military assistance. It was in that final form that the measure was enacted.

It was with reference to the preceding background that Mr. E. C. Hadley spoke when he informed Senator Dodd's subcommittee of the position, with respect to S.1592, that had been assumed by the Sporting Arms & Ammunition Manufacturers' Institute:

"One of the most significant proposals recommended by the President is a ban on imports of surplus military firearms and other weapons not suitable for sporting purposes. The need for gun control legislation has been generated in large part by just such imports. As early as 1958, the sporting arms industry sought to obtain a ban or restriction on these imports on trade and national defense grounds. We wish to make it clear that we did not then and do not now oppose the importation of quality sporting firearms of new manufacture." (CC–p. 409)

Subsequent to the appearance of Mr. E. C. Hadley before Senator Dodd's subcommittee, several cogent comments were made with respect to certain portions of his testimony by Samuel Cummings, President of International Armament Corp., who submitted them to the subcommittee in the form of a written memorandum. Some pertinent portions follow:

"It is interesting to note that Mr. Hadley himself admits that the S.A.A.M.I. endeavors to embargo importation of military surplus rifles were based on 'trade and national defense grounds' and not on any grounds of crime prevention. Inasmuch as crime prevention is the purpose of S.1592 now before Congress, Mr. Hadley's reasons of 'trade and national defense' do not have any place here whatsoever.

Just to set the record straight, between 1957 and 1964 the New England manufacturers have been responsible, directly or indirectly, for 11 separate attempts before the legislative and executive branches of the Federal Government to eliminate the importation of military surplus rifles. . . ." (CC–p. 717)

Samuel Cummings went on to call the subcommittee's attention to an apparent inconsistency between Mr. Hadley's testimony in 1958, which had mentioned, as being among the problems of the domestic firearms industry, "the importation of foreign made commercial arms", and his current testimony which had asserted that the industry wished "to make it clear that we did not then and do not now oppose the importation of quality sporting firearms of new manufacture". Mr. Cummings dryly observed that:

"We cannot account for this discrepancy in testimony, but this committee should be aware of the fact that in the meantime Winchester has opened a factory in Japan and is importing shotguns from Japan to the United States, presumably in an effort to counter the serious competition always furnished by the Browning Arms Co. which imports their shotguns from Belgium." (CC–p. 717)

In detailing the eleven attempts by the domestic arms industry to eliminate the importation of military surplus rifles, Mr. Cummings included within his memorandum certain facts concerning one of those attempts which may prove enlightening. It represented the ninth attempt in his series:

"On June 30, 1960, the so-called Dodd amendment was passed by the Senate as a rider to a State Department appropriation bill. The Dodd amendment stated that it was 'the sense of the Senate' that the State Department 'should take action as may be necessary to prevent the importation of all military firearms.' It was included by action of the Senate Subcommittee on Appropriations for State, Justice, and the Judiciary, whose chairman was Senator Lyndon Johnson and included both Senators Dodd and Saltonstall. There was no explanation in the Appropriation Committee report and no comment on the floor of the Senate. Upon being informed of the Dodd amendment, various importers, manufacturers, gun dealers, gun enthusiasts and the National Rifle Association acquainted the members of the Senate-House conferees of their concern and as a result the Senate-House conferees removed this rider from the State Department appropriation bill (H.R. 11666). Congressman Rooney reported to the House that this action was taken because 'this language might raise havic with the small sporting goods dealers and gunsmiths all over the country.' (Congressional Record, August 24, 1960). On August 24, 1960, the Dodd amendment was again introduced as a rider to the Mutual Security appropriation bill (H.R. 12619). On August 25, the Senate-House conferees on the Mutual Security appropriation bill (a different group from the State Department appropriation bill conferees) also struck the Dodd amendment from that bill." (CC–p. 719)

It should be noted that during the period of 1955 through 1958 the impact of military surplus rifles on the sales of domestically produced small arms reportedly was so great that American arms manufacturers had been obliged to lay off one-third of their production workers. It, therefore, would have been only natural for Senator Dodd of Connecticut to have been sympathetic to their plight and responsive to their needs. After all, as he had stated before the Senate Committee on Commerce in 1963:

"In my own State we have quite an arms industry. We have the Colt Co., we have Winchester, we have Remington, we have HI-Standard. It is quite a factor in the State of Connecticut." (BB–p. 15)

Another witness who appeared before the House Committee on Ways and Means with respect to Senator Dodd's S.1592 and whose thoughts paralleled those which had been expressed by Samuel Cummings was Leslie E. Field, an attorney who represented Mars Equipments Corp., and Shore Galleries, importers, wholesalers, and dealers in firearms and ammunition. The penetrating questions raised by Leslie Field during his testimony were never really answered by anyone throughout the entire course of the hearings.

"It must be pointed out that over the last decade representatives of domestic industry have made repeated attempts upon a number of pretexts, to halt or impair the flow of imported firearms, especially military surplus, into the United States.
    It seems to me that the position that the proponents are taking is that American military firearms, American sporting rifles, are all right, but if the thing happens to come in from abroad, then there is something inherently wrong with it.
    I would like to know the logical distinction between a crime committed with an American-made firearm and a foreign-made firearm. I would like further to know what is the difference between the military training value of an American-made firearm and a foreign-made firearm where they both approximate the same characteristics.
    The subject of such a prohibition has not been one which has not

183

received some attention before. On about 11 previous occasions when amendments to the IAW Act, amendment to the Mutual Security Act, and other means have been suggested, various enterprises in the northeastern part of the United States who have a semi-interest in the production of center-fire arms have attempted through their representatives to impose a ban on this type of importation.

I don't think that one can say honestly that the reasons that were in their hearts were those of preventing crimes.

These attempts have been defeated after due consideration by the Congress in each session. Nonetheless, the congressional representatives of the Eastern States now persist in attaching a ban on the importation of surplus military rifles to what is claimed to be an anticrime measure." (EE–p. 456)

Mr. Field also commented that, as of that time, there were two domestic firearms firms which controlled about 45 percent of the manufacture of all center-fire rifles and at least 80 percent of the manufacture of metallic cartridges. Although not mentioned by name, the firms referred to were undoubtedly Winchester-Western and Remington Arms Co., both of which were located in Senator Dodd's State of Connecticut.

The reader should also not forget that the National Rifle Association had actively opposed the attempts by the domestic small arms industry to ban the importation of foreign war surplus rifles during the late 1950s. That fact should be remembered and later compared with the studied efforts of the anti-gun claque to have the National Rifle Association portrayed to the general public as constituting nothing more than a mercenary "front for the munitions manufacturers".

The tremendous psychological disadvantage which was inherent in all military rifles, whether of foreign or domestic manufacture, and one which they shared with those weapons within the destructive devices category, was the fact that to most people their general appearance was unesthetic. They were designed for reliable battlefield performance under climatic extremes, with dull non-reflective metal parts enveloped in an unattractive piece of plain and discolored wood, featuring oversized protected battle-sights and bayonet mounting lugs. This "killer" appearance was effectively exploited by the anti-gun claque showing photographs illustrating such firearms, frequently stacked like cords of firewood. The truth, generally ignored, however, was that these superficially rough and unattractive exteriors often harbored attributes of a suprisingly superior nature.

Knowledgeable riflemen understood that once the non-essential external trappings were removed from military rifles, they would have a generally high quality bolt-action mechanism and barrel remaining which would serve admirably as the nucleus for making a superb custom-built hunting rifle. Best of all, the finished custom rifle would still cost only a fraction of its domestically-produced counterpart. It was not at all uncommon for sportsmen to purchase a military rifle built around a Mauser bolt-action with the intention of discarding both the barrel and wooden stock merely in order to obtain the prized Mauser action itself. Such actions were world-renowned for possessing outstanding characteristics of simplicity and strength.

Such rebuilt rifles were both safe and accurate, and they provided a lifetime of reliable service. All experienced riflemen knew that fact, and they resented the constant allegations by the anti-gun media that military surplus rifles were unsafe and inferior junk. How was the general public to know all of the facts so that an intelligent opinion might be formed, when all that they ever received through the mass media were those syndicated predigested "facts" that were deemed suitable for their thought-conditioning by the interpretative journalists and commentators?

Additional enlightening facts concerning the custom rifle business that had burgeoned in the United States were discussed by Samuel Cummings who also provided Senator Dodd's subcommittee with some comparable cost figures which prevailed at that time:

"One aspect of this type of business is that companies such as Winchester and Remington have consistently refused to sell their actions to gunsmiths until approximately 1 year ago; a gunsmith, if he wanted to make a custom rifle, had to buy either a military surplus action or a foreign commercial action imported from Finland, Sweden, or Belgium. Today, Winchester Model 70 actions are available for the price of $115 each (note that the entire M-70 rifles cost $139 complete). A small gunsmith can get this action at a discount of 25 percent or at about $76.25. In comparison, new, commercial actions such as a Finnish-made Sako, cost $54. On the other hand, we charge between $14.50 and $24 for our military Mauser actions, depending on the type." (CC–p. 720)

Even those military surplus rifles, which were not completely rebuilt into custom rifles, were normally modified by cutting down, reshaping and refinishing their wooden stocks, shortening the barrel, replacing the sights and generally lightening and dressing up the rifle. The technique was referred to as "sporterizing", and many small gun shops across the country specialized in such jobs. That activity alone provided employment for a significant number of people, a number comparable to those employed by some of the large domestic arms manufacturers, and they and their families felt that their livelihood in an old and honorable trade was threatened by Senator Dodd's S.1592. Samuel Cummings expressed it extremely well:

> "The hundreds of small manufacturers and gunsmiths which serve the large market in barrels, stocks, sights, ammunition, spare parts, and other accessories do not think of themselves as engaged in a marginal business to be sacrificed." (CC–p. 696)

The reasons now begin to emerge why such a controversy raged over the not-so-simple issue of banning the importation of foreign military surplus rifles in the light of Senator Dodd's obvious inability to demonstrate their peculiar or significant use in crime. There was a well justified and shameful suspicion that possibly a crime bill, trading on the emotionalism of a presidential assassination, was being used to protect a key industry in the sponsoring senator's home State.

It should already be quite obvious that gun control is by no means a simple issue. It is one that instead poses many vexing problems each often as difficult to perceive as to comprehend. It is simple only for those in the news media who intuitively know what is best for the American public, who then proceed to tell the public what is in their best interests, and simultaneously protect the public against the incursion of incompatible facts and opinions.

Another problem was the flamboyant advertisements through which many military surplus rifles were sold. Some of these ads caused serious and conservative riflemen to wince, and caused nonshooters to conclude that the ads were designed to attract the lunatic fringe. In most instances such ads were merely written with a "tongue in cheek" approach in the hopes that their distinctive format would prove more eye-catching than the ads of other dealers who were selling identical merchandise for identical prices.

Although firearms users may have regarded some of the advertisements which were regularly run in certain hobby magazines as gauche or ridiculous, they nevertheless understood the product which was being offered. That was not the case, however, with the anti-gun crowd who delighted in indignantly holding up such ads as documented evidence of the irresponsibility of the "gun nuts" for whom they were intended. Oddly enough, many of those same people were not in the least offended by items in their family newspapers featuring movies claiming to portray in true-to-life color—for the titillation of popcorn munching voyeurs—every conceivable variety of degenerate human behavior.

186

13

*". . . and he that hath no sword, let him sell his
garment, and buy one."*

LUKE 22:36

UNFORTUNATELY, CONSPICUOUS ADVERTISING OF MAIL-
order military surplus small arms tended to obscure the
more important mail-order sales of merchandise related to a broad
variety of perfectly legitimate shooting activities. Many people, unfamiliar with the scope of firearms use in this country, simply concluded
that no real inconvenience would result to sportsmen from prohibition
of shipping and receiving firearms in interstate commerce. Such ignorance
was often quite innocent. For example, Sheldon Cohen, before the House
Committee on Ways and Means, grossly understated the effect to be produced by mail-order prohibition:

> "Only two minor inconveniences may occur for the sportsmen of this
> country. They will not be able to travel to another State and purchase

a pistol or concealable weapon, and they will not be able to obtain a mail-order shipment from another State of any type of firearm. On this latter point, the inconvenience is more apparent than real because the large mail-order houses have retail outlets and the bill will permit intrastate mail-order shipments to individual citizens from these outlets.

Such minor inconveniences cannot be avoided if the legislation is to make it possible for the States to regulate effectively the acquisition and possession of firearms." (DD–p. 28)

The fact is the states did not require any Federal help other than that which was already embodied within the original Federal Firearms Act of 1938, namely, that firearms dealers were required by law to honor the licensing requirements of their customers' states. Any state, whose legislature felt the necessity of controlling mail-order shipments to their residents, was free to enact a simple licensing statute to acquire the protection of the Federal Firearms Act. What bothered the anti-gun claque was that only seven state legislatures had decided to enact such a license law. Consequently, they were adamant in their insistence that those other remaining states would be "helped" whether or not they wanted to be. The fourteen states whose legislatures adopted resolutions opposing Senator Dodd's S.1592 clearly wanted no part of such "help" and that was their prerogative as sovereign states.

The other portion of Sheldon Cohen's reassurance to the committee was based on the proposition anyone who wanted a firearm of any kind could simply order one from their nearest general merchandise catalog sales office. For those persons whose sole familiarity with firearms was gained through a casual perusal of a Sears, Roebuck catalog, that proposition might have seemed plausible and one no doubt reinforced by the well known, if somewhat extravagant, slogan "Sears has everything." But obviously, Sears does not have everything in either the field of firearms or of ammunition, to say nothing of the countless important accessories which make up the paraphernalia of a dedicated shooter-sportsman.

Visualize the facial expression of a helpful clerk in the employ of one of the mass merchandising chains if a competitive pistol shooter were to attempt to order an accurized .45 semiautomatic pistol, almost invariably sought for serious competitions, with precision micrometer rear sight, undercut post front sight, heavy duty barrel bushing with accessory wrench, adjustable trigger pull with a backlash adjustment, recoil buffer, stippled forestrap, flat mainspring housing, modified thumb rest wood grips, and balanced to handle 185-grain semi-wadcut-

Highly specialized target rifle and pistol used in Olympics and other International shooting events.

ter bullets propelled by 3.5 grains of smokeless powder. What about the small bore match competitor who wants the latest model imported match rifle equipped with a two stage set-trigger, a Schutzen hooked butt-plate, a beavertail fore-end with long swivel rail equipped with an adjustable walnut palm rest and swivels, an international type walnut stock with thumb-hole and cheek piece, and fitted with Olympic style micrometer sights?

Is it ridiculous to expect any large mail order house to carry such highly specialized shooting gear, but that is exactly what tens of thousands of competitive shooters in this country were told over and over again when they protested that they would be cut off from their equipment sources by a total ban on interstate mail order sales. Numerous specialized dealers were also alarmed. They handled little besides highly sophisticated competitive shooting supplies, and faced the prospect of being neatly and summarily severed from their only customers by mailorder prohibition.

The building of custom rifles was another legitimate activity which relied heavily on the interstate shipment of the finished product to mail order customers throughout the country, and often such a rifle would move back and forth several times between the customer and different gunsmiths each of whom performed distinct and specialized services in its gradual fabrication. For example, the author's own custom-built rifle began as a high quality imported Mauser action. The action was mailed to a Pennsylvania gunsmith who was instructed to install in it a special type of adjustable trigger, to engine-turn and polish the bolt for enhanced appearance and improved oil retention capabilities, and to install a precision button-rifled heavy-weight barrel to be furnished by a West Virginia gunsmith who manufactured superbly accurate barrels. The finished product was then shipped to the author, who inspected the work which had been done, and who then immediately shipped the barreled action to still another gunsmith in Illinois, whose specialty it was to finish both interior and exterior barrel surfaces with a tough scratch resistant black chrome plating. After inspecting this process, the author once again shipped the plated barreled action to a Missouri gunsmith, who specialized in stockmaking to the individual customer's personal bodily measurements and detailed specifications, and who used nothing but the finest quality kiln dried selected imported and domestic woods. The then nearly completed rifle was returned to the author who personally attached to it an expensive adjustable-powered telescopic hunting sight, which was purchased by mail order from a New Jersey dealer whose scopes were more competitively priced than anywhere else in the country. The completed custom-built rifle traveled through Pennsylvania, Illinois and Missouri, and it used an imported Swedish-made Mauser action, a West Virginia precision barrel, and a New Jersey scope.

Why do shooters "need" a custom built rifle? For the same reason that everyone does not own and drive a Volkswagen, in spite of its economy, durability and reliability. Competitive shooters, hunters and gun collectors are no different in their varying needs and desires.

It was with reference to the custom gun business that Senator Paul J. Fannin spoke when he addressed Senator Dodd's subcommittee. Senator Fannin's home State of Arizona was especially well known for its many skilled gunsmiths, and he expressed concern for their future if S.1592 were to be enacted:

"There are many small businesses in my State and throughout the country which would suffer severely under this bill. Many of these are small custom shops that produce fine sporting and target arms for mail-order sale all over the world." (CC–p. 241)

Quite apart from the previously discussed problem which had been presented to gun collectors by the broad language of S.1592 in defining destructive devices as including firearms having a bore larger than one-half inch in diameter, they also became alarmed at the prospect of being denied use of interstate commerce to acquire and dispose of antique and obsolete firearms which they collected and which would never be fired.

190

The Government evidently felt compelled to offer some kind of exempting language which supposedly would have removed antique firearms from the scope of the bill. But the Government did not obtain advice from the most experienced commercial dealers in antique firearms to arrive at their definitions. That would have been the intelligent thing to do. Instead, the off-hand ideas of the manufacturers of modern firearms were accepted and the government thought it "pretty reasonable".

After a brief discussion, the following suggested new language was then inserted into the record:

"The term 'antique firearms' means any firearm utilizing an early-type ignition system, including but not limited to, matchlock, flintlock, percussion cap or the like, and of a design used before 1870, whether actually manufactured before or after that date, but not including weapons designed for use with smokeless powder or using rimfire or conventional center-fire ignition with fixed ammunition." (DD–p. 65)

Several shortcomings of the Government definition were immediately apparent to Leon C. Jackson, expert on early American firearms, who pinpointed the several deficiencies to the committee and offered alternative wording to correct them:

"To accept the definition of the Internal Revenue Service rather than the definition offered by the collectors would fail to exclude from the act such historic arms as those used by Custer at the Battle of the Little Big Horn, the single-shot rifle which Buffalo Bill used to make his mark in Western folklore, the fabled Sharps rifles of the buffalo hunting era, and thousands upon thousands of similar obsolete arms.

Remember that similar collections in the years past are the very basis today of the outstanding exhibits of the Smithsonian Institution, the Metropolitan Museum, and others who seek to educate in the methods and implements of the past." (DD–p. 351)

Continuing with his informative explanation, Mr. Jackson explained:

"To further explore this point, unless the recommended change is made we have an utterly ridiculous situation. As an example, the Volcanic pistol was the forerunner of both the Smith & Wesson revolver and the Winchester rifle. It fired an ineffective and today almost an unobtainable cartridge but which under the Government's proposed definition would still be fixed ammunition.

The gun was manufactured from the early 1850's until about 1860 and has value only as a curio or collector item. While a muzzle-loading arm made last week would not be subject to the controls, this antique Volcanic pistol would be.

Even more striking would be the inclusion as a modern arm of the Spencer repeating carbine which was the principal cavalry arm of the Civil War. It fires an unobtainable rimfire cartridge but, still, under this definition would be controlled just as a modern magnum caliber." (DD–p. 351)

Pointing out to the Committee that no modern nation in the world, including Soviet Russia, prohibits or attempts to control such antique firearms, Leon Jackson then read the definition which was submitted by the various gun collector organizations as the product of their best thinking:

"Provided, That nothing contained in this section shall be construed to include those firearms which are designed for use with loose powder and ball or which are incapable of being fired with self-contained primed cartridges; nor shall it apply to firearms held as a curiosity or decoration manufactured prior to 1898 that would require cartridges of an obsolete pattern no longer manufactured and readily available through commercial channels." (DD–p. 350)

The gun collector would have been seriously hurt by the prohibition of mail order purchases and interstate shipments because of the fact that, in order either to acquire or dispose of a representative collection, it was necessary that a collector have access to a nationwide market so as to be able to buy, sell, and trade with both dealers and other collectors. Jackson explained that it is often necessary for a collector to canvass the whole country due to the scarcity of some models.

"Even then sometimes money will not buy the object and only a mutually agreeable trade would accomplish its acquisition." (DD–p. 349)

It is axiomatic that in order to understand a collector, you, too, must also be a collector of something; of anything, but a true collector. There is a vast difference between the person who collects and the person who accumulates. Accumulations are haphazard, indiscriminate, often of mediocre quality, of no historic value, and little economic value apart from their intrinsic worth. The person, whose habit it is to pocket a book of matches taken from various restaurants and service establishments, and at the end of the day to throw them into an old cigar box, may think of himself as a collector, but in reality he is nothing more than a junk accumulator. Similarly, people whose concept of stamp collecting is limited to the hoarding of peculiar stamps received on correspondence addressed to them are no more philatelists than the persons who rummage through pocket change for "old pennies" are numismatists.

Gun collectors, like true philatelists and numismatists, in the majority of cases, are responsible business and professional people, whose interest in the prevention and control of crime is just as sincere as that professed by the advocates of highly restrictive firearms legislation. They collect guns for any one of a number of entirely legitimate reasons and follow a collecting pattern established by their own individual interests and philosophy. This was explained by Mr. Jackson to the House Committee on Ways and Means in this manner:

"For example, one man may wish to collect the handguns used by the military forces of the United States. To be complete, these would include the handmade pistols of individual craftsmen used in the Revolution, and from the first officially adopted pistol, the Model of 1798, to those in current use.

Another collector might wish to collect only the products of an individual maker and, in some cases, only the variations of one model.

Their interests could range from a fascination with the mechanical complexity of rotation and ignition to their importance in some phase of our Nation's history. Others might be interested only in the artistic decoration of beautifully designed pieces that were intended for presentation to prominent people. An example would be the beautiful mounted pair of revolvers now in the Franklin D. Roosevelt Library presented by President Abraham Lincoln to the Governor of Adrianople." (DD–p. 351)

The guns which gun collectors collect frequently cost from several hundreds to several thousands of dollars each, depending upon such factors as scarcity, state of preservation, and demand. It, therefore, should be obvious that a lifetime collection of fine firearms could represent a sizeable percentage of a collector's estate, which, if it is to be sold to produce a maximum return upon disposition, must be sold on the national market rather than merely among whatever potential customers might happen to reside within the same state as did the collector at the time of his death. This aspect was also discussed by Leon Jackson:

"In addition to these many reasons for direct interest, collectors have looked upon their hobby as a serious investment, the liquidation of which will be an important asset to their estates. To deny them or their heirs access to a reasonable market to liquidate these collections would be destroying an economic investment without due compensation." (DD–pp. 351–352)

At the time of the hearings by Senator Dodd's subcommittee, gun collectors who bought, sold and traded firearms with fellow collectors and dealers throughout the country often acquired a Federal Firearms Dealer License with which to facilitate such transactions. Competitive pistol shooters frequently did so as well. Their reasons had very little to do with any desire to purchase guns "at discount prices", as was suggested by Government witnesses. Such remarks showed a complete lack of familiarity with the processes involved. A question concerning the number of persons having dealers licenses without actually being in the commercial trade was asked by Senator Hiram L. Fong and answered by Henry H. Fowler, Secretary of the Treasury:

"Our best estimate, Senator Fong, is that out of the approximately, I think this is a fairly accurate figure for 1964, 99,544 licensees, it is our estimate that less than half of the licensed dealers are actually engaged in the business as dealers and that more than half are persons who are using the simple device of becoming a licensee for their own personal nonbusiness purposes." (CC–p. 33)

Large numbers of people resorted to securing a Federal Firearms Dealer License because the United States postal law and its regulations prohibited the shipping of concealable firearms, such as pistols, through the mails except as between certain specified classes of exempt individuals, which included federally licensed firearms dealers. There was also an exception for antique and unserviceable pistols.

The ban on the shipment of operable handguns and semi-modern collector-quality pistols meant that private citizens, who wished either to ship or receive such items, had to do so by common carrier truck. Disadvantages, as compared to shipping by the U.S. mails, were cost, convenience, and safety.

Obviously, common carrier truck service is not designed for tiny shipments to and from individual persons, but rather it is completely oriented towards truckload and carload volume shipments from basic manufacturers to warehouses, to distribution centers, and to the larger retail stores. Individuals who wanted to ship their pistols to an out of state pistolsmith for repairs, adjustment or modifications, were obliged to travel many miles to the nearest freight terminal with their tiny three pound package. Once there, they were charged the minimum freight rate assessed on the basis of a 150 pound to a 200 pound shipment, the same rate basis that would be charged to a manufacturer shipping from 50 to 100 pistols! In addition, the small size of such consignments, combined with their nature and value, contributed greatly to both loss and pilferage.

In contrast, the U.S. Post Office was nearby, was geared to the personal delivery of small parcels, operated under tight security measures, bolstered by heavy Federal penalties for tampering with the mails, and the cost was a small fraction of common carrier truck charges. The choice was obvious, and anyone who had occasion to ship or receive handguns even once or twice a year was ahead in both money and trouble by acquiring a Federal Firearms Dealer License for the $1 annual fee which then permitted the use of Parcel Post for both the shipment and receipt of handguns.

Most non-shooters are completely unaware that tournament level competitive pistol shooting requires more highly refined handguns than are available through normal retail outlets. Serious match shooting demands that such handguns be substantially modified by competent pistolsmiths, who specialize in such "accurizing" work so as to obtain their maximum performance potential. While the out-of-the-box quality of match-grade handguns has been greatly improved lately by major manufacturers, for those competitors who seek the finest possible battery of tournament handguns, the services of a first rate pistolsmith are indispensable. For example, the author owns several handcrafted revolvers, built upon the manufacturer's original frame, cylinder and trigger mechanism, but which were fitted with extra long and heavy custom-made barrels. In addition, each handgun has certain internal modifications and improvements with respect to their springs and critical bearing surfaces. In each instance, one by one, the revolvers moved back and forth over the 1,000 mile span that separated the author from the pistolsmith whose specialty was that kind of unusual work.

This discussion leads up to the issue which developed over the amounts of the various categories of license fees specified in Senator Dodd's S.1592. To provide perspective on what had occurred between the time that the fee schedule had been set in the old Dodd bill, S.1975, and the new schedule listed within S.1592, it is only necessary to review the observations and remarks of James V. Bennett, which he made during the preceding year, 1964, while testifying before the Senate Committee on Commerce with regard to the old S.1975:

"The Dodd bill would raise the manufacturer's fee to $50, dealer's fee to $10, and also establish a new category of pawnbroker, where the fee would be $50.

I approve these provisions and the avowed purpose but I think that if these fees were increased to $300 for manufacturer's, $100 for dealers, and $200 for pawnbrokers, it would stop this use of purchase of a dealer's license in order to circumvent State laws." (BB–p. 101)

As of the time Bennett spoke those words, there had been full support for Senator Dodd's S.1975, including its increased fee structure, by organizations representing both sporting and commercial interests. It should be noted that the purpose for increasing the fees was not intended originally to be punitive in nature, but was to help to defray the costs of an investigation of new applicants for such licenses.

The fee schedule in Senator Dodd's S.1592 had been raised substantially. The annual fee for a dealer in either firearms or ammunition was to be $100 and the annual fee for a manufacturer of either firearms or ammunition was to be $500. That enormous increase was yet another factor in precipitating the controversy over S.1592.

Senator Paul J. Fannin spoke critically of punitive license fees and cited his opinion as to their probable effect on the many small dealers who could not afford to pay them:

"In addition to these small dealers, there are many sparsely populated areas of Arizona where service stations and small general stores handle firearms and ammunition as an accommodation to the ranchers and farmers who need them. They also serve the more than 150,000 Arizonans who engage in hunting and whose sport is an important part of game and range management in our State. They could ill afford the drastic increase in dealer fees and recordkeeping contemplated by S.1592." (CC–p. 241)

Similarly, Senator Gordon Allott appeared before Senator Dodd's subcommittee and told his views as to how such fees would affect his home State of Colorado by forcing small stores out of the firearms and ammunition business:

"The high cost of licenses proposed for dealers under S.1592 is, of course, designed to, and I believe will, stamp out the carrying of guns and ammunition in stock by small stores. It will lead to further concentration of the industry in a few sources, and these sources would presumably be located in the metropolitan areas. This is simply one further facet of the hardship imposed on the people who live in rural areas, or small communities." (CC–p. 249)

196

Senator Quentin N. Burdick, a member of Senator Dodd's sub-committee, agreed.

The impact of the increased firearms dealer license fee would have been enormous. It prompted an appearance before the House Committe on Ways and means by Robert P. Beamer, a representative of the National Retail Hardware Association. He told the committee that the association had a membership of approximately 20,000 hardware dealers located in communities throughout the United States most of whom were in towns under 10,000 population. He then observed that:

"While these truly small businessmen may be thought by some to be individually of relative insignificance, collectively, and in their own communities, they represent a substantial position in the economy. Local people in small communities rely upon the hardware dealer to supply the daily hardware needs of the community." (EE–p. 513)

He summed up by this cogent observation:

"We submit that the amount of the fee does not determine the fitness of the dealer to handle firearms; raising the fee merely eliminates smaller dealer competition." (EE–p. 514)

Normally, when the word "manufacturer" is mentioned, the picture which comes most readily to mind includes large factories, whose mass production assembly lines are manned by numerous employees turning out huge quantities of whatever product they manufacture. An annual manufacturer's fee of $500 for such factories would not appear to pose any serious problems, and it would not have, if all manufacturers conformed to that image. An insight into the realities of how modern day muzzle loading rifles are "manufactured" was provided by Vaughn K. Goodwin:

"These bills as written will seriously affect, if not completely eliminate muzzle loading shooting and the custom gunsmiths whose livelihood depends on making and repairing muzzle loading rifles.

These fine craftsmen do not make sufficient guns to stand the 100 times increase in dealers licenses or to afford working through a distributor. Consequently, their sales would be limited to over-the-counter purchases within their state, a condition under which they could not survive.

I might add that many of our people are in the Appalachia area, the makers of these guns. They have carried these crafts from father to

197

son generation. In fact, one of the rifles was given to the President just last year for his aid in the Appalachia program." (DD–p. 319)

We have referred to NRA members who reloaded some 2,000,000 cartridges during the early days of World War II when the shortage of brass made it extremely difficult for police, plant guards and home guardsmen to obtain adequate quantities of ammunition for training purposes. The reloading of fired cartridge cases had become of increasing importance to serious shooters with the passage of years. There were two reasons for that development—economy and the desire for precision shooting.

Center-fire cartridges, commonly and erroneously referred to as "bullets" by newspaper reporters, consist of four separate and distinct component parts of which only three are irretrievably expended upon firing: the primer cap which contains the ignition charge is struck by the firing pin. This ignites the powder charge, the burning of which produces the high pressure gases which propel the projectile (correctly called the "bullet") through the barrel and on to the target. The primer cap, powder charge and bullet are held together by the brass cartridge case.

After firing such a cartridge, the average shooter ejects the empty cartridge case and discards it wherever it happens to fall. That is not done, however, by the experienced rifleman or pistol shooter who regularly reloads such empty brass cases. The latter realize the empty brass case represents approximately 80 to 90 percent of the original cost of the factory-made cartridge, and, at a cost of only a few cents and a small amount of time, it can be reloaded with a fresh primer cap, new powder, and another bullet. Best of all, such reloaded cartridges not only will shoot just as well as did the original factory cartridge, they can, and usually are, made to perform better. The process of handloading cartridges is almost of as great interest to serious marksmen as is the competition itself, because in a very real sense it is a test of his knowledge and workmanship, in addition to his shooting skill.

Not only is it possible to reload cartridges for greater accuracy, it is also possible to reduce powder charges from factory standards so as to produce a softer recoil, less noise, and reduced barrel throat erosion. Brass cartridge cases are satisfactory for several such reloadings; often as many as a dozen before they have to be discarded for excessive wear.

In addition to reloading of rifle and pistol cartridges cases, which are made from brass, it is also possible and extremely popular to reload plasticized paper shotgun shells using primer cap, powder, wads, and

198

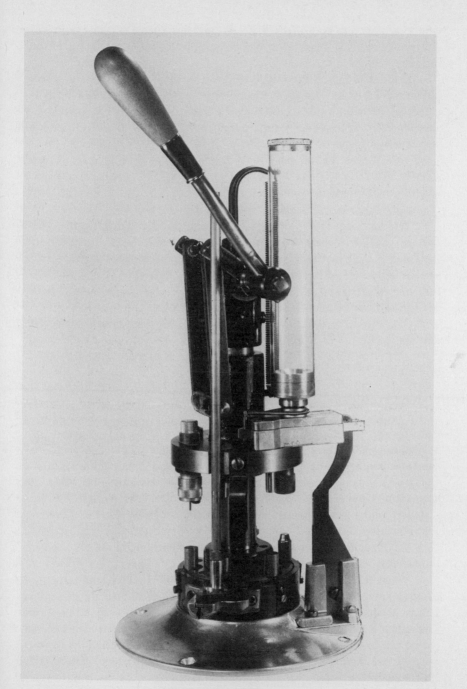

Typical handloading press.

whatever size shot is desired. If it were not for such reloading activities, the cost of serious shooting would be prohibitively expensive for all but the very wealthy.

Hand-loading of cartridges and shells can be done on a purely individual basis; or, for greater economy and efficiency, it can be delegated to one member of a club for all other members of that group on a rotating basis. Occasionally such reloads may be sold to non-club members, such as guests or visitors.

Thus it was that thousands of shooters across the country reacted sharply to the provisions of Senator Dodd's S.1592 which would have levied a $500 annual manufacturer's license fee on individuals who reloaded ammunition for sale or distribution.

The language of the bill made no distinction between the giant factories of Winchester-Western and Remington Arms Companies and the small club, where one member reloaded rifle or pistol cartridges for sale, usually very near cost, for fellow shooters. It should be noted that trap and skeet clubs, which were engaged in reloading shotgun shells, would not have been included because shotgun ammunition was omitted from the definition of "ammunition" in S.1592. The concern for rifle and pistol clubs, which were not so excluded, was expressed by Howard Carter Jr., an attorney and Director of the National Shooting Sports Foundation:

> "Many persons who reload ammunition sell or distribute such ammunition to their friends. In addition, one or two members of a gun club will do the reloading, often at cost, for the members. Under this definition any person carrying on such reloading could be classified as a 'manufacturer' and would be subject to the license fee of $500 a year. Such a broad restriction could curtail much of the reloading being conducted by an estimated 2 million persons in this country." (CC–pp. 316–317)

Franklin Orth also expressed similar views on behalf of the National Rifle Association.

When it is considered that Senator Dodd's S.1592 was supposed to have some relationship to crime control, it was ironic that its most severe effects were reserved for hard working and peaceful people of rural communities and not for the large metropolitan cesspools of crime.

This obvious discrimination in the actual effect of S.1592 was pointed out by Mr. C. R. Gutermuth, Vice President of the Wildlife Management Institute:

"Elimination of the mail-order sale of firearms would not be as inconvenient to residents of the larger metropolitan areas, because they live closer to retail stores and have a broader selection from which to choose. The bill discriminates mostly against the farmer, rancher, and other person who does not live in, or who does not want to live in, a metropolitan area. Interestingly, it is in the metropolitan areas where the crime problem is most disturbing and where the pressures of population appear to create the most cases of emotional instability." (CC–pp. 298–299)

Using the analogies of automobile dealerships, department stores and supermarkets, Franklin Orth sought to demonstrate the gross impracticability of a total ban on the interstate shipments of firearms to individual purchasers:

"One thing to be considered is the fact that no one commercial outlet handles all of the many types, calibers, gages, and variations of firearms manufactured in this country and abroad. No one dealer handles all of this merchandise, either directly or by catalog. As a matter of fact, I do not know of any dealer in any type of merchandise who handles every conceivable type of merchandise in which he is specialized. I know of no automobile dealer that deals in all brands. The implausibility and, very definitely, the impracticality of such a happenstance is true in the case of supermarkets, department stores, or any other retail trade outlet. Most retail outlets deal with the complete line of one manufacturer. The result of this legislation would be to eliminate the small dealer in order to 'manage' the smaller number of large dealers for the convenience of enforcement of such regulations which the Secretary or his delegate might find convenient for him.

While controls on the interstate shipment of firearms are definitely needed, the complete prohibition of such commerce to all but the licensed few is not the answer." (CC–p. 202)

It is seen there were indeed many substantial and legitimate reasons for apprehension on the part of millions of Americans for the consequences of the enactment of Senator Dodd's S.1592. Note these reasons existed independently of any suggestion that S.1592 violated the Second Amendment of the U.S. Constitution. Yet, for those people whose impressions as to the nature of the opposition to S.1592 were gained solely from reading newspaper and magazine articles and listening to television commentators, there would have been no doubt that witness after witness appeared for the sole purpose of vacuously reciting the last half of the Second Amendment of the Bill of Rights. Not so!

This is not to say that that issue was not raised, and quite properly so, but even had there been a complete absence of a Second Amendment in the Bill of Rights there was more than ample cause for the Congress to summarily reject the entire Dodd bill as patently undesirable.

Had it been possible for the millions of law-abiding citizens in the United States who really understood the issues to have collectively and succinctly expressed their many and varied attitudes towards Senator Dodds' S.1592, they could not have phrased it any better than Senator Gordon Allott in these very appropriate words:

> "I believe that the basic philosophy expressed in S.1592 is that guns are somehow bad per se and must be heavily regulated. With this philosophy, I cannot agree. The word 'guns' is not a four-letter, Anglo-Saxon word with dirty connotations, as some seem to think, and putting the epithet 'mail order' with it still does not make it unclean." (CC–p. 247)

An interesting collateral issue, which had been raised by S.1592 was the one which gravely concerned the nation's professional conservationists who feared that the harassment of law-abiding citizens in their efforts to acquire and become proficient in the use of firearms could eventually result in a diminution of funds for the management of wildlife. Their fear was based on the little known fact that virtually every dollar generated for this country's wildlife conservation programs was directly derived from one or more of the many fees paid each year by nearly twenty million hunters and sport shooters.

A superb summary of the prominent role played by firearms owners in wildlife management programs was presented by Mr. C. R. Gutermuth, Vice President of the Wildlife Management Institute. The Wildlife Management Institute was the successor to the old American Wildlife Institute, which dated back to 1911 in its concern for the restoration and improved management of natural resources. A representative of the American Wildlife Institute testified in favor of the 1937 Copeland bill which became the Federal Firearms Act of 1938.

Mr. Gutermuth's presentation to Senator Dodd's subcommittee is most informative:

> "Every State has a fish and wildlife department, and more than 99 percent of the money available for wildlife law enforcement, research, management, land acquisition, development, and other necessary programs is obtained from the sale of hunting licenses and permits. Less

than 1 percent of the money for these essential activities comes from general revenue in any of the States.

In addition, the hunter indirectly pays the manufacturers excise tax of 11 percent on sporting arms and ammunition. This amounted to nearly $17 million during the last year of record. Under the terms of the Pittman-Robertson Federal Aid in Wildlife Restoration Act, this money is credited to a special fund in the Treasury and subsequently allocated under a prescribed matching grants formula to all of the States for approved wildlife restoration projects.

There were in the United States in 1963, the latest year of record, 14,122,659 paid hunting license holders. The actual number of hunters is believed to be at least 20 percent greater, because landowners, tenants, and certain others are not required to obtain licenses in some States.

The gross cost to hunters of all licenses, tags, and permits was more than $72 million that year. This brings to $1,123,054,481 the amount that hunters have contributed to essential State wildlife restoration work since recordkeeping began in 1923. In addition, the excise taxes which they have paid willingly on sporting arms and ammunition and whose continuance they have supported from time to time have made still another $255.7 million available for wildlife restoration programs in the past quarter century.

Many sportsmen also buy the $3 migratory bird hunting stamp, the so-called Duck Stamp, issued by the Federal Government, the proceeds of which are used to purchase and develop wetlands necessary for the preservation of ducks, geese, and other migratory birds. This currently amounts to $5 million to $6 million a year, and under the terms of a recent enactment, duck hunters have pledged to repay from future duck stamp sales the $105 million authorized for a 7-year program of speeding wetlands purchases.

I mention these factors, Mr. Chairman, to point out that the hunter-shooter has a prominent role in protecting America's wildlife. Without his contributions there would be no way to buy and develop land for wildlife, to provide law enforcement, and to underwrite research to gain knowledge with which to blunt the effect of urban and industrial expansion that destroys wildlife irrevocably by eliminating its habitat. We must make sure that the rules and regulations that are adopted in an effort to curb crime do not so inconvenience and discourage sportsmen that wildlife restoration programs fail to get necessary financing. That assurance is lacking in S.1592." (CC–pp. 304–305)

The funds raised by the various taxes, licenses, fees, permits, tags, and stamps are not used exclusively for the perpetuation of merely game species, but are used equally as well to protect song birds, insectivorous birds, birds of prey, furbearing animals, and other valuable species. Over many years that money has been used to purchase wildlife refuges, wildlife management areas, waterfowl production areas, and other types of land which are open to all the public for recreational use, regardless of whether or not such use involves hunting during established open seasons. The law enforcement services financed through these hunting fees also protect non-game as well as game species.

It should also be noted that the excise taxes paid on the huge amounts of ammunition expended by competitive target shooters vastly exceeds that which is generated by an equivalent number of hunters. Therefore, non-hunting target shooters contribute significantly to the preservation of the nation's wildlife through tax support of conservation programs. The man who boasts that he has never owned a gun in his life and prefers "hunting game with a camera" may be quite correct in saying that he has never killed any kind of game, but on the other hand neither has he ever contributed anything to prevent their starvation or destruction by the inroads of thoughtless men.

Later, it will be seen how the funds of conservationists and sportsmen were used in a heavy-handed attempt to intimidate the States into compliance with demands of the Federal Government that they enact restrictive gun control legislation undesirable within their respective borders. (See report of the President's Commission on Law Enforcement and Administration of Justice.)

On August 11, 1965, less than a month after the two committees had terminated their hearings on S.1592, the arrest of a young Negro by a Los Angeles patrolman for a speeding violation touched off a series of circumstances which exploded into what has become known as the Watts riot of 1965. There was widespread window smashing, looting of stores, and firebombing. When the National Guardsmen eventually arrived, they, together with police, reportedly made heavy use of firearms in an attempt to bring the rioters under control. Reports of "sniper fire" were also received during the turmoil.

When the riot was concluded several days later, it was found that 34 persons had been killed, hundreds injured, and over 4,000 arrested. Total property damages were estimated at approximately $35,000,000. Watts was only the first of several major riots that played a role in the developing controversy over gun control.

Commenting on the Watts riot, one TV show moderator observed that Los Angeles citizens rushed to their neighborhood sporting goods stores in a record wave of gun buying, and in a filmed interview Senator Dodd included these comments:

"I say this is a vicious circle, because many of these guns were bought by frightened people. What were they frightened of? They were frightened of other people who had guns, who stole them, or got them from mail-order houses, or some improper way. And the thing goes round and round. The person who shouldn't have a gun gets one, so the man who's responsible and doesn't have a gun thinks he has to go out and get one." (ABC-TV Oct. 9, 1965)

If one were to take Senator Dodd's words literally, then one would conclude that the people who bought a gun during the Watts riot were completely unmindful of the prospect of having their homes burned down from Molotov cocktails, the real danger, but instead were concerned only about the far less likely prospect of being shot. There also seemed to be a strong implication that people who did not have guns were somehow more "responsible" than those who happened to have one for some legitimate purpose, such as for hunting, competitive shooting, or home defense.

The first session of the 89th Congress came to an end October 23, 1965, and Senator Dodd's S.1592 had not gotten out of committee.

Exactly one year to the day from its introduction, Senator Dodd finally managed to secure the approval of an amended version of S.1592 by his subcommittee following a vote of 6 to 3 taken on March 22, 1966. In order to accomplish that result it was necessary to amend the bill to remove the absolute ban on the interstate sales of rifles and shotguns, and to provide instead for their controlled sale by reverting to the system of a sworn affidavit plus notice to the highest local police official. The interstate mail-order sale of handguns, however, continued to be prohibited. Furthermore, proposed license fees for firearms dealers was reduced from the proposed $100 per year to $25 for the first year, and $10 annually thereafter. Senator Dodd's subcommittee then filed its full report endorsing the amended version of S.1592 with the Senate Judiciary Committee on May 19, 1966.

On August 1, 1966, a young ex-Marine, who had been suffering from excruciating headaches and who had been under psychiatric care, made his way to the top of the tower on the University of Texas campus in Austin and opened fire with a high powered rifle on passersby down below. Before he himself was shot down by police, he had killed 13 persons and wounded 31 others.

During the subsequent investigation of the background of Charles Whitman, the ghastly fact was reported that, in the weeks immediately prior to the mass slaying, he had repeatedly detailed to his psychiatrist his dreadful fantasy of wanting to shoot people from the University of

Texas tower. It was also later determined through an autopsy that Charles Whitman had been suffering from a previously undetected brain tumor, apparently the cause of his aberrant behavior.

As might have been expected, the Austin slaughter immediately prompted demands that the Congress act at once on Senator Dodd's bill. It did not seem to matter that, up to the very moment he went berserk, Charles Whitman enjoyed an exemplary record without the least blemish that would have constituted a legal impediment to his lawful purchase of any firearm.

The Austin tragedy prompted CBS-Television to dust off their then two-year old program "Murder and the Right to Bear Arms" and re-broadcast it on August 7, 1966, with a special introduction by Mike Wallace which began in this manner:

> "Good afternoon, I'm Mike Wallace. Last Monday on the campus of the University of Texas at Austin, Charles Whitman shot 13 persons to death and wounded 31 others. Earlier, he had killed his wife and mother. It was a day of senseless massacre by a young man in a state of virtual mental collapse.
>
> Whitman had climbed to the University of Texas Tower with an arsenal consisting of 2 rifles, a sawed-off shotgun, a high-powered revolver, a semi-automatic pistol, and a great deal of ammunition. No one has seriously suggested that Whitman's act could have been averted had his guns been registered, but the massacre immediately spurred fresh debate over the question of weapons controls.
>
> The morning after the tragedy, President Johnson urgently called upon the Congress to bring the long delayed debate over gun control legislation to a climax and a vote. He called for passage of legislation which had been introduced by Senator Thomas Dodd in 1963, but still had not reached the Senate floor. Two years ago, following similar clamor for weapons control after the assassination of President Kennedy, CBS-Reports did a film study of the subject of gun control legislation. It was produced by the late David Lowe and was entitled 'Murder and the Right to Bear Arms' ". (CBS-TV: Aug. 7, 1966)

Then the entire program originally broadcast on June 10, 1964, was repeated, but without commercial breaks. As if it were not sufficient that the program's original distortions of the issues surrounding S. 1975 had been presented two years previously, they were once again paraded and passed off as though there was no significant difference between the mail order affidavit provisions of S. 1975 and the total ban on the interstate sales of handguns under amended S. 1592—to say nothing of all of the many other unresolved issues.

At the conclusion of the rebroadcast of "Murder and the Right to Bear Arms", there was added the following excerpt taken from the message of President Johnson made on the day after the Austin slaying:

"The shocking tragedy of yesterday's events in Austin is heightened because it was so senseless. While senseless, however, what happened is not without a lesson, that we must press urgently for the legislation now pending in Congress to help prevent the wrong persons from obtaining firearms.

The bill would not prevent all such tragedies, but it would help to reduce the unrestricted sale of firearms to those who cannot be trusted in their use or possession. Many lives might be saved as a consequence. The gun control bill has been under consideration in Congress for many months. The time has come for action, before further loss of life that might be prevented by the passage of this bill." (CBS-TV)

In order to relate the reference made by President Johnson to the bill that was "pending in Congress" with the old original S. 1975, Mike Wallace then made the following simplistic assertion:

"The bill President Johnson referred to was essentially the same bill you have heard about during the past hour." (CBS-TV)

While Senator Dodd's amended S. 1592 might have appeared "essentially the same" as the old S. 1975, in the opinion of CBS-Television, it most assuredly was not the same, in the opinion of those millions of sportsmen who knew all of the facts and understood the ramifications which flowed from them.

It should be noted that on July 14, 1966, only two weeks prior to the horrible Whitman massacre in Austin, the nation had been shocked by the savage slaughter of eight student nurses in their Chicago dormitory by a knife wielding murderer. Coming within such proximity of each other, the two mass murders, one committed with a gun and the other with a knife, produced a nationwide sense of frustrated anguish largely expressed in a wave of revulsion against any and all manifestation of violence in general, and against firearms in particular. It was in that unhappy atmosphere that the fate of Senator Dodd's S. 1592 continued to be weighed in the Congress.

On August 16, 1966, gun control legislation was the subject of extensive debate in the Senate. One of a number of senators to arise in opposition to the Dodd bill was Senator Hruska, a member of the subcommittee that had conducted the hearings on it. In carefully measured words Senator Hruska cautioned the senators that although the senseless and shocking tragedy in Austin was abhorrent to all of them, they nevertheless had the duty to act with care and deliberation rather than under the stress of emotion. It was on that same occasion that Senator Hruska announced he was drafting a substitute bill which would return to the principles which had been contained in Senator Dodd's earlier measures.

Senator Hruska's bill was eventually filed and even came officially before the full Senate on October 19, 1966, bearing the number S.3767. However, because the Senate was near adjournment, the bill could not be brought up in the few remaining hours and, like Senator Dodd's S. 1592, it died with the conclusion of the 89th Congress.

The year was not yet over when once again newspaper headlines reported still another multiple murder occurring on November 13, 1966, in Mesa, Arizona. Four women and a little girl were shot to death by a youth using a .22-caliber pistol. It was reported he had been planning a mass murder for three months, ever since the Chicago nurses had been knifed to death, saying, "I just wanted to get myself a name. I wanted to be known."

The succession of the three heinous wholesale slayings, and the resultant mood into which they had plunged the country, produced a vague sense of anxiety and apprehension among many firearms owners in anticipation of what they believed would be new and repressive gun control proposals introduced into the next Congress. They had good reason for their uneasiness. The anti-gun forces were even then readying their arsenal of stratagems, tactics, ploys and propaganda. One primary target was the National Rifle Association.

It is appropriate at this point to preview an admonition that was delivered by Congressman John Dingell on April 5, 1967, before the House Judiciary Subcommittee No. 5, which was holding hearings on gun control measures at that time:

"I have always believed as the Bible says that by their deeds you shall know them and there are a large number of people who are actively sponsoring this legislation in the other body and in the executive department who have made a 'cause' out of this kind of legislation. They have been agitating and pushing and stirring up trouble on this subject for as long as I have been in Congress and I can point out that there are a lot of bureaucrats downtown in the Treasury Department and some in the Attorney General's office that have been circulating drafts of legislation even more oppressive than the outrage before this committee. I say that these people constitute a group of willful men bent upon the disarmament of the American people, inconvenience of the law-abiding citizen, the destruction of a prosperous industry, and determined in every way that they can to limit or eliminate the acquisition of firearms for legitimate purposes by law-abiding citizens." (FF–pp. 470–471)

Strong words? Perhaps. But true.

14

"Ye shall know them by their fruits."

MATTHEW 7:16

WHEN THE 90TH CONGRESS CONVENED IN JANUARY, 1967, Senator Dodd's newest gun control bill was ready and waiting, bearing the easy-to-remember number, S.1. Shortly thereafter, the Administration had Senator Dodd introduce an amendment to his S.1, referred to as Amendment 90.

A barrage of sensational magazine articles and newspaper editorials greeted the new Congress. It was an incredible feat of publicity coordination by the advocates of anti-gun legislation. Among the national publications which expressed various views on the need for some kind of immediate gun control legislation were: *McCall's*; *Life*; *Coronet*; *Harper's*; *Ebony*; *New York Times Sunday Magazine*; *Together* (Methodist); *Presbyterian Life*; *The National Police Gazette*; *Medical*

Economic; *Reader's Digest*, and *Good Housekeeping*. An examination of the contents of the latter will prove informative and provide a degree of insight into the emotionalism saturating the country at the time.

The January 1967 issue of *Good Housekeeping* magazine carried a four-page article by Adlai E. Stevenson III entitled "Let's Muffle The Sounds Of Guns". Citing as an example of why he was particularly sensitive to the "menace of guns", Adlai Stevenson began the article by relating a tragic incident which had occurred in the life of his father who had been both Governor of the State of Illinois and the U.S. Ambassador to the United Nations.

The incident which was described took place just after Christmas 1912, at a children's party in the Stevenson home in Bloomington, Illinois. One of the older boys at the party happened to have been a cadet at a military academy. He performed the manual of arms with the aid of an old .22 caliber rifle which had been kept in the attic. In Adlai Stevenson's words:

> "The cadet carefully examined the barrel and the magazine of the gun to make sure they were empty. When he was satisfied, he performed for the group, marching up and down and demonstrating the manual of arms. When he finished, he gave the gun to my father to return.
>
> As any other 12-year-old boy would, my father tried imitating the maneuvers he had just seen demonstrated. Suddenly there was a shot and one of his cousins, Ruth Merwin, fell dead. The gun had gone off in his hands and a bullet had entered her forehead."

Continuing, Adlai Stevenson described still another family incident involving a tragedy with a firearm:

> "It was not this incident alone that has made me, his son, particularly sensitive to the menace of guns. Another accident shadowed the life of my grandfather, Lewis G. Stevenson. When he was a teenager, a gun freakishly backfired while he was hunting. The blast caught him in the shoulder, and he developed tuberculosis of the bone. To the end of his life he never fully recovered; his shoulder remained stiff."

The next several pages told readers of many additional examples of accidents and misuses of firearms by the mentally ill, the retarded, the criminal, the narcotic addict, and the immature. He then went on to describe the failure of the Illinois General Assembly of which he was a member at the time, to enact a gun registration bill which he had sponsored in 1965.

One may reasonably wonder how gun registration would have prevented either of the two sad accidents which marred the lives of the Stevenson family. Obviously, gun registration was totally irrelevant.

Further evidence of rampant emotionalism and extremism lies in 77 consecutive editorials in the *Washington Post* pushing in favor of Dodd's measures. (*Congressional Record,* July 18, 1968, Wm. G. Bray.) When can one remember having seen even as many as seven consecutive editorials on one given subject, much less 77 editorials?

In addition to the spate of articles and editorials published concurrently with the introduction of Senator Dodd's new bill, S.1, there was also the release just weeks later, in February, 1967, of the long awaited report *The Challenge of Crime in a Free Society* by the President's Commission on Law Enforcement and Administration of Justice.

The ultimate outrage of that report was contained in its official recommendations with respect to gun control law:

> "*The Commission recommends*: Each State should require the registration of all handguns, rifles, and shotguns. If, after 5 years, some States still have not enacted such laws, Congress should pass a Federal firearms registration act applicable to those States." (p. 243)

Gun registration was the one kind of control in particular which for years had been strenuously resisted by sportsmen's groups knowing very well that registration could serve no purpose except to facilitate total gun confiscation in this country during some future period of national hysteria. That fear of gun registration by firearms owners undoubtedly was the reason for the following statement of reassurance by Attorney General Katzenbach to the members of the House Committee on Ways and Means during their hearings on Senator Dodd's S. 1592:

> "This legislation will not force sportsmen to register their guns, and it will not prevent them from carrying their guns." (DD–p. 72)

Ten days later Katzenbach became Chairman of the President's Commission on Law Enforcement and Administration of Justice whose final report contained the recommendation to require total gun registration in America! This subject is mentioned here, not for the purpose of discussing gun registration now, but rather to cast light on the credibility of the Government's position.

Another noteworthy event occurred in February 1967. The formation of an anti-gun lobby to be headquartered in Washington, D. C., was announced. Its avowed purpose was to campaign for continuously more restrictive gun legislation. A brief excerpt from a news article described it in this fashion:

"A lobby to champion gun control legislation at federal, state and local levels has been established. Its first task may be lining up suppor for President Johnson's proposal to restrain the sale of firearms.

Illinois Treasurer Adlai E. Stevenson III and New York Mayor John V. Lindsay have been elected to the board of directors of the new group. It is known as the National Council for a Responsible Firearms Policy and is headed by James V. Bennett, former director of the U.S. Bureau of Prisons. J. Elliott Corbett, a former Chicagoan who is an official with the Methodist Board of Social Concern, was credited with a major role in organizing the group." (*Chicago Daily News*: Feb. 25, 1967)

The article went on to tell how President Johnson had received 50,000 letters against Senator Dodd's S.1592 during 1965, and less than 20 letters in favor of it. Then, in typical fashion, the article offered its readers, as the only reason for the opposition to S.1592, the following explanation:

"John Coggins an Internal Revenue Service attorney, was asked about the NRA's contention that gun control laws are unconstitutional because they infringe on the right to bear arms. 'That's part of the propaganda against firearms legislation,' he said. 'There's no merit to it whatsoever. Courts have held . . . that it protects a state militia and not private gun-bearers.'" (op. cit.)

It was exactly that type of simplistic and misleading information which was continuously fed to the public through virtually all of the major channels of communication. After thoroughly saturating the country with such "facts", the media then had the audacity to point to public opinion polls as demonstrating what the "enlightened" public thought with respect to the gun control issue.

Another interesting gentleman was on the scene. Carl Bakal, who authored a provocative book in 1966 sarcastically titled *The Right to Bear Arms*, and who also assisted in the organization of the National Council for a Responsible Firearms Policy. Both Carl Bakal and his book are interesting because his book was so very frequently and widely quoted by top level Government officials, as well as segments of the news media, much as though it were revealed gospel. The publisher of the soft cover edition of Carl Bakal's book described it in a sales brochure as being the book which was quoted daily by the major

213

radio and television networks; quoted daily in the *Congressional Record*; quoted by *Time, Reader's Digest, Life, Coronet* and almost every major magazine in the country; quoted by the U.S. Attorney General Ramsey Clark, Mayor John Lindsay, Governor Nelson Rockefeller, Senator Thomas Dodd and other legislators; and the only book which spelled out the dangers of the gun lobbies. Suffice it to say, the publisher was obviously correct in the assertion that the book was very widely quoted.

The paperback edition of Carl Bakal's book even carried the imprint of approval from Senator Dodd in the form of an official letter stating that his committee had "worked closely" with the author for years and that Carl Bakal's "well-balanced and outstanding . . . encyclopedia of information . . . was widely quoted by witnesses before our recent hearings on firearms legislation."

The very first page of his book began with this very impressive statistical representation:

> "A strange and peculiarly American plague has long swept our land—a plague of guns. Every year, firearms claim more and more lives in this country. Since the turn of the century, this plague has brought death to the astonishing total of more than 750,000 Americans—men, women and children—a figure based on official, though incomplete, government records." (p. 1)

Carl Bakal quoted that same figure when he testified for enactment of Senator Dodd's S.1 before the House Judiciary Subcommittee, but he was not allowed to escape without Congressman Thomas Railsback making this incisive observation:

> "Are you aware that J. Edgar Hoover in a letter to Gun Week dated November 1, 1966, said that his Bureau does not have any reliable figures or estimates on the total number of Americans killed by firearms since 1900?" (FF–p. 739)

Naturally, the Federal Bureau of Investigation did not have such figures, and neither did any other governmental agency. It should interest the reader to learn that homicide statistics were not kept at all in the United States prior to 1910, and that those which were accumulated after that date were done on a spotty and very incomplete basis for a great many years.

After more prodding by Congressman Railsback, Carl Bakal finally made the following admission:

214

"As the Government facilities increased, they included more and more of the population, but I believe it was not until 1930 or so, that statistics were gathered from the entire population." (FF–p. 739)

An insight into the reliability of whatever figures were used in projecting that astronomical total can be obtained by comparing the number of homicides which were listed by Carl Bakal for the year 1933 with the number of homicides reported by the U.S. Attorney General of that period, Homer Cummings. Carl Bakal's figure was 7,863 murders by firearms alone in 1933, (*The Right to Bear Arms*, Carl Bakal, p. 354) compared with 3,514 murders in total that were cited by Homer Cummings for that same year! (Homer Cummings quoted, *Chicago Herald and Examiner*, April 22, 1934) Further, Homer Cummings cited that figure during the course of his deliberate effort to build up the impressive figure of 533,796 "armed criminals" so as to shock the country and the Congress into enacting gun registration which would have included ordinary pistols and revolvers.

Being a careful researcher, as one might assume he was, Carl Bakal might very well have been familiar with the technique employed by Homer Cummings to produce shocking and astounding statistics. He even referred to the incident in the following paragraph taken from his book, without benefit of the statistical derivation, of course:

"At a hearing before the House Ways and Means Committee in April 1934, the Attorney General pointed out the need for the proposed legislation: 'All of these bills . . . are predicated upon the proposition that there has developed in this country a situation which is far beyond the power of control of merely local authorities.' He took occasion to reaffirm a statement which had previously astounded the country. He declared there were at least 500,000 lawless persons 'who are carrying about with them, or have available at hand, weapons of the most deadly character.' " (*The Right to Bear Arms*, pp. 169–170)

It is small wonder that the U.S. Attorney General's remarks "astounded the country". They were an absolute fraud contrived for the express purpose of shocking the country and motivating the Congress into enacting gun registration laws.

Let's proceed with a further examination of the book by Carl Bakal which was characterized by Senator Dodd as being "well-balanced and outstanding". Those male readers who own a firearm might choose to engage in a bit of personal introspection to ascertain whether the following characterizations fit their particular personality. It is, after

215

all, how they are regarded by many of those persons among the anti-gun crowd.

Bakal related the following conversation he had with a psychiatrist:

"I asked a psychiatrist friend, Dr. Alfred J. Siegman, to expand on the thesis which sees guns as sex symbols. 'Is such symbolism attached to the gun because of its size and shape?' I asked. 'Well, not only for that reason,' he said. 'It pierces, it penetrates, it discharges, much like the penis.' " (op. cit. p. 88)

Continuing with his explanation, the psychiatrist responded to more of Carl Bakal's questions and made this observation on masculinity:

"The idea of being masculine is perceived as involving the use of penetrating, aggressive, hurting things. And there may be people who, because of the need for particular reassurance about their masculinity, resolve their problems by means of guns." (op. cit. p. 88)

In 1965, during the hearings on his S. 1592, Senator Dodd remarked:

"Before I ask a question I want to say to you for the record that I am not against guns. I own some myself." (CC–p. 61)

Carl Bakal's book came out in late 1966, and during the mid-1967 hearings on S. 1 Senator Dodd did this sudden about face:

"I never saw any sense to guns anyway, and I do not go backward by saying so." (GG–p. 140)

One cannot help wondering whether or not the speculations of Carl Bakal's psychiatrist friend cooled off certain people's enthusiasm for proclaiming their interest in guns.

Continuing in his "well-balanced and outstanding" book, Bakal quoted still another doctor on the possible association between hunters and homosexuality:

"In a letter to me, Dr. Stickney said he has noted a 'shy, inarticulate aestheticism' in many hunters. He has also been impressed by the sadistic love many hunters have for the animal victim as well as the totemic and 'latently homosexual quality' of, say, big Southern deer hunts. In his manuscript for the book, Dr. Stickney also wonders if there is something homosexual about a hunt." (op. cit. p. 90.)

216

Incidentally, the theory of sexual symbolism of guns has been explored with several psychologists and psychiatrists who themselves own and use firearms. The symbolism seems agreed upon, but the interpretation differs. The view was expressed that guns may indeed be symbols of the male organ to some people, but that those males expressing the greatest fear and revulsion over them may be manifesting either a repressed fear over their personal sexual inadequacies, or simply rejecting their own masculinity and thereby disclosing a tendency towards latent homosexuality.

When one prominent public figure, conspicuously in the forefront of the anti-gun movement, pompously proclaimed that pistols were sexual symbols, and then, in almost the same breath, disparagingly said that they were merely "ugly little weapons" having scant practical utility, one may wonder whether the gentleman had not unwittingly disclosed something rather personal about the way in which he regarded himself. Some psychiatrists so conclude.

This interlude is inserted only because the phallic symbol issue was raised (no pun intended) by the antigun claque. It is best to terminate this nonsense by recalling an incident in the life of Sigmund Freud, the originator of the Freudian concept of phallic symbolism, when on one occasion a colleague reminded him that the cigar upon which he was puffing was a phallic symbol. It was reported that Freud's unappreciative response was:

"Sometimes a cigar is just a cigar."

Bakal suggested that the extinction of the passenger pigeon was helped along by sport shooters and market hunters, when even the rankest amateurs among conservationists acknowledge that the passenger pigeon became extinct as a result of the deforestation of millions of acres of trees which were their natural habitat providing them with refuge, food, and nesting grounds. Contrary to Bakal, it was the hunters who, through their National Wildlife Federation and Wildlife Management Institute, first called the Nation's attention to the wanton despoliation of the fields and streams by the greedy Eastern money interests. It was the millions of hunters and their licenses, permits, tags, stamps, and the excise taxes collected under the Pittman-Robertson Act of 1937 on the guns and ammunition they used that produced over a billion dollars in three decades to establish and maintain the only existing game conservation and management programs in this country.

One might properly ask the anti-gun claque, what monies have they contributed to conservation? What fish have they stocked? What wildlife have they nurtured and preserved? The survival of what species can be credited to their efforts?

In his attempt to link gun ownership with various extremist groups, Bakal made two very thought provoking commentaries:

> "In fact, guns are valued accessories of the ultras, antis, fanatics and assorted crackpots who hold that crack shots are our last defense against Communist enslavement and, accordingly, profess that firearms legislation is part of a vast Communist conspiracy to disarm red-blooded American citizens." (*The Right to Bear Arms*, p. 105)

In order for the reader to understand at least a portion of the basis of the fear among some Americans that gun registration is a part of an all-pervasive Communist conspiracy to disarm this country there will be reprinted here an article which was originally printed in the *New World News*, February, 1946. It has not been established whether the document was authentic or originated in the manner described. Its parallel with contempory events in America is most interesting when one considers that it dates back at least a quarter of a century. Here it is, intact:

"RULES FOR REVOLUTION

On a dark night in May 1919, two lorries rumbled across a bridge and on into the town of Dusseldorf. Among the dozen rowdy, singing 'Tommies' apparently headed for a gay evening were two representatives of the Allied military intelligence. These men had traced a wave of indiscipline, mutiny, and murder among the troops to the local headquarters of a revolutionary organization established in the town.

Pretending to be drunk, they brushed by the sentries and arrested the ring-leaders—a group of 13 men and women seated at a long table.

In the course of the raid the Allied officers emptied the contents of the safe. One of the documents found in it contained a specific outline of 'Rules for Bringing About a Revolution.' It is reprinted here to show the strategy of materialistic revolution, and how personal attitudes and habits of living affect the affairs of nations:

'A. Corrupt the young. Get them away from religion. Get them interested in sex. Make them superficial, destroy their ruggedness.

B. Get control of all means of publicity and thereby:

1. Get people's minds off their government by focusing their attention on athletics, sexy books and plays, and other trivialties.

2. Divide the people into hostile groups by constantly harping on controversial matters of no importance.

3. Destroy the people's faith in their natural leaders by holding these latter up to ridicule, obloquy, and contempt.

4. Always preach true democracy, but seize power as fast and as ruthlessly as possible.

5. By encouraging government extravagance, destroy its credit, produce fear of inflation with rising prices and general discontent.

6. Foment unnecessary strikes in vital industries, encourage civil disorders and foster a lenient and soft attitude on the part of government towards such disorders.

7. By specious arguments cause the breakdown of the old moral virtues: honesty, sobriety, continence, faith in the pledged word, ruggedness.

C. Cause the registration of all firearms on some pretext, with a view to confiscating them and leaving the population helpless.' "
(BB–pp. 85–86)

These "Rules For Revolution" are not reproduced here to endorse them as proof that the movement towards gun registration is Communist inspired, but rather as a means of revealing some of the background necessary to understand why some people do regard them as such. The reader may decide that question upon completion of this book.

The second remark by Bakal appeared in a later part of his "well-balanced and outstanding" book. Still ridiculing the notion that gun control laws were a facet of a giant and all-embracing Communist conspiracy, he remarked:

"Why, in the face of this, the Communists condone the shipment of Russian rifles and revolvers here for purchase by American civilians is a rather puzzling maneuver in this imagined 'conspiracy.' " (*The Right to Bear Arms*, p. 275)

The Russian rifles and revolvers to which Carl Bakal referred were undoubtedly the same ones over which Carl Perian, the Staff Director for Senator Dodd's subcommittee, expressed amusement when in the original 1963 hearings he stated:

"I think one of the humorous comments on this is the fact that tens of thousands of these pistols and revolvers and rifles are being shipped into this country as surplus from Russia and from the Iron Curtain countries." (AA–p. 3382)

Carl Perian was wrong. He apparently made an innocent mistake based upon a perfectly natural assumption, and before the true origin of

219

those weapons had been clarified. That clarification was made twice, however, during the 1965 hearings of Senator Dodd's subcommittee, the year before Carl Bakal's book was published. Here is the first of the two explanations of the origin of the Russian weapons as was presented by Robert N. Margrave, the Director of the Office of Munitions Control for the Department of State:

> "The particular weapon, sir, to which I believe you refer I recall vaguely may well have been manufactured prior to World War II, and in my memory had actually been captured by Finnish Defense Forces in the so-called winter war." (CC–p. 128)

Continuing, Robert Margrave told the subcommittee that it was the policy of the Department of State to ban the importation of Soviet-bloc weapons so that they would not benefit from their sale in the United States.

If that were not a sufficient explanation, then this clarification by Samuel Cummings, President of International Armament Corp., the world largest dealer in surplus weaponry, should establish the cold facts:

> "It has been alleged the United States is being inundated with military surplus weapons from behind the Iron Curtain. The testimony of Mr. Robert N. Margrave, Director of the Office of Munitions Control of the Department of State, would indicate that it is impossible to import any firearms from the East bloc and that most thorough investigations are conducted by the U.S. Embassy's staff abroad to establish the bona fides of each transaction before an import license is granted to the importer.
>
> We find that only two Russian rifles are involved; one the model 1891 Nagant, and the other the Tokarev. Both these weapons were imported from Finland under State Department licenses No. 794 dated February 23, 1960, No. 1040 dated March 4, 1960, and No. 3451 dated October 11, 1961, and were captured by the Finns in their heroic resistance against the Russians in 1939–40. These rifles are clearly marked with the Finnish Army abbreviation 'SA' meaning 'Suomi Armi.' Many, if not all, of the Russian M1891 rifles imported by us were actually made under contract for the Czar in World War I by Remington and Westinghouse, respectively. The Finnish Government has sold these weapons in an effort to obtain cash and thus strengthen their economy which, due to the closeness of the Soviet menace, suffers greatly from a drain caused by military requirements." (CC–p. 715)

In the face of that kind of documentation, which was readily available to Carl Bakal, it is difficult indeed to understand why he persisted in maintaining the fiction that Russia was condoning the shipment of Russian rifles into the United States. There even existed the possibility that a cursory knowledge of Russian history might have familiarized him with the Finnish origin of Russian guns, especially in view of the report that his parents allegedly emigrated before World War I from Kishinev, capital of the then Czarist Russian province of Bessarabia and presently a part of Soviet Russia.

Gun owners of this country have been so frequently ridiculed and berated in the press and TV as anti-communist crackpots they generally cut and run at the first accusation that their possession of guns has something to do with fear of communism or communist inspired riots and civil disorders.

Let the facts, however, stand on their own merit and leave it to any man to feel inwardly or to respond as he will. The fact is that in this country and in many others there are long and sad records of murder, turmoil, arson, riot and rebellion inspired by or fought by communists.

The fact is the Communist Party line has been expressed repeatedly and on the record that members should oppose the open democratic possession of arms in this country, though making careful and cynical provision for their own.

The *New York Times* reported on May 20, 1966, that the Soviet Union "had ordered an intensification of paramilitary training of civilians" and listed rifle marksmanship training for youngsters first among the activities ordered. This was at a time when the same program for American youngsters was under bitter attack here and was later curtailed by action of Secreatry of Defense Robert Strange McNamara after vigorous importuning by Senator Edward Kennedy. Any intelligent man will be concerned that communists can develop and promote a military sport in their homelands and at the same time eliminate it in America.

The National Rifle Association was attacked in *The Worker* June 18, 1967, with malicious and false statements by Communist Party National Chairman Henry Winston and General Secretary Gus Hall.

As far back as World War II communist party functionaries have appeared at hearings in opposition to the right to keep and bear arms. They have seemed to be as much opposed to arms for our police as for our ordinary citizens.

On January 10, 1965, *Komsomolskaya Pravda* vigorously attacked the National Rifle Association for its stance on the right of citizens to training with arms and suggested NRA members were tapping Senator Dodd on the shoulder for having "gone soft on communism". It must have been embarrassing, if not galling, to that old commie-fighter to find his gun control plans for America applauded and supported by *Pravda*.

Lenin said the workers must be armed and the property owners disarmed—that "The oppressed class that does not aspire to learn to handle weapons or be armed only deserves to be treated as a slave class. . . ." Thus a permit system—licensing and registration—is a perfect device to deny arms to certain people and grant them to others.

Serious students of the gun prohibition movement in America are justified in their concern for the ultimate goals of these prohibitionists.

It is clear that the communists seek to deny individual Americans the right to keep and bear arms. It is not clear why so many sincere and presumably intelligent Americans agree with them.

Now that the reader has been introduced to Carl Bakal, the discussion will proceed to the next link in the fascinating chain of circumstances which tied together the world of the anti-gun people. The reader may rest assured, however, that the ideas, opinions, and quaint attitudes of Carl Bakal will be further touched upon somewhat later in this book.

As a matter of fact, Carl Bakal served as a consultant for the one-hour NBC-Television special entitled "Whose Right to Bear Arms?", which was broadcast on March 19, 1967, during the first week of the hearings on Senator Dodd's newest bill, S. 1. (FF–p. 730)

The two opening paragraphs of a lengthy review of the NBC-Television special was published on March 28, 1967, by the *Manchester Union-Leader* which characterized the program in the following manner:

> "The most outrageous hour of political propaganda ever aired on television was the NBC 'news inquiry report' called 'Whose Right to Bear Arms?' which was broadcast Sunday evening, March 19. This unobjective epic was shown 6:30 to 7:30 so as to catch children and little old ladies, too. The title itself arrogantly challenges the validity of the U.S. Constitution, as if the right did not exist for all citizens but those who prove themselves unworthy. The impression aimed for throughout and intended to be left in the minds of viewers: 'Isn't it simply awful that a U.S. citizen may own a firearm? Quick, we must do something like they're done in foreign countries!' "

The program itself opened with these words:

222

"We are a gun loving, gun toting, gun shooting, nation." (NBC-TV)

The next several minutes were punctuated by the activity and sounds of frenetic shooting from a New York Penny Arcade, a Dallas shooting club, a violent segment of a typical late Western movie on television, duck hunters, and a rerun of the killing of Lee Harvey Oswald by Jack Ruby.

The next scene showed a man dressed in military regalia marked with Nazi insignia. On the wall to his rear was a giant red and black flag with the swastika of Nazi Germany. Holding out a rifle, he was heard to shout out:

"There's a race war coming, and you'd better get ready. You better get a gun!" (NBC-TV)

The response from the other men present, similarly attired was:

"Seig Heil! Seig Heil!" (NBC-TV)

Following another round of "Seig Heil!", the program faded off into a commercial to allow the viewer time in which to contemplate what had just been witnessed. The program opened once more with these reassuring words:

"This is an inquiry. Its subject is, are guns too readily available to the wrong people? This program is not about the 30-million hunters, target shooters, and others who use guns legally and properly." (NBC-TV)

Next, the viewer was transported back to August 1, 1966, by way of a film clip showing the University of Texas tower in Austin under heavy seige by police. The air is filled with gun fire, police sirens and ambulance sirens, and still more ricochetting bullets, and more sirens. Then President Johnson's message to the nation was superimposed against the activity and his voice was merged and carefully blended with the background sounds of the Austin tragedy. Then, in an instant, the viewer was whisked to Mesa, Arizona, where the killing of the four women and little girl was described by a police official. Following that, the next tale of horror was set in Detroit where a Rabbi had been shot to death in his synagogue by a mentally disturbed member of his congregation. Then the scene switched to Chicago to the aftermath of the killing of two automobile dealers which took place in the automobile showroom. The moderator then intoned these chilling statistics:

"Think of this fact, 17,000 people will die in the United States this year by gun fire, by murder, accident or suicide, at the hands of criminals, narcotics addicts, children, the mentally ill, the temporarily deranged, the jealous, the enraged. Three times the number of Americans who will die in Viet Nam, 50 a day, two while this program is on the air, two dozen before you leave your house tomorrow morning." (NBC-TV)

The moderator then described how on the preceeding November 22, 1966, NBC-Television filmed religious services in Dallas in the memory of President Kennedy's assassination while simultaneously an NBC hireling went into a sporting goods store just ten blocks away and purchased the same kind of 6.5mm Carcano carbine which Lee Oswald had ordered by mail, plus 10 rounds of ammunition. The NBC-TV camera then followed the man as he walked through the streets of Dallas with progressively more and more of the carbine being allowed to protrude from its wrappings until finally all of the wrappings were removed. The point to all of that was that no one in Dallas paid the slightest attention to the man and his carbine, not even a Dallas police officer directing traffic on a street corner.

The moderator droned on with the theme of the program:

"Guns of all kinds are easily, and usually legally, available in this country to almost anyone who has the money to buy them." (NBC-TV)

Next, after showing how easily pistols could be bought in a Phoenix, Arizona store, the scene switched to New York City where the moderator told of how another NBC stooge had purchased a semi-automatic shoulder arm by only displaying his driver's license. The stooge reported on his purchase in these words:

"For $99.95 I was able to buy this. It's an Eagle .45-caliber carbine. The clip holds 30 rounds. He described it to me as being capable of cutting down a tree by simply shooting across it. He didn't have ammunition for it at the store, but said I could get all I wanted just up the block. At the same counter I was also able to purchase this. It's a German Nazi armband. It cost $9.99. On display in the same counter were various other types of Nazi insignia." (NBC-TV)

The NBC-TV camera did a gradual close-up, to the dramatic roll of drumbeats, as he slowly slipped on the Nazi armband. The scene immediately burst back to the room full of marching Nazis and three choruses of "Seig Heil!; Seig Heil; Seig Heil!" The Nazi attired leader brandished a carbine:

> LEADER: "You're going to need one of these things. You're going to need to know how to use it, and the Communists know it, and that is why they're having a program, a campaign, to take away from you your right, your constitutional right, to keep and bear arms!"
> ANOTHER VOICE: "What do we want?"
> RESPONSE: "We want power; white power; white power!"

Next, a reporter interviewed one of the Nazi-dressed men:

> REPORTER: "What is your policy concerning guns?"
> NAZI MAN: "I advocate that every white man in America today, if he has any brains at all, he's going to get himself a gun. He's going to learn how to use it. He's going to get his wife a gun. He's going to teach his wife how to use it, because they're going to need it." (NBC-TV)

Instantly, the next switch was to an apparent spokesman for the Ku Klux Klan who was heard to say:

> "We in the Klan advocate that everybody in America buy a weapon but keep it in their home, do not carry it around with them. We feel that in due time they're going to need these weapons." (NBC-TV)

The scene next whisked the viewer to the State of New York where police were shown taking a group of men into custody while the moderator described the action:

> "These men belong to an organization called 'The Minutemen.' They were arrested in Queens, New York, on October 21st, 1966. Police said they'd planned to blow up three camps in New Jersey."
> POLICE OFFICIAL: "Going through their homes and secret hiding places, digging up buried weapons and ammunition and recovering a huge arsenal of destructive weaponry of which this is only just a mere sampling. We've actually recovered at this time truckloads and tons of weapons, rifles, eleven .30-caliber machineguns, more are on the way, rocket launchers, bazookas. As far as I know this is the greatest haul of weapons and ammunition and destructive death dealing equipment

that has ever been grabbed in this area in the memory of many long time and veteran police officers."

MODERATOR: "It is not legal to try to overthrow the government with weapons like these, or to blow up people you don't like, but it is perfectly legal to buy these weapons and store them and have them ready for whatever you plan to do." (NBC-TV)

It apparently did not bother the moderator in the least that possession of an unregistered .30-caliber machinegun was a violation of the National Firearms Act of 1934 carrying with it a penalty of up to five years in a Federal penitentiary and/or up to a $2,000 fine. No mention was made either of the Voorhis Act of 1940 which required the registration of every weapon owned by any group whose intent it is to "overthrow the government". No doubt the general public sat transfixed watching their television sets muttering to themselves that what was needed in the country was a gun registration law. With the resumption of the program the moderator then asked the key question, and then proceeded to answer it in the typical fashion:

"Do we need stricter gun control laws? Those who oppose such laws say the Second Amendment to the Constitution guarantees the right of every citizen to bear arms. As a result, its possible in this country for a blind man to buy a gun legally, a narcotics addict, someone who is mentally ill, in most States a minor. You can clip a coupon from a magazine and send away for guns like these." (NBC-TV)

Switching once again to another kind of sport shooting, the viewer is shown hunters preparing their gear and hunting dogs to embark upon a hunt while the moderator clucked over how the hunter's automobile was licensed, how their dogs were licensed, and how they bought a license to hunt, but feared having their guns licensed. The moderator did not mention no one intended to confiscate their automobile or their dogs.

The NBC-News special, "Whose Right to Bear Arms?," contained all of the classic ingredients necessary to brainwash the American public. It employed the most basic propaganda techniques—sensationalism, smear by association, misrepresentations, and a continual appeal to the emotions. The program throughout associated the National Rifle Association with the Nazis, Ku Klux Klan, and Minutemen. Viewers were given the general impression that America was swarming with Nazis, dope addicts, nuts, kooks, and the mentally deranged, all of whom shared the interest of the legitimate sportsman in firearms, and all of whom vigorously opposed Senator Dodd's bill.

Not a single argument was properly presented as to the true reasons

226

for the tremendous national opposition which was responsible for the failure of the Congress to enact Senator Dodd's S. 1592. The moderator, as the reader will recall, dismissed that key issue with a rhetorical question which he both asked and answered:

"Do we need stricter gun control laws? Those who oppose such laws say the Second Amendment to the Constitution guarantees the right of every citizen to bear arms." (NBC-TV)

With such a representation of the position of the legitimate citizen concerning national firearms legislation, there should be little cause to wonder why public animosity was engendered, and why many people began to think of the National Rifle Association as some kind of anachronistic relic of pre-revolutionary America whose members went charging around with a Kentucky rifle in one hand a copy of the Second Amendment clutched in the other. It must not be forgotten that Carl Bakal was a consultant to NBC-News in the preparation of that program.

It was many months later that a most interesting report was published in the form of an expose written in a nationally-syndicated column co-authored by Drew Pearson and Jack Anderson. Their column opened in the following manner:

"Locked in the files of the Senate Junveile Delinquency subcommittee is evidence that the television networks have helped to spread violence in this country. This may well have contributed to the recent wave of assassinations." (*Chicago Daily News*; June 13, 1968)

Gradually warming up and continuing in the same vein, the column further reported:

"Juvenile delinquency committee documents fix the blame squarely on the networks which, in pursuit of higher ratings, have filled the video tubes with sex and violence. Staff studies accuse the networks of putting profits ahead of public responsibility." (op. cit.)

Now, here was the bombshell allegation that the column charged:

"These studies, written more than six years ago, were suppressed, ironically, by the same Sen. Tom Dodd (D-Conn.) who introduced the gun control bill to curb violence. His staff felt violence could be reduced by restraining the TV networks from teaching it to children. But

227

Dodd didn't want to embarrass the powerful networks. He went after guns instead." (op. cit.)

The Pearson and Anderson column went on at length to disclose that in a report dated as far back as January 22, 1962, Staff Director Carl Perian had recommended legislation to compel the networks to practice better broadcasting standards. It was explained that legislation was being drafted to give the Federal Communications Commission increased power to insure that the networks adhered to their own standards of broadcasting. It was also stated that Senator Dodd's subcommittee had subpoenaed documents from the networks proving that they were in a position to and did control program content.

In still another shocking column under the by-line Drew Pearson and Jack Anderson, the following allegation was also made with regard to the relationship between Senator Thomas Dodd and certain of the television networks:

"Again, during his investigation of violence on TV, he accepted personal gifts and campaign contributions from officials of the NBC and Metromedia networks. Both networks were spared the embarassment of hearings." (*Washington Post*: April 13, 1968)

If one were to speculate upon reasons for the enthusiasm displayed by certain persons within the television industry for vigorously supporting Senator Dodd's gun control bills, and for attacking the National Rifle Association simultaneously, then what conclusion springs most readily to mind?

15

"The Bill of Rights—with the judicial gloss it has acquired—plainly is not adequate to protect the individual against the growing bureaucracy. He faces a formidable opponent in government, even when he is endowed with funds and courage. The individual is almost certain to be plowed under, unless he has a well-organized active political group to speak for him. *** But if a powerful sponsor is lacking, individual liberty withers—in spite of glowing opinions and resounding constitutional phrases."

JUSTICE WILLIAM O. DOUGLAS

AS STATED EARLIER, AFTER SENATOR DODD HAD PRE-filed his original S. 1, the Administration presented him with an amendment which substantially modified the provisions of S. 1. He filed it, and the amendment became known as Amendment 90. Generally, Senator Dodd's bill was thereafter frequently referred to as S. 1—Amendment 90. For convenience, however, we will simply refer to either of them as S. 1, or Senator Dodd's bill.

The bill which was discussed, debated, and seriously weighed was S. 1, modified by the Administration's Amendment 90, and not the original S. 1. It will be illuminating briefly to touch upon some of the distinctions between the original S. 1 and the Johnson Administrations's Amendment 90.

"CLYDE, ARE THEY CLOSING IN ON US?"

Miscellaneous cartoons designed to promote emotional anti-N.R.A. sentiment.

BELOW OLYMPUS

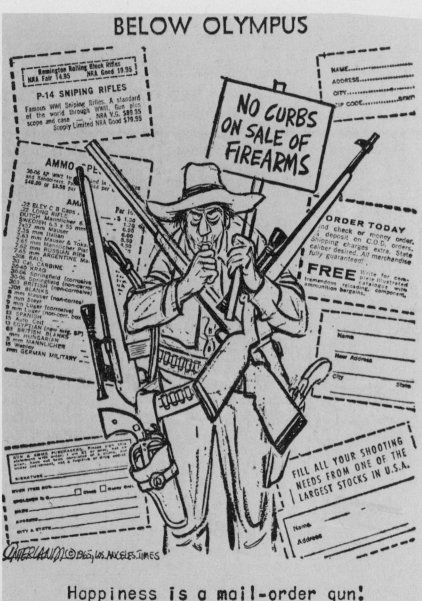

Happiness is a mail-order gun!

Miscellaneous cartoons—*continued.*

Miscellaneous cartoons designed to promote emotional anti-N.R.A. sentiment.

"Both Sides All Ready?"

Miscellaneous cartoons—*continued*.

"WE CAN'T LET ANYTHING SPOIL THE SACRED DEALER-PATIENT RELATIONSHIP."

Miscellaneous cartoons designed to promote emotional anti-N.R.A. sentiment.

"PARDON ME, ARE YOU TWO FELLOWS ACQUAINTED?"

Miscellaneous cartoons—*continued.*

"AIN'T NOBODY HERE BUT JES' US SPORTSMEN."

Miscellaneous cartoons designed to promote emotional anti-N.R.A. sentiment.

"Cease-Fire Over Here? "Are You Nuts?"

Miscellaneous cartoons—*continued*.

"PRAISE THE LAWS AND PASS THE AMMUNITION."

Miscellaneous cartoons designed to promote emotional anti-N.R.A. sentiment.

"SHUCKS, IT WAS JUST ONE MORE
LITTLE KILLING."

Miscellaneous cartoons—*continued.*

'It's like the the gun lobby guys say --laws interfere wit' us sportsmen'

Miscellaneous cartoons designed to promote emotional anti-N.R.A. sentiment.

Senator Dodd's original S. 1 would have permitted the mail order purchase of rifles and shotguns, which were not of war surplus origin, through means of the notarized affidavit system by which notice of the sale, including a duplicate copy of the affidavit, was to be forwarded by registered mail to the highest local police authority in the area of the purchaser's residence. This was the same method which had been incorporated in the final version of old S. 1975, the bill which previously had the support of the National Rifle Association, the sporting and conservation groups and the small arms industry. By having excluded handguns and war surplus rifles from such affidavit mail-order provisions, Senator Dodd had not returned precisely to the terms of the old S. 1975, but it appears significant that he did make an attempt to maintain some kind of a compromise between S. 1975 and the extreme position reflected by the original S. 1592. It is perhaps more significant that the Johnson Administration did not permit that to occur and, instead, thrust forth Amendment No. 90. One might also speculate on the amount of confusion which was caused among people who were unaware that there were, in effect, two different so-called "Dodd" bills.

The general provisions of S. 1, as modified by Amendment No. 90, are set out below, and all subsequent discussion of the measure will proceed on that basis. If Senator Dodd's S. 1—Amendment 90 had been enacted, then it would have produced the following results:

(1) It would have prohibited the interstate mail order sale of all firearms, but would not have prohibited intrastate sales where both the purchaser and firearms dealer were located within the same State.

(2) It would have allowed a purchaser to travel to another State and, in person, buy a rifle or a shotgun, which the firearms dealer could then ship to the home of such out-of-State purchaser.

(3) It would have prohibited the sale or delivery of handguns to anyone who was not a resident of the State in which the firearms dealer's place of business was located.

(4) It would have provided for an increase in firearms dealer license fees from $1 to $25 for the first year and $10 annually for each year thereafter.

(5) It would have prohibited a firearms dealer from selling or delivering a rifle or a shotgun to any person under 18 years of age, and a handgun to any person under 21 years of age.

(6) It would have prohibited firearms dealers from selling or delivering any firearm to any person whom the dealer believed

was prohibited by state or local law from receiving or possessing a firearm.

(7) It would have prohibited the interstate transportation of destructive devices, machineguns, sawed-off shotguns and sawed-off rifles, except as between licensed firearms dealers.

(8) It would have banned the importation of other foreign firearms to those particularly suitable for, or readily adaptable to, sporting purposes.

The above enumeration is merely the briefest sketch of the major provisions of S.1—Amendment 90 and is intended only to provide a frame of reference from which more detailed discussions will come from time to time. It is important to recognize yet another bill at this point, a measure introduced by Senator Hruska.

Senator Hruska's bill, although clearly a product of intelligent contemplation and the best intentions, would come to be disparagingly referred to by the news media as a "weak, watered down, compromise measure". Embodying several of the principles of Senator Dodd's earlier S. 1975, it had its own distinctive features and carried the identifying number of S.1853. It also had the unanimous support of the National Rifle Association and every other major sporting and conservation organization in the United States. For convenience sake, it will hereafter simply be referred to as the Hruska bill, and its specific differences from Senator Dodd's S.1 will be set out later so that the reader will not be overburdened with excessive details at this point. There were also other bills similarly supported by the National Rifle Association, but which were generally ignored by the news media who found it more to their purpose simply to assert to the American public that the NRA was opposed to all firearms control legislation:

Again, there were two hearings on Senator Dodd's bills. One hearing was conducted, as usual, before the Senate Judiciary Subcommittee to Investigate Juvenile Delinquency, and the other before the House Committee on the Judiciary Subcommittee No. 5. For convenience, as was done previously, discussions of pertinent issues herein will disregard the forum in which they originated. The narration to follow will mingle the germane considerations presented to the Congress by interested parties both in support of, and in opposition to, Senator Dodd's S. 1. This will represent a distillation of approximately 2,000 pages of testimony and statements submitted for the official records of the two subcommittees.

The strategy of many of the proponents of S.1 centered around the extravagant crime statistics presented in the book by Carl Bakal, which they claimed reflected an escalating national crime rate, attributed, in part, to the easy availability of mail order guns, coupled with the "inability of States to protect themselves" without the aid of additional Federal legislation. Their justification for the gross intrusion upon the traditional prerogatives of State police power was bolstered by continual reference to several public opinion polls, including one conducted immediately after the mass slayings in Austin, which they claimed to reflect the will of the American public.

Extravagant and sensational references were made to alleged extremist groups, such as the Minutemen, the Ku Klux Klan, the Black Muslims, the Black Panthers, and assorted others falling somewhere within that same general category. It might be noted that the only extremist groups not mentioned were those Communist-oriented.

The several racial riots which occurred during 1967, particularly those in Tampa, Cincinnati, Newark, Plainfield, and Detroit, were grist for their mill and, they argued, showed need for the inclusion of rifles and shotguns in Senator Dodd's S.1. An attempt also was made to establish, as a general principle, that once handguns were no longer readily available, the criminal element would substitute rifles and shotguns. This was part of the effort made to justify the application of legislation to all kinds of firearms, long guns, as well as handguns.

Evidently frustrated to the point of near rage at their previous inability to obtain the acceptance of the principles contained in either S.1592 or the amended S.1592 by a Congress which had not been convinced of its merits and whose millions of constituents would have been severely hindered by its unnecessarily harsh provisions, the gun prohibitionists began an undisguised campaign of vituperation against the National Rifle Association.

All manner of efforts were exerted to intimidate the NRA into a docile compliance with the authoritarian demands of the anti-gun claque, and to undermine and destroy its programs which had so well served the needs of America for many decades.

That campaign should be viewed in light of the thesis of this book, namely, that it is the ultimate goal of certain influential persons within the anti-gun movement in the United States to achieve the elimination of the private possession and ownership of firearms in this country.

That campaign was aided and abetted by innumerable persons who may have had the best of intentions, but who were completely unaware of the movement's ultimate objective, and who were thoroughly convinced that what they were doing had some direct relationship to national crime control.

Opening statements July 10, 1967, by Senator Dodd and Senator Robert F. Kennedy fairly well set forth the position of most proponents of restrictive gun control legislation, namely, that crimes of violence were allegedly increasing, that many such crimes would not have been committed had it not been for the availability of guns, and that the number of violent crimes with guns could be significantly reduced by further restricting the channels through which guns were commercially available. Dodd committee hearings in S.1 had begun.

Those propositions will now be examined starting first with the allegation that crime was rampant and literally increasing minute by minute. Let us cite several gentlemen who could scarcely be considered gun enthusiasts. The first of them is Professor Karl Menninger, whose negative attitude towards guns had been shown by his statements and by his membership in the National Council for a Responsible Firearms Policy. (*Chicago Daily News*, Feb. 25, 1967)

Professor Menninger was the author of a book released in 1968 which was entitled *The Crime of Punishment*, and he was widely quoted by the press on the occasion of its publication. A few examples follow. In a news article captioned "Menninger Disputes Rise In Crime", the following three sentences summarized that contention:

"Dr. Karl Menninger argued Tuesday that there has been no real increase in violent crime in America and said the idea behind the phrase 'law and order' is self-destructive. 'More murders have taken place by far in the past than today,' the psychiatrist said. 'Violent crime has been diminishing all the time.'" (*Chicago Sun-Times*: Oct. 30, 1968)

Dr. Karl Menninger was also quoted as making one additional comment which the reader might note for whatever it may be worth:

"If you are feeding the people's fears you'll always attract attention." (op. cit.)

For the next authority on the rate of crime, reference will be made to several published commentaries by Professor Marvin E. Wolfgang, recent Chairman of the Department of Sociology of the University of Pennsylvania. Wolfgang advocated removal of all guns from private possession. (Wolfgang, *Time* Magazine, July 5, 1968)

On that basis, attention should be given other reported statements by Professor Wolfgang with respect to the alleged increase of national crime. In 1967, *Look* magazine was exploring the question of murder in the United States and quoted Professor Wolfgang as follows:

"Several leading criminologists are reluctant to acknowledge that there is any alarming increase. Dr. Marvin E. Wolfgang of the University of Pennsylvania says: 'I know the public is concerned about the volume of murders, but the murder rate hasn't really changed.' He insists that our burgeoning population, with its large numbers of young people in murder-prone ages, is a major factor."

Essentially that same position also was reflected in a major essay by *Time* magazine on "Violence In America", also published in 1967, which contained this enlightening bit of intelligence:

"Above all, there is evidence to show that—some statistics to the contrary—violent crime in the U.S. is not really growing relative to the population. After massive researches, the President's Crime Commission admits that crime trends cannot be conclusively proven out by available figures. According to FBI reckoning, crimes of violence have risen about 35% so far in the 1960s. But these figures fail to consider two important factors: population growth and changes in crime reporting. Experts believe that part of the apparent increase is caused by the fact that each year the police grow more thorough—and the poor are less reluctant—about reporting crime that previously went unrecorded. Says Sociologist Marvin Wolfgang, president of the American Society of Criminology: 'Contrary to the rise in public fear, crimes of violence are not significantly increasing.' " (*Time*: July 28, 1967)

For the final piece of evidence, one is directed to the explanation offered by Professor Norval Morris, at the time a co-Director of the Center for Studies of Criminal Justice at the University of Chicago. Professor Morris stoutly opposed private ownership of firearms. The following was taken from a book which he co-authored:

"We seek a disarmed populace. We are confident this offends no constitutional sanctity; we do not oppose a militia whose right to bear arms is guaranteed by the Constitution. Disarmament of the rest of us, unless we can show good cause to have a gun, must rest on positive or inclusive licensing." (*The Honest Politicians Guide to Crime Control*, p. 65)

So as not to avoid credit where credit is due, it should be noted those words were taken from *The Honest Politician's Guide to Crime Control* whose other co-author was Gordon Hawkins, also affiliated with the University of Chicago. Professors Morris and Hawkins made the following points.

"What appear to be categorical factual statements are often extremely dubious inferences from unreliable data. Consider, for example, the statement in the Uniform Crime Reports, 1960, that the 'first year of the sixties recorded a new all-time high, with 98 percent more crime than in 1950.' Such a statement is patently liable to mislead any 'general reader' who fails to reflect that there was a substantial increase in the United States population between 1950 and 1960. When the crime rates, i.e., crimes per 100,000 inhabitants, are calculated and adjustments necessary for valid comparison are made, the actual increase was only 22 percent. And this increase was almost entirely confined to property offenses. In relation to population, murder remained unchanged, and in proportion, aggravated assault and robbery decreased." (op. cit. p. 32)

Are these rabid gun prohibitionists saying crime in this country is not increasing? If crime is not their reason for seeking gun prohibition, then what is their real reason?

It was not really necessary to resort to evidence from professional sociologists and criminologists for substantiation of facts concerning the actual rate of crime, for such facts were very well understood by a great many intelligent people as is clearly demonstrated by this portion of the testimony presented by Congressman John Dingell before the House subcommittee:

"According to the most recent FBI figures I could find, the absolute number of homicides with firearms has actually decreased from 1940 to 1963. The rate per 100,000 of population has declined in those years from 3.5 to 2.2. As I pointed out to the gentleman from Ohio, the decline has been not only in terms of absolute numbers of persons but also on a per capita basis. When you consider the increase in population, it becomes very plain this would indicate that there is no great need for legislation of this kind." (FF–p. 463)

Several years ago, Professor Marvin Wolfgang prepared an exhaustive study of various homicides in the City of Philadelphia. That study was eventually published in a volume entitled *Patterns In Criminal Homicide*, and, bearing in mind that Professor Wolfgang apparently had little use for firearms, in fact has manifested a positive aversion to them, one should find especially interesting several statements taken from that work:

"Several students of homicide have tried to show that the high number of, or easy access to, firearms in this country is causally related to our relatively high homicide rate. Such a conclusion cannot be drawn from the Philadelphia data." (*Patterns in Criminal Homicide*—Marvin Wolfgang, p. 81)

Professor Wolfgang continued on that theme and commented about the difference in homicide rates in the United States as compared with various European countries:

"While it may be true both that the homicide rate is lower in Europe and that fewer homicides abroad involve use of firearms, it does not necessarily follow that the relatively high homicide rate in this country is merely due to greater accessibility of such weapons.

Comparison of a general homicide rate with percentage use of firearms is not an adequate comparison. Unless all methods and weapons used in homicide are compared between two areas or communities, the proportionate use of firearms compared in isolation is not convincing evidence of a causal relation between a high homicide rate and the number of shootings. Moreover, comparison of like cultural areas having similar homicide rates but vastly dissimilar proportions of deaths caused by firearms would tend to reject an hypothesis of a causal nexus between the two phenomena." (op. cit. p. 82)

Professor Wolfgang further developed the idea that the kind of weapon employed was only incidental to the intention to commit the assault and only superficially related to causality, and he concluded:

"It is the contention of this observer that few homicides due to shootings could be avoided merely if a firearm were not immediately present, and that the offender would select some other weapon to achieve the same destructive goal." (op. cit. p. 83)

It should be noted that Professor Wolfgang's personal antipathy towards firearms was a product of what he apparently regarded as ethical considerations. If that is correct, then they are in no way inconsistent with his empirical findings. A man's ethical feelings are his own concern, and they ought not be subject to criticism by those who do not happen to share them. Neither should they be the basis of public legislation affecting those who do not happen to share them.

The third premise which was implicit in the testimony of Senator Dodd and Senator Kennedy was that the number of violent crimes committed with the aid of guns could be reduced by restrictive firearms legislation. That exact premise was the subject of a study begun in 1964 and concluded in 1967 by the American Bar Foundation. It had this to say with respect to the causal relationship between guns and crime:

247

"A fundamental assumption of those who support the drive for stricter regulation of firearms is the belief that easily available weapons are a stimulus to crime and that absence of the weapons would significantly reduce criminal activity. This assumption is much debated at conferences of law enforcement officials, in legislative halls, and in the professional journals. In our own inquiry we have discovered no convincing evidence on the question. However, the opinions of knowledgeable people suggest that considerable caution be used in hypothesizing a close causal relation between firearms and the commission of crimes. In the published materials and in our interviews, there is a respectable body of opinion that legal restraints on weapons have little effect on crime and criminals." ("Firearms & Legislative Regulations" Amer. Bar Foundation–p. 3)

In his written statement filed with the House subcommittee, Congressman Ray Roberts demanded evidence to substantiate the naked allegations made by the proponents of Senator Dodd's bill, and he threw down this challenge:

"HAS SUCH A LAW EVER CLEARLY DECREASED THE NUMBER OR THE SEVERITY OF CRIMES INVOLVING FIREARMS? I challenge you to point to clear and convincing proof that the approach taken by this bill works." (FF–p. 727)

Somewhat more restrained, but equally pointed, was the conclusion which had been reached by Senator Bourke B. Hickenlooper who told Senator Dodd's subcommittee:

"In my opinion, S. 1, sponsored by the chairman of this subcommittee, is, in its overall approach, unnecessarily restrictive and burdensome. I have seen nothing since public hearings were initiated on this question in 1963 to support a total ban on the transportation, shipment, or receipt of all firearms by nonfederally licensed individuals in interstate or foreign commerce. If there is evidence to substantiate the direction taken by S. 1, then the record does not reveal it." (GG–pp. 163–164)

Compounding the fact that the Dodd bill proponents were unable to adduce convincing proof for the need of a total ban on interstate sales, there was the embarrassing fact that the Government had made only token efforts, or less, towards the enforcement of the Federal Firearms Act of 1938. That fact was demonstrated both by testimony and by the record, which disclosed that in its thirty years of existence, there had never been a single conviction made under Section 2(c) of the

248

Federal Firearms Act of 1938. (19) Not one conviction! Recall that Section 2(c) read:

> "It shall be unlawful for any licensed manufacturer or dealer to transport or ship any firearm in interstate or foreign commerce to any person other than a licensed manufacturer or dealer in any State the laws of which require that a license be obtained for the purchase of such firearm, unless such license is exhibited to such manufacturer or dealer by the prospective purchaser." (AA–p. 3216)

There had been extensive testimony presented during earlier hearings which tended to establish an indifferent attitude on the part of the Federal prosecuting authorities with respect to violations of both the National Firearms Act of 1934 and the Federal Firearms Act of 1938. Mr. Frank Foote, Section Chief for the Nebraska Game Forestation and Parks Commission, told the members of Senator Dodd's subcommittee of his experience in that regard:

> "We think that, in some cases, duly constituted authorities are not using fully the tools available to them now, the National and Federal Firearms Acts. At this point, with your permission, I might cite some examples of this to bear this out.
>
> In our enforcement work we occasionally apprehend individuals in violation of game laws or in routine checking who are in possession of weapons that are in clear violation of the National or Federal Firearms Act. Such weapons as sawed-off rifles, sawed-off shotguns. As a matter of course, we seize these weapons and turn them over to the proper authorities of the Alcohol and Tobacco Tax Agency. To our knowledge, there has never been a prosecution resulting from these seizures."
>
> * * *
>
> "It has been reported to me by these men, good officers, that they have apprehended individuals in serious violations of the present Firearms Act, men with a record, convicted felons, transporting weapons across State lines—they got the information, the evidence, turned it over to the proper prosecuting authorities. The U.S. Attorney's Office, representatives of Mr. Katzenbach, and formerly Mr. Kennedy, have been before this committee requesting more stringent laws. And yet no action has been taken. This concerns us." (CC–p. 549)

Corroborating evidence from an exceptionally knowledgeable witness was provided to Senator Dodd's subcommittee by John M. Schooley, a lawyer who had been the Manager of Safety for Denver for 25 years and, in more recent years, ex officio Sheriff at the city and county levels. John Schooley had also been a past President of the National Rifle Association of America as well as having been an investigating officer of the Treasury Department for 20 years. He was eminently well qualified to have expressed the following views on the procedure followed in Federal prosecutions under one or the other of the two national acts:

"In those areas where enforcement personnel charged with the enforcement of the Federal Firearms Act are stationed and where they have close working relationships with the local officers, they are alerted by the local officer when an arrest is made that has the apparent color of a Federal violation. When so alerted, the Federal officer investigates and if adequate proof can be obtained that the person arrested is one prohibited from transporting a firearm in interstate commerce and that he did in fact transport a firearm in interstate commerce, a report of these facts is prepared and forwarded to the U.S. attorney having jurisdiction for prosecution. During my 20 years of actual experience with such activity, it was only infrequently that prosecution was a result of such investigation and report. Prosecution would be declined generally on grounds that the defendant received adequate punishment by the State courts, or that it was a minor violation and that the Federal court was not to be turned into a police court by handling such minor matters. I do not think anyone can honestly state that the Federal Firearms Act has been used effectively as a deterrent to the illegal transportation of firearms by persons sought to be prevented from such transportation." (GG–p. 967)

The new U.S. Attorney General, the Honorable Ramsey Clark, was closely questioned by Congressman Byron G. Rogers regarding the number of prosecutions and convictions obtained under the two national acts. Mr. Clark replied there had been "a good many prosecutions each year. We have statistics here for fiscal 1966, which indicates violations of these two acts, National Firearms and Federal Firearms, that 244 cases were filed, 252 terminated, 183 guilty, 117 not guilty."

In the fact of the small number of prosecutions, to say nothing of convictions, during the course of an entire year in a country of over 200,000,000 persons where it had been alleged that crime was running rampant, is it reasonable angry men asked why? Echoing those millions of Americans was Mr. C. R. Gutermuth, Vice President of the Wildlife Management Institute:

"They ask, and rightfully I believe, why they should accept further restrictions and inconveniences when the record shows clearly that the

250

Federal Government has not made the maximum effort to enforce the existing Federal Firearms Act. The potential effectiveness of that Act is virtually unknown. What assurance is there that a new law will be enforced any better?" (GG–p. 622)

Then came the race-oriented riots in several large American cities in mid-1967.

The two attracting the greatest public attention were Newark and Detroit—attention traceable to the hysterical reports by the news media of extensive organized and "deadly sniper" shootings in those cities. Stunned home television viewers watched their screens as excited police and firemen scurried back and forth against a backdrop of the blazing inferno that was engulfing one city block after another while security was provided them by National Guardsmen and federal troops. The sounds of rifles punctuated the night air with intermittent bursts of what sounded like the firing of automatic weapons. Both riots occurred during the hearings on Senator Dodd's S. 1.

Senator Dodd took note of the riots which had just terminated in Newark with these words, which he addressed to his subcommittee:

"The rioting is over in Newark, though possibly not in other towns. So far there is only a minimum count of the toll. As of now 25 are dead and more than 1,500 injured. Beyond the lives, it is impossible to measure the property loss, business loss, and the setback to efforts to solve local problems.

The killing, the maiming, and the rioting could continue in other towns. It was disasterous that legitimate nonviolent, civil protest was exploded into violence by a handful of agitators, many with criminal records, who armed themselves in advance knowing that peaceful protest could be turned into civil riots with a few murderous sniping incidents." (GG–p. 281)

Using the opportunity to stress the role which rifles and shotguns played in the alleged Newark snipings, Senator Dodd later went on to claim:

"I think you will find and certainly we are informed by the authorities in Newark that the long gun was very widely used in the sniping." (GG–p. 813)

In a letter written to Senator Edward M. Kennedy, a member of Senator Dodd's subcommittee, in response to his request for an appraisal of the New Jersey weapons control law following the Newark riot, Arthur J. Sills, Attorney General of New Jersey, included this conclusion:

"Certainly the devastation wreaked upon the City of Newark in recent days is conclusive testimony to the ineffectiveness of our law in preventing the importation of firearms into New Jersey by persons with criminal intent. We know that many of the weapons used by snipers and rioters during these catastrophic days could not have been purchased legally in New Jersey." (GG–p. 995)

Based upon the evaluation of the New Jersey Attorney General, Senator Edward Kennedy stated that the evidence was clear that a Federal law was needed to assist such States as New Jersey:

"As a result of the Newark riot we now have decisive evidence of what the absence of a Federal means to a State where the elected officials have done their best to protect the citizens." (GG–p. 994)

Bear in mind that portion of the previous statement regarding how the "elected officials have done their best to protect the citizens", as that subject will receive further attention before this issue is closed.

It would be an understatement merely to state that the news media exploited the Newark riot to the fullest possible advantage in editorially demanding prompt enactment of Senator Dodd's S. 1. Typical of the many editorials of this period was this blast by the *New York Times*, July 19, 1967:

"If ever a message came through clearly, it was the crack of rifles, shotguns and even automatic weapons in the hands of lawless rioters in Newark. But one circumstance that led to their criminal actions—the possession of these arms—was in most cases perfectly legal.

How many more police officials and innocent bystanders will fall under rifle fire before Congress and the states get the message? How many more self-righteous statements will be issued by the gun lobbyists —completely distorting the meaning of the constitutional right to bear arms—while citizens are shot down like deer in the hunting season?"

It was not even one week from the holocaust in Newark that riots in Detroit erupted and dominated the nation's headlines. Once again the subcommittee heard Senator Dodd's ominous words:

"Last night helicopters equipped with floodlights and manned by uniformed men armed with submachine guns flew over a large city in

252

search of rooftop snipers. This wasn't in Vietnam. This was in Detroit, Mich.

As if we didn't have enough proof of the need for strong Federal firearms controls, for the second time during these hearings a major riot has erupted in which weapons of all kinds have played a major role.

First reports from Detroit, Mich., follow the pattern of last week's riots in Newark and previous riots studied by this subcommittee. Once the original rioting takes hold, the criminal residents in the communities who own firearms begin to take over entire neighborhoods. As in Watts, once the fires of the Molotov cocktails begin, firefighting companies and law enforcement agencies are reduced to helplessness by hidden snipers from rooftops and barricaded apartments. We have been told that in Detroit, firemen attempting to fight the blazes were hindered mainly by snipers.

Sniping was light during the daylight hours on Sunday but as evening came on, it picked up and became heavy. Heavy smoke haze made the targets of the snipers, policemen and firemen, almost invisible." (GG–p. 735)

Another editorial by the *New York Times* August 2, 1967, captioned "Disarm the Snipers" devoted its attention to the sinister new development in the summer rioting, the sniper:

"A sinister development in this summer's riots is the presence of snipers who for days at a time have held off police and National Guardsmen. The snipers, engaging in deadly and deliberate violence, is a much more menacing figure than the reckless teen-ager or the casual looter."

Using its editorial comments about the riots as a point of departure the *New York Times* then went on to urge enactment of the Johnson Administration's Amendment 90 to S. 1 so as to totally ban all interstate mail-order sales of firearms, and, at the same time, it used the opportunity to characterize the moderate Hruska bill as weak, feeble and ineffective against rifles and shotguns:

"These are the deadly weapons that snipers are using."

Among the witnesses testifying before Senator Dodd's subcommittee who attempted to link sniper firearms with mail-order purchases was Senator Joseph D. Tydings. Senator Tydings, himself a member of that subcommittee, reminded the other members of the reports that had been

253

received from the riot areas that the guns taken from rioters had been purchased by mail-order:

"My strong feeling is, Mr. Chairman, that the time for debate is long since over and the need for action is urgent. I don't think that I have to repeat to you the intelligence which has come out of Newark or Detroit, where weapon after weapon after weapon taken from the snipers by the hoodlums rioting, were acquired through mail-order purchase. Governor Hughes of New Jersey spoke publicly and on national television of the tremendous need for this legislation, if we are going to make any dent at all in the easy acquisition of firearms by the hoodlums and snipers involved in these riots." (GG–p. 872)

Once again, the *New York Times* August 27, 1967, ran another article headed "Debate on How to Disarm the Sniper", in which this generalization as to the seriousness of riot sniping appeared:

"Almost every urban riot this summer has witnessed snipers perched in windows and on roof-tops sending a fusilade upon police, firemen and others—with weapons that could be purchased in any sporting goods store merely by putting down the necessary cash."

During the course of the testimony U.S. Attorney General Ramsey Clark was asked specifically by Senator Dodd whether he thought that passage of S. 1 would have helped the officials in Detroit and Newark maintain law and order. The unequivocal response was:

"It will unquestionably, Mr. Chairman. It would not make a vast, immediate difference. But this country has to act to control firearms. If Detroit does not demonstrate that, if Newark does not demonstrate that, then nothing can. Thousands and thousands of rounds of ammunition have been fired, lawlessly. And we should not tolerate it. We ought to move now, we ought to move firmly, we ought to move effectively to bring this under the control of the Government." (GG–p. 929)

In an emotional editorial which appeared in the *Washington Post*, July 28, 1967, the writer explained the methodology attributed to the organized band of snipers:

"In front of us as this is written, for example, is a banner headline which says: 'SNIPERS KEEP DETROIT IN TURMOIL.' And the current issue of *Life* tells of a sniper organization, members of which were moved into Newark from other cities for the express purpose of distracting the attention of the police from looters."

Following the testimony by the U.S. Attorney General, on July 29, 1967, the *New York Times* reported on the possible new strategy being considered by Senator Dodd:

"Because of the large number of weapons used in the recent riots, Mr. Dodd said, he will attempt to add the gun control bill to the antiriot legislation. Senator Edward M. Kennedy, Democrat of Massachusetts, endorsed such a move last week. In the past, the Administration has had trouble getting a strong gun control bill out of committee. Congress has refused to act on the issue, partly because of the strong pressure exerted by the gun lobby."

Putting the final grim and dramatic touches on the subject of riot sniping was Quinn Tamm, Executive Director of the International Association of Chiefs of Police. Quinn Tamm informed Senator Dodd's subcommittee that he represented 6,200 U.S. police executives who comprised the majority of the association's international membership. He characterized the reported sniping incidents for the Senators in the following vivid terms:

"I would like to mention that we of the police have evolved a name for the age in which we are rather precariously living now in America. It is a grim name, but we believe a most appropriate one—the age of snipers.

Until the past few years of social strife in this Nation, sniping was a tactic almost exclusively confined to infantry combat between warring nations. Now this means of inflicting death by Americans upon other Americans has become an appallingly standard tactic of the vicious malcontent, the misguided and the subversive to use against constituted authority to demonstrate their discontent with real and imagined social and economic inequities.

In Detroit, this deadly procedure was refined to the point where snipers were roaming in squads. They were reported as firing upon two police precinct stations, a fire station, and a National Guard Command Center. The final death toll in Detroit has exceeded that of the Watts holocaust." (GG–p. 1053)

On July 29, 1967, President Lyndon B. Johnson issued Executive Order 11365 which established the National Advisory Commission on Civil Disorders and charged it with investigating the origins, causes and contributing factors which had led to the major civil disturbance. One

255

of the major research studies prepared for that commission was a little publicized report by the Stanford Research Institute entitled *Firearms, Violence and Civil Disorders*. The reason it was not widely publicized will be quickly grasped when the following excerpts have been read. After a five-month in-depth study of the role of firearms in urban civil disorders, the report had this to say:

"The findings show that violence by firearms on the part of participants in the disorders of 1967 was substantially exaggerated by the communications media and by public officials. The impact of this exaggeration has already changed the environment with respect to attitudes of many black and white citizens as to the role that firearms may play in future riots and has contributed to the development of a domestic arms race that has not yet fully run its course." (HH–p. 295)

So, the news media stood charged with contributing to—with causing, perhaps—what they pretended to deplore. As to Detroit and Newark the report continued:

"Neither Detroit nor Newark experienced the widespread sniping activity described by the media and public officials. In Newark, where there were more than 1,500 persons apprehended on various charges, seven individuals were arrested under circumstances that led police to consider them snipers." (HH–p. 296)

Commenting on the total number of deaths in the Detroit and Newark riots which were related to snipers, the report stated:

"An analysis of the deaths and injuries in these two cities indicates that the number of casualties that could be attributed to snipers was minimal. Five out of 43 deaths during the Detroit disorder could be attributed to sniper fire. In Newark, two of the 26 deaths could be attributed to sniper fire. In the other cases where the assailant was unknown, testimony before a Grand Jury indicated that public security officers could well have been the source of gunfire." (HH–p. 296)

An interesting insight into how "the elected officials have done their best to protect the citizens" was provided by this shocking revelaon:

"A month before the riot, a Newark Police Department patrolman warned the Mayor of the existence of an 'armed camp' of potential rioters and complained that shotguns, riot guns, helmets, and tear gas for policemen were either unavailable or in short supply. The Mayor's office ordered a survey of available police equipment. Except for the delivery of 25 shotguns one week before the riot, no steps were taken by the Newark Police Department to order special equipment or to train a tactical force." (HH–p. 309)

A survey of the ammunition expended in New Jersey by troopers accounted for the firing of the following numbers of shots: 1,187 rounds of .30-caliber rifle ammunition; 1,168 rounds of .45-caliber; 350 rounds of .38-caliber pistol ammunition; and, 198 rounds of "00" buckshot, plus 2 rounds of No. 9 birdshot. No tear gas was used at all. (HH–p. 310)

The embarrassing facts continued to pour through the report which described the testimony of the Newark Director of Police as follows:

"Newark Director of Police Dominick A. Spina stated to the Governor's Select Commission on Civil Disorder, State of New Jersey: '. . . a lot of the reports of snipers was due to the—I hate to use the word—trigger-happy Guardsmen, who were firing at noises and firing indiscriminately sometimes . . .' Appearing before the Kerner Commission, the Director said: '. . . down in the Springfield Avenue area it was so bad that, in my opinion, Guardsmen were firing upon police and police were firing back at them . . .'

An Essex County (New Jersey) Grand Jury investigated 25 riot deaths and determined that there were examples of excessive use of firearms by local and state police and National Guardsmen. The Governor's Select Commission found that: 'The amount of ammunition expended by police forces was out of all proportion to the mission assigned to them.' " (HH–p. 311)

Continuing with its assessment of the Newark and Detroit disorders, the report contained sharply critical words for the news media:

"Confusion, inexperience, multiple reporting, and excessive firing by law officials explain most of the exaggeration of sniping. However, the media must bear some of the responsibility for the inflated stories of sniping that have prompted many Americans to purchase firearms. In the words of one newspaper editor who appeared at a conference sponsored by the Kerner Commission on the role of the media:
    We used things in our leads and headlines during the riot I wish we could have back now, because they were wrong and they were bad mistakes . . .
    We used the words "sniper kings" and "nests of snipers." We found out when we were able to get our people into those areas

and get them out from under the cars that these sniper kings and these nests of snipers were the constituted authorities shooting at each other, most of them. There was just one confirmed sniper in the entire eight-day riot and he was . . . drunk and he had a pistol and he was firing from a window." (HH–p. 327)

Seven months following the publication of the Stanford Research Institute's study there was published still another independent review of the riot data by the Lemberg Center for the Study of Violence at Brandeis University. Among its findings concerning sniping were the following:

"Initial vs. later reports of sniping showed many discrepancies concerning the amount of sniping. These discrepancies included a downward revision of early sniping figures, particularly where the following items were concerned: the number of snipers involved, the number of shots fired, and the number of policemen involved as targets.

The press—at both the local and national level—was inclined toward imprecise, distorted, inaccurate reporting. In some instances, the press revealed a tendency to needlessly sensationalize the news." (pp. 19–20 *Sniping Incidents—a New Pattern of Violence?* Lemberg Center for the Study of Violence, Brandeis Univ.)

After researching dozens of riots taking place in almost every section of the country and following through on the actual instance where sniping took place in comparison to reports carried by the news media, the report had this to say:

"It is especially significant that in more than one-quarter of our cases in which sniping was originally reported, later indications were that no sniping had actually occurred. Let us turn to specific examples which illustrate our finding." (op. cit. p. 30)

Among the examples which the report went on to enumerate was the following one which was described to the RDC, the Riot Data Clearinghouse:

"A more dramatic illustration is found in the case of East Point, Ga. Although 50 shots were reportedly fired at the time, Acting Chief of Police Hugh Brown informed the RDC that no shots were fired." (op. cit. p. 32)

Next, after an exhaustive survey of the report from many cities,

258

attention was directed to the role of the news media in accounting for the numerous exaggerations and errors:

> "In a few instances, discrepancies between first reports and sober reappraisal can be traced to the policemen themselves. However, most of the discrepancies already cited throughout this report can be attributed to the press—at both the local and national level. In some instances, the early press reports (those appearing at the time of the incident) were so inexplicit as to give the *impression* of a great deal of sniping. In other instances, the early figures given were simply exaggerated." (op. cit. p. 33)

Continuing, the report described the effects achieved on the general public merely by the mental image conveyed through the use of certain headlines and captions:

> "A few individual acts of violence were so enlarged as to convey to the reader a series of 'bloodbaths.' . . . In some cases, an explanation of the circumstances surrounding the injuries was buried in the news story. In other cases, no explanation was given." (op. cit. p. 34)

It was pointed out that the report did not make any attempt to single out particular newspapers for criticism, and it was also observed that in all probability very few newspapers could withstand that kind of critical scrutiny. Summarizing their assessment of the role of the press in distorting the riot reports, it was said:

> "Few of the nationally-known newspapers and magazines attempted to verify sniping reports coming out of the cities; few were willing to undertake independent investigations of their own; and far too many were overly zealous in their reports of a 'trend' based on limited and unconfirmed evidence. Stated very simply: the national press over-reacted." (op. cit. pp. 35–36)

The report characterized as both surprising and reprehensible that the press, particularly at the national level, showed so little initiative with regards to checking their facts and investigating the riots with greater care. The report also ended on somewhat of an ominous note:

> "Unwittingly or not, the press has been constructing a scenario on armed uprisings. The 'story line' of this scenario is not totally removed from reality. There *have* been a few shoot-outs with the police, and a handful may have been planned. But no wave of uprisings and no set

pattern of murderous conflict have developed—at least not yet. Has the press provided the script for future conspiracies?" (op. cit. pps. 36–37)

Although at this point, one can well well realize the kind of impact the mass media had on the gun control controversy; the full story has not yet been told. But, bear with us. The truth will be told.

Ever since the first hearings were held in 1963 on Senator Dodd's original proposal, the one that was made prior to the assassination of President Kennedy, the anti-gun groups had attempted to bolster their meager list of contrived justifications for additional restrictive firearms legislation by constantly harping on the alleged demand for such measures by the American public as evidenced by one or another public opinion poll. Such polls, in addition to being based upon an infinitesimal sampling, were not infrequently conducted immediately following some national tragedy as, for example, the presidential assassination in 1963 or the Austin tower slayings in August 1966. It was to a Gallup Poll taken following the latter incident that James V. Bennett addressed himself when testifying before the House subcommittee urging enactment of S. 1:

"Let me say in conclusion that public attitudes are overwhelming only for firearms control. Increasingly, the public is becoming aware of the dangers involved in easy access to firearms and other weapons, even though it is admitted that there is no way to eliminate all gun deaths by suicide, accidents, or murder. Still, many can be prevented if the gun is not ready at hand. This conclusion is reflected by the Gallup poll reported last September when 68 percent of those polled indicated they favor requiring a permit for the purchase of guns. Fifty-seven percent of the gun owners themselves, I believe, also favor such control." (FF–pp. 494–495)

Besides his penchant for quoting public opinion polls, another characteristic of James V. Bennett's presentation was his usual reference to legislation of a type which was considerably more severe than that to which the attention of the Congress was then directed.

On the Senate side of the Capitol, Senator Tydings had attempted to assure the members of Senator Dodd's subcommittee that the majority of Americans were ready and eager for laws which would require them to register their rifles and pistols, citing as his authority for so audacious an assertion another Gallup Poll as reported in the *Washington Post*:

260

"I think, Mr. Chairman, we have got to have an end to propaganda and a beginning of reason. Most Americans favor gun control. They are waiting our action. A 1967 Gallup poll shows that 75 percent of all Americans favor even stronger gun proposals than any bill before the subcommittee prescribes. The substantial majority even go so far as favoring registration of all rifles and pistols; the ending of mail-order-sales period, and restrictions limiting those who can buy weapons. A 1966 poll indicates that 56 percent of all gun owners actually favor a police permit requirement before a gun purchase. In fact, the majority of gun owners in America demand provisions similar to the strictest laws of any of our States. And yet Congress has not enacted even the mild measure suggested in S. 1." (GG–p. 876)

After listening patiently for some time, Senator Hruska who quite obviously was unimpressed with the quality of the evidence dryly retorted:

"Well, that is fine. One of these days it would be well to put a rider on a bill saying 'now, we shall go by what the Gallup poll says.'" (GG–p. 881)

Knowledgeable people understand that the outcome of any particular poll can be influenced by many factors, including: the size of the sampling, the particular segments of the population which are sampled, the interviewing technique of the pollster, the way in which the questions are phrased, the timing of the polls, the use of "loaded" questions designed to reflect those specific points best serving the interest of the sponsor of the poll (polls have to be paid for), and, most important of all, the level of comprehension of both the issues involved and their various ramifications by those persons sampled.

The value, if any, of an individual opinion depends upon a great deal more than mere intuition or a Pavlovian conditioned response to a particular set of verbal clues provided by a pollster. There are few things of less value than an uninformed opinion. An intelligent opinion, on the other hand, derives its value from the fact that it is a rational conclusion derived from a disciplined body of knowledge which has been formed from an extensive and systematically acquired fund of information concerning a particular subject. It has been said, and quite rightly so, that it is a wise man indeed who understands the implications of his beliefs. It is fatuous to suggest that a public opinion poll reveals anything other than the interests and goals of its sponsor.

The allegations made by the proponents of Senator Dodd's bill as to the nature of the crime problem in the United States, and of the relationship of guns to the causes of that crime, were incorporated into the bill itself by means of a section called the "Findings and Declaration". It was apparent, that although convincing evidence could not be marshaled by those who supported the measure, the evidence of their naked and unsubstantiated assertions within the bill itself would have derived a certain superficial legitimacy if the Congress could have been persuaded to accept them as a prefatory part of the substantive bill. The inclusion within the bill of the so-called "Findings and Declaration" therefore was a matter of great consequence to those who regarded their presence in such a piece of legislation as constituting further grist for the anti-gun mill which would have been used next as the "official" premises for still greater demands for gun registration, licensing, and ultimately, gun confiscation. Easily the most potentially damaging of the findings was the one which made the following unsupported claim:

> "that the ease with which any person can acquire firearms. . . . is a significant factor in the prevalence of lawlessness and violent crime in the United States;" (GG–p. 12)

Among those witnesses expressing concern over the sweeping language which permeated all nine of the major "findings" in addition to the final declaration, was Franklin Orth, who summed it up in these words:

> "This olympian approach is, at the very least, open to question. I should like to inquire how such conclusions can be reached when based only on very limited facts or on no evidence whatever. Mr. Chairman, although these 'findings and declaration' do not affect the substance of the bill, as such, they do, nevertheless, set the 'tone' and justification of the measure so as to affect the scope of its operation and the nature of its intent and interpretation by administrative or judicial action." (FF–p. 621)

Thomas Kimball of the National Wildlife Federation was even more pointed when he commented specifically on the finding that equated firearms availability with violent crime, remarking, as he did, that it constituted far more than just a mere implication that the only solution to crime in America was to make firearms completely inaccessible and unavailable to the public.

Powerful evidence of the fact that firearms were not in themselves considered to be the cause of crime was contained in the annual listing by the Federal Bureau of Investigation in their *Uniform Crime Re-*

ports of those eleven significant "Crime Factors" which did affect the amount and type of crime which occurred in the United States. Although that list had been compiled and published annually for a great many years, it had never included within it as a crime factor the availability of firearms. The list of conditions and factors which did affect crime, in the experience of the FBI, was as follows:

"Density and size of the community population and the metropolitan area of which it is a part.

Composition of the population with reference particularly to age, sex and race.

Economic status and mores of the population.

Relative stability of population, including commuters, seasonal and other transient types.

Climate, including seasonal weather conditions.

Educational, recreational, and religious characteristics.

Effective strength of the police force.

Standards governing appointments to the police force.

Policies of the prosecuting officials and the courts.

Attitude of the public toward law enforcement problems.

The administrative and investigative efficiency of the local law enforcement agency, including the degree of adherence to crime rporting standards."

The FBI crime report also contained an admonition to the reader to exercise caution in attempting to draw conclusions from direct comparisons of crime figures between individual communities without first considering the various factors involved.

The integrity of the FBI, under the administration of J. Edgar Hoover, has been consistently maintained for four decades. One can only speculate as to the great pressures that must have been brought to bear on the FBI in an effort to have firearms availability included as one of the significant factors contributing to crime. It is a testimony to the professional integrity and unimpeachable honesty of the FBI that although Mr. Hoover supported certain gun control measures he never prostituted truth by inclusion of firearms in his formal statement of the conditions and factors which did affect crime.

Lest the reader think that such an apparently simple finding which sought to link the mere possession of firearms with crimes of violence was too weak a basis to support serious fear, consider these words of one nationally syndicated columnist which were spread by newspapers from one end of the country to the other during 1967 when the Congress was weighing Senator Dodd's S.1:

"The mere possession of a gun is, in itself, an urge to kill, not only by design, but by accident, by madness, by fright, by bravado." (Sydney J. Harris, *Chicago Daily News*: April 18, 1967)

It was not merely the millions of sportsmen in the country who were concerned over the ultimate intentions of the proponents of the Dodd bill, but also many knowledgeable, experienced and sophisticated members of Congress who recognized the danger signs implicit within the bill, and which were subtly hinted at by various of its supporters. Senator Peter H. Dominick expressed his alarm to Senator Dodd's subcommittee with these words:

"I was somewhat alarmed by the individual views of Senator Kennedy of Massachusetts filed in the report of the Judiciary Committee in October 1966, stating that he considered the Dodd bill introduced in the last Congress a 'first step' in controlling firearms abuse. And I use that first step in quotes because those are his words.

Some measure of the dissent this bill has caused is amply demonstrated by the point raised earlier before the subcommittee that the legislatures of eight States have adopted resolutions in opposition to it—Alaska, Alabama, Arkansas, Louisiana, Michigan, Montana, Oklahoma, and Texas. If a measure this severe is to be only the first step in new Federal Government regulation of guns, what lies ahead? I would like to make it crystal clear that I, at least, as a junior Senator, will fight to the finish any steps to require a national registration system for firearms." (DD–p. 911)

Also reflecting the views of many other members of Congress was Congressman Robert L. F. Sikes whose carefully chosen words carried this note of warning to the members of Senator Dodd's subcommittee:

"I feel positively that this bill, S. 1, is the entering wedge for universal gun registration in the United States." (GG–p. 979)

Consider also these rhetorical questions posed by Senator Frank Church, who prognosticated as to the future of Federal gun controls once the pattern had become established:

"If Federal control of firearms becomes our chosen method for dealing with big city crime, do we not stand now at the beginning of the course? Once commenced, who here can foretell how far the pursuit will carry us? Will it stop with the enactment of the moderate Hruska bill, limited to mail-order and out-of-State purchase of handguns? Or is this the opening wedge, the first concession to Federal control which will then grow even larger with the passing years? The truth is that, once the process starts, no one here can prophesy, let alone guarantee, what the final price will be." (GG–p. 417)

The same type of exhortation was made before the House sub-committee by Congressman John Dingell who called the attention of the group to the gun registration recommendations which had been released by the President's Commission on Law Enforcement and Administration of Justice during the preceding month:

"The President's Commission on Crime has recommended registration of all firearms, including shotguns, rifles, and pistols, in the country. The Commission also recommended that where States, in 5 years, have not enacted a registration law dealing with such firearms, the Federal Government shall do so.

And, so we see the forces at play here. They include the concerted effort to achieve this legislation as a 'first step' in the words of one of the proponents in the other body. The very ineffectiveness of each step will be an invitation to newer and more repressive actions to further disarm and harass the law-abiding citizen, while the criminal goes on his way, armed, capable of striking at the time, place and in the manner he finds best against his governmentally disarmed victim." (FF–p. 467)

In an attempt to assuage whatever fears concerning the prospect of gun registration that might have been entertained by members of the two Congressional subcommittees, a procession of witnesses who had appeared in support of the enactment of Senator Dodd's S. 1 were careful to utter various kinds of reassurances as to that issue. Among such witnesses was James V. Bennett who told the House subcommittee that:

"The legislation does not require or contemplate Federal registration of firearms. There is nothing in the bill which either directly or indirectly would constitute or require registration of firearms by private citizens." (FF–p. 493)

Similar promises were made by Sheldon Cohen, Commissioner of Internal Revenue, who observed:

"There is no attempt by these proposed measures to in any way license or register firearms at our Federal level." (GG–p. 55)

Even the anti-gun radical Leonard S. Blondes, added his words of pacification. One should also note that Leonard Blondes, in the meantime, had become Vice President of the National Council for a Responsible Firearms Policy, a fact which makes his testimony of particular value and interest:

"I might further state that none of us are, again, antiguns, nor are we interested in restricting the rights of individuals, nor are we trying to combine for any selfish or business reasons." (GG–p. 842)

In a brief discourse with Senator Hruska, he appeared quite agreeable to dismissing gun registration from anyone's thoughts:

"SENATOR HRUSKA. . . . we find the recommendation of the Crime Commission to register guns, and if the States won't make registration laws, the Federal Government, says the Crime Commission, should impose them on these States and they don't like that very much.

MR. BLONDES. I don't blame them. And that's why I say to them, and to us, let's enact S.1, which is reasonable legislation, and forget about registration." (GG–pp. 862–863)

Several other remarks made by Leonard Blondes, although not directly relating to the issues at hand, should prove illuminating. In response to an observation made by Senator Dodd that the State of Maryland had recently enacted one of his gun control bills he said:

"Yes, it was quite a struggle. And you know, Senator, I would like to point out one more thing about the legislation. When we passed the legislation 2 years ago we had to eliminate rifles to be able to successfully pass it. Many times we bargain for things because we feel that it is so important to get part of what is necessary. We went back again to this last session and introduced legislation to include rifles." (GG–p. 849)

Those words should have been neither shocking nor surprising to Senator Dodd, if what Carl Bakal wrote about the original S.1975 was true: In his book, which Senator Dodd himself had praised as being "well-balanced and outstanding", Carl Bakal wrote the following of the first Dodd bill, S.1975:

"For tactical reasons, the bill had been drafted to cover only pistols and revolvers; its sponsors had so hoped to neutralize the opposition of the hunting interests." (p. 193)

266

Even Senator Dodd presented his own assurances, in this case to a representative of the National Grange, which strongly opposed the registration of guns, especially rifles and shotguns. Senator Dodd quieted that concern by saying:

"Mr. Graham, there is nothing in any bill before us that calls for the registration of rifles and shotguns." (GG–p. 832)

Many people were not overly receptive to Senator Dodd's protestations, however, and found it difficult to reconcile several of his apparently divergent positions with respect to firearms. Some recalled his words back in 1965 when ABC-Television raised the same question in their program "Gun Fight". The program moderator explained the feelings of some sportsmen toward the Senator, and then permitted him to respond:

MODERATOR. "The bill is backed by Senator Dodd who is cast as a villain by many shooters. They believe Senator Dodd has no understanding of guns."

SENATOR DODD. "My answer to that is, I've owned guns all my life and I've handled guns all my life. I own guns now. I have shotguns and rifles and handguns. I think I know how to handle a gun! I think I've known how since I was a boy; and I've taught my four sons, I think, how to properly handle a gun, so there's nothing to that legend at all. I'm not anti-gun."

Now, the reader may try to square those remarks with the following dialog which occurred between Senator Hruska and Senator Dodd during the hearings on S.1:

"SENATOR HRUSKA. Some say the ideal situation would be to pass a law abolishing, prohibiting, and destroying all guns.

CHAIRMAN DODD. Well, some people would be for that.

SENATOR HRUSKA. Well, I would not.

CHAIRMAN DODD. I would be for abolishing all guns, all bombs and all destructive weapons of all kinds if they did not have any legitimate use. But what about murders by knife? Nobody ever cut bread with a gun. I never saw any sense to guns anyway, and I do not go backward by saying so. I think maybe it is impractical now, but I hope someday the world comes to the place where they will say just what you suggested—destroy them all." (GG–p. 140)

One can well imagine the degree of trust and confidence that was engendered among firearms owners by Senator Dodd's inconsistencies and apparent vacillation.

The repeated unsuccessful attempts by Senator Hruska to elicit a simple answer from U.S. Attorney General Ramsey Clark concerning his personal position with respect to the President's Crime Commission's recommendations as to gun registration would have been humorous, if the subject were not so serious. Here was the first question, and the response:

> SENATOR HRUSKA. "Let me ask you whether you subscribe to the recommendations of the President's Crime Commission that there be a national Sullivan law if the States of America do not enact into law in their respective legislatures a Sullivan law within 5 years.
>
> ATTORNEY GENERAL CLARK. I do not believe we need to face that question or can really wisely face it at this time. I think we desperately need Federal legislation, such as S.1, Amendment 90. I think it will provide great protection to the public from firearms which cause so much grief and crime." (GG–p. 937)

A few moments later, the question was repeated by Senator Hruska:

> SENATOR HRUSKA. "The President's Commission has said if the States do not enact a Sullivan law within 5 years, there ought to be a law—there ought to be a national Sullivan law. Do you favor that kind of a recommendation?
>
> ATTORNEY GENERAL CLARK. Let me say first that I do not say that there would be no immediate impact because of this legislation. There will be immediate impact." (GG–p. 938)

Several minutes later, after still not having had his question answered directly, Senator Hruska tried a third time to get a straight answer from the U.S. Attorney General:

> SENATOR HRUSKA. "The Commission's recommendation has stirred a lot of people into thinking that this bill which will not have much great impact immediately only is the first step; it is the beginning. There is great opposition to registration of firearms, as you know, and one of the fears that was expressed by many people in the early stages of consideration of this legislation was that there would be registration of firearms.
>
> Well, the day this Presidential Crime Commission published its report, the blueprint was there. Mr. Barr comes here and says this bill, that we considered in the House of Representatives, is to implement

and put into force the substance of the recommendations contained in the President's Crime Commission report.

Do you think Amendment 90 is just the beginning and the start if it enacted into law?

ATTORNEY GENERAL CLARK. We favor S. 1 Amendment No. 90. We then would like effective State action. And that is the best way for the United States, under its Federal system, to meet this problem. I am confident that with a solid Federal base, the States will meet their responsibility to their citizens, and it is premature to look beyond that at this time." (GG–p. 938)

Less than one year later, U.S. Attorney General Ramsey Clark stood before that identical subcommittee and spoke these words:

"Today, I appear to urge passage of President Johnson's proposal for registration and licensing of firearms. They are essential to comprehensive control." (HH–p. 57)

Senator Dodd's S.1 revived other issues. Among them was the old canard regarding destructive devices.

It will be recalled destructive devices were those war surplus military crew-served weapons of foreign origin which were used by the anti-gun claque to sensationalize the hearings of Senator Dodds' subcommittee in order to gain public attention and support for the balance of the legislation which had nothing whatever to do with destructive devices. In short, it was easier to frighten people with pictures of old mortars and bazookas for which live ammunition was not available, than it was to frighten them with rifles and handguns which superficially resembled domestically manufactured firearms.

The capability of destructive devices to produce fear in many people was cleverly played upon by a number of newspapers and magazines in such a manner as to leave the impression that such ordinance was being sold with "live" rockets and shells, and that the only way in which to prevent their importation and sale was through the enactment of Senator Dodd's bill. Also, the manner in which some articles and editorials were written frequently created the false impression that destructive devices were issued under the Civilian Marksmanship Program to members of the National Rifle Association.

Recall that the artificiality of the destructive device issue was exposed by Senator Roman Hruska during the 1965 hearings on S. 1592 when he pointed out that the importation of such heavy military weapons of foreign origin had been subject to complete control of the President of the United States under the terms of the Mutual Security Act of 1954. During these, the 1967 hearings on S.1, Senator Hruska called the attention of Senator Dodd's subcommittee to his earlier argument and then cited as proof of its validity the following fact:

"No license for destructive devices has been granted for at least 2 years and maybe more they are not imported and that was accomplished under the authority of the Mutual Security Act." (GG–p. 91)

In precise corroboration of Senator Hruska's assertion, John W. Sipes, Director of the Office of Munitions Control for the Department of State, made the following remarks at another point in the hearings:

"The regulations require that all imports and exports of arms, ammunition, and implements of war be licensed by the Department's Office of Munitions Control."

* * *

"Additionally, the Department does not license the import of large caliber weapons for resale, on the basis that there is no legitimate market for these types of weapons." (GG–pp. 192–193)

Unswerving in his pursuit of the truth, Senator Hruska used every opportunity to clear the record of all vestiges of erroneous accusations concerning destructive devices and the Civilian Marksmanship Program. He also demolished the myth concerning the vast cost of the ammunition being distributed through the DCM. Consider this pertinent interrogation by Senator Hruska of David E. McGiffert, Under Secretary of the Army:

SENATOR HRUSKA. "Mr. Secretary, could you indicate what kinds of weapons have been distributed under the civilian marksmanship program?

MR. MCGIFFERT. There are two parts to the program in this connection, Senator. The first is the equipment loaned to our clubs. We have about 38,000 weapons on loan to our clubs. The three categories of weapons that make up most of that 38,000 are the .30 caliber M-1 rifle, the .22 caliber Remington rifle, and the .45 caliber pistol.

SENATOR HRUSKA. Have any destructive devices ever been distributed under this program?

MR. MCGIFFERT. None.

SENATOR HRUSKA. Any cannon?

MR. MCGIFFERT. None.

SENATOR HRUSKA. So if anybody referred to distribution of cannon or destructive devices under this program, he would be in error?

MR. MCGIFFERT. That is correct.

SENATOR HRUSKA. Is not a major cost item of the Civilian Marksmanship Program the book value of obsolete ammunition? Is that the way it is set up in your analysis?

MR. MCGIFFERT. Well, ammunition is certainly a major cost.

SENATOR HRUSKA. Let me put it this way: Large quantities of obsolete ammunition are made available to this program. When a cost is attributed to that type ammunition it is put on the basis of original cost; is it not?

MR. MCGIFFERT. That is correct. It is put on the basis of cost.

SENATOR HRUSKA. What would happen to this ammunition if it were not distributed in this fashion?

MR. MCGIFFERT. To the extent it is obsolete it would presumably be destroyed.

SENATOR HRUSKA. Junked. That means dumped to the bottom of the Atlantic or the Pacific Ocean, or some other similar disposition?

MR. MCGIFFERT. That is correct." (GG–pp. 774–775)

It is illuminating here that the great costs said to exist concerning the Civilian Marksmanship Program reflected the new cost of ammunition now old and obsolete which if not used would be dumped into the ocean.

Bear in mind that, in spite of the fact there existed no opposition to the enactment of legislation to further "strengthen controls" over destructive devices, per se, that particular portion of the Dodd legislative package was nevertheless not enacted and merely continued to linger on without any decisive action. That fact was conspicuous and many people began to ask pointed questions concerning it.

The importation of war surplus foreign military small arms was, of course, still very much a part of the controversy swirling around Senator Dodd's S.1. One of the basic techniques employed in an attempt to marshal support for their total import prohibition in the case of handguns, and their discriminatory stringent regulation in the case of rifles, was the continual disparagement of their quality by characterizing them as "cheap unsafe junk" from which Americans must be protected. The superficial appearances of many such firearms lent credibility to those assertions among people unfamiliar with the inherent worth of certain models.

A typical example of the kind of representations which were made with respect to such guns by the proponents of S.1 was contained in the testimony of Sheldon Cohen before Senator Dodd's subcommittee:

"Under the bills as proposed, the surplus military handgun would be prohibited. There is little or no use for these kinds of weapons in normal civilian purposes." (GG–p. 85)

In a more generalized comment, revealing again lack of knowledge of his subject, Sheldon Cohen expressed indignation over the alleged poor quality of surplus military small arms:

"I personally feel very strongly when once we get beyond bazookas we get to the surplus military weapon, really, that is a travesty. People are trying to pass off junk on American citizens that is dangerous to user and potential victim, and it is just unconscionable." (GG–p. 91)

As the Commissioner of the Internal Revenue Service, Sheldon Cohen may have been an expert in revenue matters, but he did not know guns. His personal feelings were not an acceptable substitute for facts.

In order to provide Dodd's subcommittee with the opinions of a genuine expert in the field of mechanical, structural and design features of foreign military rifles, William D. Dickinson was called. Mr. Dickinson was the manager of the H.P. White Laboratory, a very unique testing laboratory which had for many years performed analytical work on firearms for the U.S. Government, for foreign governments, for domestic industry, and the like. In the words of William Dickinson:

"Mr. Chairman, I represent an organization that is uniquely objective. In the first place, the Secretary of the Treasury many years ago designated my laboratory as exempt from the provisions of the National Firearms Act; bill S. 1853 provides for a like exemption. In the second place, we are allied with no particular group, since we perform tests for domestic industry, for foreign industry, for the U.S. Government, for the National Rifle Association, for private citizens, and for a variety of law enforcement agencies. We have also done some work for CBS, and they are at absolutely opposite poles from the National Rifle Association on firearms legislation." (GG–p. 255)

The testimony of William Dickinson was strictly confined to the technical aspects of the questions which had arisen concerning the quality of foreign surplus firearms:

"From the technical standpoint, S.1 and Amendment 90 suffer several deficiencies. For example, both presuppose that surplus foreign military firearms are inferior, per se, and should be subjected to standards that are not applied to domestic firearms, either military or sporting

272

types. This conclusion is not consistent with the experience of the H.P. White Laboratory. Our many tests have shown that surplus foreign military rifles are generally of good design and construction, and usually have safety features not found in many rifles made specifically for sporting uses. There is a good reason for that. A rifle must be subjected to GI's of all sizes and shapes for long periods of very rough use, and they do not have some of the refinements that sporting rifles have, and hence they can be much more regulated." (GG–p. 255)

In order to clarify the nature of some of the tests which had been conducted on foreign military surplus rifles by the H.P. White Laboratory, Senator Hruska requested that specific examples be given:

"SENATOR HRUSKA. Mr. Dickinson, on the first page of your statement you say, 'Our many tests have shown that surplus foreign military rifles are generally of good design and construction.' Could you give us specific examples of tests that you made in that connection?

MR. DICKINSON. We just made one of a Swiss Smith-Reuben, which is a rifle that someone contemplated importing and modifying the chamber. They modified the chamber to fit our ammunition—I mean caliber .30, I believe, which was somewhat smaller than the other, and put an insert in so that it effectively weakened the—they weakened the gun. We fired it with larger and larger propelling charges, and we got to over 90,000 pounds per square inch before anything happened.

Then the primer blew—then the gun blew up. That was the weakest of those three. The other three did not blow up. And that is exactly 100 percent more pressure than the pressure of ammunition for which it is designed.

SENATOR HRUSKA. But it is the type of test you engaged in?

MR. DICKINSON. Yes, yes. And we did another test of a large number of foreign weapons, and by adding proof pressure, which is some 30 or 40 percent higher pressure—then we added proof pressure plus 15 percent. In other words, about 40 or 50 percent higher in a large number, and the rifles held up." (GG–p. 262)

The reader will recall that a very substantial number of foreign military rifles were purchased for the purpose of rebuilding them into sporting rifles chambered for American cartridges in newly manufactured American barrels. One of the foremost precision barrel manufacturers in the country appeared before the House subcommittee to provide background information as to the nature, size and scope of the sizeable domestic industry that had grown up around the conversion and modification of such foreign rifle actions. This was Mr. G. R.

Douglas, President of the G. R. Douglas Company. As an aside, it might be mentioned that the author owns one rifle and one pistol whose exceptional accuracy can be attributed to the quality of the custom barrels produced by that small company, and both firearms were acquired through mail-order purchases.

The following profile of the custom gun industry was outlined by Mr. Douglas:

"Gentlemen, I am a small business owner and manager of a West Virginia corporation employing 28 employees. Specifically, we manufacture commercial rifle and pistol barrels, and are currently engaged in performing contracts with the U.S. Government in supplying much needed ammunition test barrels which are used to evaluate the performance of combat ammunition, for small arms. We have been a corporation since 1958, in business since 1948, and our roots go back to 1930."

* * *

"In performing the foregoing, we pay wages of approximately $200,-000 a year; we buy and consume 300,000 pounds or more of high quality alloy steel; we buy $3,600 worth of electricity, and approximately $2,500 of natural gas.

In addition, we buy approximately $100,000 worth of operating supplies, tools, and so forth per year, and last but certainly not least, we pay our share of both State and Federal taxes.

Our personnel are unionized, and among them we have three severely handicapped people who carry their own load, and receive wages fully equal to what an able bodied person could earn doing the same work."

* * *

"Since the beginning we have possibly used as many as 100,000 of these surplus military rifles in converting them to recreational use and currently have on hand a substantial quantity so as to continue our business as before, in helping to build a better sporting rifle utilizing a highly satisfactory basic mechanism, obtained from the surplus imported or domestic military rifle as a starting point." (FF–pp. 593–595)

Not only did the G. R. Douglas sporterize foreign military rifles, but they also manufactured thousands of barrels for numerous gunsmiths and private individuals who preferred to make modifications according to their personal concepts of what should be included in a fine custom-built rifle. Remember, too, that for every rifle, there was a stockmaker, or a dealer in special woods semi-finished and inletted for such rifle actions. There were also hundreds of small specialists in the manufacture of iron and telescopic sights and mountings; of leather slings and the various kinds of sling swivels by which they were attached to the rifles; of leather, canvas, wood, and aluminum carrying cases; of shoulder pads, metal butt plates, grip caps, and hosts of gadgetry that goes with a fine rifle. There were the specialists in barrel bluing and chroming, and those who did fancy engraving in metal surfaces for decorative purposes. All of those, and many others, were dependent to a significant degree on the stimulus provided by the importation of military small arms and the use of mail orders between consumer and artisan or supplier.

The testimony with respect to small arms of foreign origin was summed up by Richard S. Winter, Vice President of the International Armament Corp., the leading importer of such firearms:

"In the last several years of hearings in both Houses on this subject, we have yet to hear hard evidence or logic which justifies taking firearms out of commerce, by means of import embargoes or otherwise, solely on the grounds that they are foreign or that they were made to military specifications and sold as surplus. On the contrary, the evidence of past hearings is clear that imported small arms, military or commercial, are inherently identical to sporting firearms manufactured in the United States, and available at any store under generally applicable regulations. The foreign origin of a firearm, or the fact that it was made to meet stringent military specifications, has nothing to do with a gun's susceptibility to criminal use." (FF–p. 597)

Responding to the general allegations that such guns were not suitable for sporting purposes, Richard Winter made this trenchant observation:

"The fact is that our company alone has sold over a million of such rifles in the United States over a decade. Most of these sales in the last three years have been at prices ranging from $25 to $40. This many Americans would not be likely to spend this much money on junk. Neither would responsible merchandisers such as Sears and Montgomery Ward who make use of their product testing laboratories. The fact is that men who know guns recognize that these weapons have been manufactured to specifications far more stringent than most of the sporting firearms on the market today." (FF–p. 599)

If there had been any lingering doubts among the members of the House subcommittee, they should have been dissipated by the testimony from the representative of the American small arms industry, Mr. J. G. Williams, who presented the joint views of both the National Shooting

Sports Foundation and the Sporting Arms and Ammunition Manufacturers Institute. Altogether, those two industry organizations were composed of 112 companies that not only manufactured guns and ammunition, but various component parts, accessories, shooting clothing, boots, hunting paraphernalia, and books and magazines devoted to outdoor sports and shooting activities. Mr. Williams, speaking for all of those American companies, made their position, with respect to foreign surplus firearms, unequivocal:

> "On the question of imports, I would like to make clear that our member companies do not engage in the business of importing surplus military firearms. As a matter of fact, from a trade standpoint, some industry groups have opposed the importation of military surplus rifles in the past. But with regard to the problem of keeping firearms out of the hands of criminals, we can see no real basis in distinguishing between a surplus military rifle and a newly manufactured rifle of domestic origin." (FF–p. 605)

Congressman Robert Sikes also lashed out at the discrimination against rifles of foreign origin and defended their utility in comparison to their higher priced American counterparts:

> "I must assume that weapons of foreign origin are discriminated against in this bill because it is thought that they are politically vulnerable. The administration's testimony has offered no better reason. Foreign surplus is particularly vulnerable. We are all familiar with the bogey of dumping on the American market. But what about looking at this problem from the standpoint of the American citizen who resents a paternalistic government deciding for him whether he must spend over $100 for a deer rifle made in Connecticut, or $30 for a foreign military rifle which he thinks is good enough for him?" (FF–p. 545)

In addition to military surplus rifles, there were also the various handguns among which were included: .38 caliber Smith & Wesson revolvers; .45 caliber pistols; 9mm Brownings and German Lugers, just to mention a few. Aside from having a military parkerized nonreflective finish, those pistols were identical in all respects to their commercially produced counterparts selling for several times their price. Many people felt that they were willing to sacrifice a highly polished finish for a mechanically sound pistol in view of the significant cost differential. Those handguns sold in the United States between $35 to $55 each.

It should be noted that, in the case of the Smith & Wesson revolvers and the .45 automatic pistols, those handguns had been originally

276

manufactured in the United States, yet their importation would have been banned completely under Senator Dodd's S.1. It was with respect to that discrimination that Congressman Sikes next addressed himself:

"The drafters of this bill had the problem of how to exclude the cheap .22-caliber revolvers which are not surplus. I fear they have taken the easy and deceptive course of using the 'surplus' label to get at the less definable cheap new revolvers about which the city law enforcement agencies have been complaining." (FF–p. 546)

* * *

"The discrimination between identical categories of firearms is too obvious to overlook. The focus on surplus takes the attention away from the difficulty of providing a legislative standard on which to exclude cheap .22-caliber handguns, which are not surplus. Is Congress prepared to legislate against cheapness? This might get at the problem, but it is not appealing to imply that the responsibility of the buyer depends on his pocketbook." (FF–p. 547)

Another area that had still not been resolved from the hearings on S.1592 two years previously was the simple problem faced by gun collectors whose old collector arms frequently had bore diameters of one-half inch or larger, thus placing them automatically in the destructive device category. Also, in spite of the detailed explanations of the problems which would have been caused by the use of 1870 as the cut-off date for antique and obsolete firearms, rather than the more logical 1898 date, Senator Dodd's S.1 still stubbornly retained the original troublesome language.

All of this raised serious questions in the minds of many people as to whether there was a deliberate intent to restrict and impose controls on all persons having an interest in firearms as opposed to those with a criminal relationship.

The attack upon the National Matches at Camp Perry, the Civilian Marksmanship Program, and the National Rifle Association by prominent supporters of Senator Dodd's bill convinced many firearms owners that crime control was not their goal; that instead they sought controls over law-abiding men for some reason not yet out in the open.

Franklin Orth requested the House subcommittee on behalf of the gun collectors to insert language in the bill excluding firearms of a kind which representatives of the Government piously denied intent to affect. Definitions in harmony with stated intent seemed impossible.

"The National Rifle Association with good reason is sensitive to matters ill defined or left undefined. In over 30 years of experience in the field of firearms legislation, the association has found that many unfortunate consequences could have been averted had statutory or regulatory terminology been clear and precise." (FF–p. 624)

Once again, further elaborating on the reason for the request that 1898 be designated as the date of demarcation between obsolete and modern firearms, Leon C. Jackson appeared before the House subcommittee. His testimony was made at the request of approximately eighteen groups of gun collectors numbering in all about 25,000 persons:

"One of the things we object to is the cutoff date of 1870 as it relates to antique or museum-type firearms. I don't know where that came from. It is certainly not the transitional date for any development of firearms or for any particular period.

This thing includes such guns as the Spencer Carbine which was tested by President Lincoln, and I believe that gun is housed in the Smithsonian Institution. But under the 1870 date and the fixed ammunition restriction, that gun would be controlled because you could not ship it in interstate commerce. It is a great historical item.

There are many arms in this period from 1870 forward, for about a quarter of a century, that have no record of criminal use, at least in the last half century, and we feel that these should be excluded.

Now, the collectors have for a long period of time, offered a cutoff date of 1898 and seek to exclude those arms using loose powder and ball, or using fixed ammunition which is no longer manufactured nor readily available in commercial channels. The reason for the 1898 date is twofold; that is, the date used in the Mutual Security Act, that arms being imported into this country, which were manufactured prior to 1898, do not require an import license. The second point is that 1898 is the approximate transition date from black powder to smokeless powder, or the modern powder that is now in use." (FF–p. 700)

Pointing out the absurdity of the 1870 date specified in Senator Dodd's bill, Leon Jackson gave two examples of the kinds of antique guns it would include:

"Some of the things that would be included are rather ridiculous. One of these is a Colt .36 caliber Police Thuer Conversion. This cartridge sells for $60 to $75 and its use in crime is somewhat problematical."

* * *

"Another item of interest would be the Remington 1865, Navy, which is a .50 caliber pistol. There are probably not more than 300 of them in existence, but in addition to being banned from interstate

278

commerce, it would be a destructive device under this bill." (FF–p. 700)

The last pistol referred to was originated in 1865, but because it was continually manufactured beyond the date of 1870 as a popular type of pistol it would have been included in the "modern" category and thus have been banned from interstate commerce among private gun collectors.

As simple as it would have been to modify the language of the offending sections without in the least affecting the substance of S.1, the anti-gun crowd permitted it to carry over for two years from S.1592 as a needlessly festering source of discontent and suspicion among a completely legitimate class of firearms owners, people who never even fired the guns they so carefully preserved as cherished relics of Americana.

One can gain a further insight into the gross insensitivity displayed by certain Government representatives concerning the issues raised by Senator Dodd's S.1 from the response by Joseph W. Barr, Under Secretary for the Department of the Treasury, to a question propounded by Congressman Edward G. Biester during the course of the House subcommittee hearings:

"MR. BIESTER. If that number of sales is a large figure and if most of them are for legitimate purposes, there must be some reason why people obtain these guns by mail order. Do you know what those reasons are?

MR. BARR. No, sir, Mr. Biester, I do not. I counted my guns before I left this morning and I am the proud possessor of three rifles and six shotguns and I have never bought a gun by mail in my life. I cannot understand why you want to buy a gun by mail in the United States, but evidently a lot of people do." (FF–p. 556)

Perhaps Marie Antoinette could not understand why the people did not eat cake when there was no bread! Here were leaders in Government proposing the most drastic control of firearms while not understanding why people would want to purchase firearms by mail-order. Really sad, indeed.

Joseph Barr speculated that perhaps price had something to do with it, or maybe even accessibility to well stocked retail outlets. Then the latter possibility was dismissed as unlikely because he could not personally think of any area so remote as to necessitate the use of mail-order.

One can only wonder where Joseph Barr was during all the previous hearings when there was clear testimony as to why people bought guns by mail-order. Facts and circumstances not in the interest of furthering Government controls were simply dismissed as frivolous, unreasonable or irrelevant. Barr should have informed himself as to earlier testimony at hearings before both the House and the Senate subcommittees. Senator Frank Church had laid a stack of petitions on the table of the Dodd subcommittee and then spoke the following words:

> "Mr. Chairman and members of the committee, the people of Idaho are overwhelmingly opposed to the new Federal gun legislation. The proof is laid out before you, opposing the enactment of new Federal gun laws, signed by nearly 44,000 Idaho residents. In my hand, I hold five letters from Idaho, favoring stronger Federal gun controls, the total number I have received. The ratio of opponents to proponents, as registered with my office, is nearly 10,000 to 1.
>
> If there is a better way to ascertain the opinion of the people of my State on the subject of Federal legislation regulating the purchase of firearms, I do not know of it. These petitions are not the work of any lobbying organization; the signatures bear no correlation with the membership list of the National Rifle Association or any other organized group.
>
> The signatures come from the rank and file of Idaho citizens, from husbands and housewives, from lawyers and loggers, from farmers and bankers and policemen—from the customers who came, last month, into country stores, sporting goods shops, and gas stations throughout Idaho, and found this petition lying on the counter.
>
> They volunteered their signatures in such numbers that we couldn't furnish enough petition forms. The torrent of names pouring back into my office was so great that we had to call a halt; we lacked the physical capacity to process the returns. Even though Idaho is a sparsely populated State, I have no doubt, had we left these petitions in circulation another month, I could have come here armed with a hundred thousand signatures." (GG–pp. 415–416)

Senator Church drove home the point that, even though the ownership of firearms in Idaho was far greater per household than in the eastern United States, Idaho did not have as high a crime rate as did the eastern States:

> "I would emphasize that most Idaho families keep guns. The percentage of our people owning guns is much higher than the national average. But our crime rate is much lower. We have not found it necessary to restrict the purchase of firearms.
>
> Idaho doesn't ask to write the gun laws for California or Illinois.

We ask only to be left the master of our own house. We are against new Federal gun controls because they wrap all States, large and small, in the same blanket." (GG–pp. 420–421)

Paralleling the statement of Senator Church was the one presented by Senator Peter H. Dominick who also addressed Senator Dodd's subcommittee:

"Mr. Chairman, Colorado issued 424,806 firearms hunting licenses in 1966. Of course, there are, in addition to this, many guns held for target, skeet and trap shooting or other wholesome nonhunting purposes which are not included actually in the hunting license figure. Since our population is approximately 2 million people, the heavy concentration of guns is obvious. We are not a crime-free State, but our citizens do not live in perpetual fear of being robbed, yoked, or mugged on the streets. Our State general assembly has not found it necessary to enact tight restrictions on guns. The firearms problems of Colorado, and I emphasize this, simply are not the same as those of New York or Washington, D.C." (GG–p. 910)

The plight of the sparsely settled States was also brought out by James R. Jungroth, President of the North Dakota Wildlife Federation. A practicing lawyer and a former State legislator, James Jungroth concisely expressed his objection to the total ban on the mail order sales of firearms in this manner:

"Sportsmen and collectors in areas remote from metropolitan centers do not have access to large and varied inventories of sports equipment. Many of us cannot afford a trip to Minneapolis or Seattle to buy the particular gun we would like to have. Many of us cannot afford to forego the economy available to us through comparative catalog shopping." (GG–p. 599)

Congressman William H. Harsha further echoed the protests of those less densely populated sections of the country stressing that small dealers simply did not have sufficient stock from which to make selections on the basis of particular needs.

The rejoinder to such arguments and protests from rural areas was generally typified by the kind of statement that was submitted by Leonard S. Blondes:

"Companies such as Sears Roebuck & Co., Montgomery Ward, etc., have thousands of local stores throughout the country and in every

281

state. These outlets carry large stocks of firearms and could undoubtedly satisfy any individual's needs." (GG–p. 844)

Senator Edward Kennedy was also quick to push Sears and Wards as providing the solution to all gun owners problems. As he evidently visualized it, anyone would soon be able to purchase everything from custom-built precision rifles, accurized target pistols, imported Olympic-style Free Pistols, big-game guns, and every one of nearly 100 different brands of firearms in their approximately 5,000 variations of models, calibers and features. That was about as likely a prospect as Senator Kennedy doing his family wardrobe shopping at Sears or Wards, a fact which he ignored. On the other hand, perhaps he believed that, with the cancellation of the National Matches, there would be progressively less demand for required highly specialized firearms. In any event, here was his cavalier assertion:

> "It is self-evident, and I would expect that if these stores, Montgomery Ward and Sears, Roebuck, have these outlets, and this legislation passes, then with the demand which would be built up, I am sure, Montgomery Ward and Sears, Roebuck would necessarily take the appropriate actions to have in their inventory the kinds of weapons for which there is demand." (GG–p. 611)

The subcommittee contacted both Sears and Wards and obtained from them a list of all retail and catalog sales offices from which a customer could order and pick up a firearm. The lists indicated that nationally Sears had a total of 2,276 such outlets, and Wards had 1,366.

But was the answer really that simple? Could Sears and Wards satisfy the needs of all individuals? The answer was that quite obviously they could not. Both of those highly competent and efficient mass merchandisers were oriented towards the 80 percent or so of the mass market, excluding both the low-end and the high-end trade, because it was only by selectively merchandising their stores and catalog pages for the tastes, needs, and financial capabilities of the masses that they were able to maintain the level of sales, turnover, and profits necessary to sustain their enormous operations. There was no room for the needs of the discriminating firearms specialist within the stocks of either of those companies, and their management no doubt would have readily acknowledged that fact, had they been asked. Senator Hruska recognized that fact and commented upon the list of stores that had been placed before Senator Dodd's subcommittee:

282

"Mr. Chairman I would have no objection to putting the list in, but it would not count for much. It would not indicate the type of guns they handle, nor would such a list indicate the number or the extent of the selection from well-known brands that would be in demand. It might lead to the wrong conclusion." (GG–p. 611)

What Senator Hruska probably was referring to was the heavy emphasis placed upon their own private brands by both Sears and Wards, as opposed to the merchandising of so-called famous national brands. There are several very sound reasons for that practice and, in general, they operate to the advantage not only of Sears and Wards, but also to their customers as well.

Part of the basic cost price charged to retail and catalog merchants includes a proportionate share of the cost to the manufacturer of the product for national advertising to familiarize the public with the features and quality of its products. However, when Sears or Wards purchases such items from nationally known manufacturers with the private brand name of Sears or Wards attached, rather than that of the manufacturer, then they normally obtain a special lower cost which is achieved in part by deducting the proportionate expense of the manufacturer's national advertising which neither Sears or Wards require. Thus, Sears and Wards frequently are able to enjoy either one of two competitive advantages. They can sell the item, substantially identical to the nationally known brand of the manufacturer, for significantly less money, or they can order superior features added to the merchandise for the cost difference and thereby sell a better product for the same money. In either case, the consumer benefits very directly through lower prices or superior product features in most private brands of those two very excellent merchandising firms who have so measurably contributed to an improved standard of living in this country.

Smaller independent stores unable to command the volume of purchases necessary to sell private brands are obliged to pay full costs, including the national advertising needed. They must sell the nationally branded items at what are often fair-traded and maintained prices. The tremendous natural advantages enjoyed by the merchandising giants was well understood by many. To propose that they were to reap further profits from business torn away from thousands of small gun distributors and gunsmiths, whose livelihoods depended upon their individualized services, did not sit well with many people, including Senator Hruska who observed:

283

"In fact one of the objections to the bill, as the Senator will recall, that it establishes a monopoly. It is fine for Sears, and for Montgomery Ward. That is fine. They have 49 States in which they have outlets. A lesser mail-order house, or even a man who is in an individual business of mail order does not get that chance. He does not get that chance, and therein lies the danger of monopoly." (GG–p. 612)

One of the amusing incidents which occurred during that portion of the hearings, which dealt with the adequacy of those kinds of firearms available through Sears and Wards, even for general farm use, came in the midst of testimony from Harry L. Graham, Legislative Representative of the National Grange. For those not familiar with the National Grange, suffice it to be said that it was the Nation's oldest farm organization and a highly respected one. Harry Graham made it quite clear that firearms played an indispensable role in rural communiies:

"But for rural areas and for the farmer, with livestock to protect, and property to protect, they are an absolute necessity. And most of the time they are available best of all from the mail order houses." (GG–p. 834)

In commenting on the sufficiency of the variety and types of firearms available through Sears or Wards, Harry Graham remarked in passing:

"In terms of shotguns and rifles, the ordinary mail order house, such as Montgomery Ward and Sears, Spiegel, carries a rather limited line of well-known common caliber common-gauge shotguns that the average person can order, know what he is getting, and he does not have to worry about how it is going to handle or anything." (GG–p. 833)

Harry Graham evidenced some reluctance to speak too critically about whatever shortcomings he felt might have existed in looking to the giant mail-order houses for all shooting needs when he let pass the following remark:

"We certainly could not testify very much against the Sears foundation with good faith, because they have given us a hundred thousand dollars a year for 20 years, for community service contests." (GG–p. 833)

When Senator Dodd persisted in pointing to the long list of Sears and Wards outlets across the country as providing adequate sources for firearms acquisition, Senator Hruska continued to squelch his remarks with the following type of response:

"In the case of Sears or Montgomery Ward. Yet there are many mail-order houses, and it is necessary again to channel this business into the hands of monopolists—I think they would be just tickled pink. But it would keep out of the mail-order business many hundreds of legitimate mail-order houses who are not in every State." (GG–p. 810)

Not content to allow the matter to rest there, Senator Dodd told Senator Hruska that firearms dealers who did not have their own locations established in each of the States could nevertheless sell their products through other dealers who were so situated. Senator Hruska, in reply, pointed out the substantial additional expense entailed by so cumbersome an arrangement, if it could be made to work at all. Senator Dodd's response only revealed his ignorance of the economics involved in adding a middle-man to such transactions:

"I do not have great knowledge about it, I do not pretend to, but I do not think it will necessarily raise the cost." (GG–p. 810)

Senator Dodd seemed to think that commercial establishments rendered services, incurred expenses, and assumed responsibilities without added charge. Some privileged people have no doubt been the recipient of such magnanimity, but they should not confuse its special nature with the pay-as-you-go world of the average hard working tax-payer.

One major facet of the gun control controversy churning in the Congress during 1967 that was rarely mentioned by the news media except disparagingly, was the unanimous support for Senator Hruska's bill, S.1853, by all major shooting organizations, the domestic firearms industry, and the conservation groups. The anti-gun claque was very careful to avoid publicizing the fact that there existed a Hruska bill which was an alternative approach to the repressive Dodd measures, and when unavoidably forced to recognize its presence they did so grudgingly and characterized it as a weak and watered down measure.

Speaking loudly and clearly on behalf of the then 833,000 member National Rifle Association of America, Harold W. Glassen, a distinguished attorney and President of the NRA, told Senator Dodd's subcommittee and Senator Dodd of their support of Senator Hruska's bills:

> "MR. GLASSEN. We are in favor of S.1853 and S.1854. It has our unqualified support. We have stated this openly many times. It appears in our magazine. It has the endorsement of our board of directors.
> CHAIRMAN DODD. I am well aware of that." (GG–p. 546)

In spite of the support of the National Rifle Association for the alternative Hruska bill, the news media, possibly taking their lead from the statements of Senator Edward Kennedy, consistently presented the NRA in a negative light as opposing all Federal legislation. The reader will recall that major article attributed to Senator Kennedy which placed the blame for Congressional inaction in these words:

> "And why hasn't something been done about this carnage? Because the anti-gun bill lobby, led by the National Rifle Association, has opposed responsible federal gun control legislation at every step." (*San Francisco Examiner*: July 30, 1967)

If one were to interpret literally the words "has opposed responsible federal gun control legislation", then it would appear Senator Hruska and all of the numerous Members of Congress who backed his alternative measure were irresponsible, a proposition at once ridiculous and reprehensible.

Once again, consistent as it had always been in the past in its support of well drawn and properly tailored legislation, the position of the National Wildlife Federation was presented by its Executive Director, Thomas L. Kimball:

> "The time has come for action, rather than study and further delay. Two of the bills before you today—S.1853 and S.1854—have finally emerged as the best answer, in our opinion, to the firearms problem in the United States. They deserve the support of every responsible citizen, firearm owner, and dealer." (GG–p. 244)

Statements such as the previous one, made by the spokesman of an organization which included 1,199,048 individuals, who were members of 7,459 local conservation clubs in 49 states, plus some additional 260,000 individual associate members, who were not affiliated with any local clubs, were completely ignored by the press, which continued ruthlessly to misrepresent the position of the NRA and those other independent organizations whose views coincided with its position.

Consider the following simplistic characterization so typical of the anti-gun press during that period:

"The NRA, through no special calculation of its own, has fallen into an extreme position of advocating free trade in guns. This may, and has already begun, to react against the interests of the legitimate hunters and target shooters it is supposed to protect. It simply opposes all gun controls." (*The Ottawa Journal*: June 12, 1968)

One should note the progressively increasing membership size of the National Rifle Association during the period in which it was being most intensively attacked by the news media, a clear reflection of the fact that those people who understood what was happening were more than willing to stand up and cast their lot with that of the National Rifle Association.

The editor of one excellent firearms publication, *Gun Week*, appeared before Senator Dodd's subcommittee and left no doubt as to the support both by that weekly publication and its readers for the Hruska bill. *Gun Week* editor Neal Knox expressed himself in these words:

"I fail to see how the States would receive any greater assistance by the passage of S.1 then they would by the passage of S.1853. I fail to see why it is necessary to prohibit mail-order sales of all guns and prohibit the out-of-State gift or sale of handguns when the same objectives can be met by the reasonable and sensible regulations proposed by Senator Hruska. The stated objective is to assist the States, and I agree with that stated objective. Senator Hruska's bill, S.1853, will do it, and I endorse it, and I have editorially endorsed it since the first issues of Gun Week—and the vast majority of Gun Week readers have agreed with that endorsement." (GG–p. 663)

Making a broad general reference to the anti-gun claque and the members of the mass media who so willingly did their dirty work, Neal Knox continued:

"We have attempted to act responsibly by consistently supporting legislation such as S.1853 and S.1854, which would impose reasonable, effective controls, and we have argued in vain for legislation which would reduce gun crime—swift and severe punishment of those who misuse firearms. Yet we have been slandered and threatened because of our refusal to accept the so-called reasonable regulation of S.1 and Amendment 90. We find these bills to be not regulation but prohibition —and we find prohibition both unreasonable and unnecessary.

287

Every stated objective of assisting the States which is included in S.1 and Amendment 90 will be met by the passage of S.1853 and S.1854. I urge the adoption of these sensible bills." (GG–p. 664)

It should also be noted that the fairness and objectivity of *Gun Week* newspaper, and Neal Knox personally, was confirmed and commended by Carl Perian, Staff Director for Senator Dodd's subcommittee. (GG–p. 665)

The 103 member companies of the National Shooting Sports Foundation also gave their support to the Hruska bill before Senator Dodd's subcommittee through the presentation of its President, Warren Page:

"Realizing that there is a need to consider the legitimate interests of the many millions of law-abiding firearms owners, we approve of the basic philosophy of S.1853, which seeks to regulate specifically, rather than to ban broadly, the interstate shipment of firearms. We believe that when a person is lawfully entitled to purchase a firearm in his own State, he should be able to do so either over the counter in another State or by mail, subject to the controls and regulations established in S.1853." (GG–pp. 798–799)

A Chicago newspaper pointed out that as yet no law had been enacted by Congress, which would have stopped another Lee Harvey Oswald from purchasing a carbine by mail order—as if any law would be an obstacle to international political assassination! That particular paper never seemed adverse to acceptance of advertisements from Sears and Wards for the sale of guns and ammunition during the pre-hunting season, two of the giant companies least likely to have been affected by Senator Dodd's bill.

Franklin Orth called the attention of the Dodd subcommittee to the manner in which the press was so patently misrepresenting the NRA's position on the issues:

"MR. ORTH. The patent unilateral presentation by the press in certain areas of the NRA approach to gun regulation can be simply demonstrated by the first Dodd bill, introduced as S.1975 in the U.S. Senate in August 1963. You know better than anybody, Mr. Chairman, that since the launching of the full inquiry by the Senate Subcommittee on Juvenile Delinquency into the matter of firearms and crime that the NRA for many months had worked closely with the staff of the subcommittee to formulate legislation that would both meet the requirements of the problem and not unduly impinge upon the legitimate interests of firearms owners. S.1975 in its original form and sponsored by you in the 88th Congress was a workable measure to which all legitimate interests, public and private, could be drawn without undue infringement of any area of legitimate concern.

CHAIRMAN DODD. General, I remember that. I remember how helpful you were." (GG–p. 495)

Governor Richard J. Hughes of New Jersey engaged in an interesting colloquy with Senator Hruska revealing typical prejudice and/or misunderstanding:

"SENATOR HRUSKA. Governor, I have the highest respect for you, and a great deal of admiration. But you do put the National Rifle Association into the position, no matter how one looks at it, of supporting of selfish and encouraging of violence with guns. Awfully harsh language; don't you think so?

GOVERNOR HUGHES. It is harsh language. And I use it because I am really upset, Senator, about the way that many people, including sportsmen and decent American citizens, have been hoodwinked by this group into thinking they are not going to be able to buy guns if this kind of law were passed.

SENATOR HRUSKA. You see, there is not only S. 1, and the provisions of that bill, nor the provisions only of the Administration's is Amendment 90. They do not have a monopoly on fair arms control provisions. There are other bills, other approaches, and other ways. It seems that the National Rifle Association and many others have seen fit to opt for other bills than S.1, and Amendment 90. For that you would condemn them?

GOVERNOR HUGHES. Yes. Because that is in their interest. These other bills would not disturb them so much."

* * *

"SENATOR HRUSKA. Now, you spoke of the legislators of other States being buffaloed and being led astray by the position of lobbyists that have a pecuniary interest. Would you consider that Senators like Senator Metcalf or Senator Mansfield, both of whom are for the Hruska bill—have been buffaloed? Are they using bad judgment? Are they benefited by pecuniary interests? Is there position reprehensible?

GOVERNOR HUGHES. No; I do not apply any of those adjectives to those fine men. I think if they are not in favor of this strong legislation, they are wrong. But I think, as I have mentioned in respect of your position, Senator, that it was sincere and honorable. I do not apply these adjectives to them. I apply those adjectives, sir, to the lobbyists who make money out of selling guns indiscriminately to people who are insane and criminal and addicted to narcotics, and who ought to be

289

ashamed of themselves. And they not only ought not to influence Congress, they ought not to be allowed to come near Congress.

SENATOR HRUSKA. Well, of course, we do have a Bill of Rights, and we do have freedom of speech, and we do have freedom of the press. Now, maybe if we are going to say that lobbyists against gun legislation of a certain kind should be denied those rights, then we would be entering a new field of jurisprudence, wouldn't we?

GOVERNOR HUGHES. Yes, we would. Everybody is entitled to talk just so long—

SENATOR HRUSKA. Would you say that Senator Dirksen, Senator Hickenlooper, former Governor Jordan, former Governor Fannin, former Governor Thurmond, are they reprehensible? Have they been buffaloed, have they distorted or been victims of distortion of what S.1853 contains, and what S.1 and Amendment 90 contain?" (GG–pp. 1018–1019)

Later during his testimony Senator Hruska asked Governor Hughes an elementary question in order to test his knowledge of the National Rifle Association which he so freely castigated:

"SENATOR HRUSKA. I am rather intrigued by your reference to a pecuniary interest of the NRA in this matter. Are they a profit or a nonprofit corporation?

GOVERNOR HUGHES. I do not know.

SENATOR HRUSKA. The National Rifle Association, are they a profit corporation or a nonprofit corporation?

GOVERNOR HUGHES. I am sure I do not know, except insofar as—

SENATOR HRUSKA. I will tell you, they are nonprofit, because they do not pay taxes on any of their income." (GG–pp. 1026–1027)

On the House side of the Capitol, Carl Bakal also was berating the National Rifle Association. It will be recalled, Bakal was the author of the book characterized by Senator Dodd as "well-balanced and outstanding", and who admitted to having served as a consultant to the NBC-Television hour-long special "Whose Right To Bear Arms?" Carl Bakal included the following remarks about the National Rifle Association in his written statement submitted to the House subcommittee:

"Does all this mean anything to you? Or will you, like other congressional committees of the past, heed the voice of the small but clamoring minority led by the National Rifle Association which, in the words of the highly respected Catholic monthly, The Commonweal, has 'the megalomanic conviction that its members are the only patriots and the

290

sole sovereign power in this republic, and that any gun law whatsoever is treasonous, Communist, sacrilegious and insulting and to be thwarted by any means, even to ostensible cooperation with the lawmakers, hypocrisy, and treachery.' " (FF–p. 731)

Carl Bakal closed his lengthy statement with this parting salvo directed at the National Rifle Association. It should convey a great deal of information about Carl Bakal:

"In opposing such preventive laws, the National Rifle Association is a threat to our internal security and a menace to our peace and well-being. So I say that it is about time that we stopped listening to the lies of this lobby and stopped watching the slaughter in our streets and homes. It is about time to begin listening to reason and truth instead of to hypocrisy and hysteria. It is about time to heed the voice of the people—the majority of the people—instead of the voice of an irrational, irresponsible, selfish special interest minority seeking only to profit at the expense of the public good." (FF–pp. 732–733)

After telling the House subcommittee how he had helped to organize the National Council for a Responsible Firearms Policy, Carl Bakal was quizzed by Congressman Robert McClory concerning that organization and about statement which he had made about the National Rifle Association:

"MR. MCCLORY. Well now, when you refer to the National Rifle Association as a lobby in opposition to this legislation, would you not characterize yourself and your organization as a lobbying group?

MR. BAKAL. Yes, I would say that we are, but unfortunately, since we are an honest lobby, we do not have the tax exemption privileges that the National Rifle Association has.

MR. MCCLORY. Are you a registered lobbyist, Mr. Bakal?

MR. BAKAL. No, sir.

MR. MCCLORY. You have not seen fit to register as a lobbyist under the Federal statute?

MR. BAKAL. No, sir. I am not paid.

MR. MCCLORY. Well now, you say that the other members and you are supporting the activities of the organization and you say you are not paid. They are supporting your activities, are they not?

MR. BAKAL. No, sir.

MR. MCCLORY. Well, what do these contributions to the organization go for?

MR. BAKAL. Well, when you say contributions, these could be measured in pennies, really. These go for postage and mailing. That is

about all. More or less internal communication between members."
(FF–p. 737)

At the conclusion of the testimony by Carl Bakal he was asked this important question by Congressman Railsback concerning the nature of his interest in gun legislation:

"MR. RAILSBACK. Are you primarily concerned about keeping guns out of the hands of narcotic addicts and the incompetents, and other persons that might be able to use the weapon in a hazardous manner? Isn't that primarily your purpose? Or would you prefer to see gun sales prohibited altogether?

MR. BAKAL. Oh, not at all. Not at all. I simply feel, as the President does, as the American Bar Association does, as the chiefs of police do, that guns should be kept out of the hands of people who are most likely to misuse them. That is my only interest." (FF–p. 740)

During the testimony of Franklin Orth, the question of the applicability of the Lobbying Act to the National Rifle Association was raised by Senator Edward Kennedy:

"SENATOR KENNEDY. I would like to direct this question to any of the members of the panel. I would like to ask whether the NRA has to register under the Lobbying Act?

MR. ORTH. No; we do not.

SENATOR KENNEDY. Do you know why the NRA does not have to register under the Lobbying Act?

MR. ORTH. In the first place, we are organized under 501(c)4, our exemption as a nonprofit organization, which is quite different from 501(c) (3), and there is no requirement for us to register in respect to lobbying, because as long as we speak for our membership, why this is all the requirement that is put upon us.

Now, furthermore, the total amount of our assets in respect to what we use of our total substance in our budget comes to something between 3 and 6 percent. In other words, it is not our principal business to lobby. That is quite something else. It is just in recent years when we have had this harrassment with respect to some of these legislative problems that we have spent as much time lobbying as we have.

But, in any event, there is nobody who spends as much as 50 percent of his time on legislative work. Now, in my own work. I certainly spend less than 30 percent of my time on anything having to do with legislative matters. Most of my time is spent in direction of the activities of the organization." (GG–pp. 528–529)

292

When Franklin Orth was asked by Senator Edward Kennedy whether he thought that there had been sufficient hearings on the various bills he responded:

"Yes, sir. We are prepared to support Senate S.1853 and S.1854. That is the position of our board, of our officers, and the position of our members. We have notified them through the magazine. I mean any implication that we have not is not true. We have given them every opportunity to respond, Senator." (GG–p. 530)

Refreshed by a new epithet, "Lobby", that could be mindlessly thrown at the National Rifle Association, another spate of news articles and editorials lashed out reviling "the powerful and well-financed lobby" which was single-handedly dominating the most complex and awesome legislative body in the world, the U.S. Congress. Even a Canadian newspaper innocently added its interpretation of the American controversy for its readers by reporting:

"The principal opponent of gun control laws is the National Rifle Association, an affluent 'non-profit' lobby which has a striking head-quarters building here. With the suport of hordes of senators and congressmen, it opposes interference with the constitutional right of Americans to keep and bear arms." (*The Montreal Star*: Aug. 8, 1967)

See how very simple it was to capsulize the entire gun control issue into only one or two brief sentences? The press so often saved its readers the chore of thinking for themselves.

In a class by itself, and without competition when it came to hurling brickbats at the National Rifle Association, the *Washington Post* summed up the entire history of the NRA for its readers in this fashion:

"If you want to acquire a magnificent edifice like the house that the National Rifle Association built recently on 16th Street, you must study the strategy of the NRA. First, you must get yourself chartered as a nonprofit organization dedicated to education, social welfare and the promotion of public safety. With this facade to protect you from taxation and from any obligation to register as a lobby, you can begin to lobby to your heart's content in the interests of an industry which will, of course, advertise lavishly in the slick-paper magazine which you will distribute to your 800,000 members. And on top of all that, if you'll just get yourself a steady, solid subsidy from the Government, you'll have it made, man; you'll have it made." (*Washington Post*: June 17, 1967)

The publisher of the *National Police Gazette* similarly labeled the National Rifle Association as the lobby for the firearms industry in the following audacious characterization:

"Although organized as a non-profit organization, this group, financed by the munitions trust, is the industry lobby in Washington. Does this powerful, well-financed lobby have *your* Congressman in their hip pocket? Instead of protecting *your* life, is the man you sent to Washington protecting the gun industry's profits?" (*National Police Gazette*: August, 1967.)

Happily, the refutation of such charges are greatly facilitated by pertinent facts, conspicuous among them the undisguised firearms industry goal for more than a decade to secure a ban on the importation of surplus military rifles, a goal strongly opposed by the National Rifle Association. Another matter vexing to the domestic firearms manufacturers was the availability of certain firearms through the Civilian Marksmanship Program, which was strongly supported by the National Rifle Association.

For ready reference, the following statement was issued on March 25, 1958, by Mr. E. C. Hadley, President of the Sporting Arms and Ammunition Manufacturer's Institute, before the House Foreign Affairs Committee:

"There are four sources of the industry's problem. First, the importation of American-made rifles declared surplus by our allies abroad; second, the importation of surplus used and new foreign made military surplus rifles; third, the importation of foreign made commercial arms; fourth, the sale of surplus military firearms by the U.S. Government within the United States." (CC–p. 717)

It was hardly possible for the NRA simultaneously to lobby both for and against the arms industry, but that was the substance of allegations against the NRA—obviously untrue. The National Rifle Association has always had as its sole concern the legitimate interests of law-abiding American citizens, without regard to race, religion, national origin, or color. The NRA has always stood squarely on the principle that all such persons should be free to purchase, possess, and to use firearms responsibly for all legitimate purposes. The NRA draws its strength from law-abiding citizens in all walks of life and all social strata, who have been welded together by a century of integrity and fidelity to the principles upon which this Nation was founded.

Many members of Congress, as well as the members of the National Rifle Association, were aware that, in addition to the Hruska bill, the NRA fully supported other crime-control bills, which were pending in the Congress. All together, the positive side of the NRA's legislative posture was encompassed in a four-point program about which Franklin Orth testified before Senator Dodd's subcommittee:

"There are four bills which we have been supporting since announced, actually, in 1966, in the January issue of our magazine.

The truth of the matter, Mr. Chairman, is that the NRA does have a positive, overall program for additional Federal firearms control, if the Congress deems such legislation necessary or desirable. This program has been widely publicized and consists of four approaches:

1. A bill to provide a mandatory penalty for the use in the commission of certain crimes of firearms transported in interstate commerce.

2. A bill to provide that no licensed manufacturer or dealer may ship any firearms to any person in any State in violation of the laws of that State.

3. A bill to place 'destructive devices'—bombs, grenades, mines, crew-served military ordnance, and similar items—under the tax and registration provisions of the National Firearms Act.

4. A bill, the principal feature of which is that a person who orders a handgun by mail, or over the counter in a State other than his own, submit a sworn statement containing certain information, with such information to be forwarded to the chief law enforcement officer of the locality to which the handgun will be shipped, and that shipment of the handgun not be made until at least 7 days have elapsed following receipt of notification to the local law enforcement officer.

This four-point program is reflected in bills introduced in the House of Representatives by Congressmen Casey, Sikes, King, Dingell, and others. In the Senate, points three and four of the NRA program are manifested in S.1853 and S.1854, by Senator Roman L. Hruska of Nebraska.

Mr. Chairman, the National Rifle Association is in accord with and supports the bills introduced by the distinguished Senator from the great State of Nebraska, S.1853 and S.1854. They represent a sound and balanced approach to the question of the enactment of additional Federal firearms controls, amending the Federal and National Firearms Acts." (GG–p. 496)

Franklin Orth's reference to the NRA's support of a bill to provide for stiff mandatory penalties for crimes committed with firearms was not a sudden and recent departure from past positions, but rather a reaffirmation of an NRA policy dating back nearly forty years ever since the principle had been enunciated by the National Conference of Commissioners on Uniform State Laws and the American Bar Association at their gathering to initiate a study of existing State laws. In their commentary preparatory to the formulation of the Uniform Firearms Act in the early 1930s, the National Conference of Commissioners made this determination with respect to the deficiencies of various state pistol laws apart from their lack of uniformity:

> "Still more objectionable is the wrong emphasis in most pistol legislation. It is aimed at regulating pistols in the hands of law-abiding citizens rather than at punishing severely criminals who use pistols. Of course, no legislation can prevent gangsters and other dangerous criminals from securing and using pistols, but legislation can make it to the interest of criminals not to use pistols and can send to prison for long periods those caught doing so." (AA–p. 3482)

The very first reference to that part of the NRA policy, which was made during the hearings on the Dodd bills, was made by Franklin Orth on May 2, 1963, before the original subcommittee that conducted the hearings on the proposal by Senator Dodd that three months afterward emerged as the original S.1975:

> "The NRA has consistently favored increased and mandatory sentences where armed force has been used in the commission of a crime. We repeat again that this seems to us a logical and sensible approach." (AA–p. 3484)

There was good reason for calling attention to the penalties imposed by the courts for serious crimes involving violations of existing national and local firearms laws. That reason was based on the fact that such penalties frequently constituted only token reprimands rather than being commensurate with the seriousness of the offenses for which they were imposed. That fact was continually brought out during the various hearings by Senator Dodd's subcommittee, and sometimes by the anti-gun proponents.

The original Dodd subcommittee heard this testimony from William J. Gilmore, Assistant Superintendent of the Pittsburgh Bureau of Police, who described an individual who was found in possession of an arsenal of weapons which included fully working machineguns, clearly a gross violation of the National Firearms Act:

"The machineguns were turned over to the Federal Alcoholic Tax Unit for prosecution. On March 28, 1962, he was adjudged guilty and fined $50 and cost of the prosecution. On a local charge he was found guilty and is serving probation for 1 year." (AA–p. 3456)

Other examples of the incredible sentencing meted out by the courts for serious offenses were cited for the original Dodd subcommittee by Franklin Orth:

"The District of Columbia law provides a maximum penalty of $1,000 fine or imprisonment for not more than 1 year, or both, for those found guilty, for the first time, of illegally carrying a concealed weapon. Anyone previously convicted of a weapons violation or a felony can be imprisoned for as much as 10 years. Nevertheless, a survey of the District of Columbia court of general sessions indicates that in 1962 less than half of the 236 persons found guilty of illegally carrying a concealed pistol received a jail sentence—56 were permitted to pay a fine, 62 were placed on probation, 88 charges were dropped." (AA–p. 3482)

Continuing, Franklin Orth brought to the attention of the subcommittee the results of a study of assaults on police officers, which had been made by the Citizens' Crime Commission of Metropolitan Washington:

"This study reveals that in the District of Columbia during the fiscal year 1961 there were 167 such offenses commited by 153 individuals. This crime is a felony under existing law and carries a fine of not more than $5,000 or imprisonment for not more than 5 years or both. Anyone in the commission of such acts who uses a deadly weapon or dangerous weapon may be imprisoned not more than 10 years. In spite of the severe penalties provided, only 23 of the criminals were held for the grand jury. No papers were issued on 10; 12 were dropped; 71 cases were reduced to misdemeanors, and 24 were turned over to juvenile authorities. Of the 23 which went to the grand jury, 11 received a fine or jail sentence—only 1 for more than 2 years.

In one case in which an officer was stabbed in the abdomen with a knife, the defendant was sentenced to 30 days for three counts of assault, one count of prohibited weapon, and one count of disorderly conduct. In another case where a policeman was deliberately run down by an automobile and required hospitalization, the offense was reduced to simple assault and the defendant given a fine of $25 or 30 days in jail. In the 71 cases in which the offense was reduced to a misdemeanor, it was further reduced to simple assault in 50 of them. As a result of this study, the crime commission concluded that 'the sentences are so lenient, that they tend to create a lack of respect for law and order.' " (AA–pp. 3482–3483)

The documentation of the most extraordinary leniency granted to persons convicted of serious crimes, particularly those involving firearms and machineguns, continued to be presented to Senator Dodd's subcommittee. Here, for another shocking example, is an excerpt from the testimony of Sergeant J. C. Gonzalez of the Los Angeles Police Department describing the outcome of the prosecution of a California man who had been apprehended with what was said to be a massive arsenal that allegedly included machineguns and submachineguns:

"It included everything necessary to train an army. He was convicted of the illegal possession of automatic weapons, explosives, and tear gas grenades, and was fined and placed on probation." (CC–p. 167)

During the House Committee on Ways and Means hearing concerning one of the Dodd bills, Congressman Frank M. Karsten quizzed U.S. Attorney General Nicholas Katzenbach on the percentage of armed robberies solved by arrest, and, more important, the number of convicted persons receiving maximum sentences for their crimes. Katzenbach testified that probably less than 20 percent were solved by arrest and that "very few would receive maximum sentences by the court." (DD–p. 111)

That House Committee on Ways and Means also received details of arrests and convictions for the offense of illegally carrying concealed weapons in the City of St. Louis, Missouri. The St. Louis Police Department furnished a table listing the statistics covering a period of three and one-half years. It showed that during that time a total of 3,508 persons were arrested on the charge of illegally carrying a concealed weapon. Of those 3,508 persons, warrants were actually issued for only 468 of them. Of course 468 persons for whom warrants were issued, only 283 were found guilty of that charge, 90 received reduced sentences.

In a similar vein, Senator Strom Thurmond called attention to a statement attributed to a Northwestern University Professor of Law, Fred E. Imbau, who had reported that:

"In Chicago in 1966 over 6,000 people were arrested while carrying guns, and 200 of them went to jail." (HH–p. 226)

In an impressive piece of documentation of the recidivism rate of persons charged and convicted of serious offenses, who were then subsequently released from penal institutions, was published by the Federal Bureau of Investigation in 1967. Captioned *Careers In Crime*, in provided some remarkable insights into the nature of the administration of criminal justice in the United States.

The FBI study began in January 1963 with a systematic accumulation of information on the criminal histories of individual offenders. Three years later, in order to trace the careers of criminal repeaters, the FBI made an analysis of the records of 41,733 persons who had been arrested in 1966 for a serious crime after having been included in the FBI study program as a result of having had a prior arrest after January 1963. It was found that leniency in the form of probation, suspended sentence, parole and conditional release had been afforded to 51.6 percent of such offenders, and that following the first leniency, that group of persons each averaged more than 5 new arrests. Of the entire 41,733 offenders, it was found that 36,506 had a prior arrest record on the same charge. Further the criminal careers of those repeaters averaged out to more than ten years from the time of their first to last arrest, and during that interval the group averaged over 6 arrests each, 3 convictions and 2 imprisonments.

In a separate study which followed up the criminal careers of those persons who were released from custody in 1963, a total of 17,837 such persons, 55 percent were rearrested for new offenses within the next 30 months.

Interestingly enough, the FBI figures also indicated that of 139 persons whose paroles were handled by so-called Pre-Release Guidance Centers, so-called Half-Way Houses, 75 percent were again arrested within 30 months!

Further, of 965 persons who were acquitted or whose cases were dismissed in Federal courts during 1963, the FBI found that 83 percent had been rearrested by mid-1966.

During 1963, there were 5,761 persons released for such crimes as: murder, forcible rape, aggravated assault, burglary, robbery, larceny, and auto theft. The FBI reported that those persons then accumulated 13,180 new criminal charges collectively during the next 30 months.

The general subject of policemen killed by criminals also received careful attention from the FBI who had compiled the following shocking statistics since 1960:

"Since 1960, there have been 442 persons involved as offenders in the 335 police murders. In reviewing the prior criminal histories of these 442 offenders, the records disclose 76 percent had been arrested on some criminal charge before becoming involved in the police killing. Over one-half of those with prior criminal arrests had been previously taken into custody for an assaultive-type crime such as murder, rape, robbery, assault with a deadly weapon, assault with intent to kill, etc."

* * *

"Among the 442 persons who were involved in the police killings, 67 percent had prior convictions on criminal charges and 69 percent of this group had been granted leniency in the form of parole or probation on at least one of these prior convictions. In fact, 3 of every 10 of the murderers were on parole or probation when they murdered a police officer." (FBI Uniform Crime Reports 1966: p. 48)

Thus comes enlightenment on the broad and interrelated subjects of crime, punishment and gun control. Not everyone agrees with the anti-gun movement in the United States.

The President's Commission on Law Enforcement and Administration of Justice which made the following recommendation in February 1967:

"Each State should require the registration of all handguns, rifles, and shotguns. If, after 5 years, some States still have not enacted such laws, Congress should pass a Federal firearms registration act applicable to those States."

The May 22, 1967, *Chicago American* newspaper contained a little noticed, but highly informative article titled "Crime Report Slaps Tough FBI Stand," which opened with these words:

"A Presidential crime commission report recommends that ex-convicts be given the right to serve on juries, hold public office, and vote. Contrary to the views of FBI Director J. Edgar Hoover, the report says rehabilitation is the key in returning a convict to society."

* * *

"The report on corrections, released Saturday night, is the fourth of nine released by the President's commission on Law Enforcement and Administration of Justice, which directed a massive study of crime in the United States. The report urged that parole be considered a prisoner's right, rather than a privilege."

The various recommendations of the President's Crime Commission drew a sharp reaction from Congressman Bob Casey, who, on numerous occasions, had voiced strong demands in Congress for legislation which would provide strict mandatory penalties for crimes of violence. Congressman Casey, sponsor of one of the bills—which enjoyed the full support of the National Rifle Association—made these remarks to the House subcommittee:

> "With all due respect, I say to the Crime Commission and the Justice Department—do not point the finger of blame for this shocking situation at 20 million decent citizens who bought hunting licenses last year. Do not point the finger of blame at the other 30 million who legally own guns to protect their homes and businesses and their loved ones from the scum that lax courts and lenient prosecutors and lenient juries turn loose to prey on us.
>
> I find it unbelievable that in this same report—filled with inadequate facts and distorted logic—recommendation is made for rigid control on sale, registration, and possession of firearms for law-abiding citizens. And at the same time, it is recommended that all mandatory prison sentences and long maximum prison terms be abolished, and sentencing be left to the discretion of the courts.
>
> I say it is time the people removed from the courts the discretion in sentencing that has led to such terrible abuse of the rights of the innocent." (FF–p. 481)

The conflict which arose between proponents of heavy mandatory penalties for serious violent crimes and proponents of progressively restrictive firearms control legislation may be glimpsed, albeit fragmentarily, from some of the writings of one of the Directors of the National Council for a Responsible Firearms Policy, Dr. Karl Menninger. In his book entitled *The Crime of Punishment*, Dr. Menninger made the following observations in a chapter headed "Crimes Against Criminals":

> *"I suspect that all the crimes committed by all the jailed criminals do not equal in total social damage that of the crimes committed against them."* (p. 28)
>
> * * *
>
> "For inexplicable reasons, to deprive a man of decent social relationships, palatable food, normal friendships and sexual relations, and constructive communication is not—in the eyes of the law—cruel or unusual." (p. 72)
>
> * * *
>
> "The mugging process is reminiscent of calf branding: when the hot iron is withdrawn, the calf struggles to his feet and staggers off in the direction indicated by his stony-faced handlers." (p. 72)

In another chapter, "Vengeance Is Mine, Saith the Lord", Dr. Menninger added these assertions:

"Being against punishment is not a sentimental conviction. It is a logical conclusion drawn from scientific experience." (p. 204)

* * *

"But to renounce vengeance as a motive for punishing offenders leaves us with the equivocal justification of deterrence. This is a weak and vulnerable argument indeed, for the effects of punishment in this direction cannot be demonstrated by sound evidence or research." (p. 206)

* * *

"The principle of *no* punishment cannot allow of any exception; it must apply in every case, even the worst case, the most horrible case, the most dreadful case—not merely in the accidental, sympathy-arousing case." (p. 207)

* * *

"If society were able to catch most offenders, and then if it were willing to punish them promptly without any discrimination, inflicting the penalties fairly but ruthlessly, as it were, most crime could be prevented. But society is neither able nor willing to do this." (p. 208)

Dr. Karl Menninger also favored the National Rifle Association with this brief reference in his book:

"The National Rifle Association and its allies have been able to kill scores of bills that have been introduced into Congress and state legislatures for corrective gun control since the death of President Kennedy." (p. 184)

Another member of the National Council for a Responsible Firearms Policy, its President, James V. Bennett, while seeking maximum gun controls, vigorously opposed mandatory minimum punishment for crime.

Both Dr. Karl Menninger and James V. Bennett were members and Directors of the National Council for a Responsible Firearms Policy. Their names also appeared in the published list of "Advisors" to the President's Crime Commission. The Chairman of the President's Crime Commission was none other than former U.S. Attorney General Nicholas Katzenbach. Mr. Katzenbach was also asked for his position with respect to mandatory penalties during the same hearings as was Mr. Bennett. It was Congressman James A. Burke who raised the issue as to whether the penalties for violation of the two national firearms acts should be strengthened:

"MR. BURKE. Mr. Attorney General, the penalties here under the Federal Firearms Act and National Firearms Act have a ceiling of a fine up to $2,000 and imprisonment for not more than 5 years.

Under this legislation here you seem to be delegating power to the States, and don't you find in your experience as Attorney General that there is severe criticism of the courts for the light sentences and the soft handling of known criminals when they are apprehended and they go before the courts?

Do you not think that this section here should be strengthened? Do you not think that we should set some minimum sentence for those criminals found in violation of this act?

MR. KATZENBACH. No, Congressman, I don't. I have never believed that minimum sentences were a particularly wise thing for Congress to enact in any area." (DD–p. 100)

Mr. H. Rap Brown, a militant black-power advocate, had been charged with transporting a carbine across state lines on an airliner while knowing that he was under indictment on charges of inciting to riot and arson in violation of the National Firearms Act. The *Washington Post* May 24, 1968, had this to say:

"The conviction of H. Rap Brown in New Orleans for violation of the National Firearms Act was a salutary application of the principles of law and order."

* * *

"Yet there is already much controversy over the wisdom of Judge Mitchell in imposing the maximum sentence of five years in prison."

* * *

"But Judge Mitchell could have handed down a stiff sentence commensurate with the offense without throwing the book at this black-power advocate. To many the maximum sentence of five years for carrying a gun will seem vindictive."

An additional problem has been created in the last few years by the U.S. Supreme Courts detailed demand for procedural and technical niceties in criminal proceedings. The net result has been a series of legal decisions which have had the effect in the lower courts of freeing many criminals on purely procedural grounds without regard for their guilt or innocence. It was with regard to precisely those conditions that Congressman Speedy O. Long referred when he addressed the following words to the House subcommittee:

"On the one hand, therefore, we have the Supreme Court of the United States releasing convicted criminals and other persons accused of crime

303

simply because of technical constitutional interpretations rendered in their favor, while on the other hand, Congress, by this bill, is attempting to limit and restrict the constitutional right of free and honest, law-abiding citizens in their right to keep and bear arms. The situation, I submit, is incongruous and inequitable. I submit that criminals are walking the streets of America today, not because of their right to bear arms, but because of the handcuffs and limitations which have been imposed on America's law enforcement officers and agencies in the apprehension of criminals and in gathering the evidence to convict the guilty before the bars of American justice." (FF–p. 763)

The gradual weakening of law enforcement in the United States in recent years, as a consequence of all of the preceding factors, can be clearly demonstrated by careful study of the following chart compiled by Congressman Bob Casey, who had been actively working towards the enactment of federal legislation to provide for a system of mandatory minimum penalties for crimes of violence committed while armed with a firearm:

Year	Arrests For Serious Crime	Total Criminal Offenses	Federal And State Prison Population	Federal Court Prison Sentences	Criminals Executed
1961	871,700	2,068,400	220,149	13,745	42
1962	892,750	2,198,900	218,830	14,042	47
1963	937,350	2,420,000	217,283	13,639	21
1964	1,059,600	2,737,300	214,336	13,273	15
1965	1,088,000	2,911,400	210,895	13,669	7
1966	1,136,350	3,264,200	199,654	13,282	1

In 1967, the most recent year for which complete figures were available at this writing, the combined Federal and State prison population dropped still further to only 194,920 persons! Seventy-three new Federal judgeships were created in 1961, and an additional 45 created in 1966, yet the number of prison sentences imposed by the Federal courts continued to dwindle in the face of rising arrest rates. The inescapable conclusion was expressed very well by Congressman Bob Casey:

"Too long have we listened to the sociologist, the social do-gooders, and the theorists who bleed about the poor misguided criminals who have no way of making a living except through robbing, raping or murdering. For six straight years we have succumbed to their cry that

304

society is at fault, that punishment, including execution, is no deterrent to crime, that probation and not a prison cell is the answer. And for six straight years, our prisons have spewed forth case-hardened convicts to continue preying upon us to the point where our prison population is at an all time low—and our crime and arrest rate is at an all time high." (HH–p. 767)

16

"Those who would give up essential liberty to purchase a little temporary safety deserve neither liberty nor safety."

BENJAMIN FRANKLIN

A SYNONYM FOR "GUN REGISTRATION" IN THIS COUNTRY since 1911 has been the so-called New York "Sullivan Law", the name of which was derived from its chief sponsor, Timothy D. Sullivan, a Tammany Hall politician. Political good fortune had smiled on Sullivan until, like Senator Dodd years later, he was caught up in scandal—in Sullivan's case a racing scandal. Caught in the turmoil of rapidly changing political fortunes, and manifesting signs of acute paranoia which preceded his eventual insanity, he exerted what little was left of his declining political influence to obtain enactment by the New York State Legislature of the bill that was destined to bear his name.

The bill that became known as the Sullivan Law was introduced in

Albany, New York on January 5, 1911, only a few months before the world of Timothy Sullivan completely disintegrated. According to the *New York Times*, after his "wife died and with the strain of public scandal coming close to him, he broke down completely and had to be sent to a sanitarium. His friends and relatives cared for him, but he never completely recovered and it was necessary to keep a close watch over him until the day he died."

Signed into effect by the Governor on May 25, 1911, the Sullivan Law was assailed and its repeal demanded after it had been in operation for only one year. On April 16, 1935, Col. Calvin C. Goddard, the Director of the Scientific Crime-Detection Laboratory of Northwestern University, testified before the U.S. Senate Committee on Commerce:

> "The Sullivan law had the intent, as all such laws do, of disarming the crook and reducing crime. Murders increased 18 percent in New York State within the first year after the Sullivan law was enacted, and, for example, companies writing burglary insurance, casualty and insurance companies petitioned the Legislature to repeal it in the first year because burglaries and robberies increased so much that they had to increase their premiums to a point where they were not able to sell insurance.
>
> My authority for that is a bulletin published by the United States Fidelity & Guaranty Co. of Baltimore, which was one of the petitioning companies.
>
> The law has operated in this fashion: A man in Buffalo, seeing a burglar effecting an entry in his home through a window, secured the family revolver and held up the burglar. He called the police. The police arrived, arrested the intruder, arrested the householder for owning a weapon without a permit, having a weapon in his possession without a permit. They hied them both to the hoosegow. They had to appear in court the following morning. The would-be burglar was fined $25, which fine was suspended, and the householder was also fined $25, which he had to pay, and his gun was confiscated." (KK–p. 39)

On May 24, 1913, less than two years after the Sullivan Law went into effect, an editorial in the *New York Times* made the following observation:

> "The concealed weapon law has not worked as well as was expected by those of us who commended it. This is a fact too obvious for denial. Criminals are as well armed as ever, in spite of the sternness with which the law has been applied to a few of them. There is the impres-

sion among honest men, mistaken but none the less real, that they were wrongly deprived of the means for defending themselves and their property."

In the course of the next fifty-two years the Sullivan Law was amended no fewer than 67 times in an effort to correct its various deficiencies, but it still survived as the same unworkable and discriminatory piece of legislation it was when first enacted in 1911.

The original Sullivan Law was applicable only to handguns, and it required a permit to purchase one plus a license to possess it. In addition, there was yet another special license for the carrying of a handgun on the person such as would be required by a security guard. In more recent years, the few remaining target shooters are obliged annually to file a special Targeteer's Affidavit describing when and where the licensee did his target shooting, the number of times such firing took place, the kind of targets used, and the caliber of pistols fired during the course of such target practice. None of the licenses referred to are issued merely for the asking, but rather the procedures necessary for obtaining them are prolonged in time, detailed, complicated, and calculated to discourage all but the most determined applicants.

It should be pointed out that when the Sullivan Law was first enacted the application fee for a pistol permit was only fifty cents, but in less than 10 years that fee was raised to a non-refundable $20. The reason underlying that abrupt increase as well as a highly enlightening insight into the administration of the Sullivan Law by the police authorities, can be readily obtained from the following excerpt taken from the annual report of the New York City Police Department just prior to the raising of the fee:

". . . an effort was made during the latter part of the year to secure authority for increasing the fee for the issuance of pistol permits. Since the prerogative of issuing them was taken from the police magistrates and given to the police department, less than half as many have been granted. With a view to building up the police pension fund—which will have its main contribution cut off through the enforcement of the Prohibition Amendment—it was sought to raise the fee from a trifling sum as at present to a substantial one, such as $10 or, perhaps, $20. . . ." (HH–p. 478)

A resident of New York City who wants to apply for a permit to purchase a handgun, first must visit his local police station where he will be interviewed by the precinct police captain who endeavors to learn *why* the would-be applicant thinks he *needs* a pistol. If the applicant is

308

one of the rare fortunates to be given an application form, then he faces two pages of approximately thirty-eight personal questions which he is obliged to answer. In addition to completing the questionnaire, he has to furnish the police with references from three local acquaintances who are willing to vouch for all that he had represented in his application form. He also then must pay the application fee of $20 which goes directly into the police pension fund and is not refunded even in the probable event his application for a permit is refused. Furthermore, he is obliged to furnish four current photographs of himself, at a cost of several more dollars, as well as to permit several sets of his fingerprints to be recorded. Only after all the foregoing is accomplished will the actual investigation begin.

A fingerprint check is requested from both the Federal Bureau of Investigation and from the New York State Identification and Intelligence System. The Pistol License Bureau also checks with the New York State Department of Mental Hygiene in an effort to determine whether the applicant has had any history of mental disorder. Other investigators search the files of such agencies as the Bureau of Criminal Identification, the Bureau of Special Services, the Central Investigation Bureau, the Old Record Unit, the Information Unit, and the Known Gamblers file.

The three personal references provided by the applicant are independently investigated by the same agencies. They are personally contacted and interviewed by the police who also make similar checks with the neighbors and business associates of the applicant.

Upon completion of all of the many investigations, the application is returned by the Pistol License Bureau to the police precinct station from which it originated. Thereupon a report is prepared along with a recommendation for approval or disapproval. Such recommendations have to be endorsed by the precinct detective commander, the precinct police captain, the division commander, and ultimately by a representative of the Police Commissioner. If everything is approved, a most unlikely event, then a permit to purchase is issued and the applicant once more is thumbprinted. That is not the end of the processes under the Sullivan Law; it is really just the beginning.

In New York City, the license to possess the pistol has to be renewed annually at a cost of $10 plus the additional cost of furnishing four more photographs. Also, the signatures of the three personal references similarly have to be renewed. If for any reason one of the three vouchers is no longer available, then the entire process must be repeated for an alternate voucher. (BB–p. 150)

New York City pistol licensees also receive periodic notifications from the police ordering them to show up with their pistol, or pistols, at the local precinct police station to have their registered description verified. Approximately once each year the police make a surprise visit to the homes of such licensees to inspect the pistol and verify its registration. That is still not all. (GG–p. 504)

On the death of a pistol licensee, the licensed and registered handgun becomes ipso facto a public nuisance and thereupon is immediately confiscated by the police Gun Sergeant and rarely, if ever, seen again. (EE–p. 480) There is no compensation whatever paid to the estate of the decedent. That particular practice has prompted some licensees to remove their pistols from New York City prior to undergoing serious surgery so as to protect the guns in the event of their death on the operating table.

In a classic example of understatement, Leonard E. Reisman, Deputy Commissioner of the New York City Police Department, replied to a question from Congressman Clark W. Thompson:

> "MR. THOMPSON. Commissioner, if a householder in New York wanted a pistol to keep in the house for protection of his home how much trouble would it be for him to get it, or could he get it?
> MR. REISMAN. He could get it. It would be a fair amount of trouble for him to get it. He would have to make application, be fingerprinted, have persons vouch for his good character, and his house, his premises, would be checked to see if they are reasonably secure for the possession of such weapons. We do issue some. We do not issue many.
> MR. THOMPSON. You, in other words, discourage the ownership of a pistol under any conditions?
> MR. REISMAN. Yes, we do." (EE–pp. 363–364)

One's attention should also be directed to one other set of facts, namely, that once a permit is issued to purchase a pistol, that pistol is licensed for only one fixed premise and can not be transported to any other location without having another license issued to carry. If a shopkeeper were licensed to have a pistol in his place of business, then that pistol will have to remain there and can not be taken home over a weekend, or to the country, or to a target range, without first having secured the separate license to transport it. Similarly, if a homeowner were licensed to have a pistol in the home, then that pistol can not be removed from those premises legally without a separate license to carry it. That is one of the reasons for the once a year surprise visit by the

310

police—to insure that these provisions of the law are obeyed by the licensees.

Licenses to carry are restricted to security guards and to other individuals similarly employed who are required by the nature of their jobs literally to wear their pistols on their persons. Special targeteer licenses theoretically are available to members of gun clubs so that they might transport their target pistols to and from a target range, but they are virtually non-existent in New York City. Furthermore, licenses to carry which are issued by other jurisdictions in the State of New York are not recognized in New York City and persons traveling through that city literally are forced to by-pass it in order not to be in violation of the Sullivan Law.

In order to provide a complete understanding of the impact which the Sullivan Law had, as it was administered in New York City, the table below will prove enlightening. It compares, for those years where the information was available, the total number of pistol licenses issued for both premises and for carrying, and the total number of reported murders, assaults, robberies, and rapes for those same years. Quite clearly, as the pistol licenses were decreased, the crime rates increased!

Year	Pistol Licenses For Premises	Pistol Licenses To Carry	Murders	Assaults	Robberies	Rapes
1940	2,956	24,174	275	2,551	1,393	862
1945	2,601	23,741	292	4,924	1,234	597
1950	1,563	21,847	294	7,097	2,457	704
1955	987	21,827	333	27,075	7,438	1,322
1960	474	16,473	394	34,472	6,629	1,390
1964	346	17,150	552	38,504	6,850	1,349
1965	307	17,844	634	45,918	8,904	1,574
1966	282	18,256	653	62,080	23,539	1,901

It should also be noted that police strength in 1940 was 18,177 for New York City, and by 1966 it had increased to 27,429 officers. The police department expenditures for 1940 was some $67,000,000, and by 1966 this had leaped to nearly $364,000,000.

Now for another insight into the woes of New York City, consider this revealing excerpt taken from the February 8, 1965, issue of *U.S. News & World Report* magazine concerning that sick, sick city:

"The city has a police force of nearly 27,000 men. Grand juries return between 4,500 and 4,800 felony indictments each year. But the court dockets are so jammed that only 10 percent of these are resolved in trials." (CC–p. 256)

It would appear the City of New York has only managed to intimidate and harass law-abiding citizens who desire to have some means at their disposal for the defense of their person, families, or property. Small wonder so many people have commented that while New York City might be a nice place to visit, they would not want to live there. Some people now even fear to visit there.

The experiences which New York City residents have had to endure in the process of trying to obtain something as simple as a targeteer's carrying license can be illustrated by a letter submitted to Senator Dodd's subcommittee by Woodson D. Scott, a prominent New York City attorney, and, at the time, President of the National Rifle Association. The letter was written by a New York City resident and told of its writer's experience under the Sullivan Law:

"Herewith attached is a receipt showing that on October 5, 1962, I filed an application for a pistol permit giving this reason 'Being a member of the National Rifle Association (Washington, D.C.) and of the Eureka Rod & Gun Club Inc. (Mount Vernon, N.Y.), I want to be legally protected while carrying a pistol to and from target practice.' Fourteen months later apparently no action has been taken thereon as to date no pistol permit has been issued to me." (BB–pp. 151–152)

A second letter, also submitted for the information of Senator Dodd's subcommittee by Woodson Scott, related to an elderly gentleman who had owned a pistol during the course of his employment for many years. The letter was a copy of the original which had been addressed to a New York State district attorney:

"For over 15 years I carried a pistol and a permit for my work for the Higgins Co. here necessitated my going very frequently to piers, etc. It got harder and harder each year, and most expensive. In my many years, at least 15, I furnished photographs, fingerprints, and letters from six reputable men as to my character, and then I decided finally that it was becoming a nuisance and more and more expensive, and that eventually the Police Department would, literally, have hundreds of my photos and fingerprints and got along without the permit for I gave up the pistol. This I sent to my son-in-law who lives in New Jersey, owns a home and is permitted to have a pistol at home for self-

312

protection. The police here, however, went so far as to have the chief of police at my son-in-law's home call on him to examine the pistol I had sent him, compare the number, etc., and advise the police department here. I was treated from beginning until past the end as a thief or criminal. I was born and have lived in New York all my life, 85 years, and have never been accused or tried for any sort of a crime." (BB–p. 151)

These are not isolated examples. They are simply the routine methods of pushing around little people who are not big enough, influential enough, or financially able to protect either themselves or their rights. Here is an example from a letter by a Brooklyn cab driver who had applied for a pistol permit so that he could join a gun club for the inexpensive recreation of weekly target shooting:

"I have been interested in obtaining a pistol license in order to participate in the team. I am a New York City licensed cabdriver. I have been a licensed cabdriver for the past 12 years. I also work as a machine operator on ladies' coats. I am a ladies garment worker which is seasonal work. There is a time when the industry is slow or no work at all. Then I drive the taxi steady as a supplementary income. I am a family man with three children. During the regular season I drive the cab on weekends. That is on Saturdays and Sundays. Without the hack license I would be forced to apply for unemployment insurance during the slow or no-work season.

I have recently applied for a target pistol permit. Enclosed is the reply I received. Is this the price I must pay for the privilege of obtaining a pistol license to target practice one night a week?" (EE–p. 482)

The letter to which that cab driver referred was from the Pistol License Bureau of the New York City Police Department in response to his application for the license:

"Your pistol license application is being held at this office, pending surrender by you of current hack driver's license, issued to you by this department. It will be necessary for you to surrender this license in person at this office before a pistol license may be issued to you. Please phone beforehand for an appointment." (EE–p. 482)

The reader should clearly understand there is absolutely nothing in the Sullivan Law to require the surrender of the taxi cab drivers license in exchange for the pistol license. That demand was nothing more than

313

an exercise of arbitrary departmental policy that anyone who had the one license could not have the other.

The classic example of recent years concerning the inequitable operation of the Sullivan Law related to the events surrounding the attemped rape and felonious assault on the person of a 27-year-old New York University secretary. The young woman had begun carrying a three-inch switchblade knife, illegal under the Sullivan Law, ever since the savage murder of Kitty Genovese, whose screams for help were heard and ignored by 38 New York neighbors on the night of March 13, 1964. As she explained it, she just did not want to become another Kitty Genovese.

Three months after the Genovese murder, the secretary attended the New York World's Fair with several girl friends. Afterwards each of them had walked back to their respective homes in Forest Hills. While walking the last several blocks to her home she was grabbed by a man who tried to drag her into the shadows. Reaching into her purse for the knife she pressed the button which snapped the blade into position just as her attacker threw her to the ground and leaped upon her. Falling upon the upturned blade of her knife, he suddenly released her and fled bleeding.

Afterwards, when the secretary summoned help and reported the attack to the police she was promptly arrested and arraigned for the illegal possession of a weapon prohibited by the Sullivan Law. The news story which carried the details of that sad event opened with the following words:

"A 27-year-old New York University secretary complained today she was 'treated just like a criminal' after she thwarted rape by a sailor by stabbing him with a small switchblade knife she carried in her purse for protection." (*Fort Lauderdale News*: July 6, 1964)

The national outcry that occurred when her story was spread coast to coast by national news magazines eventually influenced the outcome of the matter, and the grand jury refused to bring in an indictment.

It might be noted that at the very moment this New York secretary was defending her own life another young woman who had just returned from a gay evening at Coney Island was dying in the hallway of her Brooklyn home, the knife of an unknown assailant plunged into her heart.

The incident involving the switchblade knife was mentioned in passing by Congressman John Dingell when he presented his opinion of

314

the New York Sullivan Law to Senator Dodd's subcommittee back in 1965:

> "Consider the fact that in New York, where the stringent Sullivan Act is aimed at disarming the individual, a soaring rate of violent crimes has made city streets unsafe for the unarmed, law-abiding citizen.
>
> Not long back a young woman was assaulted by an individual, and in defense of herself pulled a switchblade knife. It was rather promptly reported in the papers. And as a result of this, in defense of her virtue and chastity, having exercised what I regard as the common and ordinary right of self-defense, she was threatened with prosecution, and indeed was actually brought into the criminal procedures for prosecution by the authorities of that State—while she was seeking solely to defend her person as a law-abiding citizen." (CC–p. 376)

Over the past half-century, through progressively more stringently administration of the Sullivan Law, law-abiding residents of New York City have been systematically denied their right to possess pistols by police authorities who claimed that ordinary citizens had no need for pistols. On the other hand, certain members of the elite class of citizens —those possessing wealth and commanding political influence—have suffered fewer impediments to possession or to carrying of pistols. Note an article which appeared in the *Chicago Tribune* on April 12, 1970, appropriately captioned "Pistol-Toting Judge Foils Attack in N.Y.":

> "A state Supreme court judge, returning home late last night, shot and wounded two youths he said he caught beating an elderly neighbor. He held them at gunpoint until police arrived."
>
> * * *
>
> "Brownstein, armed with a .38 caliber revolver, surprised the youth as he entered the lobby. As they attempted to flee, he fired four shots hitting both in the arms. Neighbors called police while the judge stood guard over the two boys."

What a pity one of the 38 neighbors of Kitty Genovese had not been a judge, but, after all, there just are not enough judges numerically to match the criminals.

The sum and substance of the experience with the infamous Sullivan Law was concisely expressed by Woodson D. Scott:

> "Our experience in New York with the Sullivan law has been so unfortunate that any registration law at any level of government is considered undesirable and unacceptable." (BB–p. 152)

Approximately fifty years ago, the State of Illinois experimented with a law which provided for a license to carry a pistol on or about the person. The intent of the law was to permit reputable individuals legally to go about armed with a concealed handgun. It failed completely, and was repealed in the 1920s.

With few exceptions, no reputable citizen living in Chicago could acquire such a permit, and no criminal who was able to pay $50 to some corrupt official was without one. It was to that situation which Col. Calvin Goddard referred when he testified back in 1935 to the Senate Committee on Commerce:

> "In this country I have talked with people in New York State and in Chicago, where a license is required for the purchase of weapons, who have met the most supreme indifference on the part of the police, an indifference to their needs and an indifference to their reputable records.
>
> I know of one retired colonel of the Regular Army, in Chicago, who was denied a permit for a .22 caliber target pistol because the police felt he did not need one. At the same time, when the permits were issued in Chicago, every hoodlum had one." (KK–p. 39)

As the foremost American expert in the field of scientific crime detection methods, and as a man who had studied extensively in the crime detection centers of thirteen western European countries, Goddard knew better than any other man in the country that there was absolutely no crime prevention or detection value in gun registration, but that such fraudulent gun control schemes were fraught with potential for great abuse, and, therefore, should be vigorously opposed wherever encountered. It was in November 1934 that he wrote these prophetic words of warning to his fellow Americans:

> "In the case of arms legislation, an active minority is, and has been, working incessantly for increased restrictions upon the sale, possession, and use of firearms."

> * * *

> "The danger is greater than ever before, while preparations against it are for the most part still vague and indefinite.
>
> The N.R.A. in Washington is active and vigilant, but it cannot alone carry the country. We must reach those groups of sportsmen who are friendly but as yet not enlisted in our cause. And, more important still, we must reach that great mass of American citizens who do not know what it is all about, and who will fall prey to the insidious efforts of the would-be reformers if we do not enlighten them.

These uplifters are leaving no stone unturned to deceive the uninitiate as to the issues involved. By radio, press, and public orations, they inculcate their insidious doctrines. We dare no longer leave the issue to be fought out in committee. We must kill the monster at birth, and fight fire with fire. Education, education, and still more education should be the watchword." (*The American Rifleman*: November 1934, pps. 9 and 19)

One of the organizations with which Col. Goddard was most influential was the Illinois State Rifle Association. The ISRA was founded by a group of Army Reserve officers in 1903 immediately following the establishment of the National Board for the Promotion of Rifle Practice in that year. As it grew in size and increased the scope of its marksmanship activities under the guidance of such men as Col. Francis W. Parker Jr., Col. Calvin C. Goddard, and Chicago attorney Morrison Worthington, it also maintained a watchful eye on the State Capitol at Springfield, lest some well intentioned but uninformed legislator unwittingly unleash the plagues of another Sullivan Law in Illinois.

Over the years there were occasional overtures toward consideration of a Sullivan Law for Illinois, but wise Illinois legislators were sufficiently well informed as to its abject failure and gross abuses in New York. They would not seriously consider inflicting it upon their own state.

Despite various efforts over the years and despite that modifications of the law were sought by both sides of the gun control issue in Illinois, an opportunity to remedy the firearms section of the criminal code of Illinois did not occur until 1964. The opening opportunity was the appointment of "The Mayor's Committee on Organized Crime" by Chicago Mayor Richard J. Daley. This committee was assigned the task of formulating legislative proposals for combating organized crime in the aftermath of more than 70 restaurant bombing and arson cases in the greater Chicago area.

Unhappily, just as had happened earlier, the "official" drafting subcommittee completely ignored the helpful overtures, not only of the Illinois State Rifle Association Legislative Committee, but also of those made by other interested and capable parties who had manifested a desire to render assistance. The subcommittee attitude was simply that the members were thoroughly conversant with everything necessary to know about firearms and firearms control legislation. They closed the door in the face of all legitimate sportsmen, dismissing them as though they and their opinions were of no consequence whatever.

It later developed that the Subcommittee had been considering two kinds of legislative approach to gun control, both pertaining only to handguns. The first would have absolutely prohibited the possession and sale of any firearm which could be concealed upon the person. The second would simply have provided a Sullivan Law for Illinois. Eventually, the subcommittee selected the second proposal for their recommendation, and no doubt regarded themselves as magnanimous for having done so. The organized sportsmen of Illinois did not see it that way, and they carried the fight to the State Legislature.

In addition to opposing the Chicago sponsored gun registration bill, Illinois sportsmen supported another pending bill which would have provided for mandatory penalties for crimes of violence committed while armed. That mandatory penalty bill had been sponsored by Illinois State Senator W. Russell Arrington who made the following comments on the occasion of being interviewed by WBKB-Television on March 6, 1965:

> "MODERATOR. Mayor Daley is backing an Illinois House bill that would require licensing of every concealable firearm. Now, State Senate leader Russell Arrington opposes that bill, but offers a substitute bill that would provide a new scale of penalties for crimes committed with weapons."
>
> * * *
>
> "SENATOR ARRINGTON. Registration doesn't assure that the criminal is going to register his gun. He disobeys all other laws, there's no reason to assume that he would obey this law. The ones in my opinion who would not register would be the criminals. They have no reluctance to commit an illegal act, so I don't think that would deter them at all. They don't mind violating the law. Mine is that, if you've committed a crime, when you have possession of a whole variety of deadly weapons, then throw the book at him.
>
> * * *
>
> All the mail that I've received with respect to the bill that's now in the House have been against it, and I would judge that we have more mail on that issue than perhaps any that we have pending before the legislature."
>
> MODERATOR. "Gun fanciers admittedly have organized letter writing and lobbying efforts to defeat proposed firearm legislation, but the sportsmen are considered only a minority by the other side of the controversy."

The pistol registration bill was soundly defeated in the Illinois General Assembly. Abner J. Mikva, who had been one of the sponsors of that bill, subsequently commented that there were over five thousand letters and telegrams received in opposition to that measure, and

318

only six favoring it. He further stated that 30 of the original 38 sponsors of the registration bill deserted it. Obviously those for gun control did not feel very strongly about it.

One after the other, the majority of Chicago newspapers bemoaned the loss of the pistol registration law, and asserted that the will of the people, manifested by opinion polls, had been thwarted by a well organized and financed lobby consisting of a tiny minority of gun owners. Throughout their lamentations it was often repeated that the registration bill would not have been a burden on the rights of anyone, and that the bill had been only moderate measure. In their vain struggle to contrive some kind of a suitable explanation of the reason for the bitter antagonism towards gun registration among knowledgeable gun owners, the Chicago press most frequently attributed it to nothing more substantial than a rote recitation of the second half of the Second Amendment to the Constitution. They evidently did not know the facts, or they did not dare disclose those facts to their readers.

Certain elements among the press did not hesitate to misrepresent the legal consequences of the failure of the pistol registration bill to be enacted. Consider the absolute falsehood that was contained in a *Chicago Daily News* editorial June 23, 1965, entitled "Gun Lobby Cracks the Whip":

> "In losing, it leaves Illinois without any specific prohibition against the sale of handguns to persons under 18, to narcotic addicts, or to convicted felons."

That statement was demonstrably false, as every organized gun owner well knew, because the 1961 Revised Criminal Code of Illinois had specifically declared unlawful the sale of any and all firearms to either a narcotic addict or an ex-convict within five years of release from the penitentiary. A copy of the text of that law was immediately forwarded to the editorial offices of the *Chicago Daily News*, but apparently no notice was taken of the facts contained within it because, on a subsequent occasion, one of their editorial contributors, Sydney J. Harris, repeated the falsehood in his column August 6, 1965, captioned "Our Peanut Legislators" in which he wrote:

> "As a result, Illinois now has no specific bar against the sale of handguns to minors, to addicts, or even to convicted felons."

What was this? A mistake? A deliberate lie?

Two years later, there was another attempt on the part of the City

319

of Chicago to impose its will on the people of the State of Illinois by forcing a gun registration bill through the General Assembly. The events which transpired during that period were important because of similarities they had with the mammoth national campaign which took place the following year, almost as though it constituted a practice run in order to perfect the techniques utilized. Interestingly enough, Carl Bakal had paid a visit to Chicago exactly three weeks before Chicago Mayor Richard J. Daley officially announced that the city would sponsor a bill to require the registration of every firearm in Illinois, including rifles and shotguns, as well as handguns. (WBBM-Radio, Feb. 2, 1967)

Dishonesty and little knowledge of guns were matters of small interest to the gun prohibitionists whose objects were best served by having the facts obscured by journalists who were not well informed of the issues. The real issues in gun control around the obvious ineffectiveness of gun registration as a method of crime control, together with the gross abuses that were known to have taken place under the Sullivan Law and under the administration of the Chicago pistol purchase permit ordinance for several decades.

Typical of the administration of the Chicago pistol permit ordinance was the case of a Chicagoan, a man in his early forties, married, the father of three children, and having a continuous record of employment with the same company for 15 years. The applicant also happened to be a skilled competitive target shooter who had requested a permit for the purchase of a highly sophisticated single shot .22 caliber Swiss-made Olympic-style target pistol which he intended to fire in International Pistol Matches. Such Swiss pistols were the finest quality available in the world and were virtually made by hand to critical tolerances for exceptional accuracy. At that particular time they sold for approximately $285 each. This man's application was rejected.

A letter of protest to the Superintendent of Police resulted in the following response:

"We follow a policy in the Police Department of not issuing a permit to purchase unless the applicant can show a strong need for the weapon in addition to the fact that he is a person of good character. Apparently in your case you did not succeed in convincing the personnel in our Records & Communications Division that you had a need for the weapon in question.

We think this policy is wise for there are too many people purchasing weapons that really don't need them. The weapon can get into the wrong hands, individuals may be injured through careless or misuse of the weapon and it may be stolen from the person who owns it." (Author's personal file)

The letter speaks for itself. It clearly reveals what may be expected anywhere when the law-abiding citizen must prove need. Such abuses of the pistol purchase permit ordinance in Chicago were common knowledge not only amont those who had been aggrieved, but also among the many thousands of persons who had been actively engaged in the various legitimate shooting sports throughout the State of Illinois. Such documented facts could not be successfully hidden from the public at large who were captives of misleading reports of the news media. As a case in point, consider the following excerpt taken from a major news article published during the critical period in 1965 when the Illinois Legislature was considering the pistol registration bill:

"Opponents fear the law would not be properly administered and that the ownership of weapons would simply be denied. They maintain this already has happened in Chicago and that Chicago wants to spread the policy statewide. Kukla charges that the Chicago Police Department has made it a hard and fast rule never to grant a pistol purchase permit to a civilian, no matter how good his character or reasons."

*   *   *

"That charge was denied by Col. Wilson, who said the Chicago police grant permits when an investigation shows the applicant 'has a reason that is not frivolous.' Home protection, target competition and collecting are all good reasons, said Wilson." (*Chicago Sun Times*: Feb. 28, 1965)

The Col. Wilson referred to in the preceding article was Col. Minor K. Wilson, the top aide to Superintendent of Police Orlando W. Wilson who, in another news article during the same critical period, was quoted as having said:

"I have no objection to a law-abiding citizen having a gun in his house if he is in fact a law-abiding citizen." (*Chicago Tribune*: Feb. 6, 1965)

How would the reader reconcile those statements with the policy set forth in the previously quoted letters released by the Chicago Police Department? What does all this suggest to the reader about the Chicago Police Department?

The chief reason specified in the form letter used by the Chicago Police Department first to reject pistol permit applications contained this paragraph:

"A study of the beat plan covering your place of residence indicates that there is a sufficient number of patrol vehicles assigned within close proximity to your home, assuring fast and protective response to

321

any grievious calls for police service which you might make."
(Author's personal file)

The implication was quite clear that no one required a handgun for home protection because the Chicago Police Department was capable of providing ample and rapid protection. Did they really? On those occasions where that "fast and protective response" did not happen to arrive on time and the robbed, raped or assaulted citizen wrote an indignant letter of complaint to the Superintendent of Police, the Chicago Police Department had the appropriate answer neatly prepared, in another form letter. Two paragraphs from that exculpatory missive read as follows:

> *"The police cannot be everywhere all of the time.* It costs a great deal of money to run a police department. Just as the average person does not have enough funds to do everything he would like to do, the police do not have enough funds and personnel to place a police officer wherever a crime may occur in order to prevent that crime from occurring. We undertake to deploy our manpower in such a manner as to have policemen in locations where crimes are most likely to occur and during the hours when they are most likely to be committed in the belief that a criminal ordinarily does not commit a crime in the presence of a policeman.
>
> *All crimes cannot be prevented.* Even if it were possible to assign a police officer to each citizen, there is no assurance that all crimes can be prevented. Many crimes occur in private premises and originate in the back reaches of a person's mind and are the result of a sudden impulse. No amount of police protection can prevent such crimes."
> (CPD–11.149–S163)

Thus we have an excellent grasp of some of the reasons why law-abiding citizens anywhere cannot trust the big city influence to guide either state or national gun legislation.

At the beginning of the 1967 gun registration campaign launched by Chicago Mayor Daley, the author received a telegram at his office from the Mayor's forces of a nature and under conditions designed to embarrass him in his position as an executive for a large merchandising company.

Mayor Daley led off with requests that Illinois state officials and representatives be flooded with letters, petitions and telegrams in support of gun control.

The effort by Daley and his forces were organized tightly and

ONLY <u>YOU</u> CAN

PASS

the

GUN
RESPONSIBILITY
BILL

Cover of Chicago's gun responsibility kit.

efficiently. Sophisticated and artistically developed work kits were distributed.

The gun registration bill was euphemistically called the "Gun Responsibility Bill". Inflammatory illustrations were circularized and the common lack of truth started with an inaccurate copy of the bill itself! There were pledge cards, montages of sensational news reports, lists of the members of the Illinois General Assembly—little was forgotten in this high pressure effort to force Daley's will on all of Illinois. A campaign headquarters with volunteers, petitions, propaganda distribution and telephones were provided. The Chicago newspapers blossomed with support for the mayor. Honest reporting was forsaken; reporting for a purpose was rampant. Gun advertising was sensationalized by indicating machine-pistols were for sale, cheap, where—although the picture of a machine pistol was shown—in fact only the stock of that type was

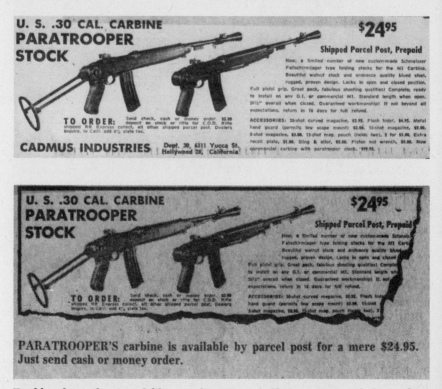

Double photo showing deliberate distortion of *Shotgun News* ad for carbine folding-stock.

for sale for fitting to a perfectly legal U.S. .30 caliber carbine.

Without doubt the most professional assistance given Mayor Daley's gun registration legislation was the advertising campaign by the Edward H. Weiss & Co. advertising agency of Chicago. That agency prepared superb posters on behalf of the gun registration bill. The posters were designed to focus attention on the dangers associated with firearms, and urged viewers to contact their legislative representatives in the State Capitol and request they enact the gun registration bill into law. Reportedly, the posters had been prepared free of charge for the Mayor's Citizens Committee for the Passage of the Gun Responsibility Bill. The size and scope of that advertising campaign was described on the advertising and marketing page of the *Chicago Tribune* on May 10, 1967, as follows:

"The campaign now consists of more than 3,200 transit cards for subway, bus, and railroads, as well as one and two-sheet posters. Space for the campaign was donated by Metromedia, Inc., and Trans Displays, Inc."

It was interesting that Metromedia donated space for the anti-gun posters because, as the reader will recall, on occasion their name had appeared in the newspapers linked with that of Senator Thomas J. Dodd by columnists Drew Pearson and Jack Anderson, who wrote of Senator Dodd that:

"Again, during his investigation of violence on TV, he accepted personal gifts and campaign contributions from officials of the NBC and Metromedia networks. Both networks were spared the embarassment of hearings." (*Washington Post*: April 13, 1968)

One should attempt to visualize 3,200 posters urging people to write to their legislators demanding gun registration. That is a large number of posters, and they obviously cost a great deal of money to produce and distribute. The jumbo size poster measured a full five feet in width and nearly four feet from top to bottom. Even the medium sized poster measured just under two feet square. The posters were made up in ten different varieties, adding considerably to their overall cost of production.

Can you imagine what would have been said by the news media had the National Rifle Association dared to engage in such a bold advertising campaign in opposition to some ill-conceived piece of legislation? Indeed, the news media had already severely castigated the

325

Don't be dead wrong.

Help pass the gun law.

WRITE AND ASK YOUR STATE REPRESENTATIVES AND SENATOR IN SPRINGFIELD TO VOTE FOR THE ILLINOIS GUN RESPONSIBILITY BILL. TO GET THEIR NAMES CALL 744-4056.

The Handy Death Kit.

WRITE AND ASK YOUR STATE REPRESENTATIVES AND SENATOR IN SPRINGFIELD TO VOTE FOR THE ILLINOIS GUN RESPONSIBILITY BILL. TO GET THEIR NAMES CALL 744-4056.

Six emotionally-loaded anti-gun ads used in Illinois.

Six emotionally-loaded anti-gun ads used in Illinois—*continued*.

Anti-gun ads used in Illinois—*continued.*

NRA for merely writing letters to its membership furnishing objective information concerning provisions of proposed firearms legislation.

On March 27, 1967, the *Chicago Tribune* ran a story entitled "Two Crime Fighters Rip Mob Dinner" which described the cavorting of some 200 allegedly top hoodlums at a lavish dinner-dance attended by more than 1,000 persons and held at the Edgewater Beach hotel. The affair was supposedly billed as a social gathering for members and friends of the Santa Fe Saddle and Gun Club, and the article stated that it was held under the watchful eyes of various law-enforcement investigators. One of those investigators was the Executive Director of the Illinois Crime Investigating Commission, whose remarks the *Chicago Tribune* reported as follows:

"He suggested that one aspect of the meeting may have been to discuss ways to defeat the gun responsibility law, which was introduced by Mayor Daley. 'Here you have a meeting that includes hoodlums who all but admit they are members of a gun club and silently proclaim, "What's wrong with carrying guns?" It just annoys me. The mayor has launched a terrific program for the gun bill, and it must be passed.' "

Did you catch that part about the silent proclamation? If not, then read it over once again slowly for a classic example of how to go about putting words of your own choosing into mouths of your own choosing. There is no end to the possibilities! Anyone can be made to "silently proclaim" anything. Magic! It is as good as interpretative journalism, perhaps even better.

The next day, March 28, 1967, the *Chicago's American* rushed in with a follow-up story on the allegedly hoodlum infested Sante Fe Saddle and Gun Club, and purported to quote the Operating Director of the Chicago Crime Commission as saying that the gun club was probably a shooting range for mob firearms specialists, and that:

" 'Skeet shooting ranges have always been a prime training ground for gunmen. It provides them with a moving target,' he said."

That was not the first nor the last occasion on which legitimate sportsmen were subtly associated with the disreputable or criminal element by those persons anxious to procure enactment of the gun registration law. The most frequently employed technique was the use of so-called "political cartoons" which graphically and quite unmistakably projected the desired impressions to the viewers.

On April 24, 1967, Illinois State Senator W. Russell Arrington

'They wanna deprive us of the right to bear arms, boss'

Chicago's American anti-gun cartoon.

introduced a gun control measure in the Illinois Legislature to require the licensing of persons in possession of either firearms or ammunition. The *Chicago Sun-Times* reported the filing of the bill on the following day and quoted Senator Arrington as follows:

" 'Gun registration does not prevent crimes. It is only an impediment which may or may not stop a killing. Real firearms control must directly involve the person,' Arrington said he had not consulted the National Rifle Assn., chief opponent of gun control legislation, but he hoped for support."

Apparently upset by the announcement of the Arrington firearms owners licensing proposal, Chicago Mayor Richard J. Daley quickly issued a proclamation that April 28, 1967, was to be "Gun Letter" day in Chicago, and according to the Chicago's American the Mayor asked citizens to write letters to the Legislature favoring his gun registration bill before the public hearings were commenced the following week. It was also reported that:

"The mayor also urged that citizens who back the bill try to appear at the hearings next week 'to make your presence and wishes known.' "

One official witness for the gun registration bill was the Chicago Superintendent of Police, Orlando W. Wilson who, upon being pressed by a legislator, testified that in the year preceding the Chicago Police Department had issued only 11 gun permits under the city ordinance. Little chance any law-abiding citizen of Chicago had to get a gun permit!

Following the three and one-half hours of hearings, the House Executive Committee voted 18 to 13 to send the Mayor's bill to a subcommittee for study along with 13 other proposals relating to gun control. Daley was defeated. Arrington prevented him from dominating Illinois.

Mayor Daley attended the hearing in Springfield. He had been accompanied in his trek to the State Capitol by representatives of five of the highest ranking religious officials in Chicago. It was reported that the religious dignitaries did not ride in two buses which had been used for transporting more ordinary citizens from Chicago to Springfield, but instead flew with Mayor Daley in a chartered Ozark Airlines plane. Neither was it mentioned whether they had worn the large yellow and black lapel buttons, provided Daley supporters, or were paid the ten dollars plus two free meals allegedly received by the shirtsleeve followers.

During the course of the hysterical gun registration campaign the Illinois State Rifle Association summoned a council of the major firearms oriented sporting organizations in Illinois, so that a logical and consistent position, with respect to the several major firearms control bills, might be adopted. After analysis of the pending legislative proposals, and a discussion of their respective merits and shortcomings, it was agreed they would offer their collective support to the firearms owners licensing proposal, sponsored by State Senator W. Russell Arrington, as an alternative to other unreasonable and unworkable measures proposed.

Upon learning of the fact that the Illinois firearms owning sportsmen were supporting his licensing bill, Senator Arrington requested that the Legislative Chairman of the Illinois State Rifle Association testify to that effect before the Illinois Senate Judiciary Committee. That request was promptly honored, but without benefit of the noisy fanfare and lapel button claque which had accompanied the earlier appearance by representatives of Mayor Daley of Chicago on behalf of gun registration. One man, alone, and fortified only with a rational presentation, was quite sufficient.

On May 22, 1967, Senator Arrington's bills came up before the full Illinois State Senate, and once again he called upon "the man from the rifle association," Robert J. Kukla, to appear before the Senate in support of his measures, and, as before, it was done. The results were noted with amazement by the *Chicago Sun-Times*, which reported on May 23, 1967:

> "Gun-owner licensing legislation passed the Illinois Senate Monday by a surprisingly overwhelming vote. Three measures sponsored by Senate Majority Leader W. Russell Arrington. . . . were sent along to the House by votes of 48 to 7 on the main owner-licensing proposal and 50 to 5 on two companion measures."

The very next day the *Chicago's American* ran an editorial titled "Killing In The Streets" which commented on a recent shooting rampage in the city. It should be observed that the editorial was published on May 23, 1967, eleven days *after* the Illinois State Rifle Association testified on behalf of the Arrington bills before the Senate Judiciary Committee, and one day *after* its Legislative Committee Chairman had again appeared in support of those same measures before the full Illinois State Senate. The *Chicago's American*, however, opened its editorial May 23, 1967, with the following statement:

332

"The powerful pressure groups opposing gun control legislation cannot advance any argument that would justify legal ownership of firearms by the four youths accused of killing one person and wounding 10 others Saturday in what police termed a 'mad dog' rampage on the west side.

Yet this, in effect, is what they are doing as they step up their efforts in Springfield to block any type of effective gun control legislation—including that designed to keep guns out of the hands of irresponsible minors."

The concepts of integrity and intellectual honesty subscribed to by the anti-gun forces in this country are beginning to become clear, are they not?

This particular episode clearly illustrates the lengths to which certain people will go in disarming of free and law-abiding citizens under the guise of preventing crime. They did not succeed.

Chicago Mayor Richard J. Daley was not about to allow the matter to be dropped merely because his gun registration bill had been overwhelmingly defeated in the State Legislature. On January 2, 1968, he began the new year by calling for a special session of the Chicago City Council on January 5, 1968, to ask that they adopt a city ordinance which would require the registration of all guns by residents of the city. In a gross understatement, the *Chicago Sun-Times* tendered the following explanation on January 3, 1968:

"Details of the proposal were not disclosed. But Daley is known to have been deeply disappointed at the refusal of the Illinois General Assembly last year to pass a law requiring the registration of all firearms in the state."

On that same day, the *Chicago's American* purported to quote one of the Chicago aldermen, A. A. Rayner, Jr., as responding to the Mayor's proposal with his pocorobian suggestion:

"Rayner said he would like to see all guns taken out of the hands of citizens. 'If people want to hunt,' Rayner said, 'they could rent guns from the state and if they just want target practice, they could use realistic toy ranges.' "

On January 5, 1968, Mayor Daley called for registration of all firearms owned by Chicago residents, including rifles and shotguns, with the City Collector beginning 60 days after the passage of the ordinance. The *Chicago's American* also helpfully reported a remark allegedly made by the Mayor, which was reminiscent of Gestapo tactics under Adolf Hitler:

> "Daley called for all citizens to cooperate with his proposed ordinance by reporting all owners who fail to register guns."

In the event one is not familiar with the manner in which the City of Chicago was run during that era, then it should be understood there was never any question as to whether or not the Mayor's gun registration ordinance would be adopted. The moment Daley called for a gun registration ordinance for Chicago, that was the moment its passage was assured. In the opinion of many knowledgeable observers, everything which followed thereafter was strictly for the purpose of maintaining an illusory appearance of democratic government, while the ultimate conclusion of the whole procedure had already been preordained.

For the television cameras and the typically uncritical news media, one of the Mayor's representatives rolled out his tour de force, an unbelievably enormous stack of new petitions having so many signatures calling for gun registration within the City of Chicago that it boggled the imagination. The *Chicago Daily News* solemnly described the presentation of the petitions in an article published on January 10, 1968, the day of the hearings:

> "AT THE start of the hearing, Ald. Matthew Danaher of the mayor's own 11th Ward submitted petitions bearing 1,200,000 signatures of persons favoring passage of the ordinance. Daley last week had ordered a door-to-door canvass in the city's wards to obtain a large number of signatures."

Imagine, 1,200,000 signatures in a city whose total population of men, women and children was only about 3,550,000. Imagine, 1,200,000 signatures collected in less than one week and during the coldest month of the year, January. Magic! It was far better than public opinion polls, and certainly more reliable than either newspaper clip-out coupons or form letters torn off at dotted lines. Even the *Chicago's American* was impressed with that astounding total and took pains to refer to it in their editorial of January 17, 1968:

> "This gun control ordinance, which has received the indorsement of 1.2 million Chicagoans including the citizens committee for enactment of gun-control legislation, certainly isn't the whole answer to the abuse of firearms. But it is a sound, legal way to increase the personal safety of everyone in Chicago."

334

On January 16, 1968, one wonderfully honest and courageous woman apparently solved the mystery of the 1,200,000 signatures, and a popular newspaper columnist named Mike Royko had the moxie to tell her story in print, once, in the *Chicago Daily News*. He began his excellent article in this manner:

"A South Side woman says her son's eight-grade class was used to forge voters' names on Mayor Daley's gun-control petitions. She said a man, believed to be a Democratic precinct worker, brought a list of voters to the class last week and the teacher told the students to copy the names on the gun-control petitions."

The author received a report during the petition gathering project of another incident in which a Democratic precinct captain, who was employed as a night security guard for a large company, was caught copying voter registration lists onto the Mayor's gun control petitions. His explanation had been that with the three days given everyone to produce their quota of signatures there simply was no other way in which to obtain the number which was required. Perhaps, it wasn't magic, after all, but interesting anyway.

The reader should not forget those 1,200,000 signatures. They cost too much time and effort to be used only once. As will be seen, they popped up once again, at another time, and in another place, but also in support of gun registration.

Exactly one day before the Chicago City Council had been scheduled to enact Mayor Daley's long sought-after gun registration ordinance the United States Supreme Court, in the landmark decision of Haynes vs. United States (390 U.S. 85 [1968]), invalidated a very significant portion of the gun registration provisions of the National Firearms Act of 1934. On the following morning, January 30, 1968, the *Chicago Sun-Times* carried this front page announcement in bold letters:

"GUNS: 1934 Firearms Registry Act is Invalidated."

Pandemonium reigned on the fifth floor of Chicago's City Hall. Last minute efforts were desperately made to rationalize the irrational act of forcing through a registration ordinance following the same principle which had been the basis of the national law since 1934—now found unconstitutional. The problem arose over the fact that the U.S. Supreme Court had ruled that, under the terms of the Fifth Amendment of the Constitution, the constitutional privilege against self-incrimination provided a full legal defense to criminal prosecution either for failure to register a firearm or for possession of an unregistered firearm under the National Firearms Act of 1934.

Recall the testimony of Charles V. Imlay, the District of Columbia member of the National Conference of Commissioners on Uniform Laws, who had flatly told the Copeland committee in 1935 his legal opinion of the National Firearms Act which at that time had been in effect for less than one year. He had expressed his views in this one concise statement:

> "I submit that the National Firearms Act, limited as it was, after these hearings last year, is based upon a specious question of taxing to supply the only element of constitutionality that can be found." (KK–p. 28)

The quandary of the Mayor's minions must have been considerable, but in a city known for its "magic" solutions to vexing problems an answer was inevitable, and this occasion was no exception. The decision arrived at was simply to exclude from eligibility to register guns any person whose possession of any firearm was prohibited under any State or Federal law relating to firearms. In other words, none of the following classes of persons were "eligible" to register their guns: persons under 18 years of age; narcotic addicts; persons convicted of a felony within 5 years of release from a mental institution or custody of the Illinois Youth Commission; persons mentally retarded; and, persons possessing any firearm which was prohibited by any State or Federal law as, for example, sawed-off shotguns or machine guns.

Absurdly, only decent and law-abiding citizens remained to be forced to register every individual firearm they owned. It was in that precise manner the obedient Chicago City Council enacted the city's first gun registration ordinance on January 30, 1968.

The ink was scarcely dry on the new Chicago ordinance when the *Chicago Sun-Times* conclusively confirmed the extent of its small knowledge of matters pertaining to firearms by offering the following pocorobian suggestion on its editorial page on February 1, 1968:

> "All guns should be 'fingerprinted'—test-fired for ballistic markings. If that were required by law a gun could be identified by the markings it put on the bullets fired from it.
>
> Such a ballistics test-firing program would have to be carried out on a statewide basis. It would be futile to do it in one or two municipalities. We suggest, also, that federal laws be passed to require gun manufacturers to test fire the weapons they produce, so ballistic-marking information could be supplied with the gun when it is sold to

a dealer, who would forward the information to the local police department when the gun is sold. In time, every legally owned firearm would be fingerprinted and the job of identifying a gun made easier for the police."

The proposal for fingerprinting bullets stems from the same kind of mentality that is unable to discern any distinction between the registration of an automobile and the registration of a firearm, and therefore blithely makes the assumption that if people can be fingerprinted, so can firearms. That is completely fallacious, as anyone knows whose knowledge of firearms and identification techniques has not been derived from reading detective comic strips or watching the mystery movies on television.

It should be understood that human fingerprints remain unchanged during the entire lifetime with a constant pattern of whorls, arches, and tented arches which permits a system of logical classification, coding, retrieval, and comparison for identification purposes. No such system exists in the case of firearms, and none can ever be realistically devised. This is due in part to the fact there are an infinitely greater number of variables among firearms and the bullets fired through them than there are in the case of human fingerprints produced with the consistency and monotonous regularity of type by Mother Nature. In addition, those distinguishing characteristics of microscopic size found within rifled bores, and which are the very basis of bullet identification, are subject to constant change with use, with the abrasions of regular cleaning, with the corrosion of neglect, and with normal erosion. They can also be changed deliberately in a matter of only a few seconds by anyone desiring to do so.

The International Association for Identification, composed of approximately 2,000 experts in the field of fingerprints, documents, and firearms identification, rejected as utterly useless any scheme for mass testing of firearms for the purpose of fingerprinting bullets. They went further and said such schemes were detrimental to criminal investigation.

Chicagoans did not have long to wait before beginning to enjoy the full benefits of the gun registration law. On July 30, 1969, readers of the *Chicago Sun-Times* were greeted with this bit of information:

"Police have arrested a patrolman who they charge was selling gun permits to ex-convicts employed as 'Rent-a-cops,' The Sun-Times learned Tuesday.

* * *

"The possibility existed that dozens of ex-convicts may have obtained gun permits. Persons with criminal records are not allowed to possess firearms.

Clark was reluctant to comment on the case but it was learned police believe permits were sold for as much as $300 each to unauthorized persons."

On April 8, 1970, syndicated columnist Mike Royko's entertaining column captioned "Chicago Punishes a Victim" described how the new Chicago gun registration ordinance had been applied to a hapless burglary victim. The victim, who had recently moved to Chicago from the State of Wisconsin, returned home from shopping one evening to discover that his apartment had just been ransacked. Rushing out into the back alley he apprehended one of three young men who had been holding two rifles which belonged to him. The police were promptly summoned, and when they arrived they arrested both the burglary suspect and the burglary victim who had failed to register his rifles when he moved into Chicago. Both were locked up in the same jail.

When the matter finally came up in court, typical Chicago justice prevailed. Although the burglary suspect had pleaded guilty to possessing the stolen guns, the presiding judge dismissed the charges. Then, turning his attention to the burglary victim, the judge fined him $500 for not having his guns registered. Not having the $500, he was once again locked up in jail.

Eventually, the poor man's wife was able to raise the $500 fine and thereby obtain his release from jail. Mike Royko recorded his understandable reaction to his experience with the Chicago style of justice and the gun registration ordinance:

" 'I am getting out of this goofy town,' he says. 'I'm the one who was burglarized, and I'm the only one convicted of anything.'

" 'They got my guns, and I can't get them back, and I still haven't got my $100 bond back. So I'm out my property and $600.' " (*The Cleveland Press*: April 8, 1970)

Probably the only persons in Illinois who were not in the least bit surprised over the "problems", to say nothing of the lack of effectiveness of the Chicago gun registration ordinance to prevent crime, were the organized firearms owners in the State who had known exactly what might have been expected. After all, they were the real experts when it came to firearms and to firearms legislation.

17

*"We see Americans behaving like children, parroting
nonsense, accepting unproved theory as fact and
reacting as the Germans did in the 1930s as the
Goebbel propaganda mill drilled lies into their
subconsciousness."*

HAROLD W. GLASSEN

LET US RESUME TRACING THE PROGRESS OF SENATOR
Dodd's S.1 through the Congress. The point of resumption will be August 25, 1967, with the National Rifle Association being further castigated in the press.

Reporting on the testimony given by Senator Robert F. Kennedy before the New York City Council Committee on City Affairs and the Joint Legislative Committee on Crime, the *Washington Star* stated on August 25, 1967, that:

"Kennedy said under questioning that the National Rifle Association was 'one of the strongest lobbies' in the country financed by 'tremendous resources,' the Associated Press reported.

339

He said that since 1954 the association had 'successfully lobbied' against stronger federal gun-control legislation, which he termed 'a great disservice to the country.'

'Because of what they've done,' Kennedy said, 'the association must take a share of the responsibility for the deaths of many Americans.' "

The accusations of Senator Kennedy reverberated throughout the country as one newspaper columnist after another echoed and re-echoed his charges. Referring specifically to the remarks of Senator Kennedy with respect to the National Rifle Association, columnist Inez Robb (the *Courier Journal and Times*) used them as the springboard for these indignant remarks on September 10, 1967:

"There is no desecration of the flag more offensive than its use as a wrapper by self-anointed patriots. Members of the association, as well as those adherents of paramilitary groups on the lunatic fringe, have spread the word that any gun-control measure, no matter how needed or sensible, is part of a great Communist conspiracy. They have wrapped themselves in the Stars and Stripes as superpatriots and as the only force that stands between you and me and a Communist takeover. It is a despicable stance and a preposterous creed."

It should be noted that the National Rifle Association was not the only object of vilification during this lengthy period. Hunters also received their share, as did anyone else who owned and used firearms for legitimate purposes. Consider, if you will, the manner in which hunters were characterized in this excerpt taken from a *Saturday Evening Post* article Oct. 21, 1967, which had been descriptively entitled "Hunting Is A Dirty Business":

"Physically they run to paunch and red faces. They are slow of foot, expensively dressed from the tips of their down bootees to the knobs of their silver hip flasks. They have little desire to search for game, but a great desire to kill something that can be tied to a fender or held up in a bar-room."

The *Detroit Daily Press* January 22, 1968, chimed in that ". . . this barbaric practice (hunting) should be outlawed. . . ."

Inundated by an absolutely incessant barrage of vitriol at times seemingly unleashed on command, beleaguered firearms owners began to flood the National Rifle Association with membership applications at a rate that soon exceeded 20,000 per month.

On February 7, 1968, President Lyndon Johnson again called for prompt enactment of a law which not only would forbid interstate mail order shipment of firearms but also over-the-counter sales of handguns and out-of-state customers. In commenting on the President's message a *Washington Post* columnist explained his interpretation of the conflict between the demands of the Johnson Administration and the adamant opposition of the National Rifle Association:

"The disagreement between President Johnson's gun control views and the National Rifle Association's poses no problem for me. President Johnson has no money interest in this matter. The NRA does have. It collects millions in advertising revenue from gun manufacturers and sellers. It collects millions more in dues from members who are told by the NRA that it is protecting them from a Government that is trying to 'disarm' them." (*Washington Post*: Mar. 8, 1968)

This is as good a place as any in which to discuss the economic facts of the NRA's life, using the most recent available figures as a basis from which to proceed. In 1969 the NRA's earned income was $7,410,389. Of that moment, 66 percent was derived from the annual membership dues, 21 percent came from the sale of advertising space in *The American Rifleman* magazine, and the 13 percent balance resulted from various other income-producing services and activities.

It cost the NRA a total of $6,997,704 to service its membership, and the remaining $406,925 was placed in reserves to offset the cost of servicing life memberships over future years. Of the $6,997,704 in operating costs, a total of 37 percent related to the Office of Publications which published and distributed the NRA's monthly magazine, *The American Rifleman*, to more than 1,000,000 NRA members; 27 percent was accounted for by the Membership Division which was responsible for membership promotion and the enormous job of maintaining membership records, and the remaining 36 percent was expended for such services as firearms safety and marksmanship training, organized shooting competitions, hunting and game conservation programs, firearms legislative information bulletins, and general Headquarters operations.

As the governing body of U.S. competitive rifle and pistol shooting as well as a member of the U.S. Olympic Committee and International Shooting Union, The National Rifle Association coordinated, sanctioned, and maintained detailed individual marksmanship records for the following numbers of competitive shooting events: 486 high power rifle matches; 883 smallbore rifle matches; 1,400 pistol and revolver matches, 2,830 moving target competitions, which includes international skeet, international clay pigeon, international running boar, and international running deer; 530 shooting league matches; and hundreds of postal matches.

As a not-for-profit membership association, the National Rifle Association's 75-member Board of Directors has general charge of its affairs and property. The Directors are elected from among the Life Members of the association and serve a three year term. The President and Vice Presidents of the National Rifle Association are, in turn, elected for a one year term by the Board of Directors from among its own members. Neither members of the Board of Directors, nor the President or Vice Presidents, receive any salary, compensation, remuneration, or other emolument arising out of their service to the National Rifle Association. Quite to the contrary, they regard the singular privilege of being permitted to serve their fellow members according to their respective abilities as a great honor.

As a personal aside, the author was cautioned upon the occasion of having been first elected to the Board of Directors that he could reasonably expect to incur as much as $1,000 per year in out-of-pocket and non-tax-deductible expenses to discharge the responsibilities of that position. Suffice it to say that the aforesaid estimate proved to be quite conservative, to say the least.

The day to day business of providing the NRA's many excellent services to its huge membership is performed by a paid executive staff of exceptionally fine, highly qualified and dedicated people for whom NRA employment means far more than merely another job. Altogether, including clerical assistants of every variety, the NRA employs approximately 260 men and women.

It was in the very midst of the continuing turmoil raging over the Administration's gun control proposals that yet another shocking tragedy occurred. On April 4, 1968, the Reverend Martin Luther King Jr., the eminent Negro civil rights leader, founder of the Southern Christian Leadership Conference, and Nobel Peace Prize winner for his advocacy of non-violent protest, was slain by a man armed with a rifle in Memphis, Tennessee. In the ten days which followed, there were 129 recorded incidents of racial violence in 29 states.

Prior to the murder of the Reverend King, Senator Dodd's bill had advanced from the House Judiciary Subcommittee to the full Judiciary Committee on November 7, 1967, by a vote of 7 to 6. On the day of Reverend King's death, the Senate Judiciary Committee approved the Administration's sweeping anti-crime bill after a series of close votes on amendments, among which was one by Senator Dodd to exclude long guns from its provisions, so that S.1 could be voted out of the committee. It was disclosed that the vote to ban the mail order shipment of handguns had been approved by a vote of 9 to 7.

On April 14, 1968, *The Boston Sunday Globe* ran a revealing article purporting to survey the gun control controversy in Congress and the role of the NRA in opposing the total prohibitions contained in the Administration's bill. The article concluded with the following gratuitous observation by a foreigner:

"Gunnar Myrdal, prominent Swedish sociologist discussed that point when interviewed after the riots in America's cities last week.

'I am against all your gun laws,' he said. 'It is argued that the Constitution supports them by holding that every citizen has the right to bear arms. Then to hell with the Constitution.' "

There is nothing quite so edifying as a calm, rational, emotionally detached, and professional assessment of complex sociological phenomenon, is there? Indeed.

On April 29, 1968, Senator Roman Hruska introduced his own amendment to the Administration's omnibus crime bill which was being touted by the appealing name of the "Safe Streets Bill." The Hruska amendment would have prohibited any firearms manufacturer or dealer from shipping or transporting any firearm to any person in any state where the receipt or possession of such firearm would be in violation of any statute of such state or of any published ordinance applicable to the locality in which such person resided. The amendment was based upon a recognition of the diversity of conditions which exist in different parts of the United States and would have permitted the states to control the circumstances under which their residents would have been able to acquire firearms by mail-order purchases. The *Rochester Courier* May 9, 1968, published this editorial reference to that amendment:

"Sportsmen's organizations, including the prestigious Outdoor Writers Association of America and the National Shooting Sports Foundation have and are continuing to support the Hruska amendment."

On May 14, 1968, Senator Everett M. Dirksen and Senator Hruska combined forces to propose a series of amendments which, if passed, would have resulted in the substitution of the Hruska bill for that of Senator Dodd. However, the amendment was voted down by a vote of 45 to 37 on May 16, 1968, along with Senator Dodd's attempt to add long guns to his bill, which lost by a vote of 54 to 29.

Three weeks later the Nation was shocked to its very core as it learned that on June 5, 1968, Senator Robert F. Kennedy had been shot by an anti-Jew alien while campaigning for the presidency of the United States in Los Angeles, California. He died early on the following morning.

The heinous assassination of Senator Kennedy triggered a series of reactions and occurrences which were without parallel, and virtually all of them focused on the subject of firearms legislation. Promptly, the pressure upon Congress to enact gun control laws was literally irresistible, and on the very day of Senator Kennedy's death the President's omnibus crime bill, which was composed of eleven separate measures, including the ban on mail-order sales of handguns, was passed by the House by the overwhelming vote of 368 to 17 after having been previously approved by the Senate.

Shortly after the Congress had enacted the measure, President Lyndon Johnson spoke out on nationwide television and described the bill as a "watered down" version of what he had been seeking through all of the days of his presidency. Then, calling for still more comprehensive controls, he said:

> "Surely this must be clear beyond question: The hour has come for the Congress to enact a strong and effective gun-control law, governing the full range of lethal weapons." (*Chicago Sun-Times*: June 7, 1968)

Four days later, President Johnson established a "National Commission on the Causes and Prevention of Violence, and named as its chairman, Milton S. Eisenhower, the brother of the late President Dwight D. Eisenhower. That Commission will be the subject of a subsequent examination insofar as the subject of firearms control legislation is concerned.

On the very same day that President Johnson set up his Violence Commission, June 10, 1968, the weekly journal of the advertising media, *Advertising Age*, ran an editorial which was concisely captioned "GUNS MUST GO", and presented a three-point plan to achieve that purpose.

In mid-June, a full page ad signed by hundreds of prominent show business, church, government, medical, and legal personalities, appeared in the *New York Times*, in the *Washington Post*, and in the *Los Angeles Time*. The ad ended with an urgent plea to readers to write immediately to their Senators, Representatives, state legislators, and

344

Presidential candidates, asking that they join in the support for strong gun legislation.

Even the bubble-gum set received its own, tailored for the adolescent, propaganda appeal in the form of a special editorial inserted in the August 1968, issue of *Teen Screen* magazine. The editorial, the first ever run in that magazine, was built around the assassinations of Reverend Martin Luther King Jr. and Senator Robert F. Kennedy. Some excerpts follow:

"How would you like to kiss your father tonight, go to sleep, and wake up tomorrow morning and find that he had been shot to death by a kook who didn't dig your father's opinions?

*   *   *

"But you can do something to help prevent your father getting shot to death. You can write to your senator—while you still have a senator—and tell him you want him to do his best to stop the killing. You can write to him and tell him that all guns and ammunition should be registered. Tell him you want all mail order sales of guns and ammunition stopped now."

As the reader can surmise, the anti-gun campaign was of no small proportions, and as time went on the campaign intensified and became the catalytic agent through whose stimulus there burgeoned forth an absolutely astounding variety of monomaniacal reactions against guns of any and all kinds, and against the National Rifle Association of America.

Beginning with the morning on which Senator Robert Kennedy was shot in Los Angeles, the switchboard of the National Rifle Association was bombarded with telephone calls from people expressing their abhorrence to violence, and protesting killings. They did so by twice stating that they placed a bomb in the NRA building, and by uttering such epithets to the telephone operators as:

"All you people in the NRA should be shot."
"You murderers. . . ."
"I'm going to kill all you people." (Author's personal file)

By noon on June 5, 1968, there were an estimated two hundred pickets marching back and forth in front of the NRA headquarters building carrying signs bearing such slogans as: "Blood is the color of the NRA"; "NRA stop the gun lobby"; "Lobby for Murder"; "Ban Weapons"; "Disarm the NRA"; "Stop Violence, Stop the NRA". The demonstrations, mostly over the noon hour, lasted for seven days.

On June 10, 1968, the newspapers carried the story of how several chains of discount stores had decided to discontinue selling guns and ammunition, and how a national movement to turn in guns was being encouraged by some persons. Three days later, June 13, 1968, the *Chicago Daily News* told of a manufacturer of plaques and trophies which had announced that it was discontinuing the manufacture and sale of marksmanship trophies and awards. The president of the company was quoted as having said:

> "The time has come when we must do something about the popularity of guns in the hands of Americans. We refuse to add any admiration or enthusiastic interest to gun awards, whether for sporting or skill. We are especially concerned about the young people who look to the trophy award as a symbol of great achievement. We do not want to further this interest."

Chicago's new Superintendent of Police called for private citizens to turn in their personal firearms according to *Chicago's American* which reported on June 18, 1968, as follows:

> "Police Supt. James B. Conlisk Jr. today urged Chicago gun owners to turn in their weapons 'to prevent bloodshed and tragedy that can result from misuse or accident.' He said if the owners will call PO 5-1313 police will pick up guns and ammunition from any Chicago home without questions, even if the guns are not registered."

In a separate article on the following day, the *Chicago Sun-Times* reported how the Superintendent of Police had warned against the dangers of having firearms around the home and cited as an example a recent case where a 16 year old boy held a pistol to his head, pulled the trigger, and killed himself in the mistaken impression that he had earlier unloaded the pistol:

> "The boy had emptied the weapon's ammunition clip but, unfamiliar with automatics, had overlooked a shell in the chamber. That killed him. The pistol had been stolen in a burglary."

The article went on to assert seriously that if only the original owner of the pistol had surrendered it before it had been stolen by the burglar, then the boy would have still been alive. Think about that one for a while.

In a follow-up article, the *Chicago Sun-Times* June 25, 1968,

346

reported that as of that time 934 guns had been turned in to the Chicago Police, and that the turn-in rate was from 75 to 80 guns a day:

> "Chicagoans are turning in their guns 'so fast that we have hardly had time to catalog them,' Gen. Francis P. Kane, head of the city's gun registration program, said Monday."
>
> * * *
>
> "He attributed the response to the 'realization by citizens that they have no need for weapons' and also to the assassination of Sen. Robert F. Kennedy."

In one specific incident on the East coast, an 80 year old man turned in his shotgun to police and was widely quoted as saying he no longer felt like going hunting. Small wonder, at his age. In another case, a very much younger man who suddenly was overcome by a deep sense of remorse, on a momentary impulse surrendered two fine quality and expensive hunting rifles to local police, thereby unburdening his guilt-ridden conscience. The rifles had belonged to a friend from whom the young man had borrowed them for use over the weekend.

An interesting postscript to the gun surrender drive in Chicago popped up unexpectedly over one year later when the *Chicago Sun-Times* headline of October 7, 1969, reported "Quiz Told How General Sold Chicago Guns." The opening words told most of the story:

> "Maj. Gen. Carl C. Turner (Ret.), using his high office of Army provost marshal as a front, persuaded two police departments, including that of Chicago, to donate confiscated guns and then sold them 'for personal gain,' a Senate investigator testified Monday.
>
> The witness, Philip R. Manuel, testified that 'under the color of his official position' as provost marshal, Turner obtained at least 700 firearms—handguns, rifles, sawed-off shotguns, and machineguns—from Chicago and Kansas City (Mo.) police, and from Fort Bliss in El Paso, Tex."

The front page story in the *Chicago Tribune* on the same day contained this statement as to the occasions upon which the guns were allegedly selected from the Chicago Police Department:

> "Lt. Paul Duellman, commanding officer of the evidence recovery department of the Chicago police department, said Turner selected the weapons during four separate visits last year on May 23, on Aug. 1, on Aug. 30, and on Nov. 14."

The *Chicago Daily News* added this additional information to the rapidly unfolding story:

"On at least one occasion when he picked up firearms from Chicago police, Manuel said, Turner already had been in retirement from the Army for two weeks." (*Chicago Daily News*: Oct. 6, 1969)

Police Superintendent Conlisk appeared before the Senate subcommittee and testified that all weapons which had been turned over to the General were turned over for use by the United States Army, both for training and for exhibition in Army museums.

One of the gun surrender programs which produced no scandalous aftermath was the one participated in by the children of various schools, who were persuaded to surrender their arsenal of cap pistols, pop-guns, water pistols, and B-B guns. One news article which covered the mass surrender of the toy guns explained the purpose behind the movement:

"By their simple act, the children symbolically outlawed 'cops and robbers' and all other games using toy guns. Many of the pupils among the 1,400 attending the school contributed their 'weapons' to the new cause." (*Chicago's American*: June 17, 1968)

Joining in the campaign against toy guns was one retail merchant who decided no longer to deal in toy guns. According to the news stories he invited a group of Cub Scouts to smash his store's inventory of nearly 1,000 toy guns by stamping on them and mashing them with mallets on the sidewalk fronting his establishment as grinning adults looked on with approval.

One humorous incident occurred during the filming of a news program which had televised another incident of toy gun destruction by a police officer. One child was asked to hand the officer a toy gun which was to be destroyed, and the child responded quickly and with obvious enthusiasm. Immediately the television news reporter interviewed the little boy and asked him whether it had troubled him to give the toy gun to the policeman to be broken, and the lad cheerfully responded that it had not bothered him in the least. Thrusting the microphone once more towards the child, the reporter asked the boy to tell the people why he did not mind having the policeman destroy that toy gun. Out came the candid reply, as only a little boy could have expressed it:

"It wasn't mine. It belonged to that other kid over there." (Author's personal file)

Carrying the war against toy guns to its logical extremity, a story appeared in the *Chicago Daily News* on June 20, 1968, captioned "Gun Ride 'Disarmed' by Amusement Park" which told readers that the manager of a 17-ride amusement park intended to remove the toy guns which were mounted on one of the rides. He explained that he did not feel that guns were proper on a ride for children.

The gun control controversy had even a more substantial effect on the manufacturers of toy guns than the relatively few which were symbolically destroyed by tractable children. This brief note from *Chicago's American* on July 10, 1968, told that story:

"A number of Chicago toy dealers and department stores report they are reevaluating 'toys of violence' as a sale item, with an eye to either deemphasizing them on display counters or cutting them out.

The move was led this week by Sears Roebuck & company, which said it will eliminate toy weapons from its 1968 Christmas catalog and display them less prominently in its stores."

Two weeks later, another program to take away toy guns was descriptively labelled "Operation Gum Drop" by the Wabash Avenue police station in Chicago. The event was covered on July 27, 1968, by *Chicago's American* which reported that:

"Hundreds of youngsters appeared at the district's annual open house yesterday in response to an offer to give them bags of candy in exchange for their toy guns."

The same article went on to describe the plans of a savings and loan association to conduct a drive for toy guns through the month of August:

"The savings association has offered to pay 10 cents for every gun turned in by a youngster when he is accompanied by a parent, a spokesman said."

The national wave of revulsion over anything which in the slightest degree reminded sensitive people of violence even affected certain comic strips. An Associated Press news release of June 14, 1968, reported that the *Greensboro Daily News* had announced on its front page that it was dropping the Dick Tracy and Little Orphan Annie comic strips. The Little Orphan Annie strip had been carried by the paper since 1926, and Dick Tracy since 1939. A spokesman for the 90,000 circulation newspaper was quoted as having explained:

"We feel that their constant exploitation and advocacy of violence by law enforcement officers and the good guys outweigh any value the strips might have in promoting the theory that crime does not pay."

To fully appreciate the hysterical climate which had enveloped the United States during that extraordinary period, one need only consider the reaction to a new postage stamp which had just then been issued by the postal authorities to commemorate the patriotic frontiersman and folk hero, Daniel Boone's single shot flintlock squirrel rifle along with a powder horn, tomahawk, and belt knife. The four items, all closely associated with Daniel Boone in history, were mounted upon a rough hewn board fence into which were carved "Daniel Boone" and "1734", the latter date being the year of his birth.

The *Chicago Daily News* ran a preview article concerning the new commemorative stamp on July 20, 1968, and captioned it "A Tribute To Boone Or An Ad For Violence?" The author of that article seemed especially concerned about how the stamp would be interpreted abroad and made this assessment of the prospects:

Enlarged illustration of Daniel Boone stamp.

"Maybe those who will use or receive the stamp after it's issued at Frankfort, Ky., on Sept. 26, will appreciate the part his weapons played in the life of resourceful, heroic Boone. But the chances are that a rifle, tomahawk and knife will seem more like an advertisement for or tribute to instruments used for assassinations, muggings and devastating riots."

Needless to say, while the country was so utterly engrossed with the contemplation of its psychopathic feelings of collective guilt and its frenetic attempts to assuage its conscience, the Administration struggled vainly in an attempt to dislodge its bill to ban the mail-order sale of rifles and shotguns from the House Judiciary Committee. A motion by the committee chairman which would have advanced the proposal to the House floor on June 11, 1968, failed due to a tie vote of 16 to 16.

On the very next day, Senator Joseph Tydings and nine other senators introduced a national firearms registration bill into the Senate. On June 13, 1968, the *Chicago Daily News* also attributed the following remark to Senator Tydings on that occasion:

"Tydings said 'the gun lobby, led by paid Washington lobbyists of the National Rifle Assn., the Minutemen and other extremist groups, has without the slightest twinge of conscience' opposed all effective firearms measures."

Four days later, June 16, 1968, newspapers across the country carried headlines which told of President Johnson unleasing an all-out drive for stronger gun laws, and *Chicago's American* described the tone of that announcement in these words:

"President Johnson yesterday ordered a relentless drive to get strong, effective gun-control laws at the federal, state and local levels. The primary aim is to persuade Congress to put thru what it has balked at accepting so far—greatly expanded restrictions on sales of rifles and other long guns."

Simultaneously, the *New York Times* reported that three leading gun manufacturers had come out in substantial support of the Johnson proposal:

"The three companies—Remington, Winchester and Savage—announced they support legislation banning the interstate mail order sales of rifles and shotguns, as proposed by the administration. But the manufacturers suggested that the administration approach be modified to give individual states the right to exempt themselves from the prohibition on mail order sales."

The three manufacturers were reported as also having announced that two other gun manufacturers supported their position, O. F. Mossberg and Sons, Inc., and Ithaca Gun Company.

In reporting the occurrence, the *Chicago Sun-Times* June 16, 1968, added this detail which was no great secret to anyone other than the American public:

"A representative of a New York public relations firm for the three companies said 'there is no connection between the companies and the National Rifle Assn. There is no relationship. It just doesn't exist.' "

In the process of describing how the gun control battle was heating up, *Business Week* magazine came out in their June 15, 1968, issue with the same old accusation by Senator Tydings which had been spread from one end of the continent to the other:

"Senator Joseph D. Tydings (D-Md.) denounced the gun-lobbying National Rifle Assn. as the 'voice of munitions makers and gun sellers.' "

In the meantime, the Associated Press put out a release on June 14, 1968, which contained the following remarkable statement which the reader should read and never forget:

"The American Civil Liberties Union said today that the freedom to bear arms must be sacrificed to the more important freedom of 'free and fearless debate on which our free society rests.' "

At the precise time that the American Civil Liberties Union was mouthing its platitudes about "free and fearless debate on which our free society rests", the author was being viciously assailed in the news media on groundless charges leveled at him by one of the Chicago Mayor's legislative representatives in a deliberate attempt to cause him to be discharged from his employment.

On the day preceding the news release, the author had received a telephone call at his business office from a reporter with one of the four major Chicago newspapers. The reporter stated that he had just been informed by one of the sponsors of Mayor Daley's 1967 gun registration bill in the Illinois Legislature that the author had not registered as a lobbyist with the Legislature in spite of having appeared before it twice at the request of Senator W. Russell Arrington during 1967 to testify in support of the firearm owners licensing law. In response to the request by the reporter for comment, the author gave a completely true statement as follows:

That he was an attorney at law, licensed to practice by the Illinois Supreme Court within the State of Illinois, and licensed by the Federal District Court for the Northern District of Illinois. As an attorney whose special familiarity with laws pertaining to firearms control had been an outgrowth of an earlier interest in competitive shooting, and following the publication of his technical-legal treatise in 1958 entitled *Ballistic Evidence—Firearms Identification*, he had been requested by the officers of the Illinois State Rifle Association to serve as Chairman of their Legislative Committee. He served in that capacity for a number of years entirely as a non-paid volunteer, and provided such guidance and counsel in matters pertaining to firearms as he was able. On the two occasions during 1967 upon which he appeared before the Senate Judiciary Committee and the full Senate, he did so without pay; at great personal inconvenience and at the particular request of the President Pro Tempore and Majority Leader of the Illinois State Senate, W. Russell Arrington, who desired his testimony on behalf of the Illinois State Rifle Association in support of the pending licensing bill.

It was carefully explained to the reporter that the corporate employer of the author in no way was involved with the gun control issue, either in the State of Illinois, or on a national level; that the participation by the author in that field was a result of personal experience combined with philosophical and legal beliefs. The reporter was also fully informed that, on those occasions when the author had traveled to the State Capitol to testify upon request of Senator Arrington, he traveled on time that had been deducted from his vacation schedule, and not on time allowed by his employer. Further, the reporter was informed that any telephone calls on the subject were charged to the author's credit card, and not to the employer.

The reporter was also informed that the author's employer was not likely to view with benevolence any news story which attempted to link, in a derogatory manner, the author's personal pursuits of conscience with the corporate business, and that any such article would undoubtedly place the author's position in serious jeopardy. Specifically, the author requested that the reporter extend to him the courtesy of omitting any reference to the employer. The reporter responded by asserting that he had absolutely no intention of making any reference whatever to the employer as he did not want anyone to lose their job.

On the following morning three major Chicago newspapers ran the entire story, including the details of the author's employment, job capacity, and location of the employer. The June 14, 1968, edition of the *Chicago Daily News* opened with the following allegations in an article captioned "Pro-Gun Lobbyist Failed To Register":

> "The chief lobbyist for the Illinois State Rifle Assn. failed to register with the state as a lobbyist despite extensive activities against a stiff gun registration bill. The bill was defeated in the 1967 Legislature. It was supported by then-Gov. Otto Kerner, Chicago Mayor Richard J. Daley and former Chicago Police Supt. O. W. Wilson."

Among the immediate fruits of that exercise of the free press was an immediate letter to the editor of one paper from an indignant reader who proposed a "general customer boycott" of the author's employer until such time as he "registers with the state as a lobbyist".

The reader should understand that the Illinois lobbying act did not require that the author register as a lobbyist, nor did it require the publisher of the *Chicago's American*, Stuart List, to register in spite of the fact that he testified on behalf of gun registration in his capacity as Chairman of the Mayor's Citizens Committee for the Passage of the Gun Responsibility Bill. Neither did it require those members of Mayor Daley's entourage of religious dignitaries to register who also testified on behalf of the gun registration bill.

It is especially fitting at this time and place to dredge up an old editorial entitled "Reporters And Lobbyists" which had been published on March 8, 1967, by the *Chicago Daily News*. The following excerpts are the first and last paragraphs from that editorial:

> "The state treasurer, Adlai E. Stevenson III, says that newspaper reporters 'who in fact are lobbyists' ought to be required to register as such. We don't see the point."
>
> * * *
>
> "We are confident Stevenson did not intend in any way to inhibit a newspaper's vigorous advocacy of a good cause by raising the possibility of registering reporters 'who in fact are lobbyists.' But unless he can cite concrete examples of evil being done, he had best not tamper with a freedom so vital to the public welfare."

One need not be a particularly astute analyst in order to come rather quickly to the inevitable conclusion that there exists two stan-

354

dards of free speech in the United States on controversial public issues; one for the members of the press who increasingly and unifiedly express but one ideology and the other for their ideological opponents. As some representatives of the fourth estate evidently interpret their role in America, they are merely vigorous advocates of a good cause, while their opponents are despicable lobbyists; the press performs a laudable public service by disseminating the facts, while their opponents mislead the public with distorted propaganda; the press supports effective and meaningful legislation while their opponents favor weak watered-down substitutes; the press is motivated only by concern for the public interest, while their opponents are crass mercenaries; the freedom of the press is a constitutionally guaranteed right, while the possession of firearms by honest American citizens is only a transitory privilege subject to being "sacrificed to the more important freedom of free and fearless debate on which our free society rests."

The recital of facts in the author's case should be compared with the record of those government officials who have spoken for gun control at meetings in Miami (in winter, of course), in California and in many places in between, at the taxpayer's expense and on the taxpayer's time. Indeed, it is a harsh fact that an ordinary citizen opposing the hysterical caprices of a highly centralized and politicized government must support that government with taxes and at the same time oppose its oppression with his own money and on his own time.

On June 20, 1968, President Johnson signed into law the Administration's omnibus crime bill, which contained among its various provisions, the ban on interstate sales and shipments of pistols and revolvers. That bill was thereafter known as the "Omnibus Crime Control and Safe Streets Act of 1968." On the same day, the House Judiciary Committee voted 29 to 6 to approve the Administration's bill similarly to ban interstate shipments of long guns to private citizens. In commenting on the frenetic surge of activity relating to various gun control measures, *Chicago's American*, June 21, 1968, observed:

"The administration strategy is to get the bill acted on as quickly as possible, before the public outcry over the assassination of Sen. Robert F. Kennedy wanes."

During all those weeks there had been unleashed a continual stream of newspaper articles and editorials, radio and television commentaries and formal editorials labeled as such, and feature length articles in the country's largest news magazines, most of which exerted the maximum

355

possible pressure towards enactment of restrictive firearms control legistion.

The depths of asininity plumbed by some of the anti-gun crowd was contained in the reply to a question raised by a radio news reporter who asked a professed civil libertarian how he was able to rationalize his defense of the freedom to produce and distribute pornographic materials, while simultaneously denouncing the rights of law-abiding citizens to possess firearms. The unhesitating response was that he did so because pornography was "life-oriented" while firearms were "death-oriented."

On June 21, 1968, the public found a smoking revolver pointed straight at them from the cover of *Time* magazine suggesting the subject of its cover story "The Gun In America." Inside the magazine were five pages of copy, heavily laced with tidbits apparently plucked from the pages of the anti-gun book by Carl Bakal, plus a full page of anti-gun cartoons scavenged from among the most scurrilous produced by various newspaper cartoonists.

Apparently not even *Time* could resist resorting to the suggestion that firearms constituted a virility symbol to many people:

"Indeed, Freudians point out that the gun is an obvious phallic symbol, conferring on its owner a feeling a potency and masculinity." (June 21, 1968)

In at least one area, the *Time* article concisely and accurately characterized the fundamental, but not sole, objection to gun registration:

"The fear that the Government will end all private ownership of firearms underlies the N.R.A.'s opposition to registration of any weapons." (p. 17)

Running the gamut of anti-gun arguments voiced by the proponents of such measures, *Time* also included the pocorobian and previously explained impossible theory of finger printing bullets and dressed it up with references to modern electronic data processing computers:

"Some authorities have suggested that every firearm sold be 'fingerprinted' in advance by test-firing to determine its ballistic pattern. In the age of the computer, such distinctive patterns could be kept on file without too much difficulty." (p. 18)

356

Cover of *Time* Magazine.

Newsweek magazine stooped to an artifice with which the reader is already familiar, namely, the reproduction of an advertisement for completely harmless and inexpensive replicas of handguns which had been photographically reduced in size to a point where their accompanying descriptive text had been rendered unreadable, thus creating the false impression, conveyed by their superficial appearance and prominent price tags, that they were lethal weapons selling for unbelievably low prices. The six "pistols" which were featured in the advertisement were: a German Luger for about $17; a western six-shooter for $15; a snub-nosed detective revolver for $15; another German P-38 automatic pistol for $17; an Italian .380 automatic pistol for $15; and, a U.S. military .45 automatic pistol for $17.

What had not been so readily grasped by uninformed *Newsweek* readers was that those "pistols" were not real firearms, but rather were entirely nonfunctioning models cast from a zinc alloy and cleverly designed to resemble the appearance of popular handguns at a mere fraction of their cost for display in dens, playrooms, etc. However, the accompanying *Newsweek* subtitle merely read: "In stores and catalogues, guns of every variety and price." (June 24, 1968)

Here is the actual text of the advertising copy from that ad before *Newsweek* photographically reduced it to microscopic and normally unreadable size:

"Now, at last available in the United States! In Japan, where firearms are outlawed, collectors demand the most authentic replicas possible for display in collections. Single-action mock fast-draw models, as well as modern military types have been precisely copied. Made of cast zinc alloy, and the results of several years of design study, the models represent a totally new, inexpensive and safe outlet for the collector. Safe for a family den—these models cannot chamber or fire ammunition and are designed only for display collections—YET THEY CAN BE DISASSEMBLED like the originals! These copies of famous firearms must be seen to be appreciated."

Newsweek even dredged up the following old and discredited 1964 story, dusted it off, and presented it to readers as a "recent staff study":

"In a recent staff study of 4,000 guns shipped from Los Angeles mail-order houses to buyers in Chicago, a Senate subcommittee discovered that 25 per cent of the gun buyers had criminal records." (June 24, 1968)

Newsweek, as did so many others before and after it, apparently

Cover of *Newsweek*.

could produce no more informative insight for its readers as to the role
served by firearms in the countless legitimate activities of hunting tournament shooting with pistols, rifles and shotguns, gun collecting and
their innumerable lawful offshoots, than to undrape the old phallic
symbol explanation:

> "The basic fascination of guns is a matter of debate. Some psychiatrists
> explain it entirely in sexual terms. A gun, they say, symbolizes the
> male organ and enhances its owner's feelings of potency."

Just in case the reader was unaware of the fact, it should be noted
that *Newsweek* magazine was the wholly owned subsidiary of the *Washington Post* newspaper. Interesting, perhaps; certainly expected.

In the period immediately following the assassination of Senator
Robert Kennedy a special national committee was established for the
purpose of stampeding gun registration through the Congress. The special group was the action-arm of the National Council for a Responsible
Firearms Policy, previously mentioned. It was headed by former as-
tronaut John Glenn, who claimed to have been a personal friend of
Senator Robert Kennedy. The *Chicago's American* of June 20, 1968,
reported on the meeting which had been held in the office of the U.S.
Attorney General resulting in the formation of the group:

> "Officials of the N.C.R.F.P. and representatives of 38 organizations
> met this week with United States Atty. Gen. Ramsey Clark in Wash-
> ington to discuss firearms control. After the meeting, Clark announced
> that a committee of the council had been formed to enlist support from
> the public and organizations thruout the country. The committee is
> known as the emergency committee for gun control of the National
> Council for a Responsible Firearms Policy."

Moving rapidly, John Glenn, Chairman of the Emergency Committee for Gun Control of the National Council for a Responsible
Firearms Policy, called a press conference at which he demanded
registration of all guns and the licensing of all those who owned or
used guns, in addition to a complete ban on the interstate sale and
shipment of firearms to private citizens.

Before long the John Glenn Emergency Committee for Gun Control was generating advertisements promoting gun registration, issuing
press releases designed to enlist public support for the proposals of the
Emergency Committee, soliciting broadcasting stations around the
country to make spot announcements and editorials favoring gun regis-

There is only one thing a gun is built to do...

WRITE YOUR SENATOR...WHILE YOU STILL HAVE A SENATOR.

Five anti-gun ads used by John Glenn committee in its effort for gun prohibition.

John F. Kennedy

Medgar Evers

Martin Luther King, Jr.

Robert F. Kennedy

NEXT?

You must help stop the killing. Demand rigid gun laws. Laws that:

1. restrict **hand** guns and ammunition to law enforcement and military use — and to private citizens who meet reasonable official qualifications.

2. require registration of **all** guns and ammunition sold.

3. forbid **all** mail order sales of guns and ammunition. You can do something. Write your Congressmen. (Or sign this ad and send it.) It can't wait.

WRITE YOUR CONGRESSMEN — % HOUSE OFFICE BUILDING OR SENATE OFFICE BUILDING, WASHINGTON, D.C. 20000

WRITE YOUR SENATOR . . . WHILE YOU STILL HAVE A SENATOR.

Five anti-gun ads used by John Glenn committee in its effort for gun prohibition—*continued*.

BUY NOW

KILL LATER

You must help stop the killing. Demand rigid gun laws. Laws that:

1. restrict **hand** guns and ammunition to law enforcement and military use — and to private citizens who meet reasonable official qualifications.

2. require registration of **all** guns and ammunition sold.

3. forbid **all** mail order sales of guns and ammunition. You can do something. Write your Congressmen. (Or sign this ad and send it.) It can't wait.

WRITE YOUR CONGRESSMEN — % HOUSE OFFICE BUILDING OR SENATE OFFICE BUILDING, WASHINGTON, D.C. 20000

WRITE YOUR SENATOR . . . WHILE YOU STILL HAVE A SENATOR.

John Glenn committee anti-gun ads—*continued.*

We have written a letter to your congressman about gun control.

All you have to do is sign it, and mail it.

Dear Congressman:

Please help stop the killing. Listen to the majority (85%
according to a recent Gallup Poll) of your constituents - who want
rigid gun control laws. Please work for legislation to:

1. restrict hand guns and ammunition to law
   enforcement and military use - and to
   private citizens who meet reasonable
   official qualifications.

2. require registration of all guns and
   ammunition sold.

3. forbid all mail order sales of guns
   and ammunition.

Nothing is more urgent. Please do something.

Sincerely,

Name _____

Address _____

WRITE YOUR CONGRESSMEN — ℅ HOUSE OFFICE BUILDING OR SENATE OFFICE BUILDING, WASHINGTON, D.C. 20000

Five anti-gun ads used by John Glenn committee in its effort for gun prohibition—
continued.

More and more people
are buying guns
to protect themselves from
more and more people
who are buying guns.

You must help stop the killing. Demand rigid gun laws. Laws that:
1. restrict **hand** guns and ammunition to law enforcement and military use — and to private citizens who meet reasonable official qualifications.

2. require registration of **all** guns and ammunition sold.
3. forbid **all** mail order sales of guns and ammunition. You can do something. Write your Congressmen. (Or sign this ad and send it.)
It can't wait.

WRITE YOUR CONGRESSMEN — % HOUSE OFFICE BUILDING OR SENATE OFFICE BUILDING, WASHINGTON, D. C. 20000

WRITE YOUR SENATOR ... WHILE YOU STILL HAVE A SENATOR.

John Glenn committee anti-gun ads—*continued.*

tration, and arranging for speeches and public appearances on behalf of gun prohibition—deceptively called gun control.

Another product of the Emergency Committee for Gun Control was a full page magazine ad which included a convenient clip-out coupon to be mailed by readers to their Senators or Congressman, plus a solicitation of cash contributions to help the program. The ad opened in this compelling manner:

> "You're a good citizen. You don't break laws. You're responsible about guns. You like to hunt. To target shoot. No one has the right to take your gun away. We agree. And no one wants to. What we do want to do is take guns away from convicted murderers, thieves, psychopaths, delinquents, alcoholics and drug addicts." (New Chronicle Pub. Co., Los Angeles, Cal.)

On July 9, 1968, the Emergency Committee for Gun Control issued a press release announcing the formation of a subcommittee known as "Clergymen for Gun Control" to accomodate the widespread response by the clergy to their appeal for gun control legislation. The press release listed the names and affiliations of approximately twenty-three of the country's clergymen from virtually all faiths, and, as usual, it did not forget to end with the usual beguiling assurance as to the motives of the proponents:

> "The legislative principles we support, 'Colonel Glenn said, 'are designed to help keep guns out of the hands of criminals, dope addicts, delinquents, alcoholics and mental incompetents. Nothing in the legislation will, in any way, curtail or impair the availability of guns to collectors, hunters, sportsmen or other qualified private citizens.' "

The technique used by the Emergency Committee for Gun Control in its constant repetition of soothing reassurances to the credulous public was apparently the product of the Papert, Koenig, Lois advertising agency, known in the trade as "PKL", which was the subject of an article in June 24, 1968, issue of *Advertising Age* which reported:

> "PKL, which had Sen. Robert Kennedy as a client prior to his assassination, is serving as the volunteer agency for the Emergency Committee for Gun Control established this week by the National Council for a Responsible Firearms Policy, Washington."

The article, which bore the subtitle "Admen Advise Positive Approach 'Assure Public It Won't Lose Rights' ", went on to explain the strategy to be employed:

> "While they applaud the efforts of those in the advertising industry who have already taken a positive stand on the gun control question, the PKL execs feel that a great deal of care must be exercised in handling any advertising that may appear. Misdirected good will can result in more harm than good in persuading congressmen to support new legislation, they believe. 'A positive approach is required in the advertising,' Mr. Murphy explained. 'We've got to assure people that no rights are going to be taken away from them (a major point made by the National Rifle Assn.). We've got to spell out who should not be qualified to purchase or use guns, such as juveniles, or convicted criminals and drug addicts. We've got to reassure people that their guns won't be taken away from them.' "

Clever, huh? Anyway, prominent individuals from every walk of life were persuaded to join in the support of the anti-gun movement. One typical news story, was released from Hollywood and carried its message in the caption "Five Quick-Draw Movie Stars Plead For Stiff Gun Control". An excerpt from the release itself read:

> "Five gunslinging movie stars urged citizens Tuesday to ask their senators and congressmen to vote in favor of gun-control laws.
>   Gregory Peck, Charlton Heston, Hugh O'Brian, James Stewart and Kirk Douglas, who have been seen on the screen many times squeezing off shots at the villains, made the plea in a statement distributed to newsmen." (*Chicago Daily News*: June 19, 1968)

From the other end of the country there came an article headed "Broadway Stars Get Into Gun-Control Act" which told how a group of Broadway stars stepped into Shubert Alley and persuaded some 1,000 persons to sign petitions for stronger federal gun control. The story also made use of the reassurance technique:

> "Eydie Gorme, currently starring with her husband Steve Lawrence in 'Golden Rainbow,' said: 'I don't understand the National Rifle Assn.'s point of view. Nobody is talking about taking away or stopping the selling of guns." (*Chicago Sun-Times*: July 7, 1968)

Another Hollywood actor, Warren Beatty, who had recently achieved fame for having portrayed gangster-murderer Clyde Barrow in the motion picture "Bonnie and Clyde" a movie which, in part, made a famous Texas Ranger appear ridiculous. Beatty was reported as having appeared before 28,233 fans in San Francisco Candlestick Park baseball stadium at the start of the baseball game on July 6, 1968, calling for sound and reasonable gun control legislation. However, his attempted appearance for the same purpose at the White Sox Park in Chicago was reportedly thwarted by White Sox owner Arthur Allyn who was quoted as having explained:

"There was no authority given for him to appear in the ball park. It's as simple as that. I can't inflict political views on the fans and this is purely and simply politicking." (*Chicago Daily News*: July 18, 1968)

One of the other talented and popular Hollywood entertainers to lend his support to the gun control movement was the versatile Sammy Davis, Jr. whose name prominently appeared near the top of the membership list of the Emergency Committee for Gun Control. A subsequent news article, however, raised a few questions in the minds of many people as to whose possession of guns needed most to be controlled. The Associated Press wirephoto of Sammy Davis, Jr. in London carried the following informative copy:

"Sammy Davis Jr. breaks out in a wide grin as he accepts delivery on a Rolls-Royce in London airport, but shortly before he was chagrined and 'ashamed' when officials confiscated his pistol." (*Chicago Today*: June 29, 1969)

During this tumultuous period a message of warning to the American people was issued in the form of a press release June 13, 1968, by Harold W. Glassen, President of the National Rifle Association of America, a distinguished attorney who possessed a thorough grasp of the true nature of the anti-gun campaign. It is doubtful that it was published by more than a handful of independent newspapers in the country:

"Today we are witnessing an almost unbelievable phenomenon in America. We are witnessing the strange and masochistic spectacle of tens of thousands of normally proud and level-headed Americans begging the federal government to take from them by force of law one of their basic civil rights, the right to keep and bear arms.

Make no mistake about it—there is a step-by-step move afoot to accomplish the ultimate deprivation of the American right to keep and bear arms. We were told five years ago that the gun control legislation then being proposed would not interfere with the rights of sportsmen and other private citizens to keep and bear arms for legitimate pursuits.

We have been assured time and time again that legislation to impose restrictions on mail order sales of firearms was the final objective, and that there would not be a subsequent attempt to add further restrictions.

We have been told that there was no intention to propose a requirement for national registration of firearms. And we were accused of misrepresentation when we warned that registration was a possibility, and of being downright irresponsible when we suggested that firearms registration was being seriously considered.

Well, who's right now? The NRA voiced the suspicion that control of interstate sales of firearms might be only the 'first step' toward such measures as registration. And we were right.

Several bills have now been introduced to accomplish national registration of firearms, and pressure is being applied in Congress to rush this measure through to completion. This is the 'second step' which we feared. And now, today, we have seen the 'third step' instituted in the form of a bill in the Senate (sponsored by Sen. Joseph Tydings of Maryland) to require a license for the purchase or ownership of firearms.

Do we have to say more? Do we have any reason to believe there will not be a fourth and final step in what appears plainly a plan to disarm American citizens? Do we have any reason to trust those who have assured us that their aims fell short of this mark?

I don't think so, and I warn the American people that if Congress is lured into accepting this reassurance, the ultimate is inevitable, and there will no longer be private ownership of guns in the near future."

Hal Glassen was indeed prophetic. The cry for confiscation is already upon us.

One of the cunning techniques of propagandizing for gun control consistently employed by much of the news media from the very beginning of the controversy, was ostensibly to represent both sides to every argument, the anti-gun side and the NRA side, neatly distorted and mangled for the purpose of achieving these effects: (1) to create a superficial appearance of a fair and objective two-sided presentation (2) to present the NRA position in such a way as to offend the sensibilities of the average reader by suggesting its arrogant defiance of the public will.

Consider some interesting excerpts taken from the July 1968 issue of *The Advance*, a publication of the Amalgamated Clothing Workers of America. Its graphic title was "The National Rifle Association's Gun Lobby—MERCHANTS OF FEAR":

"The National Rifle Association is reacting to the public demand for gun controls with its usual hysteria. But for the first time in three decades, its campaign of outright lies and deception is not working."

* * *

"The NRA has successfully thwarted almost every important state and federal effort to control arms ever since a madman's bullets, intended for Franklin D. Roosevelt, killed Mayor Anton Cermak of Chicago in 1933. The nation was outraged then, but except for legislation controlling sawed-off shotguns and machine guns, gangster favorites, little was done."

* * *

" 'All that is necessary for the triumph of evil,' the great British statesman Edmund Burke said, 'is for good men to do nothing.' The NRA understands this, and has learned to take advantage of Americans' complacency. Members of the organization can inundate Congress with a million letters in 72 hours (it has done so many times), and they persist in fighting gun controls as relentlessly today as they did 30 years ago."

* * *

"The arguments of the National Rifle Association against gun controls are illogical and have been proved to be total misrepresentation of the facts."

* * *

"The argument that possible gun registration and licensing will mean that police can arbitrarily deny permits for gun ownership or have the power to confiscate arms is also a gross distortion of fact. The police could never have such authority in a democracy."

* * *

" 'The NRA's lies have had a very great effect,' Sen. Joseph Tydings (D-Md.) says, 'so great that I don't know whether we can ever reverse it.' "

Whenever it becomes possible to influence effectively 93 percent of the newspaper circulation in the United States—which the anti-gun forces have repeatedly claimed for themselves, then it also becomes possible to withhold systematically from the general public any information which is inconsistent with the carefully drawn premises and conclusions of their coldly calculated professionally guided advertising campaigns. That fact is the quintessence of successful propaganda. Substantial opposition cannot be tolerated. It must be destroyed or intimidated. Apart from the gun issue, it is to this sinister object 93% of the press circulation has bent itself in America—(their figure and their statement).

The anti-gun forces were faced with the very formidable problem of how to deal with the 1,000,000 members of the National Rifle Association who still had access to the facts through the pages of a superb magazine, *The American Rifleman*, and, whenever necessary, through special information bulletins which provided the objective information upon which informed and intelligent opinions could be based by individual members.

Recall the vigorous efforts in the year, 1967, to destroy the annual National Matches; to deprive the National Rifle Association of the use of Camp Perry for holding its national championships, and to dismantle the Civilian Marksmanship Program, which had been still further restricted again in June 1968. It was inevitable there were to be further attempts to intimidate, and further efforts to coerce the National Rifle Association into complicance with the will of those it had opposed.

On the occasion he announced his filing of a national gun registration bill, Senator Dodd was reported to have issued warnings there would be an increasing number of assassinations and attempted assassinations unless stringent measures were taken. The *Chicago Daily News* of June 10, 1968, reported Dodd had referred to the National Rifle Association as "probably the most dangerous lobby that has ever existed."

The *Chicago Daily News* June 13, 1968, also noted Senator Tyding's remarks on the occasion of his announced filing of a combination gun registration and national licensing bill:

"Tydings also said he has asked the Internal Revenue Service why the NRA 'remains unregistered and untaxed.' He said the NRA spends a large percentage of its annual $5,700,000 budget for 'lobbying against the public interest.' "

Before continuing further, it is appropriate to pause just long enough to take note of an editorial opinion which the reader would do well to remember when reading a newspaper or magazine article which proposes gun registration. It is an excerpt taken from the May 25, 1968, issue of *Editor & Publisher*, self-described as the oldest publishers' and advertisers' newspaper in America:

"The Virgin Islands comprise a territory of the United States and not a State. Nevertheless, its native-born residents are citizens of the United States and it is disturbing, therefore, to learn that its unicameral legislature has taken a step towards facism and dictatorship by adopting a registration bill for all publications in the islands.

371

The authority to register and to license carries with it the power to deny such registration and license. Therein lies government control of the press. The government of the Virgin Islands should take rapid steps to correct this affront to freedom of the press in the U.S. and in this hemisphere."

The authority to license carries with it the power to deny such license. This is our best reason for opposing licensing of guns and gun owners. By the power to deny licenses they have the power to eliminate private gun ownership—which far too many, now, have said was a righteous goal.

Once again, beginning June 26, 1968, Senator Dodd's subcommittee began hearings on national gun control, but on this occasion the hearings were largely confined to the new issues of national licensing of gun owners and the individual registration of all privately owned firearms. The hearings began in the very midst of the hurricane of anti-gun sentiment which had been fomented and encouraged by massive advertising and publicity campaigns initiated by the hard core of the anti-gun proponents. On the first day Senator Dodd presented a brief summary to his subcommittee as to how he viewed the various issues. The reader will recall that three years previously, on May 20, 1965, he had piously ridiculed some of the opposition to his old S.1592 by asserting:

"You know one of the arguments made by opponents of this bill is that it will lead to ultimate legal registration." (CC–p. 125)

Three years later, on June 26, 1968, as he opened the hearings on four gun registration bills, Senator Dodd ridiculed the notion that registration could lead to gun confiscation:

"The gun problem demands further action, and this committee will obtain as many views as possible on the legislative proposals before us, the registration of firearms, and the licensing of gun owners. We know that there will be the shrill cry of the gunrunners that we are heading for the confiscation and ultimately the abolition of the private ownership of firearms." (HH–p. 2)

Thus, after serving notice by his choice of language that he apparently regarded anyone who protested gun registration as the precursor to confiscation as being "gunrunners", Senator Dodd continued to convey his sentiments as to the reasons for his support for such legislation:

372

"Registration is a simple recordkeeping procedure which enables law enforcement agencies to identify the proper owner of an object, whether it's an automobile or a gun. Registration is directed more to the gun, than to the person who owns the gun. Identification of the gun itself along with the name, address, and perhaps the social security number, and signature of the owner are sufficient for the purposes of this recordkeeping." (HH–p. 2)

* * *

"Registration of all guns is the simple and logical complement to the new controls on the sales of handguns, and to the proposed controls on the sales of long guns. Registration is the primary means for obtaining information about the guns already owned at the time the law goes into effect. It is not enough to control the traffic in new weapons. We need at least to identify the estimated 200 million guns already in the hands of American citizens. This registered information about guns and the ammunition bought for it would be available to local police forces to assist their efforts in maintaining safe streets." (HH–p. 3)

* * *

"Registration will not overnight effect the disarmament of the several million irresponsible elements in our society who today own guns. But it will provide us with the essential machinery through which we can limit future purchasers of guns to the mature and the law-abiding, and through which we will be able to substantially reduce the number of firearms that are today in the hands of people who should not have them." (HH–p. 3)

Another of the sponsors of a gun registration and licensing bill, Senator Joseph Tydings, also made introductory remarks before Senator Dodd's subcommittee and also incorporated within them his statement made before the Senate on June 12, 1968. Some of the excerpts from the latter follow:

"I ask my colleagues to study the bill closely because, without question, it will be the subject to a propaganda drive of massive misrepresentation throughout the United States by the National Rifle Association." (HH–p. 20)

* * *

"My proposal applies both to firearms and ammunition. It will require the registration, by a simple form, of every firearm now in the United States and all firearms produced in or imported into this country in the future, and the reregistration or transfer each time a firearm changes hands." (HH–p. 23)

* * *

"Anyone who owns a firearm will be able to register a firearm, and, in fact, every owner will be required to do so. This is to provide a record of the serial number, kind of weapon, and its owner for every firearm in the Nation." (HH–p. 24)

* * *

"In addition, an applicant will have to submit a photograph and fingerprints with his application, so that his identity can be firmly established and his freedom from a criminal record confirmed." (HH–p. 24)

* * *

"The gun lobby in this Nation—led by their paid hierarchy, the National Rifle Association here in Washington—has, without the slightest apparent twinge of conscience, opposed with a vicious disregard of fact every effective piece of firearms legislation introduced since I have been in the Senate and, I am informed, since long before I arrived here. We can expect the NRA and its satellites to continue their opposition." (HH–p. 27)

The third key Senator among those sponsoring gun registration bills was Senator Edward W. Brooke who included the following among his reasons for supporting such measures:

"Mr. Chairman, a national registration system could provide a comprehensive accounting of the stock of firearms already held by private citizens in this country or transferred to them in the future. It is essentially an information-gathering device and would serve as a valuable tool for law enforcement officers all across the country." (HH–p. 47)

* * *

"In my judgment there is much to be said for registration legislation that is exclusively directed to the gathering of information on firearms and that is explicitly not a penal statute." (HH–p. 48)

The statement made on behalf of the Johnson Administration was presented to the subcommittee by U.S. Attorney General Ramsey Clark who cited as reasons for gun control an alleged 7,700 murders, 11,000 suicides, 55,000 assaults, and 71,200 robberies in a single year, all committed with guns. The U.S. Attorney General continued:

"Today, I appear to urge passage of President Johnson's proposal for registration and licensing of firearms. They are essential to comprehensive control.

The bill would require that a national registration of firearms begin 180 days after its effective date. All those who now have firearms and all those who buy them in the future would be required to register the weapons with the Secretary of the Treasury.

The registration application form would contain essential information: name, address, date of birth, social security number, the manufacturer of the gun, the caliber and model, serial number, and information as to whom it was purchased from. This information would be fed into the National Crime Information Center operated by the Federal Bureau of Investigation. By using the center's computer capacity, authorities in every part of the country would be able to trace the ownership of a registered gun in a matter of seconds." (HH–p. 57)

One is cautioned to pay particular attention to this next explanation by the U.S. Attorney General as to the manner in which he envisioned that the national licensing system would operate. Then, pause for a moment and attempt to visualize personally going through the provisions, especially the part about securing the approval of a doctor to own a gun:

"An applicant, first of all, would have to present a valid, official document from his State—such as a driver's license—showing his name, address, age, and signature or photograph. Then he would have to present a form signed by the chief law-enforcement officer in his town or county that he was not a fugitive, not under indictment, had no felony conviction record, and was not ineligible under State or local law to possess firearms.

A licensed physician would have to sign a statement that, in his professional opinion, the applicant was mentally and physically competent to possess and use a firearm safely.

A set of fingerprints, a full set of fingerprints certified by a law-enforcement agency, and a photograph also would have to be furnished by the applicant. Federal gun licenses would be valid for a maximum period of 3 years." (HH–pp. 58–59)

The next time someone tries to tell you that a federal gun owners license, such as was contemplated by the Johnson Administration, was no different than a dog license or an automobile license, ask them when was the last time they had to secure the permission of both a physician and their police chief to own either a dog or an automobile. Ask them when they were forced to submit their fingerprints and a set of photographs before being permitted to buy either a dog or an automobile. Also ask them when either their dog or automobile was subject to confiscation upon failure to register them. Ask them when it was the announced goal of some of those seeking registration of your dog or automobile to confiscate them. Automobiles are not registered for the purpose of controlling either crimes or accidents, but rather as a means of raising revenue through the registration tax in order to provide funds for the construction and maintenance of roads. It should also be apparent that unlike firearms which are small and easily concealed, automobiles are large, conspicuous, and impossible to operate over the roads without displaying registration plates which are clearly visible to all law-enforcement officers at a glance.

Before proceeding with the next "special" feature of the Johnson Administration's proposed federal licensing provision, one should recall the critical importance to the wildlife conservation programs in the various states of the excise taxes collected pursuant to the Pittman-Robertson Act of 1937. That Act assesses an excise tax varying from 10 to 11 percent on the sale of guns and ammunition which is then returned to the states by the federal government for use in the administration of wildlife management and conservation programs. The President of the National Rifle Association, Harold W. Glassen, called the critical importance of that old program to the attention of Senator Dodd's subcommittee during its 1967 hearings when he observed that:

> "Since 1937, the beginning of the Pittman-Robertson Act, over $268,-401,966 has been collected on sales of more than two and a half billion dollars in sporting arms and ammunition." (GG–p. 443)

Consider now the continued explanation by the U.S. Attorney General of how the Administration's licensing bill would have operated, if enacted:

> "The bill contains an additional provision relating to the Federal wildlife restoration fund from which States receive their proportionate shares of the Federal excise taxes on sales of guns and ammunition. After June 30, 1971, States without adequate permit laws will be ineligible to receive any of that money." (HH–p. 59)

The response by the National Rifle Association to that particular aspect of the proposal by the Administration was immediate and strong, NRA President Harold W. Glassen said:

> "This is a blow aimed below the belt of every conservationist in the land whether he is a sportsman or not.
> These funds matched by funds from the States have long been the bulwark of an American conservation effort that has lifted this country into the enviable role as the world's leader in the wise use of natural resources. This portion of the proposal is no more than a heavy-handed threat to every sportsman in the country to acquiese to political

expediency or suffer irreparable damages to the natural resources of his home State.

The claim that licensing and registration of firearms has no implied threat to the sportsman is disproved by the punitive provisions of the plan. While the monetary loss threatened is considerable on the face of the proposal, the ramification in the loss of individual recreational expenditures extends far beyond the sportsman and encompasses every facet of the business community which deals with tourists, tourism and their associated services.

The effect of this bare-faced threat if carried out includes not only the interests of the hunter and sportsman but of every American interested in the preservation of natural resources because it has been the use of the funds now threatened which has led to the establishment of sound conservation programs in all of our States." (HH–pp. 206–207)

The National Rifle Association was joined by the National Shooting Sports Foundation in expressing grave concern over the Administration's threat to the Pittman-Robertson funds. Charles Dickey, Executive Director of the NSSF, made these points in his prepared statement:

"Apportionments of Federal Aid in Wildlife Restoration Funds in fiscal year 1967–1968 were a record $35,650,000. Secretary of the Interior Stewart L. Udall has termed the Pittman-Robertson Act 'one of the most important pieces of conservation legislation that this, or any other country in the world has ever known.' When the Act was being considered by Congress, one of its chief supporters was the American firearms industry. This may be the only time in the history of the United States that an industry has asked to be taxed.

We submit that these funds should be used for no other purpose than that for which they have always been intended—fish and wildlife restoration. We believe that it is wholly improper for any of these funds to be used for administrative costs of any federal firearms legislation. We believe it to be equally improper for the Federal Government to either threaten to withhold or to withhold funds that rightfully should be distributed to the individual states merely because the individual states do not pass certain legislation at the will of the Federal government." (HH–p. 800)

One of the issues immediately raised by the proposals for national systems of registration and licensing concerned the power of Congress to enact such legislation in the face of the obvious fact that the police powers had been clearly reserved to the individual States by the Constitution. That objection had been interposed in the previous year by the

377

Treasury Department whose General Counsel severely criticised one of the provisions which had been contained in the bill by Senator Hruska making it a Federal crime for any person to possess in his home state any firearm acquired illegally outside of that state. The pertinent portion of the Treasury Department's legal opinion stated:

"It seems doubtful that the second provision can be justified under the taxing or commerce powers, or under any other power enumerated in the Constitution for Federal enactment. Consequently, the Department questions the advisability of including in the measure a measure which could be construed as a usurpation of a police power reserved to the states by Article 10 of the United States Constitutional Amendments." (HH–p. 64)

When Senator Hruska reminded the U.S. Attorney General of that legal objection which had been lodged against one of the provisions of his old bill, Ramsey Clark simply dismissed it with this flat assertion:

"As I indicated, I would disagree with the opinion of the author of the statement which you just read. In my judgment, the Congress clearly has the power under the commerce clause, and also under all of the delegated powers of the Constitution which empower the Congress to enact criminal laws for the public safety, and to do all things necessary and proper to enforce those laws." (HH–p. 64)

Senator Strom Thurmond, however, was one of the many Members of Congress who was not willing to acquiesce quietly in the intrusion of the Federal Government into matters of police power which were regarded as properly being within the purview of the individual states. He expressed this powerfully worded opinion to Senator Dodd's subcommittee:

"Conditions and traditions vary widely from State to State, and the needs of one State should not necessarily be imposed upon another. The Federal Government should take no measures which pressure or require States to adopt uniform Federal standards. Several days ago I heard a prominent official in this Government say that if the States did not act by a certain time, then the Federal Government should act. In other words, that is coercion on the States.
    The States are sovereign governments just as this central government is. Every State in this Nation, all 50 of them, have every power to act in any field they want to, except where they are prohibited by so doing under the Consitution. They have responsibilities, they should meet their responsibilities. The Federal Government has responsibili-

ties, and it should meet its responsibility, but the Federal Government should not attempt to coerce or intimidate the State to pass laws which the people of that State do not desire." (HH–p. 55)

In an effort to bolster the Administration's position that the Congress did have sufficient power to enact a federal registration law capable of withstanding a judicial attack on its constitutional basis, the office of Senator Joseph Tydings requested that a legal memorandum be prepared on that subject by the Legislative Reference Service of the Library of Congress. On June 17, 1968, the report was issued by the American Law Division of the Legislative Reference Service which candidly acknowledged that:

"The purpose of this paper is to develop a theory under which the constitutionality of federal registration could be sustained." (HH–p. 741)

After eighteen pages of detailed analysis in which it was freely admitted that different people could be presumed to answer differently the various questions upon which their conclusion rested the very best answer they could provide was that:

"We can only say that the precedents do not necessarily compel either an affirmative or negative answer, although it appears that the expansive reading given the Commerce Clause by the Court would create something of a rebuttable presumption in the affirmative." (HH–p. 759)

The highly debatable question of the power of Congress to legislate in the area of reserved police powers was only one of several legal gauntlets through which the Johnson Administration was obliged to run while at the same time being soundly pummeled by the arguments of Congressmen who were strict constructionists of the Constitution. Another problem area, you will recall, had been created by the recent decision by the U.S. Supreme Court in the case of Haynes vs. United States. (390 U.S. 85 [1968])

The Haynes decision, reduced to its simplest terms, held that a timely plea of self-incrimination would constitute a complete defense to a prosecution for failure to register a weapon proscribed under the National Firearms Act of 1934, such as machineguns, submachine guns, sawed-off shotguns and sawed-off rifles.

The impact of that decision, which was less than five months old

379

as of the time of those hearings, was expressed for the benefit of Senator Dodd's subcommittee by Sheldon Cohen, Commission of the Internal Revenue Service:

"The National Act prosecutions have fallen as a result of the *Haynes* decision. We had been averaging, under the national act, about 60 to 70 prosecutions per month for national act violations. Since the first of the year, when the *Haynes* decision was rendered, we are down to about something in excess of 40 a month. So we are talking about 35 to 40 percent in the area of prosecutions under *Haynes*." (HH–pp. 661–662)

The absolutely absurd consequences flowing from the Haynes decision with respect to any new national gun registration system were: (1) only the reputable and law-abiding citizens could be forcibly compelled to register their firearms, or (2) a special provision would have to be written into law so as to grant immunity against subsequent prosecution for any illegal act which might be revealed by the registration of a gun. That incongruous prospect, however, did not in the least dissuade the proponents of national gun registration from continuing to pursue their elusive goal.

In keeping with their traditional ritual of proclaiming the desire of the majority of Americans for the most stringent gun laws, the anti-gun claque marshaled their evidence on this occasion in the form of massive numbers of signed petitions.

One such batch was presented by James V. Bennett, President of the National Council for a Responsible Firearms Policy.

Less than four weeks before he appeared before Senator Dodd's subcommittee, a letter went out over the signature of James V. Bennett which had been addressed to the members and constituents of the National Council asking that they assist in having petitions signed urging Congress to enact the legislation under consderation. An excerpt from his letter read as follows:

"We are also including for your use a petition asking for specific gun control regulations: long gun coverage, registration, and permit purchasing. Our objective is to secure ten million signatures in ten days. Please duplicate this and get your friends, neighbors, and co-workers to gather signatures. When enough are returned, they will be presented to the President and appropriate leaders of Congress. Any that can be returned to our office by June 18th should be sent in. (Extra petitions available here.)" (HH–p. 425)

380

The petitions produced by the National Council for a Responsible Firearms Policy and its Emergency Committee for Gun Control totaled an estimated one and one-quarter million signatures. These were presented by James V. Bennett to Senator Dodd's subcommittee:

"We have here as you see, Senator, petitions from well over a million people. We estimate at least a million and a quarter people. These are petitions that are signed—addressed to the President and Members of Congress and State government officials. This is in accord with the basic constitutional right of people to petition their Congress for redress of grievances. Our grievance is the indiscriminate sale of guns. And these petitions say that they, the undersigned, favor immediate action to control the sale, possession, and use of handguns, rifles and shotguns, and that such legislation should include, first, regarding rifles and shotguns, an outright ban on mail-order sales to individuals, on sales to those under 18, and on out-of-State purchases. Second, all firearms possessed, sold, or transferred should be registered at the State and/or the National level. Third, States should require that gun purchases be made only through permits, calling for adequate identification, and a waiting period for a police check. That is the petition to which we have received at least 1¼ million signatures." (HH–p. 578)

Remember the 1,200,000 signatures demanding gun registration which were accumulated by the City of Chicago in January 1968? Do you recall how it appeared that they had been obtained? Well, those same spurious petitions were dredged up once more and used in an attempt to convince Senator Dodd's subcommittee that nearly half of the entire recorded population of Chicago was clamoring for gun registration. That particular message was presented to the subcommittee by Raymond F. Simon, Corporation Counsel for Chicago, who seemed so enthralled with the large number of signatures that he repeatedly mentioned them while Senator Strom Thurmond was attempting to establish the fact that the Illinois General Assembly had rejected gun registration on several different occasions:

"SENATOR THURMOND. The State legislature turned it down, didn't it?

MR. SIMON. Yes, they did twice. And that is why we decided we would pass a municipal ordinance even though we felt it was not nearly as adequate or desirable. But a million people in a city of three and a half million people affixed signatures to petitions, saying 'We want gun registration.'" (HH–p. 224)

* * *

"SENATOR THURMOND. Well, the State has the authority to pass it, and I am in favor of the States passing if they need it and want it. But when your States do not act, then you run to Washington to get us to do something against your people that they do not want.

MR. SIMON. Well—

SENATOR THURMOND. Let us go back—

MR. SIMON. When a million of our citizens express their desire for it, we think they want it." (HH–p. 226)

* * *

"SENATOR THURMOND. Doesn't your remedy lie in Mayor Daley and your city officials enforcing the law more strictly, and punishing people when they violate it, rather than run to Washington and shift all the responsibilities here?

MR. SIMON. Senator, we are not going to shift any of our responsibility, because we are going to continue to register guns in Chicago. We would like to see it apply throughout Illinois, and throughout the United States. We are not going to be derelict in imposing registration in Chicago. We did that in January of 1968. We did not come here and say you do it for us. We did not say we are afraid to offend somebody by passing a registration law. We did it in Chicago. We have come here to say that the people of Chicago showed us, a million of them, all the media of communication, all of our leaders in the community, our religious, our business leaders, principals from schools—

SENATOR THURMOND. You have told us that.

MR. SIMON. That is his message that we have come to tell you.

SENATOR THURMOND. You told us that two or three times.

MR. SIMON. I am sorry, Senator.

SENATOR THURMOND. They all signed a petition, a million of them. Yet the State of Illinois did not go along, did they?

MR. SIMON. The State legislature did not go along with our gun registration bill; that is correct.

SENATOR THURMOND. That is what I am asking. The State legislature did not go along—and because the State legislature did not go along, you run to Washington and want us to go along.

MR. SIMON. That is correct.

SENATOR THURMOND. Why don't you go back home and work on your own State legislature?" (HH–pp. 227–228)

The reader can be the judge as to how persuasive the evidence was which had been presented by the City of Chicago to the members of Senator Dodd's subcommittee. How many reasonable men could seriously have believed that a city of 3,500,000 people could have honestly produced 1,200,000 signatures in less than one week?

The impossibility of gun registration as a method of crime control was never more evident than when its staunchest proponents vainly sought to substantiate its value on either practical or theoretical grounds. Consider some of the attributes of gun registration, according to its supporters. Senator Edward W. Brooke expressed the following opinion:

"The mere collection of information will not deprive anyone of his rights and, by enabling responsible officials to check the pulse of firearms traffic, it can help reduce the collateral dangers in a nation which has clearly reserved the right of citizens to own weapons. Such a system, working in conjunction with State or Federal licensing arrangements, can be invaluable in the struggle to keep firearms from falling into the hands of those who cannot lawfully hold them. As a detection tool it can facilitate efforts to recover stolen weapons." (HH–p. 48)

Exactly what did the Senator mean by checking the "pulse" of firearms traffic, and how would it have reduced "collateral dangers"? How would it have kept firearms from "falling into the hands of those who cannot lawfully hold them"? In what way would it have facilitated the recovery of "stolen weapons"?

To make such a flat assertion of opinion is easy. To support it factually is impossible. In what way would registration have prevented the theft of guns either from sporting goods stores or private residences? In what way would gun registration have prevented millions of privately owned firearms from being used in crimes, or in suicides, or in accidents? By what process of legerdemain would gun registration have facilitated the recovery of stolen weapons? Clearly, such claims were nothing more than meaningless exercises in rhetoric with absolutely nothing to back them up.

Consider the following plausible explanation of the benefits of gun registration which was offered by U.S. Attorney General Ramsey Clark:

"If registration is required, people who are not permitted to own guns will be arrested when they are found with guns." (HH–p. 83)

What was clearly and absurdly implied in the statement by the U.S. Attorney General was that *it was not presently possible to arrest persons who were not permitted by law to own guns when they were found with guns*, but that by some mysterious process inherent in gun registration such an implied deficiency in the law would be corrected. That was, and is, pure nonsense!

A criminal in possession of a gun is a criminal in possession of a gun, with or without a registration law, and with or without a licensing law. It must be made absolutely clear that neither gun registration, nor firearms-owner licensing, enlarges in the slightest degree the powers of the police to arrest, or the State to prosecute or the Courts to convict. A simple illustration will serve nicely to impress the reader with that fact beyond all doubt.

One winter night, a few hours after midnight, a Chicago police patrol car turned into an alley at the rear of some commercial buildings on the south side of the city. As the squad car proceeded to drive slowly through the alley its headlights suddenly revealed the figure of a man who apparently was trying to avoid being seen by pressing himself tightly into the recess of one of the doorways. The patrol car stopped and the two police officers got out to determine the identity of the man and the nature of his business in that alley at that odd hour.

Suffice it to say that, in the course of the lively conversation which followed, the policemen were the objects of excessively intemperate use of language by the suspect. They then searched him for weapons. The policemen discovered that the suspect had been carrying a loaded sawed-off shotgun slung under his left arm by a cord, and they immediately arrested him. After one night in a warm jail, the suspect was released by an obliging judge the following morning for a very basic reason. The court had no choice except to suppress the evidence of the sawed-off shotgun and not permit it to be used against the suspect because it had not been secured during the course of a legally proper arrest for legally sufficient grounds. It was just as simple as that, or as complex, if you prefer.

The reader should understand that by his act of possessing the sawed-off shotgun, the suspect had been in undisputable violation of the following weapons laws: the National Firearms Act of 1934 which prohibited possession of an unregistered sawed-off shotgun; the Illinois State law which flatly prohibited possession of sawed-off shotguns; the Chicago ordinance prohibiting possession of sawed-off shotguns; the Illinois State firearms owners license law; the Illinois State law prohibiting the carrying of a concealed firearm on or about the person; and, finally, the City of Chicago gun registration ordinance. Had there also been a federal gun registration and licensing law in effect at that time, then they would have only constituted two more useless laws in this example.

The case just cited was by no means the exception. It was the general rule. That fact was clearly confirmed by a news story which appeared just one year after the Chicago City Council had enacted its

384

gun registration ordinance. The *Chicago Daily News* reported on March 17, 1969, that:

> "More than half of those arrested on charges of violating Chicago's new gun registration ordinance have been acquitted in Circuit Court."
>
> * * *
>
> "A total of 1,762 persons were arrested for having unregistered firearms up to March 1, but judges found 999 of them innocent."
>
> * * *
>
> "They said that the charge of having an unregistered firearm often is filed along with more serious charges. Frequently a judge will find a defendant guilty of the more serious charge and dismiss the gun registration charge, the two said."
>
> * * *
>
> "However, in some cases there was a legal defense, such as a search being made without a search warrant."

And the gun prohibitionists continue to seek more laws imposing burdens on decent people and none upon criminals.

The reader must understand that the crucial problem of crime in the United States has nothing whatsoever to do with guns, but rather it has to do with the administration of justice in this country. Until this fundamental fact is recognized and squarely faced, crime will continue unabated no matter how many prohibitory laws are enacted. This is what the American public must be made to understand because it is the very keystone to the problem of crime in the United States. That principle was recognized and called to the attention of Senator Dodd's subcommittee early in the hearings by Senator Strom Thurmond:

> "Although proper gun legislation is essential, the gun, and I would remind those who are proposing measures today to inject the Congress into every facet of this field, I would remind them that the gun is merely an instrument of crime. The real fault of crime is criminals who today are operating in an atmosphere of permissiveness and arrogance. Supreme Court decisions have severely handicapped the police in the apprehension of criminals and diminished the power of the courts to see that the guilty are punished." (HH–p. 55)

Another of the reasons cited in support of gun registration was that it would allegedly permit the tracing of firearms which had been used in the commission of crimes so as to ascertain the identity of their perpetrators. The U.S. Attorney General gave the following example as an illustration of that principle:

385

"The pistol that killed Bob Kennedy had been so registered, and that registration was most helpful in identifying the person accused of the crime today." (HH–p. 66)

It was common knowledge that the suspect in the assassination of Senator Robert F. Kennedy fired the fatal shots from a distance of only a few feet, if that far, and in the presence of a crowded room full of people who instantly seized him, wrested the pistol from his grasp, and held him immobile until police arrived and took him into custody. The prior registration of the instrument of murder had absolutely nothing whatever to do with solving the case, or with the effective prosecution of the alleged assassin for the terrible crime. If the registration of the gun proved anything at all, then it proved that it could not, and did not, prevent the assassination. Consider the audacity of the Administration attempting to prove that gun registration would prevent murders by specifically citing as an example a murder that had not and could not have been prevented by gun registration. Worst yet, many credulous Americans actually believed that nonsense.

Some of the absurdities of attributing the ability to trace guns to their registered serial numbers can be illustrated by an incident which involved, of all things, heavy caliber machineguns. It is quite obvious that, in proportion to common sporting rifles, shotguns, and handguns, a relatively infinitesimal number of heavy machineguns have been manufactured in this country, and, of those which have been, all of them were sold either to the military or to the police. It would therefore seem logical that their relatively small number, combined with an exceptional potential for illegal use, their limited sale to only governmental agencies, and the detailed registration records, supposedly maintained pursuant to the National Firearms Act of 1934, and for common security reasons, would make the tracing of any single machinegun utter simplicity. How about a truckload of machineguns?

In 1965, Senator Dodd's subcommittee heard the following testimony from Daniel R. McLeod, Attorney General of South Carolina, who was accompanied by J. P. Strom, Director of the South Carolina State Law Enforcement Division:

"In 1961, a cache of heavy weapons was found by law enforcement officers under Chief Strom in a rural county in South Carolina. It consisted of ninety-five .50-caliber machineguns; twelve .30-caliber machineguns; and 771 rounds of 20-mm ammunition." (CC–p. 659)

Chief J. P. Strom then described the attempts which had been made to trace those military machineguns:

"In 1960, we received information that these guns were located near an airstrip in a rural area. Upon investigation, we found that these guns were there. Some were in fine condition, some were not. We made every effort to trace back these guns to some agency of the government who had originally owned these guns, but without any success whatsoever." (CC–p. 660)

Franklin Orth, Executive Vice President of the National Rifle Association, called the attention of the subcommittee to the faulty logic of those who maintained that registration of firearms would somehow help to solve crimes through the tracing of guns:

"This argument would be true if the person who committed the crime used a firearm registered in his name. However, most persons who use a firearm in crime do not, use a firearm registered in their names. (This, obviously, would be sheer folly for the criminal.) Rather, such persons' firearms are either stolen or obtained from undercover sources —blackmarket rental, illegitimate dealers, personal transfer in the underworld.

In the case of the weapon never registered after initial acquisition, the trail leads nowhere. In the case of the stolen firearm, the road leads back to the law-abiding citizen, the Government installation or the police from whom the weapon was stolen." (HH–p. 194)

The reader will recall that, in one of the scenes taken from the CBS-Television special "Murder and the Right to Bear Arms", there was the following enlightening interview of a convict by a reporter which took place in cell house "B" in Stateville prison at Joliet, Illinois:

CONVICT. "Well, I rented this gun. I rented this gun from a fellow. I paid $150 just for this particular job. The more money you make on a job, the more you pay for this pistol. In other words, if you rob a bank or something for about $10,000 or $20,000 it might cost you a good $1,000,—$500 for a gun. In other words, the more money you make, the more the gun costs you."

REPORTER. "What kind of guns do they have for rent?"

CONVICT. "You can rent any kind of gun, a machinegun, a sawed-off shotgun, any make of pistol, a .45, a .38, any kind of gun you want."

Evidence was submitted over the years to Senator Dodd's subcommittee as to the number and kind of firearms which had been stolen by criminals. These numbered hundreds of thousands and frequently were from military sources. In order to provide some degree of familiarity with the more impressive of these losses, excerpts follow from various materials, much of which had been dutifully filed away by Senator Dodd's subcommittee.

On October 20, 1965, Senator Hugh Scott had submitted a table of data to the Senate which he had secured from the Department of Defense to illustrate the number of firearms stolen from various government installations. His explanation was reported in the Congressional record:

"To shed some light on this question, I asked the Department of Defense, earlier this year, to prepare a compilation of firearms stolen from Active and Reserve installations of the U.S. Army, Navy, Marine Corps, and Air Force for each of the years, 1954 through 1964. Certainly, there are no more stringent regulations covering the control of firearms than those put into effect by the military and, for this reason, I thought this information would be particularly helpful." (*Congressional Record*: Oct. 20, 1965)

The figures contained in Senator Scott's table produced the following total thefts of each category of firearm for the eleven year period: 5,300 rifles; 4,316 pistols; 231 shotguns; 141 submachineguns; and, 55 machineguns.

Congressman Dingell also submitted detailed information concerning a substantial theft of weapons from Fort Meade, Maryland, in early 1968, and introduced his exhibit to Senator Dodd's subcommittee with these words:

"I would also like to give you, if I may, for the record a bulletin by the Tennessee Bureau of Criminal Identification, showing how the criminals in Maryland procure their firearms with the theft of a significant number of .45 caliber automatic pistols from Fort George G. Meade, including not only a large number of pistols, but also a large number of submachineguns." (HH–p. 522)

The theft to which Congressman Dingell referred consisted of a total of 74 automatic pistols and 20 submachineguns, all in .45-caliber.

In January of 1969, a United Press International news release told the results of a raid which had been conducted in New Jersey by federal agents which produced weapons apparently stolen from military arsenals at bases throughout the country and which were being resold on the black market:

"Federal agents and state police seized a truckload of stolen military weapons Monday night and arrested three men, two of them National Guardsmen." (*Chicago Sun Times*: January 14, 1969)

Another massive theft of weapons occurred from an unlikely source, the Smithsonian Institute in Washington, D.C., only a few city blocks from where Senator Dodd's subcommittee held its hearings. The incident was reported on March 28, 1968, in the *Washington Daily News* whose headline read "500 PISTOLS STOLEN FROM SMITH-SONIAN". The opening lines of the story stated:

"Nearly 500 pistols have been stolen during the last three years from the storerooms of Smithsonian Institution's Museum of History and Technology, it was revealed today. District police said some of the guns have been linked to suspects involved in shootings and assaults here."

In yet another report, it was learned that a December 1968 study of 389 inmates of the Texas State prison which had been conducted by Dr. Charles M. Friel, a professor at Sam Houston State College, disclosed that 23.9 percent of the handguns which had been acquired by the prisoners were stolen.

Even the *Washington Post* carried an interesting observation regarding the source of firearms taken from offenders by police in the Capitol. In an article published May 22, 1967, it was reported that:

"Of great concern, however, is the number of guns taken by police from persons picked up for a variety of offenses ranging from robberies and assaults to minor traffic violations. Most of these gun holders have come by them illegally—through theft or purchase on the street-corner from a thief."

The examples cited are only a small fraction of many which should clearly establish that criminals are not dependent upon normal trade channels for the tools of their trade. That fact was well understood by Congressman Bob Casey who included current figures of known firearms thefts as a precursor to the conclusion at which he had personally arrived:

"On June 1, 1968, the F.B.I.'s computerized National Crime Information Center listed a staggering total of 156,386 stolen firearms. On July 1, this total jumped to 161,842. Can anyone here truly believe that this arsenal of the underworld will be registered—or that the current own-

ers will submit to federal licensing? I certainly am not that naive."
(HH–p. 766)

In view of the large numbers of firearms stolen annually, it was
only natural that those firearms owners having either a large collection
of firearms, or an especially valuable collection, would be concerned
about criminal access to the highly detailed records of their property
which would have been required by a national gun registration system.
That fear was voiced by Leon C. Jackson who represented the American Society of Arms Collectors:

"We feel, Mr. Chairman, that if these proposals are enacted, that they
will make a law-abiding citizen a target for the underworld in the
burglary and theft of his gun." (HH–p. 682)

That same thought also crossed the mind of Senator Strom Thurmond who posed the question to U.S. Attorney General Ramsey Clark
in the following brief exchange:

"SENATOR THURMOND. Criminals have a way of getting guns.
They have a way of getting information. They have a way of breaking
into places that might contain the registration of firearms. And I want
to ask you this. Would not this—these proposals make the law-abiding citizen who does register his gun a prime target for attack and
burglary by the very element of our society that you seek to control?
ATTORNEY GENERAL CLARK. I see absolutely nothing to suggest it. It
makes no sense to me, Senator." (HH–p. 643)

Although there was no survey to measure their reaction, it is undoubtedly safe to speculate that not a single major gun collector in the
country felt in the least bit reassured by the U.S. Attorney General's
assessment of the potential risks to their collections. Most serious gun
collectors had long ago learned that it was not at all uncommon for
various persons in government to adopt a cavalier attitude towards
property which belonged to other people.

A classic example of governmental insensitivity to the rights of security and privacy in matters pertaining to official records of firearms
owners was made all too evident by the story which broke in the *New
York Daily News* on February 26, 1970:

"Rep. Frank Horton (R., N.Y.) charged yesterday that the internal
revenue service is publishing what amounts to a 'national guide for
gun thieves' by peddling the addresses of gun dealers and collectors

390

who registered under the 1968 gun control law. Horton said more than 140,000 names and addresses of licensed gun dealers and collectors are being sold by IRS for $140, or about one-tenth of a cent a name."

Immediately upon being made aware of this reprehensible and dangerous practice, Congressman Horton wrote a letter of protest to the Internal Revenue Service Commissioner, saying in part that:

"This practice, contrary to the Congressional intent expressed in the State Firearms Control Assistance Act of 1968, under which these licenses are issued, would seem to invite thefts and other criminal acts against licensees by pin-pointing the whereabouts of substantial numbers of guns in every city, town and village in America for anyone who can afford the price of a mailing list." (*The American Rifleman*: April 1970)

A fundamental premise of any gun registration proposal is that it is physically possible to identify one firearm from another by means of its manufacturer's name, its model number, its caliber or gauge, and its serial number. That was not entirely true, and it was even less true with respect to those firearms which were most frequently found in the hands of criminals and irresponsible persons. Advocates of gun registration, however, have generally displayed so very little comprehension of the legal, practical, and philosophical deficiencies of their proposals that their failure to grasp that essential fact was really not surprising.

The complexities associated with the identification of firearms by serial numbers was so great that Harold W. Glassen, President of the National Rifle Association, was only able to touch upon the problem superficially during the brief time that had been allotted for his testimony before Senator Dodd's subcommittee:

"The technical problems presented by a federal law requiring the registration of all firearms can well be insurmountable. Under current Federal law individual serial numbers and model designations are not required on any shotgun or .22 caliber rifle unless such shotgun or rifle has been sawed-off or otherwise modified so as to be subject to the provisions of the National Firearms Act. So far as can be ascertained, none of the major manufacturers serially numbered any of the .22 rifles or certain grades of shotguns manufactured by them until just a few years ago.

The majority of these manufacturers still do not use serial numbers for their production. When it is considered that there are probably 180 million rifles and shotguns already in circulation, with an estimate of probably 75 percent of all .22 rifles and inexpensive grades of shotguns presently in the hands of the public containing no serial numbers, the feasibility of a national registration law is suspect on this basis alone." (HH–p. 205)

The fact that some of the gun registration proponents were dimly and vaguely aware of this problem was illustrated in the following exchange between Senator Joseph Tydings and Sheldon Cohen, Internal Revenue Service Commissioner:

> "SENATOR TYDINGS. What would you require in registering those firearms which do not bear serial number identification?
> COMMISSIONER COHEN. There must be a positive identification system, so that those firearms must be impressed with a permanent identification number—very similar, for example, in Montgomery County we have a bicycle registration rule that requires a number. Some of the bicycles that are manufactured do not bear serial numbers, so they must be stamped by the local police in that particular case with a number.
> SENATOR TYDINGS. So you would provide the administrative machinery—
> COMMISSIONER COHEN. For impressing a number on those weapons.
> SENATOR TYDINGS. So they would have a serial number even though the original product from the manufacturer did not have a serial number?
> COMMISSIONER COHEN. That is correct, sir." (HH–p. 129)

It is not quite that simple, however, as anyone knows who is more familiar with firearms than with bicycles. One of the reasons is that an absolutely enormous number of European-made firearms circulating in this country bear "serial numbers" having no relationship whatever to the consecutiveness of their manufacture and which were never intended to be used for identification purposes. That was particularly true of war-time ordnance production where dozens of different foreign factories manufactured identical models of firearms with each one of their production runs starting off with Serial Number 1.

One of the most popular German pistols is the Luger. During the many years of its production there were without question hundreds of thousands manufactured, yet it is rare to find one with more than a four digit "serial number", and in no case has there ever been one found with a serial number over 40,000. Quite obviously these numbers were used for entirely different purposes than those in the United States.

Some European factories which manufactured firearms for commercial export to the United States evidently assigned a new block of serial numbers, each beginning with Number 1, to every purchase order they received. The number of duplicate serial numbers which therefore exist from such normal practices would astonish anyone not familiar with firearms.

Further contributing to the problem of serial numbers, where they exist, is the common practice of cannibalizing damaged firearms for their useful parts. For example, a pistol, the frame of which may have been damaged beyond repair, might nevertheless be the source of a dozen parts which could be used to replace comparable parts on other pistols worn or damaged.

Frequently, many such parts bear their own assembly numbers, and on an original pistol all such numbers will match. However, after the hundreds of thousands of cannibalizations which have taken place it is not at all uncommon to find pistols assembled from a number of parts each bearing a different serial number.

As an example of a multi-numbered pistol, there is no better one than the German Luger which is generally encountered with a short four-digit number. On an original pistol the identical number will be found on the barrel, on the barrel frame, on the grip frame, on the recoil toggle bolt, on the loaded-chamber indicator, on the firing pin, on the side plate, and on the base of the magazine. The scarcity of Luger pistols having completely matching numbers is attested to by the fact that such pistols command premium prices among collectors who value the genuiness of firearms which in all respects are original and intact.

Two brief excerpts from what is undoubtedly the leading text in the field of firearms identification will clearly illustrate the problem of gun registration. They are taken from a book originally published in 1957 entitled *Firearms Investigation Identification and Evidence* written by the foremost national authorities Maj. Gen. Julian S. Hatcher, Lt. Col. Frank J. Jury, and Jac Weller:

"Based upon the experience of Eastern Police Departments known to the authors not more than one handgun in 10 used in crime is of a type that tracing by serial number is possible. More than 90% are over age or foreign. Even where tracing is possible it seldom is conclusive. Criminals seldom use a weapon that can be traced to them."

* * *

"The largest single group of shoulder weapons which come into the laboratory for identification—the cheap modern low power rifles and shotguns—will have a maker's name or a familiar trademark but no serial numbers at all. The rifles and shotguns mass-produced for the large mail order houses will be marked with trade names of the house but not the manufacturer's name and will have no serial numbers." (pp. 180–181)

The problem of criminals using firearms which cannot be traced back to incriminate them was superbly illustrated by the New York City Police Department itself in a letter of April 4, 1967, which had been incorporated in the official record of the hearings of the House subcommittee in that year. The letter was issued by the Deputy Commissioner in charge of Press Relations for the New York City Police Department. It is reproduced here in its entirety:

"Attached are the press releases requested on the subject of crime statistics. The area included in the statistics of 654 homicides is the five boroughs of the City of New York including the population of approximately eight million.

Attached is a table of homicides including the population, the number of homicides, and the rate per hundred thousand. Hand guns were used in 184 homicides in the city, 28.1 per cent of the total as against 150 in 1965, of 633 homicides or a percentage of the previous year of 23.7.

A check with our statistical bureau has indicated that no licensed hand guns were used in criminal homicides last year." (FF–p. 678)

It should also be obvious that, even in the absence of insurmountable operating difficulties entailed in a national registration program, there is also the very serious matter of the cost of such a program. On the experience of the Internal Revenue Service maintaining the records of over 100,000 firearms registered under the provisions of the National Firearms Act of 1934, IRS submitted a comprehensive estimate of the cost to establish and maintain a computerized system to register an estimated 75,000,000 firearms and 40,000,000 gun owners. Commissioner Sheldon Cohen testified as to their conclusions:

"Basically there are two separate items of cost. One is a first year or an installation cost, and then of course there is a maintenance cost. The installation cost is part of the cost of the system, and the hardware for the computer system, whether it be housed in our agency or another agency, and the outlets for it around the country, so that we can have multiple access.

Basically the starting costs are about $25 million. The ongoing costs, at least on the basis of our present estimate, that States will cooperate, that many States will enact legislation, or most of the States will enact legislation that would qualify, would be that we would need about 500 additional investigating staff in addition to that which we have today, several hundred clerical people, and that the ongoing costs, yearly costs, would be something in the neighborhood of $22 million to $23 million. Now, these are projections based on what we can see today. They may be modified or expanded by what eventually is enacted by the Congress. This does not include the local police check which of course would be required, or certain other costs that are extraneous to the registration that we would carry on." (HH–p.123)

The reader is reminded that the annual cost of $22 million to $23 million was merely the conservative estimate for physically maintaining computerized records of firearms, assuming momentarily for the sake of argument that the many impediments previously discussed could somehow be overcome. There still remained the matter of "the local police check which of course would be required." That specific subject was not brought up during these particular hearings by Senator Dodd's subcommittee, possibly for very good reasons, but it was explored by President Johnson's National Commission on the Causes and Prevention of Violence, on their own initiative.

A preliminary cost analysis of firearms control programs was prepared for the National Commission on the Causes and Prevention of Violence by the professional consultant firm of Research Associates Incorporated of Silver Springs, Maryland. The report was released by the firm on December 20, 1968. Their conclusions were not at all unpredictable.

The methodical study carefully broke down all of the individual elements of cost which would be incurred in a national firearms owner licensing system to investigate applicants, process fingerprint records, check for mental competency, and provide for the necessary clerical and supervisory personnel to administer the system. Also, the analysts calculated the costs of administrating the handgun licensing program in New York City for purposes of comparing it with less stringent and less thorough licensing systems which also could be utilized. Such other licensing programs, varying in degree of severity and thoroughness, were illustrated in a table which listed the costs per applicant on a scale ranging from "A" through "G".

Program "A" represented the least costly system which neither required the checking of fingerprints nor a particularly careful investigation of license applicants. The total cost per applicant under program "A" would have been $6.69.

Program "G" represented the most comprehensive and expensive of the seven model cost programs developed and calculated by the researchers. It entailed a detailed background check of each applicant by a professionally trained investigator, plus fingerprint record checks by both State authorities and the FBI, and a verification as to mental competency. The total cost per applicant under such a program, program "G", would have been $51.99.

Interestingly enough, the research team calculated that the total cost per applicant under the New York City handgun licensing program, the Sullivan Law, came to $72.87.

In their conclusions, Research Associates Incorporated combined the estimated annual cost of a national gun registration system, as had been calculated by the Internal Revenue Service, with a national extension of their projections of licensing costs ranging from the least expensive to the most expensive systems. This is what they reported:

> "It is of interest to conceive of a firearms owner licensing program in conjunction with a national firearms registration system. Assume that there are forty million firearms owners to be licensed at the state level and that a license must be renewed every five years. An average of eight million applicants would require investigation each year. Sample Programs A through G, as developed on the cost model, would then cost $76,020,000 to $438,420,000 per year when the $22,500,000 for the registration system is included (not including initial set-up costs at the state level.)" (pps, 30–31, Cost Analysis of Firearms Control Programs, Dec. 20, 1968, for National Commission on the Causes and Prevention of Violence, by Research Associates, Inc., Silver Spring, Md.)

It should also be noted that, if the cost basis for the Sullivan Law as administered by New York City, $72.87 per applicant, were substituted for the less sophisticated model cost systems, then the annual national cost for both gun registration plus firearms owner licensing would reach $605,460,000. Of course that would be predicated upon a license which had a five year duration, and, as the reader will recall, the Administration had suggested that such licenses be valid for only three years. Consequently, a three year period would have the effect of increasing the number of people which would have to be processed each year from 8,000,000 to 13,333,333, thus making the annual cost of both national gun registration combined with national firearms owner licensing just slightly under one billion dollars, precisely $994,099,975 per year.

In addition to the outright cash expense of registration and licensing, the report also went on to discuss the somewhat less obvious indirect costs of firearms control programs:

"Primary sources of revenue for wildlife restoration activities are sales of hunting licenses and an 11% excise tax on sporting arms (rifles and shotguns) and ammunition. In 1967, 20.2 million hunting licenses, tags, permits, and stamps were sold at a gross cost to hunters of $81.5 million. During that same year, $27.8 million was collected in sporting arms and ammunition excise taxes.

Firearms control programs that would be so restrictive as to result in a serious reduction in the use of firearms for lawful purposes could result in a drastic decrease in this combined yearly income of over $100 million." (op. cit. p. 34)

Among the other potential indirect costs of restrictive firearms control programs there was mentioned the possibility of what might happen if firearms and ammunition sales sharply decreased:

"If government subsidies were eventually required to support the firearms manufacturing industry so that it would be available for defense needs, then this cost would be paid by the general public." (Op. Cit. pps. 35–36)

Many other indirect cost factors were also detailed in that excellent cost analysis by Research Associates Incorporated which for the first time had professionally reduced the vague and indistinct hypotheses of amateurs to hard cold tax dollars.

Is it any wonder why knowledgeable men, whose entire lives reflected an intimate familiarity with firearms and firearms control legislation, felt compelled to speak out in protest against the national adoption of gun registration and firearms owner licensing legislation? Consider the following cautionary words of advice tendered Senator Dodd's subcommittee by Franklin Orth, who raised certain substantive questions which any reasonable man would surely insist be adequately answered before committing the country to a system of national gun registration:

"In approaching the matter of registration, we must ask ourselves these basic questions: What is the nature of the problem to be solved? Would registration, in the light of its nature and its history, help to solve the problem? Is registration of the kind contemplated a proper exercise of the Federal Government, or does such a power properly lie within the area of the States' police powers? Is registration administratively and fiscally feasible? Would the expenditure in time, personnel, resources and money be commensurate with any alleged benefit or gain? Would it be wise for the Congress to give the newly enacted firearms restrictions in the Crime Control Act of 1968 a chance to operate before blindly and swiftly adding other controls which may well be neither desirable nor necessary? How would registration prevent or reduce the criminal use of firearms?

So far, Mr. Chairman, I have not seen or heard anything by the proponents of gun registration which answers these compelling inquiries. Laudatory and promotional statements—general, vague, and ambiguous—are the only support and reasons given by registration advocates in support of their position. Exercise in forensic, generated by emotional momentum and widespread agitation in the press, is hardly a basis for the establishment of the validity of the registration approach." (HH–p. 193)

The anti-gun campaign was so staggering that it drew this comment from Harold W. Glassen as a prelude to the thrust of his general testimony before Senator Dodd's subcommittee:

"It is no accident or mere coincidence that certain of the mass news media for many months have been waging an unrelenting campaign of antifirearms propaganda in an obvious attempt to mold the opinion of the large segment of our population that is not informed upon the issues and who have little or no interest in firearms. In this connection, it is noteworthy that as the public outcry against violence in our society has risen, the emotion of the moment has been artfully manipulated and capitalized upon by those who have long desired strict gun control legislation of the type now proposed, but who have been fearful of making their views public. The hysteria that now prevails, however, has given these men the opportunity they have long awaited, as they cloak their actions under the guise of public demand and necessity." (HH–p. 201)

The prevalence of widespread public hysteria touches even those persons and organizations which under more normal conditions could be depended upon to exercise judgments and form opinions on emotionally neutral and objective criteria. Emotionalism rather than intelligent contemplation may have been one of the reasons why the Anti-Defamation League of B'nai B'rith called for the registration of all firearms and for a requirement that owners and purchasers of firearms obtain permits. Their official explanation was as follows:

"ADL's concern with the problem arose from the increasing accumulation of firearms by members of such organizations as the Minutemen and other private 'armies' sponsored by extremist groups." (HH–p. 776)

If the Anti-Defamation League was really concerned about alleged extremist "armies", then why did they not merely exert their very considerable influence on the U.S. Attorney General and insist that he rigorously enforce the terms of the Voorhis Act of 1940 which, it will be recalled, contained the following provisions:

"The following organizations shall be required to register with the Attorney General:"

* * *

"Every organization, the purpose or aim of which, or one of the purposes or aims of which, is the establishment, control, conduct, seizure, or overthrow of a government or subdivision thereof by the use of force, violence, military measures, or threats of any one or more of the foregoing."

* * *

"Every registration statement required to be filed by any organization shall contain the following information and documents:"

* * *

"A description of all firearms or other weapons owned by the organization, or by any chapter, branch, or affiliate of the organization, identified by the manufacturer's number thereon;"

In light of the existence of the Voorhis Act for nearly thirty years, logic compels one to conclude that there could only have been two reasons why it had not been successfully employed to control the alleged extremist groups and their private "armies." Either there existed no legally sufficient evidence by means of which the sanctions of the Voorhis Act could be applied against extremists, or else the registration provisions did not work in the manner that had been anticipated when the Voorhis Act was enacted back in 1940.

If one accepts as fact the frequently repeated assertions by high ranking officials that such illegal groups of extremists and their private "armies" actually did exist, then the conclusion is inescapable that the registration provisions of the Voorhis Act simply did not work in nearly thirty years. It would therefore appear that the proponents of gun registration as a means of controlling extremists and their "armies" constructively placed themselves in the untenable position of citing the failure of one major federal registration law as a reason for the Congress to enact still another and more costly one. They were properly repudiated.

The failure of firearms registration to deprive criminals of their guns was known to Congressman John Dingell who was also an attorney, a former criminal prosecutor and one of the foremost national authorities on laws relating to firearms. Congressman Dingell was unequivocal in his statement to Senator Dodd's subcommittee:

"I think that it is quite clear, from a fair study of the history of firearms control laws, that it should be very plain to anyone who is really interested in the proper legislative solution to the problem, that registration legislation won't stop crime, it won't stop crimes of violence.

Historically it is provable that it has not stopped crimes of violence. Historically it is provable that as a matter of fact the only concrete effect of such legislation has been to strip the law-abiding citizen of a very important right and privilege, and to deny him the means and access to an instrument which in its own nature is innocent and which is wrong only because of its capacity for misuse." (HH–p. 469)

The complete failure of registration and permit laws, coupled with many decades of their arbitrary administration in such cities as New York and Chicago, were common knowledge among informed firearms owners in the country. With knowledge of the facts, they rejected the false propaganda created by the advertising industry and disseminated by the news media for consumption by the uninformed general public. That point was clearly brought out by Thomas L. Kimball, Executive Director of the National Wildlife Federation:

"Now, everyone is aware of the public pronouncements by governmental officials that gun registration will not impair the legitimate ownership of guns in this country. May I state frankly that the law-abiding gun owners of this country simply do not believe it. If all who are truly interested will scrutinize closely the actual experience of the oldest gun registration law on the books, in New York City, over the last 47 years, they will gain some insight as to why the legitimate gun owners oppose gun registration, particularly those where police are given discretion as to whether or not a permit to possess will be approved."

* * *

"Police purposely have made the license provision as burdensome as possible with the apparent goal of elimination of handguns in New York City, except to those who must have them in the course of their law enforcement work." (HH–p. 540)

Some interesting and illuminating statistics concerning crime rates in the New York City area as compared with other cities were presented by Harold W. Glassen who first called attention to the fact that although approximately 8,000,000 people resided in the New York City metropolitan area less than 2,000 private citizens whose occupations were not connected with law-enforcement were allowed to own pistols:

"In the 1966 FBI report, of 184 standard metropolitan statistical areas, 119 had lower homicide rates than New York. Included in this number were cities across the Nation; 182 had lower robbery rates and 162 had a lower aggravated assault rate. Dallas, with a population of 1,300,-000, had an overall homicide rate of 11.4 per 100,000. Minneapolis-St. Paul, with 1,600,000, had a rate of 2.3—and both had firearms laws much more liberal than New York's where the homicide rate is 6.4.

Consider if you will that the Borough of Manhattan, with a population of 1,700,000, had a homicide rate of 15.13, and Queens, with 1,800,000, had a low rate of 3.6. It is obvious that factors more important than gun laws were operating in these areas.

It is often stated by gun control advocates that Dallas, with relatively lenient gun laws, had an 11.4 homicide rate as opposed to New York's 6.4 with strict laws, but if one compares the three main categories of crime in which firearms are involved—homicides, aggravated assaults, and robberies—New York's overall rate is much higher than Dallas', 434.2 per 100,000, as opposed to 291.2. The conclusion is definitely warranted that living under strict gun laws does not actually reduce one's chances of being the victim of a violent crime." (HH–pp. 202–203)

There have been several attempts to make statistical comparisons between the homicide rates of those cities and States having strict firearms control regulations and those that did not. One of the earliest was published in 1958 in the *South Texas Law Journal* under the title "Do Laws Requiring Registration of Privately Owned Firearms Lower Murder Rates?" That comprehensive statistical analysis included data secured not only from major American cities and all states, but also from many foreign countries. Its major conclusions were these:

"There is no evidence to indicate that, acting alone, laws requiring the registration of firearms have any effect on the rate at which murders and homicides are committed. It appears that once the homicidal intent is formed the instrument to be used is only incidental. If a firearm is handy, it will be used due to its convenience, but if a gun is not available, then a knife, a board, an ice pick or simply the bare hands will be used." (GG–p. 629)

The *South Texas Law Journal* study, interestingly enough, was published in the same year as was *Patterns In Criminal Homicide* by Marvin E. Wolfgang which included, as the reader will recall, this remarkably similar conclusion:

"It is probably safe to contend that many homicides occur only because there is sufficient motivation or provocation, and that the type of method used to kill is merely an accident of availability; that a gun is used because it is in the offender's possession at the time of incitement, but that if it were not present, he would use a knife to stab, or fists to beat his victim to death." (p. 79)

Two years later, in 1960, the California Department of Justice, Bureau of Criminal Statistics, conducted a study of 640 homicides in that State for that year and concluded:

"One of the clear conclusions of this research is that the mere availability of weapons lethal enough to produce a human mortality bear no major relationship to the frequency with which this act is completed. In the home, at work, at play, in almost any environmental setting a multitude of objects exist providing means for inflicting illegal death." (*Congressional Record*: July 18, 1968)

Also in 1960, another comprehensive study on the possible relationship between firearms regulations and crime rates was conducted by the Wisconsin Legislative Reference Library for the Wisconsin State Legislature. The results of that study reaffirmed that there existed no demonstrable correlation between firearms regulations and crime rates.

Seven years later, in 1967, the Wisconsin study was re-examined, updated, and statistically analyzed on the basis of current data to ascertain whether or not there were any statistically significant differences in crime rates between those states having firearms licensing requirements as opposed to those which did not. That study which was deliberately constructed to be consistent with the earlier Wisconsin study, was conducted by Dr. Alan S. Krug, an economist with the Regional Analysis Center of the Institute for Research on Land and Water Resources at the Pennsylvania State University. The final conclusion reached by Dr. Krug was stated as follows:

"This study tested the statistical hypothesis: *States with firearms licensing laws have lower crime rates than states not having such laws.* Statistical analysis of the latest F.B.I. crime data resulted in this hypothesis being rejected. The conclusion was reached that there is no statistically-significant difference in crime rates between states that have firearms licensing laws and those that do not." (March 27, 1967 pub. by the National Shooting Sports Foundation)

The reader will also recall that in 1967 the American Bar Foundation published a research paper entitled "Firearms And Legislative Regulation" which contained these informative observations:

"In the published materials and in our interviews, there is a respectable body of opinion that legal restraints on weapons have little effect on crime and criminals."

* * *

"Other factors almost certainly outweigh the presence of firearms as a cause of crime: for example, New York has much stricter gun control laws and a much higher crime rate than neighboring Vermont." (Nov. 6, 1967, pps. 3 and 10)

It was crystal clear to the 1,000,000 members of the National Rifle Association that its then President, Harold W. Glassen, was reciting the undeniable facts when he forcefully delivered these words of protest before Senator Dodd's subcommittee:

"The tragic assassination of Senator Robert F. Kennedy has unleashed a concentrated barrage of misleading publicity in favor of strict controls on firearms. This campaign, fostered and promulgated by those who would seize the opportunity of the moment in order to further their own ends, seeks to foist upon an unsuspecting and aroused public a law that would, through its operation, sound the death knell for the shooting sports and eventually disarm the American public. We are being conditioned to believe that there is a direct causal connection between the availability of firearms and criminal activity in this country, a premise not proven after 5 years of congressional hearings and public debate, but which is now being stated as fact." (HH–p. 201)

Senator Joseph Tydings, however, provided the Dodd subcommittee with his own personal interpretation of the reason for the opposition by the National Rifle Association to gun registration and licensing. With typical insolence he proclaimed:

"It is because their membership has been brainwashed for so long by the national leadership which is principally directed, financed by the munitions industry. They do not have a chance because they never see the facts." (HH–p. 545)

The outright hostility shown by Senator Tydings towards the leadership of the National Rifle Association was evident more than once during the course of the hearings before the Dodd subcommittee. Consider these remarks following Senator Strom Thurmond's laudatory assessment of the NRA's historic service to the United States:

"SENATOR THURMOND. I want to thank you very much for your testimony here. Mr. Glassen, you and Mr. Orth both. I want to commend you for the great service you have rendered your country. I want to commend the National Rifle Association for the thousands of men they have trained to be good marksmen, and who have used that good marksmanship in behalf of their country in time of war. Regardless of the outcome of the legislation here, I just want to say to you that there are millions of people in this country that are grateful for what you people are doing, and we hope you will continue to stand by the Constitution regardless of the outcome.

MR. GLASSEN. Thank you, Senator Thurmond.

MR. ORTH. Thank you.

SENATOR TYDINGS. Thank you very much, Senator Thurmond. Gentlemen, I might like to add for the record that I could not disagree with my distinguished colleague more in his last remarks." (HH–p. 404)

Senator Tydings then proceeded to interrogate Mr. Glassen about the role played by National Rifle Association in providing information to its membership concerning pending firearms legislation, and the subject quickly turned to the issue of whether or not the NRA was improperly engaged in lobbying:

"SENATOR TYDINGS. Mr. Glassen, are you registered as a lobbyist for your organization?

MR. GLASSEN. No, I am not a lobbyist.

SENATOR TYDINGS. Your organization is not registered either?

MR. GLASSEN. No. We are not lobbyists.

SENATOR TYDINGS. You have no compunctions about your organization contacting Members of the Congress on pending legislation?

MR. GLASSEN. As individuals they have a perfect right to do that. We contact only our members. I have never gone on national television or any other kind and asked everybody within sound of my voice to write a letter to his Congressman.

SENATOR THURMOND. Incidently, I saw a television program within the last 2 days where John Glenn did go on a television program and ask the people to write to the Members of Congress. And you have not even done that, have you?

MR. GLASSEN. We never have. Our contact is with our own members."

* * *

"SENATOR THURMOND. I just started to say—the address Mr. Glenn made, he is on the opposite side from you. As I understand it, he is favoring this stringent gun legislation, registration and so forth. And yet if the members of the Rifle Association talk to anybody, or make any move to try to protect this country from a national police state—and that is what it could result in, then you are criticized. The proponents of the legislation—they can go on television, and take other steps, and it seems to be perfectly all right."

* * *

"I am told that about June 13 or 14, the Justice Department called together about 30-odd different organizations, and from that meeting drew this committee that Mr. Glenn now heads."

* * *

"So who is really doing the lobbying here—the National Rifle Association or the Justice Department?"

* * *

"The NRA is being accused of lobbying, and here you have the Attorney General of the United States, with all of the resources of the Justice Department, and all of the resources of this administration, leading the move in proposing gun legislation, and yet they are not accused of lobbying. Does that seem to be a very fair situation?"

* * *

"I think the question answers itself." (HH–pps. 423–424)

One man who could neither be accused of lobbying nor of insensitivity to the wrongful use of firearms, but who nevertheless spoke out in strong opposition to gun registration, was Texas Governor John B. Connally, Jr. On the day following the assassination of President John F. Kennedy, the Chicago Tribune noted this now almost forgotten fact:

"Gov. John B. Connally Jr. of Texas, riding with the President, was seriously wounded by a shot fired after the bullet which killed the President."

No other man had been closer to the Dallas tragedy than Governor Connally. After recovering from his injury he remained an honest man and made the following statement during one of his subsequent annual messages to the State of Texas:

"I recognize that there is a great hue and cry in some areas of our country today for a gun registration law. I am not convinced that this is the answer to our problems for two principal reasons: (1) The criminal element could still obtain firearms legally, and (2) many of

405

our most dastardly and shocking crimes have been committed by individuals who would have encountered no difficulty in obtaining and registering firearms under even the most stringent gun registration law recommended. I believe that we should hit hard at the unlawful use of firearms and concealed weapons rather than at the right of ownership." (FF–pp. 778–779)

Hitting hard at the unlawful use of weapons meant the swift and certain imposition of heavy penalties so as to remove from society those individuals who have demonstrated their inability or unwillingness to live peaceably among decent human beings. Hitting hard at the unlawful use of weapons was the very essence of the trenchant message filed before the Dodd subcommittee by Congressman Bob Casey:

"We don't want, and we don't need, the registration and licensing program as set forth in these bills. What we want is vigorous enforcement, prompt prosecution, stern sentencing and practical parole of those who use guns in a continuing career of crime. We need mandatory sentences where the authority to turn loose this vermin on society is taken from the hands of lax judges and juries and lenient parole authorities." (HH–p. 768)

Interestingly enough, substantiation of the charges that the present weak and excessively lenient criminal sanctions had served neither to deter against crime nor to remove criminals from society came from unexpected quarters. Senator Dodd had initiated a special subcommittee study of the backgrounds of murderers from the 120 major population centers of the United States, and although the facts uncovered were widely used by the anti-gun claque in their efforts to persuade the Congress of the need for additional gun control laws they clearly established quite the contrary to Harold W. Glassen who commented on the findings:

"A recent study by this subcommittee on firearms homicides in this country disclosed that 80 percent of those who used a gun had a prior criminal record; that 78 percent of all murders studied had criminal records; that the gun killer had an average of six prior arrests before his first murder, 27 of them for serious offenses; and that 60 percent of the gun killers had been arrested for a crime of violence before the murder indictment.

These facts are being presented as further evidence for strict gun controls; but if they do not indict the present court and penal structure for a failure to punish, rehabilitate, or separate from useful society those who would destroy, I misinterpret the data."

406

"We have always been told that the greatest deterrent to crime is the prospect of quick apprehension and quick and certain punishment if convicted. Yet, with the tight rules of evidence that must be followed today; with our clogged criminal courts, and with all the appeal avenues which are available to a convicted criminal, it can, and often does, take years from the time a crime is committed to put the person responsible behind bars as punishment for his crime.

It should be obvious that if quick and proper punishment cannot be meted out to those who use guns for criminal purposes, no gun law will stop the increasing misuse of firearms. What is needed most urgently are tougher and more rigidly and quickly enforced laws dealing with the use of firearms for criminal purposes." (HH–p. 203)

Substantially the same views as to the nature of the fundamental crime problem in the United States was voiced by Senator Strom Thurmond who backed up his opinions with solid crime statistics:

"The decline of law enforcement in the country is apparent from some shocking statistics. Only one lawbreaker in eight is tried and convicted; of all persons arrested in 1966, 76 percent were repeat offenders. I want to repeat that. Of all persons arrested in 1966, 76 percent were repeat offenders."

* * *

"Why? Chiefly because the Supreme Court decisions have made apprehension difficult and made punishment uncertain and unsure, and this has encouraged criminals. This, in addition to the permissiveness that seems to pervade the atmosphere today.

Just as shocking is the rate of criminal repeaters—lawbreakers who are turned loose to prey again upon society. A recent FBI study of some 18,000 convicts released in 1963 revealed that fully 55 percent had been rearrested for new offenses by June 30, 1966. Criminals are increasingly defying the law successfully, and public confidence in our administration of justice is diminishing.

Our crime and gun problem would largely come under control if conviction rates were doubled and sentences were more severe. The chief keys to the gun control problem are swift apprehension and certain punishment for those who violate the law." (HH–pp. 55–56)

Not everyone, of course, subscribed to those views on crime, punishment, and gun control. An unusually clear glimpse was provided by the testimony of Lawrence Speiser, Director of the Washington office of the American Civil Liberties Union.

There was absolutely no question about whether or not the American Civil Liberties Union supported gun registration and licensing, as Lawrence Speiser made that fact quite clear:

"Our organization is not persuaded by cries of inconvenience or futility. And in our view both registration and licensing are indispensable to any effective gun control legislation." (HH–p. 567)

The rationale for the general position of the ACLU with respect to their support for gun control legislation appeared to have been embodied within one of the findings which had been incorporated by Senator Dodd in the preamble to his gun registration bill. That finding, to which Lawrence Speiser claimed the ACLU fully subscribe read as follows:

"That the unregistered, free flow of firearms in the United States constitutes an impediment or a threat to the exercise of free speech in the maintenance and continuation of democratic process in the United States and the free exercise of religion guaranteed by the First Amendment to the Constitution of the United States." (HH–p. 567)

The American Civil Liberties Union, however, did appear to have some reservations about several of the bills pending before the Dodd subcommittee, and the nature of those reservations will prove most informative to the reader. Some highly enlightening excerpts from the testimony of Lawrence Speiser follow:

"Licensing provisions present a number of other issues. A major purpose is to keep guns from the hands of persons considered likely to misuse such weapons, and there are in some of the bills categories of disqualifications. For example, one of them proposes to deny a license to persons convicted of any felony or convicted of any misdemeanor involving actual or attempted physical harm to himself or to another. And another provision would deny a license to anyone ever committed to an institution by a court on the ground that he was an alcoholic, a narcotic addict, or mentally incompetent, or not a citizen of the United States. In our view these disqualifications are entirely too broad. A blanket prohibition against and ownership by all those convicted of any felony would seem to be unwarranted in light of the wide variety of crimes which might be termed 'felonies' and the possibility of future rehabilitation in many cases." (HH–pp. 567–568)

* * *

"The disqualification of persons who have ever been committed to an institution by a court of the United States on the grounds, or any political subdivisions, also, we think is too broad. Alcoholism and narcotic addiction have been determined to be judicially recognized as

408

diseases and it would seem to us that rehabilitation can and should occur." (HH–p. 568)

* * *

"We also feel that the $10,000 or 10-year imprisonment that is imposed under S.3634 seems to be unduly harsh and unnecessary and unrealistic." (HH–p. 569)

Can the reader imagine the outrage and indignation which would have erupted if those statements had been made by a spokesman for the National Rifle Association rather than for the American Civil Liberties Union?

In a brilliant flash of insight into the ideological dichotomy of the gun control issue, one shrewd writer for the *Evening Star*, a Washington newspaper, made these incisive observations which struck responsive cords among many Americans:

"In the popular view, for example, these passionate advocates of gun laws for everyone are equally passionate advocates for the rights of accused persons, including persons accused because they were caught in the act."

* * *

"That's the trouble with the current gun control laws. It isn't the laws themselves so much as their advocacy by what lots of people consider the pro-criminal crowd. Looked at from that point of view, the proposals, even the most far-reaching of them, are seen as steps to disarm the citizenry completely so that criminals can enjoy even more protection than they now do and feel even freer to prey upon the householder and storekeeper."

* * *

"But the actual criminal, in this view, would be protected here as elsewhere. If his gun were confiscated, it would be discovered that the police lacked a search warrant or that their information was obtained by eavesdropping or that he had confessed without a lawyer; in any event, some flaw would put the gun back in his hands and him back on the street." (HH–p. 549)

The reference in this article to the concern shared by many Americans that gun registration and licensing were merely the precursors to gun confiscation was a real and well founded fear. It was a very literal fear frequently expressed by some of the same people who had earlier anticipated that Senator Dodd's progressively escalating bills would eventually lead to proposals of registration and licensing, which they did in fact. During the current hearings before Senator Dodd's subcommittee, Harold W. Glassen expressed his fears in these few words:

"I share the worry of all the sportsmen in America. I think that the question that we have got is, Are we going to have confiscation of firearms?" (HH–p. 423)

It was in response to such fears that Senator Edward W. Brooke, sponsor of one of the gun registration bills pending before the Dodd subcommittee, presented these assurances:

"This in no way suggests that legitimate sportsmen and those who require firearms for personal defense need be prohibited from purchasing or possessing firearms. I know of no Member of Congress who wants to impair the legitimate uses of firearms and I know of no proposal before this committee that threatens to do so." (HH–p. 47)

Thomas L. Kimball of the National Wildlife Federation drew his own conclusions from the very nature of the allegations which proponents of stringent gun control were continually making, and he did not hesitate to express his opinion:

"Now, since the inception of the proposed gun control legislation, statements have been read into the testimony presented before congressional committees to the effect that there is a close correlation between the accessibility of firearms and the increasing crime rate. This leads most legitimate gunowners to conclusion that, in the minds of some legislators and law enforcement officials, the solution to the crime problem in America is to make guns inaccessible. In short, to disarm the citizenry. Now, to make guns inaccessible would require outright confiscation of all guns in private ownership, or to obtain the same result by the slower and more devious methods of registration, ever-increasing costs of license renewals, and police harassment." (HH–p. 543)

One of the witnesses appearing before Senator Dodd's subcommittee in support of gun registration and licensing, and whose name was also prominently listed on the membership roster of the John Glenn Emergency Committee for Gun Control, was Quinn Tamm, the Executive Director of the International Association of Chiefs of Police. One should remember his interesting reply to the question which was propounded by Senator Tydings concerning gun confiscation:

"SENATOR TYDINGS. You see, there are sometimes statements made that the ultimate end of those who want so-called stricter firearms control bills is to effect confiscation of weapons or to make it impossible or impractical to own firearms. That is why I asked you if that would be in your thinking as one of the ultimate objectives of legislation.

MR. TAMM. As far as I am concerned, it would not, sir. I think that a statement of that type is completely unreasonable considering the history of our country, the nature of our country and the nature of the people living here. I just do not understand how people would think that that would occur in the United States." (HH–p. 530)

Senator Roman Hruska also engaged in some rhetorical questioning, directing his comments to U.S. Attorney General Ramsey Clark in whose offices the National Council for a Responsible Firearms Policy had reportedly met with representatives from some 38 other organizations and from which meeting there emerged the Emergency Committee for Gun Control headed by John Glenn:

"SENATOR HRUSKA. You know, it was not too long ago that the business of conjuring up the reprehensible idea of licensing and registration by witnesses opposed to pending bills here was called a sham, a misrepresentation and distortion—there was no such thing as registration or licensing of guns in the contemplation of anybody. When witnesses testified like that, they caught it from certain members of his subcommittee who would say, 'Now, you are putting in the bill something that is not there, we have no idea of putting registration or licensing in. But you know, Mr. Attorney General, we have three or four bills here, and about 50 bills in the other House over there that pertain to the very thing that was the subject, not the conjecture, but of logical development and evolution in firearms control—to wit, you start with a law, and then you progress and now we are at that second stage, that is registration and licensing.

Now, why should we call as conjecture and imagination the idea that licensing and that registration will not be used as a vehicle for virtual elimination of the gun?" (HH–p. 605)

After the kind of circumlocution that direct questions by Senator Hruska seemed to produce in the U.S. Attorney General, Ramsey Clark eventually answered the question by asserting:

"If we wanted to abolish guns, there would be no need to register them. We would just go out and pick them up and destroy them." (HH–p. 605)

411

It should be immediately apparent to the reader that, in the absence of comprehensive national gun registration lists to facilitate gun confiscation, it would have been virtually impossible to "just go out and pick them up." Pick what guns up from whom? Did the U.S. Attorney General have in mind house-to-house searches by polished black-booted storm troopers to uncover all of the firearms? Quite obviously, gun registration is an absolute prerequisite to achievement of gun confiscation unless we risk deep turmoil approaching civil war. The reader should also pause to contemplate that, if gun confiscation were effectively achieved, then there would be no cause for concern over the enormous costs projected for maintaining a huge permanent registration and licensing system. Interesting.

> "SENATOR HRUSKA. I have no doubt there are many people right now who are talking about the abolition of guns, to put us on the same basis that some of the foreign countries find themselves. These people are just waiting for the time when the American people discover that the present law won't work, and then they will begin to demand abolition.
> ATTORNEY GENERAL CLARK. I am not aware of that, Senator."
(HH–p. 607)

Finally, the Chairman of the Emergency Committee for Gun Control, John R. Glenn, Jr., appeared before Senator Dodd's subcommittee for the purpose of testifying in support of both national gun registration and owner licensing. He was accompanied by his mentor, James V. Bennett, the President of the National Council for a Responsible Firearms Policy the action arm of which was the Emergency Committee for Gun Control. Naturally, it was to be expected that John Glenn would deliver himself of the same kind of careful reassurances as to the intentions of the advocates of gun control which had been so carefully designed by the New York City advertising agency for the guidance of his committee:

> "We want to make it absolutely clear that the legislative principles we support in no way would interfere with the legitimate uses of guns by hunters, sportsmen, collectors, and many, many others. I would be first to oppose that, because I enjoy hunting myself. I enjoy target shooting, and that this type thing should not be curtailed. That is not what we are trying to do.
> The scare talk that goes on every time some legislation like this comes up is intolerable. It presents only the other side that claims this is a way of taking guns away. We have no objective of doing that at all."
(HH–p. 115)

412

Some eight months later, on March 4, 1969, there appeared in the *United States Congressional Record* a copy of a very enlightening letter which had been typed on the official stationery of the National Council for a Responsible Firearms Policy and dated June 17, 1968, exactly nine days *before* John Glenn made the above statement to Senator Dodd's subcommittee. That letter now follows in its entirety:

"NATIONAL COUNCIL FOR A RESPONSIBLE
FIREARMS POLICY
Washington, D.C.

June 17, 1968

Dear Miss:

Thanks for sharing your views. We are now supporting the President's Bill which provides stringent restrictions on rifles and shotguns. We shall also get behind the Tydings Bill which provides for national registration and licensing if the states do not act within six months and a year respectively.

I personally believe handguns should be outlawed and provided the substance for such a bill to Senator Percy and Congressmen Conyers about a week ago. Our organization will probably officially take this stand in time but we are not anxious to rouse the opposition before we get the other legislation passed.

It would be difficult to outlaw all rifles and shotguns because of the hunting sport. But there should be stiff regulations. The day may come in this country when police are issued weapons for 24 to 48 hours when tracking down armed criminals. This is what they do in Britain.

Don't give up on us. We thought the handgun bill was a step in the right direction. But, as you can see, our movement will be towards increasingly stiff controls. Thanks for writing. Hope you are circulating the petitions and encouraging letters to Congress.

Yours sincerely,

J. Elliott Corbett, *Secretary"*
(*Congressional Record*, March 4, 1969, inserted by John Dingell)

It should be noted that J. Elliott Corbett was a member of the Board of Directors of the National Council for a Responsible Firearms Policy, as well as its Secretary. He was also the Director of the Washington Study Program for the Methodist Church.

Now, consider a news article which appeared on June 13, 1968, in the *Chicago Daily News*, twelve days *before* John Glenn made his speech before Senator Dodd's subcommittee. The article which was captioned "Mayors Conference Unit Urges Ban On Hand Guns" described the action taken by the resolutions committee of the U.S. Conference of Mayors during the course of their five day conference at the Chicago Palmer House hotel. According to reports, more than 500 mayors from the largest cities in the Nation were in attendance at that conference. That article opened with these statements:

"A committee of U.S. Conference of Mayors has called on Congress to ban ownership of hand guns by all except law enforcement officials. The action was taken by the conference's important resolutions committee, headed by Mayor John V. Lindsay of New York City. . . . The committee voted 11–6 to amend a very mild firearms control resolution by inserting the ban on possession of hand weapons."

John V. Lindsay was one of the Directors of the National Council for a Responsible Firearms Policy. Note that Lindsay was also listed as a member of the Executive Committee of the Emergency Committee for Gun Control.

Is it clear what has been going on? Has anything been learned about the nature of the anti-gun crowd? Has this information suggested anything about their way of thinking, their methods of operating, and their concepts of ethical behavior?

By July 8, 1968, the House Rules Committee was deliberating the ban on interstate sales of long guns and speculating on the possibility that the Senate might decide to approve registration and licensing. Some believed that, if the House were to pass the bill banning interstate sales of long guns, and, if the Senate were to pass gun registration and licensing, then strenuous efforts undoubtedly would have followed in the Senate-House Conference Committee to work out a compromise bill embracing the features of all of the measures. It was for that reason that members of the House Rules Committee balked at approving the bill to ban long gun sales across state lines.

Finally, in order to dislodge the long gun bill, the Chairman of the House Judiciary Committee, Emanuel Celler, agreed to oppose any subsequent move to add registration and licensing to the bill. It was reported that, after two hours of questioning by the House Rules Committee, Congressman Celler made this statement:

"While I am in favor of registration and licensing, I am anxious to get a rule for this bill. I am willing to oppose any amendment on the floor providing for registration and licensing and will do the same in conference with the Senate." (*Chicago Tribune*: July 9, 1968)

On the following day, July 9, 1968, and as a consequence of that promise, the House Rules Committee relented and voted 10 to 5 to report out the long gun bill to the full House for action.

Needless to say, the John Glenn Emergency Committee for Gun Control continued its efforts to force registration and licensing through the Congress by inundating individual congressmen with quantities of mail.

The Emergency Committee for Gun Control reportedly received cash contributions of up to $40,000 during this period, and was largely staffed by part-time volunteers numbering between 50 to 80 persons at any one time. Its non-cash assistance came in the form of free office space in Washington, D. C., which was contributed by a large brokerage firm, the free printing of posters by a drugstore chain, the free printing services of a New York printing company, and the free loan of a young lawyer from the Washington law firm, which was headed by an attorney who had been on the campaign staff of Senator Robert F. Kennedy.

In spite of the obvious advantages possessed by the Emergency Committee for Gun Control, not the least of which was the uncritical attention of 93 percent of the newspaper circulation in the country, there were frequently voiced complaints that the National Rifle Association of America had more money than it to spend. The Executive Director of the Emergency Committee for Gun Control was quoted as having asserted:

"The irony of it is that contributions to NRA are tax deductible because it is chartered as an educational organization it pays no taxes." (*Chicago Daily News*: July 16, 1968)

That statement, of course, was basically false, as were so many of the utterances of the anti-gun claque. Contributions to the National Rifle Association are not, and never were, tax deductible. Suffice it to say, there are two kinds of tax exempt status. One excuses not-for-profit organizations from paying taxes on income received, and the other further permits the donors of contributions to deduct their donations from their own personal income taxes. Church organizations, such as those whose "religious dignitaries" actively campaigned for gun registration, are excellent examples of the latter category of tax status. The National Rifle Association was not within that tax category, and no contributions to it were ever tax deductible. The only tax benefit enjoyed by the National Rifle Association was its exemption from paying taxes on its membership dues and related income.

Two classic examples of outright terror techniques employed in the anti-gun campaign were exposed by the use of "scare-head" monster advertisements in several parts of the country. The first one, a hairy-faced part-animal, part-human creature of fantasy, leered at readers of the June 23, 1968, issue of the *New York Times Magazine* and was subtitled "In America Today, Even This Man Can Buy A Gun." The second one, a vague, shadowy phantasm whose indistinct features were suggestive of a smirking man, occupied a full page spread in several Chicago newspapers on July 25, 1968. The lazily scrawled caption over that menacing image read "The Man Behind You Is Thinking Of Blow-ing Your Brains Out." That particular ad was sponsored by two Chi-cago radio stations which urged readers of the ad to write letters to

In America today, even this man can buy a gun.

Grotesque anti-gun ads.

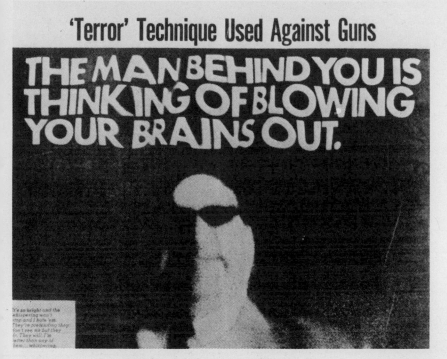

'Terror' Technique Used Against Guns

THE MAN BEHIND YOU IS THINKING OF BLOWING YOUR BRAINS OUT.

It's so bright and the whispering won't stop and I hate 'em. They're pretending they don't see me but they do. They will. I'm better than any of them . . . whispering.

Grotesque anti-gun ads—*continued.*

Congress asking for stronger gun control laws immediately. For those readers lacking a sufficiently morbid imagination, the ad also included the following interpretation of the thoughts which were to be attributed to the apparition:

> "It's so bright and the whispering won't stop and I hate 'em. They're pretending they don't see me but they do. They will. I'm better than any of them . . . whispering, whispering . . . hate 'em all . . . and I'll show 'em. I'll kill 'em."

Opportunism also contributed to the anti-gun campaign and in August 1968 movie fans across the country turned the pages of their local newspapers to the movie directory and saw huge advertisements for the new motion picture "Targets" which was just being released by Paramount Pictures. As one of the ads explained:

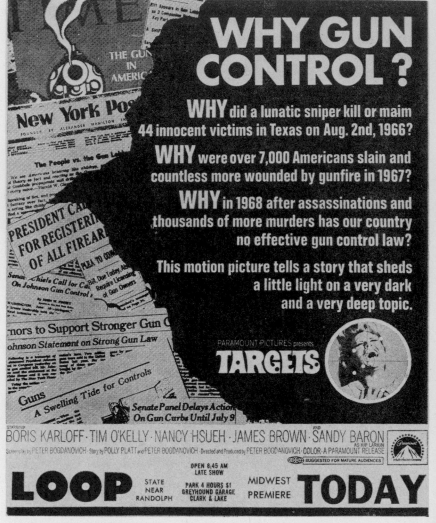

Reproduction of ad for Paramount's movie, *Targets*.

"TARGETS are people . . . and you could be one of them!"

Another ad for that movie portrayed a kneeling man sighting through a riflescope with a separate foreground illustration of the cross-hairs of a telescopic rifle sight centered on the face of a screaming young woman. Across the body of the ad and imprinted over the figure of the sniper were bold black letters which read:

"I just killed my wife and my mother. I know they'll get me. But before that many more will die . . ." (*Chicago Tribune*: August 13, 1968)

The movie was an obvious allusion to the mass slaying which had occurred in Austin, Texas, on August 1, 1966, and during its various scenes somewhere in excess of forty persons were shot by the lunatic sniper who was carefully shown using a pistol, shotgun and high powered rifle. Most of the movie ads incorporated the provocative and prominently featured question:

"WHY in 1968 after assassinations and thousands of more murders has our country no effective gun control law?" (*Chicago Sun Times*: August 14, 1968)

Newsweek magazine Sept. 9, 1968, published a review of the movie "Targets" which included this description of one of the means by which it was being promoted in New York City:

"Outside the theatre in Times Square, a machine projects a lurid loop of excerpts in which a sniper's telescopic sights are continually trained on unsuspecting citizens who continually, thrashingly die. Should such master strokes of opportunism be blamed on the film? Maybe not. They are the work of the advertising department, after all."

In the meanwhile, the House voted down gun registration on July 19, 1968, and on July 23, 1968, it rejected by a vote of 179 to 84 an amendment which would have required licensing of gun owners. The next day, July 24, 1968, the House passed the bill prohibiting interstate mail order sales of rifles and shotguns by a vote of 304 to 118. This last bill was also accompanied by three very important amendments. One amendment which passed by 218 votes to 205 exempted rifle and shotgun ammunition from the bill, thus making its ban applicable only to pistol and revolver ammunition. Another amendment provided for a special license for gun collectors so that they might have access to out of state sources and markets for collector-type firearms. The preceding amendment was affirmed by a 225 to 198 vote and it exempted shipments of firearms and ammunition by the Secretary of the Army to organizations, institutions, or individuals qualified to receive them pursuant to the various programs of the Civilian Marksmanship Program of the National Board for the Promotion of Rifle Practice.

Immediately the amendment exempting the Civilian Marksmanship Program was attacked. John Glenn issued a statement on behalf of the Emergency Committee for Gun Control demanding the elimination of the amendment, reportedly asserting:

"It is a curious result of congressional inadvertance and the National Rifle Association contempt for our process of government." (*Pensacola, Fla., News*: July 29, 1968)

On July 25, 1968, the *Chicago Sun-Times* carried an interesting reference to the source for much of the opposition to the exemption for the Civilian Marksmanship Program:

"Opponents of the amendment circulated a sheet they said came from the justice department. The statement contended the amendment 'will continue to subsidize the NRA by making it advantageous for many persons to become members of the NRA simply in order to evade the basic regulatory purposes of the act.' "

Typical of such absolute falsehoods disseminated by the news media concerning the nature and effect of the amendment was this editorial comment from the July 26, 1968, issue of the *Long Island Press*:

"Exempt every member of the National Rifle Association from the coverage of the entire act, thus making it possible to get around the law by paying $5 a year dues in the NRA. (What a boost for NRA membership!)"

Precisely the same kinds of false assertions were reported across the country, and on July 25, 1968, the *Chicago Daily News* reported:

"Critics contended that the amendment would exempt every member of the National Rifle Assn. The NRA, spokesman for the gun lobby that has been battling gun controls, has 1,000,000 members. The critics think that the amendment will vastly increase NRA membership, since anyone who wished to circumvent the gun-control law could apparently do so simply by paying $5 a year to be a member."

Extremely few, if any, newspapers carried the statement made by the sponsor of the controversial amendment, Congressman Robert Sikes, who had indignantly exclaimed on the House floor:

"Very obviously my amendment does not exempt NRA members from the requirements of the bill before the House; nor is it intended to." (*Pensacola, Fla., News*: July 29, 1968)

Strong support for the Sikes amendment, however, was voiced by Congressman John R. Rarick, who tersely commented:

"The league of anti-gun comrades are not interested in preventing criminal violence—their goal is disarming the average American citizen." (Ibid.)

The constant onslaught unleashed by the news media against the National Rifle Association continued unabated and occasionally produced such grotesque consequences as the one which was reported by an Ohio news weekly:

"The Ferndale, Mich., City Commission asked the city's Recreation Advisory Board on July 22 to discontinue rifle and pistol instruction clubs and classes because instructors are affiliated with the NRA. The proponents of the request said they were opposed to the NRA, not the instruction classes." (*Gun Week*: Aug. 9, 1968)

September 18, 1968, was the critical day in the Senate for both the vote on the prohibition of interstate mail-order sales of rifles and shotguns, and on gun registration and licensing. Headlines flashed across the country telling the news carried by the wire services. The Associated Press release opened with this neatly capsuled version of the Senate action:

"The Senate passed by a vote of 70 to 17 Wednesday a bill to ban interstate mail order sales of rifles, shotguns and ammunition. It rejected proposals for firearms registration and the licensing of owners." (*Chicago Sun Times*: Sept. 19, 1968)

The amendment which had been offered by Senator Tydings to

421

provide for both registration and licensing was rejected by the Senate in a vote of 55 to 31.

The next step in the legislative process was to send the bill which had been passed by the Senate to the Senate-House conference committee whose function it was to attempt to reconcile whatever differences there might have been between the measures recently passed by the House and the Senate. That was done, and on October 8, 1968, a measure was agreed upon by the conferees largely composed of the strongest provisions of the separate bills which had been previously passed by the two houses.

On October 10, 1968, the compromise bill was given final passage by the House in a vote of 160 to 129. Twelve days later, on October 22, 1968, President Lyndon Johnson signed the measure into law to become effective on December 16, 1968, along with the previously enacted ban on the interstate mail-order sales of handguns. In one other Executive action, there was a 30 day amnesty period declared so that persons who wished to do so could register "unconventional" weapons with the Alcohol and Tobacco Tax Division of the Internal Revenue Service. That amnesty period covered the entire month of November 1968.

18

"*Americans may like guns because they were
reminiscent of the smell of outdoors, military heroism,
the intensity of the hunt or merely because they are
fascinated by the finely machined metal parts. Maybe
the origin of a gun speaks of history; maybe the gun
makes a man's home seem to him less vulnerable;
maybe these feelings are more justified in the country
than in the city; but, above all, many of us believe that
these feelings are a man's own business and need not be
judged by the Department of the Treasury or the
Department of Justice.*"

SAMUEL CUMMINGS

EXACTLY ONE DAY BEFORE THE SENATE-HOUSE COM-
promise bill to ban interstate mail-order sales of long
guns was passed, the President's National Commission on the Causes
and Prevention of Violence opened hearings on the subject of firearms
and their relation to violence. The *Chicago's American* reported that
noteworthy event on October 9, 1968, in an article entitled "U. of C.
Prof Urges Vast Program To Disarm Civilians", the opening sentence
of which read:

"A University of Chicago professor, warning that the 'domestic arms
race' is creating a climate of fear and violence, today proposed a
unique plan to disarm the civilian populace."

423

The news story referred to Professor Norval R. Morris, a professor of law and criminology at the University of Chicago, the previous Director of the United Nations' Asia and Far East Institute for Prevention of Crime, and a co-director of the Center for Studies of Criminal Justice at the University of Chicago. This Center had been opened in 1965 with the aid of a $1,000,000 grant from the Ford Foundation. Norval Morris was born in New Zealand, raised in Australia, and had entered the United States in 1964 as an Australian citizen. He remained here as a permanent resident alien.

On January 18, 1967, a full twenty-one months prior to his testimony before the National Commission on the Causes and Prevention of Violence, Professor Morris went on record as to his personal disposition towards the private ownership of firearms. The occasion was a panel discussion on gun legislation sponsored by the Illinois Academy of Criminology of which he was a Vice President. The Academy's official archivist dryly entered the following notation into the record covering that particular session:

"Professor Morris commented that he would categorically deny the private citizen the right to bear arms." (Archivist's Report, p. 2)

It should also be noted that that entry was made months before the racial disorders of 1967, and more than a year before the assassinations of the Rev. Martin Luther King, Jr. and Senator Robert F. Kennedy.

In light of that earlier reported position it will prove enlightening to examine some portions of the testimony given by Prof. Morris before the National Commission on the Causes and Prevention of Violence:

"I am one who believes that as a first step the United States should move just as expeditiously as your leadership can achieve to disarm the civilian population, other than police and security officer, of all hand guns, pistols and revolvers."

* * *

"But the principles I would offer, if I may, sir, are that no one should have a right to anonymous ownership or use of a gun. And that just is not a right that we can safely allow anyone."

* * *

"I think the truth of the matter is that we will ultimately have a police force not equipped with guns." (pps. 1122, 1123, 1138 and 1150, Transcript of Proceedings)

During the afternoon session of the hearings, Milton S. Eisenhower, Chairman of the commission, invited questions to be asked of

Prof. Morris. He elicited this interesting one from George R. Newton, Jr., Director of the commission's Task Force On Firearms:

> "Professor Morris, you referred to a pattern of hand gun legislation which would in effect eliminate the use of hand guns. Is there any pattern of legislation or governmental activity in other countries which has indicated that legislation relating to hand guns will in the long run also be applied to long guns, so that the elimination of hand guns will lead to the elimination of long guns in the long haul?" (op. cit. p. 1145)

Now, carefully consider these excerpts from the reply by Norval Morris to that question, and his reply to another question on a closely related matter which had been raised by Dr. W. Walter Menninger:

> "There are many countries in the world in which the hand gun as a private armament at home in effect does not exist, but where shotguns, rifles, are quite widespread in the community."
>
> * * *
>
> "So I don't think there is any inexorable process here by which if you take one step towards rationality, you have to carry that beyond rationality into repression, which I think is the fear of many."
>
> * * *
>
> "What I believe, Dr. Menninger, is that the feeling of false unity is used by people who oppose rational gun legislation, that is if you touch any part of this whole system you have threatened the whole. It really relates to the earlier question." (op. cit. pp. 1145, 1146 and 1147)

Now compare the preceding statement by Prof. Morris as to there not being any "inexorable process", and his characterization of "the feeling of false unity", with the following quotation taken from the text of a book that was co-authored by him and published approximately one year later, entitled *The Honest Politician's Guide To Crime Control*:

> "Negative licensing of guns without sporting purposes, excluding a few defined categories from the right to possess a firearm, is an excessively cautious, only marginally useful mechanism, other than as a wedge to more rational legislation. We seek a disarmed populace."
>
> * * *
>
> "The President's Commission on Violence apparently believes that the benefits of ownership and sporting use of long guns outweigh the collateral social costs; we disagree, but nevertheless support their program as a first step." (pp. 65 and 70)

Has the reader formed an opinion as to the existence of an "inexorable process"? Did you also catch the part about "a wedge to more rational legislation"? Interesting.

The following list of some other legislative goals recommended by Prof. Morris in his above mentioned book should serve to assist in evaluating his efforts in gun control:

"Public drunkenness shall cease to be a criminal offense."

* * *

"Neither the acquisition, purchase, possession, nor the use of any drug will be a criminal offense."

* * *

"No form of gambling will be prohibited by the criminal law;"

* * *

"Sexual activities between consenting adults in private will not be subject to the criminal law." (p. 3)

The book also contained the two following interesting references to sexual practices, prostitution and pornography which, too, are worth noting:

"Prostitution is an ancient and enduring institution which has survived centuries of attack and condemnation, and there is no doubt that it fulfills a social function." (p. 21)

* * *

"If prurience can find satisfaction by reading books or looking at pictures, it is difficult to conceive anything less harmful to society. It is those who cannot achieve satisfaction in this way who may constitute a danger." (p. 24)

Those propositions are astonishingly similar to the Yippie "statement of demands" circulated in Chicago during the 1968 Democratic National Convention there.

The sordid details were graphically portrayed in a special report to the National Commission on the Causes and Prevention of Violence entitled "Rights In Conflict."

Among thousands of demonstrators there, were many who claimed allegiance to the so-called Youth International Party, from which the acronym "Yippie" was derived.

It was believed by substantial authorities that one of the prime objectives of this group was the disruption of the Democratic National Convention. Consequently, extraordinary security precautions were taken to prevent any such action from succeeding. The precautions included the airlifting into Chicago of 6,000 regular Army troops in full battle gear, equipped with rifles and flame throwers. In addition, another 6,000 Illinois National Guard troops had been activated to assist the 12,000 man Chicago police force.

Only the most superficial concept of all that occurred when the confrontation finally took place between the demonstrators and police can possibly be conveyed by this summary excerpt from "Rights In Conflict":

"During the week of the Democratic National Convention, the Chicago police were the targets of mounting provocation by both word and act. It took the form of obscene epithets, and of rocks, sticks, bathroom tiles and even human feces hurled at police by demonstrators." ("Rights in Conflict," p. 1)

The *Chicago Daily News* compiled a list of weapons allegedly used against law enforcement officers during the critical five day period of the confrontation. The following are a brief sampling: Cellophane bags of human excrement; cans of urine; dart guns; knives and stilettos; Molotov cocktails; potatoes with razors hidden inside; rocks, bricks and glass ash trays.

It was during that thoroughly unwholesome atmosphere a document was widely circulated among the demonstrators entitled "Revolution Towards A Free Society: Yippie!", purportedly written by "A. Yippie" and which enumerated certain specific political demands in the interests of achieving a "free society". Among their demands were included the following:

"The legalization of marihuana and all other psychedelic drugs. The freeing of all prisoners currently in prison on narcotics charges."

* * *

"A prison system based on the concept of rehabilitation rather than punishment."

* * *

"A judicial system which works towards the abolition of all laws related to crimes without victims. That is, retention only of laws relating to crimes in which there is an unwilling injured party, i.e. murder, rape, assault."

* * *

"The total disarmament of all the people beginning with the police."

The Yippie demands also expressed enthusiastic approval for totally unbridled and indiscriminate sexual relationships, but in terms

427

somewhat more explicit than the author deems suitable for language in this book.

Inasmuch as crime has so far provided the only avenue for attacks upon guns in the hands of law-abiding citizens it is disturbing to find so often that those encouraging the growth of crime are intent upon eliminating the private possession of firearms.

Prior to the commencement of the actual hearings relating to firearms by the National Commission on the Causes and Prevention of Violence a perceptive article by sociologist Dr. Susan L. M. Huck was published in the October 1968 issue of *American Opinion* magazine concerning the results of her interviews of several prominent figures connected with the research projects of the commission. The most noteworthy perhaps was with Franklin E. Zimring, Director of Research for the Task Force on Firearms, who also was an assistant professor of law and a research associate with the Center for Studies in Criminal Justice at the University of Chicago, of which Prof. Norval Morris was co-director.

One of the formidable problems facing the Task Force on Firearms was the development of reliable estimates of who had how many of what kinds of guns and for what purposes. That particular task was especially frustrating because of the reluctance of persons surveyed to give entirely truthful answers to such questions. Dr. Susan Huck discussed that aspect of her interview with Franklin Zimring and described the startling outcome in her article:

"The last doubt as to the real intentions of at least certain influential members of the Commission, with regard to privately-owned firearms, was dispelled by our Research Director of the 'task force on gun control,' Mr. Zimring. While we were discussing the polls which ask people about their weapons, and the 'downward bias' so invariably encountered, we asked Mr. Zimring why people were so suspicious.

He replied quite promptly, and with a frankness he will no doubt be made to regret: "It's because we're coming to get their guns.' "
(*American Opinion*, Oct. 1968, p. 24)

Approximately nine months following the firearms hearings by the National Commission on the Causes and Prevention of Violence, July 28, 1969, the final recommendations with respect to gun control was announced by the Chairman Eisenhower. An editorial by the *Chicago Sun-Times* Aug. 6, 1969, neatly added up the sum and substance of the recommendations in two succinct sentences:

428

"Handgun controls recommended by the National Commission on the Causes and Prevention of Violence would include confiscation of up to 90 per cent of the 24,000,000 handguns now in private hands.

The commission placed the cost of such seizure to the federal government at about $500,000,000—or an estimated $20 reimbursement for each weapon taken."

A few brief selections taken from the Staff Report to the National Commission on the Causes and Prevention of Violence will serve to provide an insight as to the intent, and the mentality, which produced the final recommendations announced by Milton S. Eisenhower.

Back in 1935 before Sen. Copeland's committee, Hector Pocoroba had suggested placing serial numbers inscribed upon small metal tape inside every bullet manufactured in the United States as a means of tracing and identifying the person firing such bullets. Compare that with the following brilliant idea taken straight out of the 1969 Staff Report to the Violence Commission:

"Another suggested method of tracing firearms is to implant an identifying capsule with a distinctive number in each bullet and require firearms dealers who sell the ammunition to maintain records of the persons who buy all such numbered ammunition." (p. 135)

Yes, incredible as it may seem, after 34 years of deserved dormancy that pocorobian proposal had been resurrected, dusted off, and presented as the latest concept in the technology of firearms control methods. There was just one slight problem which the modern "geniuses" did concede, however. They had not quite figured out how to cope with the fact that, according to their calculations the annual production of the three major ammunition manufacturers exceeded four billion metallic cartridges and shotshells.

As might have been expected, the "experts" also gave some attention to another old pocorobian proposal, the fingerprinting of bullets. Demonstrating their enlightened modern wisdom, however, they quickly pointed out that there was no known method by which rifling marks on 100,000,000 test bullets could be preserved from gradual deterioration, and also that as firearms are used their rifling and other distinctive marks imparted to bullets fired through them similarly changed over a period of time. Not content to let the impossible matter drop, the Staff Report continued and set forth the following pocorobian suggestion:

"The foregoing problems might be avoided by a system of giving each gun a number and the development of some device to imprint this number on each bullet fired from the gun." (p. 135)

The basic thrust of the recommendations of the National Commission on the Causes and Prevention of Violence was designed to confiscate 90 percent of the privately owned handguns in the United States through a system of restrictive licensing, very similar to the Sullivan Law as administered in New York City. Consider for a few moments the strategy which might be employed to entice the public into acquiescence. A clue to the plan eventually tried was contained in a few remarks spoken by Franklin Zimring when he appeared and testified before the Executive Session of the National Commission on the Causes and Prevention of Violence on October 10, 1968:

"In 1964, a national sample of shooters, and a national sample of people who don't shoot, were both asked what a good reason would be for owning a hand gun. The principal reason given by each group, by the shooters and by the nonshooters, was self protection. This is a basic theme in hand gun ownership in the United States." (p. 10 Transcript of Proceedings)

Predictably, nine months later, a campaign was launched through the mass media in an abortive attempt to convince the public that the latest in revealed truth was that handguns really were not very useful in protecting either home or business, and that people would be far safer if only they would surrender their pistols and rely entirely upon the police for all protection. *Chicago Today* newspaper commented:

"The notion that a handgun in the home is a protection against burglars is an illusion, the commission noted. In a home with children, this supposed safeguard is a constant danger, and in fact a homeowner rarely has a chance to arm himself against an intruder." (July 31, 1969)

As expected the anti-gun claque immediately began with a Messianic fervor to spread the foreign doctrine that none but the politically selected few should be entrusted with a handgun. Justification for that affront to the uniquely American tradition of self-determination was attributed to the "incontrovertible evidence" which had allegedly been adduced by the Task Force on Firearms. The official documents, however, contained little or nothing to support them.

Consider the following choice bits of information plucked from the footnotes of the Violence Commission's statement, and from the report of the Task Force on Firearms:

"With some 90 million firearms distributed among half of the households of the United States, the firearms used in crime are but a small fraction of the total." (p. 49)

* * *

"No data are available on how frequently robberies and burglaries are foiled by the householder's display of a gun that is not fired. Nor are data available on use of guns by women to prevent attempted rapes; . . ." (p. 4 of National Commission Statement on Firearms & Violence, July 28, 1969)

* * *

"The small number of burglars and robbers actually shot suggests shooting is practically no threat to the burglar but might be somewhat of a threat to the robber. It is an open question, however, whether home self-defense firearms provide an extra measure of deterrence." (pp. 64–65)

* * *

"Thus, while there are obvious limitations on the businessman's use of firearms as protection against robbery, it is not known whether, when, or how much guns protect businessmen." (p. 67)

* * *

"The trend in crimes against the home during recent years has been sharply upward in spite of the fact that the number of home self-defense firearms has also been rapidly increasing. Yet increases in the crime rate occur for reasons unrelated to home firearms possession, and it is certainly possible that the crime rate would be still higher were it not for firearms. The increase in the crime rate may indeed be a cause of the increase in firearms ownership." (p. 65)

There you have the substance of the entire farce. The recommendations of the Violence Commission were invalidated out of the Commission's own mouth and should stand forever repudiated as constituting nothing more than an insolent arrogation of the right to determine arbitrarily what is, or what is not, for the good of the American people. That right to possess arms still belongs to the ordinary individual citizen of this country, and not, as in foreign lands, to the economically and politically privileged.

Two more distinguished gentlemen associated with the National Commission were Marvin E. Wolfgang and Prof. Morris Janowitz. It was less than a month later that *Time* magazine, in their issue of July 5, 1968, published a letter from Professor Marvin E. Wolfgang which set forth his views with respect to the kind of gun control laws he thought to be desirable:

"My personal choice for legislation is to remove all guns from private possession. I would favor statutory provisions that require all guns to be turned in to public authorities."

It was exactly two weeks earlier that *Time* on June 21, 1968, had reported on the opinions held by Professor Morris Janowitz concerning private ownership of firearms:

"Some urge complete confiscation. 'I see no reason,' says University of Chicago Sociologist Morris Janowitz, 'why anyone in a democracy should own a weapon.'" (p. 17)

Subsequently, the name of Professor Janowitz was prominently listed under the heading of "The Advisory Panel" for the National Commission on the Causes and Prevention of Violence.

When the various Staff Reports were released by the National Commission on the Causes and Prevention of Violence one year later they contained a few prefatory remarks by the Chairman, Milton S. Eisenhower, including these characterizations intended for public consumption:

"These studies are reports to the Commission by independent scholars and lawyers who have served as directors of our staff task forces and study teams; . . ."

* * *

"The Commission is making the reports available at this time as works of scholarship to be judged on their merits, . . ." (p. iii)

There you have it; "works of scholarship" by "independent scholars and lawyers". See how they play the game?

All sorts of people on all sorts of occasions have come out with open demands that guns be confiscated from private citizens and from police. An especially interesting example was published in the October 1968 issue of *Esquire* magazine in an article which proposed a so-called new "Bill of Civilized Rights" written by a man who had been an editorial writer for the *Washington Post* from 1957 until 1965 when he was then made chief of the *Post's* London Bureau. Among his recommendations for a "Bill of Civilized Rights" was this one, which he dubbed "Article X":

"The right of the people to bear arms shall be promptly, effectively and permanently abridged by Congress, which shall confiscate all weapons, including those used by police: violation of this law shall be punishable by exile."

In his subsequent explanation and discussion of that proposition, he had the temerity to write:

"Even after the murder act of a second Kennedy, Congress cannot muster the will to enact a truly effective gun law and thus protect the American people from their own Bill of Rights."

On June 23, 1968, the *Los Angeles Times* ran a full page advertisement sponsored by "The Fellowship Of Reconciliation" which allegedly was affiliated with the "Jewish Peace Fellowship", the "Catholic Peace Fellowship", and the "Episcopal Peace Fellowship", among others. The ad contained this statement:

"Disarm America's private citizens—ourselves. The country needs a much stiffer gun-control law. Insist that all private ownership of guns be outlawed; that the guns now around be collected and destroyed." (p. 16, Sec. A)

On January 22, 1968, the *Detroit Daily Press* carried an editorial entitled "Outlaw Private Guns" in which it exercised its right of freedom of the press by exhorting:

"No private citizen has any reason or need at any time to possess a gun. This applies to both honest citizens and criminals. We realize the Constitution guarantees the 'right to bear arms' but this should be changed."

On May 24, 1968, the *Denver Post* ran an article written by an associate editor which made these points:

"If Congress called in all privately owned guns and banned the future sale of guns to private owners, the National Guard would still have guns and the state would still be secure—a lot more secure than it is with guns in the hands of thousands of people who can't be trusted with them."

* * *

". . . it seems to me we are reaching the point where the abolition of guns for civilians may become necessary to stem the tide of violent murders, robberies and bullet-punctured riots which mocks our pretentions to culture and a society based on law and order."

Another interesting personal view on gun ownership was attributed to the Executive Director of the Illinois Division of the American Civil Liberties Union by a *Chicago American* news article of June 20, 1968:

"Jay A. Miller, executive director of the Illinois A.C.L.U., said the state organization has taken no official position on the council's efforts, altho he personally is in favor of stricter controls. Miller said he would like to see a complete nation-wide disarmament eventually, including police forces."

Back in 1967, before Senator Dodd's subcommittee, Quinn Tamm, Executive Director of the International Association of Chiefs of Police, said:

"We of the police believe these social conflagrations could be much more effectively kept under control or confined to controllable proportions if the availability of lethal weapons was controlled by the proper Federal legislation, and generally denied to all but those of duly constituted authority." (GG–p. 1054)

Square the preceding statement of Quinn Tamm, if you can, with his other remarks in response to the inquiry by Senator Joseph Tydings previously noted in this book.

On June 22, 1968, the *New Republic* magazine ran an article captioned "The Kind Of Gun Control We Need" which opened with these lines:

"Put simply, private citizens should be disarmed. A modest effort in this direction would include the following first steps: No person should be permitted to buy or possess a hand gun or ammunition for any hand gun. Possession of all automatic or semi-automatic firearms should be banned. So should all rifles."

* * *

"Such measures should be accompanied by others to disarm the police of lethal weapons. Their casual use of these weapons merely invites response in kind."

Only one short step behind the advocates of total abolition of guns were various members of the legal profession, as is evidenced by this excerpts from the address by a U.S. Court of Appeals Judge before a 1964 panel of the American Bar Association:

434

"The manufacture and sale and possession of handguns suitable for concealed weapons should be prohibited by state and Federal law, except where sale and possession is the subject of a permit provided by state law." (*The Right to Bear Arms*, p. 330)

Five years later Abner J. Mikva was elected to the United States Congress, and in less than four months introduced a bill in the House of Representatives to prohibit the importation, manufacture, sale, transfer or purchase of hand guns. The *Chicago Sun-Times* of March 4, 1970, commented on the measure:

"The legislation, believed to be the first of its kind introduced in Congress, is aimed at drying up the supply of 24 million pistols and revolvers in private hands in the United States."

It was only two days later, March 6, 1970, that a news release in support of the Mikva bill was issued by the President of the prestigious Chicago Bar Association. It included this flat assertion:

"Possession of hand guns should be permitted only to the police and authorized security agencies."

Six months later, September 29, 1970, the Illinois Democratic Party adopted a party platform which included the following plank, which called for the abolition of private ownership of handguns:

"We urge strict enforcement of existing gun control laws and the enactment of new legislation prohibiting the ownership and possession of hand guns by other than law enforcement officials."

On January 7, 1971, the previous pronouncements of the National Commission on the Causes and Prevention of Violence, with respect to the private ownership of handguns, were bolstered by the official recommendations of yet another national commission. The final report of the National Commission on Reform of Federal Criminal Laws asserted that a majority of its Commissioners recommended that Congress:

"(1) ban the production and possession of, and trafficking in, hand-guns, with exceptions only for military, police and similar official activities; and (2) require registration of all firearms." (p. 245)

By an interesting coincidence one of the Commissioners just happened to be Congressman Abner J. Mikva, and one of the members of the commission's Advisory Committee was Professor Marvin E. Wolfgang. It should therefore come as no further surprise that the firearms consultant to the commission was none other than Professor Franklin E. Zimring.

Notwithstanding the constant barrage of propaganda claims and pious reassurances to the contrary, there exists only one reason for enacting gun registration laws; only registration makes confiscation feasible.

Confiscation of firearms in any given country can be effected either by a benevolent government, or by a malevolent government, such as an insurgent revolutionary government from within, or a foreign invader from without. The former is the law-abiding gun owner's only probable menace.

When gun confiscation is to be effected by a benevolent government, it is absolutely necessary that firearms first be registered on a national basis.

Thereafter, it is inevitable that administrative procedures, fees, police investigations and other elements of bureaucratic compliance would systematically surround gun ownership tending to reduce the number of those willing to assume the nit-picking responsibilities required for continuing gun ownership.

The noose around the neck of gun ownership would be closed—quietly and imperceptively, but steadily. The use of guns in sports would decline by the numbers of those who, although they might enjoy them, cannot spare the time for compliance with the requirements of law and regulations; or, those whose dedication to gun ownership for various reasons is not great enough to compel their continued carrying of the burdens and impositions of gun ownership. As the numbers declined of those involved it would be found that those first departing the ranks of gun ownership would be businessmen, professional and influential men, in their communities. These men are simply those who first would not have the time for multifold applications and repeated photographing and fingerprinting. Not only would they have the least time for the frivolous and repeated demands of the bureaucracy, but they would probably have the least disposition to meet the bureaucratic requirements exacted. Moreover, they would likely be among the first unable to sustain their reputations, and their careers and professions, if they should fail to meet those requirements—no matter how strongly in their hearts they might object to them.

Steadily then, the participation in gun interest would become those people enjoying the least in social approbation, perhaps because of their place at the bottom of the economic ladder and for no reason relating to their merit as citizens. The shooting sports accordingly would decline. Without the support of more respected and substantial men the question would increasingly arise, what are you trying to prove? What is your purpose?

Shooting clubs and our national shooting organizations, in a scramble to retain something of respectability, would move into areas of conservation, purity of waters, national clean-up weeks, smog control, hiking, nature studies and the like—all of which have a valuable place in contemporary life but which in shooting organizations can only tend to blur their original goals, de-emphasize the shooting sports, distract the singular attention of their participants, divert their energies into various channels, dilute their membership with factions having varied interests and finally denigrate their dedication to defense of the right to keep and bear arms. Their leaders at the same time, pressed by the economic necessities for a larger membership and more money, would deny that it is true.

The gun owners of America can be brought to this diminished condition by laws and bureaucratic procedures continually presented in the name of crime control. At the same time the crime figures can be manipulated, up and down, to suit the pruposes of the national administration in power at the time—and this is easily done.

The prestige of gun ownership would be non-existent and public toleration of gun owners would have declined. They would have become the social and political Neanderthals who, not charged with crime, would nevertheless be publicly credited with atavistic criminal attitudes and the harboring in their homes of instruments of murder and crime whether used for that purpose or not.

The organizations they first built to protect their legitimate and patriotic endeavors would be basking in plaudits for civic virtue coming from those seeking to destroy them when they represented the interest of those who founded them.

The public would be ready, then, to be easily shamed into voluntary surrender of "the instruments of murder" they kept in their homes. They would have become convinced the availability of firearms had something to do with the existence of crime. And they would find ways to prevent firearms availability on the part of family members and sometimes friends.

A bill to confiscate the remaining firearms in private hands in this country would have little or no substantial opposition. Excepting the police and military, only criminals then, with a criminal intent beyond the newly established criminal ownership of firearms, would be in possession of firearms.

Indeed, it is that our opponents all along have been the disciples of an idealistic relationship among men which has never been realized and concerning which not one bit of evidence exists to indicate will ever be realized. They profess to believe in the intrinsic goodness of man, and that all men will respond with kindness if they are treated kindly.

They will not hear that among all the scientific and mechanical achievements of man since the dark ages in Europe it has been the development of firearms more than any other one thing which has made it possible for the adherents of their philosophy to survive. They have been shielded from the natural law of survival by stronger and more realistic men carrying guns. Prior to the development of firearms it was the most muscular and brutal—the man with a club, ax, or sword who ruled our roads and streets and at their whim terrorized our homes. Today, a paunchy intellectual or a dainty and delicate woman, with courage and determination, is more than the equal of any brute who ever trampled the sands of a Roman arena. The difference is a firearm.

Guns were developed to make men equal in a most desirable and fundamental sense. Their development made possible step by step the development and the protection of the philosophy of goodness on which our opponents dwell and in which they indulge their fancies.

The handgun especially has an honorable place reserved for it in modern society. Its existence still makes possible that righteous men and good men, even when meek and physically modest, can go, when necessary, anywhere, freely, and that in doing so they can cope with any situation they encounter, avoiding that they become the victim of Neanderthals to be found lurking in dark streets and alleyways.

Of course, we know that firearms cannot be eliminated, but if it were possible for them to be eliminated, then, as once true, with the restoration of the weapons of savagery, only the muscular and the brutal would prevail—excepting only those, as typical of the ancients, who were clever and wealthy enough to surround themselves with their armed guards and torchbearers.

The firearm, and especially the handgun, is the defender of the physically weak and the more enlightened intellectually. Its presence discourages attack and so saves lives. If intellectual flabbiness is permitted to prevail in our country, the firearm will become increasingly necessary to protect those who today are all too often found bewailing its existence.

Before the proliferation of firearms in society, a gentleman spent almost all his early life learning horsemanship, swordsmanship, the value of armor and mail and the uses of mace or dirk. His oppressed serfs sweated in the fields. Today the democratic availability of firearms has made it possible for all young men to spend their lives being more useful in any field of production, of science, of medicine and of the arts, but many do not understand the basic instrument which, more than any other, made this period of ease and security possible and which even now enables men to endure in a heterogeneous, turbulent, and expansive—but still democratic society. They have come to condemn thoughtlessly the instrument which more than any other device in modern society prevents that once again our streets and byways and our homes be trampled and pillaged by those with thicker skulls and bigger biceps.

This discussion, up to now, has dealt with the possibility of confiscation of arms by a benevolent government of our own.

In the unlikely event gun confiscation was the product of revolution within our country, or of foreign invaders, gun owners would likely experience no problems in keeping and bearing arms. History so reveals.

In the latter event they would be joined by all good citizens and encouraged to assist or to spearhead all defensive efforts. In the event of revolution or civil war every able-bodied person on either side would be armed and no law could in any sense have anything to do with it.

When gun confiscation is to be imposed upon a defeated people by successful revolutionaries or foreign invaders, prior registration of arms is really not necessary, even if nevertheless helpful. Against a defeated people there need be no compunction about issuing confiscation decrees and proclamations backed up by the ultimate sanction of death for the possession of unauthorized firearms. Such sanctions after defeat historically have proved quite adequate for stimulating a massive surrender of arms. The presence of gun registration lists or licensing lists merely tend to expediency and efficiency.

Techniques for gun confiscation in foreign countries have not been uniform, but certain patterns are nevertheless discernible. For example, coincidental with the Nazi invasion of Czechoslovakia in World War II the arms registration lists of that captive country were seized by the Fifth Column and public disarmament thereby facilitated. Similarly, just before the Red puppet government assumed control of Hungary about 1948, all public and private shooting clubs were disbanded by police decree, and all private arms were taken into custody to "protect the people".

In an attempt to debunk the notion that gun confiscation took place in Europe in conjunction with the Nazi invasion of various countries Carl Bakal wrote the following in his "well-balanced and outstanding" book:

> "I also wrote to the American Embassy in each of the countries who so supposedly succumbed to the Nazis. From Denmark came this typical reply: 'The Germans did not disarm Danish civilians and so facilitate the German invasion and occupation of Denmark.' " (p. 277)

Denmark was occupied by the Germans on April 9, 1940, and was disarmed within ten weeks of that date by its own government at the direction of the German Gestapo. In its research paper covering the techniques of firearms seizure employed by the Nazis, the Legislative Reference Service of the Library of Congress wrote this somewhat cryptic reference to the Danish experience:

> "In that the occupation authorities in Denmark did not legislate, pressure was brought on the Danish Government to introduce legislation which would meet the requirements of the occupying power." (HH–p. 488)

All such firearms, confiscated on the basis of their registration with Danish police authorities, were deposited in the prison at Nyborg. Later, the Germans kept those weapons which were useful to them and had the others destroyed. The receipt below was for a pistol owned by a town judge. The pistol was confiscated by his friend, the town chief of police.

In commenting on the German technique of issuing decrees and proclamations ordering the surrender of firearms in most of the countries they invaded, the Legislative Reference Service concluded its report with these observations:

> "This sampling of German statutes, decrees, and other documents concerning firearms indicated two points: First, the profound importance the German invaders attached to the possession of firearms. Second, the importance of these proclamations and decrees as a technique used by the Germans to obtain and limit weapons in the possession of the nationals of the invaded country. These proclamations were of course accompanied with searches and severe penalties.
>
> A totalitarian society, and particularly a totalitarian society occupying a country against its will, simply cannot permit the private possession of weapons to any great extent, except by those who have proven their loyalty."

*   *   *

Skydevaaben

Undertegnede: *~~~~~~~~~~~~~~~~~~~*
(fulde Navn — Efternavn først)

Stilling: *~~~~~~~~~*

Bopæl: *Gmmy* 15

har Dags Dato afleveret til Opbevaring hos Politiet:

1 Stk. *Revolver* .... Kaliber: ....
(Vaabnets Art)

Fabrikat: *Browning* .... Fabr. Nr. *191079*

Svendborg .... , den *14 Juni* 1940

A/S O. O. B. & Co. 26889.

Udfyldes af Politiet.

Kvittering.

For Modtagelsen af det anførte Vaaben meddeles

herved Kvittering.

POLITIMESTEREN
I SVENDBORG M. V.

den *14 Juni* 1940.

(Politiets Stempel)

"It is in these German regulations applicable to the occupied territories that a relationship between firearms and resistance is most clear. The consistent issuing of these regulations with their severe penalties in the occupied territories is indicative of a profound concern over the extent to which these weapons might be used against German authority." (HH–pp. 488, 489)

One need not look back to World War II for examples of gun confiscation, however, but instead can find two choice occurrences just within the past decade. The first followed the ouster of Cuban dictator Fulgencio Batista by Fidel Castro and his guerrilla army. Utilizing the comprehensive gun registration lists established under the Batista rule to "protect the people", the Castro regime systematically confiscated every privately owned firearm in Cuba. As told by one of the Cuban refugees who fled to the United States following the takeover:

"The owner of any gun had to register it with the police. The license, filed with the police, contained not only the make, number and description of the gun, but also the owner's picture and fingerprints. Thus it was a simple matter for Castro's men to collect every gun in the Country. Today in Cuba, only those on Castro's side are permitted to own a gun of any description." ("The Armed Eagle" Dec. 1968, p. 8)

The second example would undoubtedly be familiar to the reader had not so many of the anti-gun newspapers in the United States carefully avoided mentioning the confiscation of guns and instead deceptively couched their news articles with such ambiguous and euphemistic phraseology as "a decree had been issued revoking the constitutional protection for civil liberties." The occurrence was the overthrow of the Greek government by a military junta, and the news release by the Associated Press on April 26, 1967, minced no words in reporting the actual facts:

"The law was boosted by an Army order giving military authorities the right to search private homes; require all hunting rifles, shotguns, and ammunition to be turned in to the nearest police station; cancelling all hunting licenses and forbidding all hunting; and requiring heads of households to report all persons living with them and any visitors or foreigners."

It should be apparent that, in a country the size of the United States, with its high level of education, and public knowledge of events, intent to disarm the civilian populace and the police must be disguised

442

in whatever manner best suits the immediate occasion. In all probability, the single common denominator of these continuing efforts will be some variation on the theme of "protecting the public."

It must always be remembered that gun control legislation cannot possibly succeed in curbing crime, suicides or accidents, and it is not really seriously intended to do so by many of its proponents. This is clear from the illogical and non-sequitor relationships between the alleged reasons for demanding specific laws and the actual or probable effect of such laws, if enacted. With few exceptions, they will directly and adversely affect only the decent and credulous citizens who will attempt to comply with their requirements.

It must never be forgotten that any law whose success is dependent upon the cooperation of the criminal element is doomed to failure from its inception, and the failure of such laws to function as anticipated will invariably result in continued demands for progressively harsher and more restrictive controls which will work only to the detriment of those who will comply with their terms, the honest citizen from whom society has nothing to fear in any event.

Gun permits, licenses, registration and confiscation are anathema to freedom and should be resisted by every citizen at every level of government through every available legal means. There is no rational justification in a republic for the imposition of restraints on gun ownership among responsible law-abiding citizens regardless of race, color or social class.

It must also never be forgotten that a free and essentially democratic society cannot be maintained unless government discharges its prime function of protecting society from the criminally inclined and the mentally ill. If such persons cannot be rehabilitated, cured or controlled, then they must be physically separated from useful society; permanently, if need be. The price of failure to take such steps can only result in the steady deterioration of the quality of life and the ultimate destruction of a free and open society. Stringent restrictions on the possession of firearms by reputable citizens will not solve any of the problems confronting America, but instead will merely exacerbate them to the general detriment of the country.

It would be futile to attempt any comprehensive delineation of the strategies which will continue to be employed by those who, for what they think good or evil reasons, would disarm the law-abiding citizenry. They will be as many and varied as can be contrived by the wiles of man. Beware of their employment of the dictum to divide and conquer. Freedom is not divisible. It exists for all honest men, or it exists for none.

Those who are intent upon disarming America will use every possible ruse. They can be relied upon to play handguns against long guns, cities against rural areas, race against race, values against values, the present generation against those yet unborn.

They will threaten, and they will cajole; they will implore, and they will demand; they will ridicule, and they will flatter; they will intimidate, and they will coax; they will appeal both to men's noblest and basest motives. Their techniques will include sophistry and demagoguery subtly intermixed with mellifluous blandishments calculated to seduce an unsuspecting public into acceptance of their dangerous dogma. They have demonstrated all this. There will be those among them who properly may be described as being the true masters of deceit. They must not succeed.

It must always be remembered that unlike either Europe or Asia, the right to purchase, possess and use firearms for traditionally legitimate purposes has a profoundly unique symbolism among Americans and constitutes a part of their birthright. It is only natural and proper that this should be so. Why, in America?

Why not in America, throughout whose pages of history firearms have been inextricably woven into the lives and legends of virtually all of its national heroes, who only recently, really, conquered a continent and tamed a savage wilderness; from the Pilgrim armed with his cumbersome and quaint arquebus; the Minuteman with his reliable musket; the frontiersman with his superbly accurate handcrafted long rifle, powder horn and shot pouch; the plainsman with his saddle-ring carbine and six-shooter; to Sergeant Alvin York with his bolt-action rifle and semi-automatic pistol?

Why not in America, where both the rifle and revolver were invented, and where virtually every significant firearms development for the past 160 years has taken place?

Why not in America, a country virtually unique in its vast expanses of open hunting lands available to every citizen, whatever his station in life, however humble his origin, in stark contrast to the game preserves of Europe which have been carefully tended since the 17th century for the wealthy and the politically privileged?

Why not in America, a great nation which for the first time in modern history stands for—and because of—very special kinds of freedom—the freedom of individual men, the freedom of individual responsibility, the freedom of individual accomplishment and the freedom of individual rights?

Why not in America, indeed?

444

Index

446

448